Catharina Day

SOUTHWEST
IRELAND

'Some of the jarveys' chat is
tongue-in-cheek, like this hoary
old phrase about the constant rain:
"Twasn't rain at all, but just a little
perspiration from the mountains!"

CADOGANguides

1 Staigue Fort, the Ring of Kerry

2 and 3 The Beara Peninsula

4 Coastline around Ballybunion
5 The Dingle Peninsula

6 Traditional bar on the Ring of Kerry

7 Dingle Town harbour
8 Traditional dry-stone wall on the Burren

9

9 Forest at Gougane Barra

10 Ventry strand

11 Window in Ballycotton
12 Tinker's caravan, the Dingle Peninsula

13 and 14 Bars at Annascaul and Kenmare

About the author

Catharina Day comes from a long-established Irish family. She was born in Kenya but moved to County Donegal as a small child. She attended school in Ireland, and then went to university in England. She was married in County Donegal and visits frequently with her husband and four children from her home in Scotland. She has compiled an anthology of Irish literature.

About the updater

Joss Waterfall is a regular contributor to Cadogan Guides. She loves exploring and has found Ireland to be one of the most hospitable, atmospheric and picturesque countries she has visited. She would like to thank Vanessa Letts, for updating the 'Travel' and 'Practical A–Z' chapters; Mary O'Neill, for updating the 'History' chapter; and Elspeth Anderson, whose diligence is always greatly appreciated.

Contents

Cadogan Guides
2nd Floor, 233 High Holborn
London WC1V 7DN
info@cadoganguides.co.uk
www.cadoganguides.com

The Globe Pequot Press
246 Goose Lane, PO Box 480, Guilford,
Connecticut 06437–0480

Copyright © Catharina Day 1995, 1999, 2001, 2005

Cover and photo essay design by Sarah Gardner
Maps © Cadogan Guides, drawn by
   Maidenhead Cartographic Services Ltd
Based on Ordnance Survey Ireland Permit No. 8022
© Ordnance Survey Ireland and Government
   of Ireland
Book design by Andrew Barker
Photographs: frontcover © Peter Adams
   Photography; back cover and photo
   essay © Alex Robinson
Managing Editor: Natalie Pomier
Editor: Joss Waterfall
Editorial Assistant: Nicola Jessop
Proofreading: Elspeth Anderson
Indexing: Isobel McLean
Production: Navigator Guides

Printed in Italy by Legoprint
A catalogue record for this book is available
   from the British Library
ISBN 1-86011-195-5

The author and publishers have made every effort
to ensure the accuracy of the information in this
book at the time of going to press. However, they
cannot accept any responsibility for any loss, injury
or inconvenience resulting from the use of
information contained in this guide.

Please help us to keep this guide up to date. We
have done our best to ensure that the information
in this guide is correct at the time of going to
press. But places and facilities are constantly
changing, and standards and prices in hotels and
restaurants fluctuate. We would be delighted to
receive any comments concerning existing entries
or omissions. Authors of the best letters will
receive a Cadogan Guide of their choice.

Introduction

01

You have chosen well if the southwest of Ireland is your destination. Ireland is the perfect place to take a holiday, and Cork, Kerry, Limerick and Clare make up a most beautiful and fascinating region. These counties, which together make up the province of Munster, are easily accessible from Shannon, Cork and Kerry airports, and they have all the attractions of this lovely island in abundance. The landscape is varied and unspoilt, the pace of life is relaxing, and the local people know how to make a stranger feel at home.

Munster (*Cuige Mumhan*) is the largest province in Ireland. It's a mixture of everything you would consider Irish: the purples of the mountains melt into chessboards of cornfields, in which the stooks stand like golden pieces. Houses are whitewashed, glens are deep and the coastline is made ragged by the force of the Atlantic, with sandy bays and rocky cliffs. It's a land of extremes: a large, placid, fertile plain, brooding mountain scenery, luxurious vegetation and harsh, barren land. The stately River Shannon flows out to sea between County Clare and County Limerick. The extreme southwest coast is swept by westerly gales, distorting trees into twisted shapes. The moonscape of the Burren contrasts with the softness of Killarney; the dairy pasture of the inland valleys contrasts with the thrashing sea around the Dingle and Iveragh Peninsulas.

The remarkable Burren is the youngest landscape in Europe and its carboniferous limestone hills have been shaped by intense glaciation. Spring gentian, mountain avens, hoary primrose, milkwort and orchids are among the wonderful variety of plants that flourish here. A great collection of southern and northern plants grow together in the province: the alpine or arctic plants of the Burren, and the bog violet and arbutus in Kerry. Wild goats still range the Burren and keep at bay the ever-invasive hazel scrub. The best time to see the Burren's flowers is May.

This is the land of the Mumonians (the '-ster' suffix of Munster is a Scandinavian addition to the more ancient name of Muma); the people are warm, relaxed and musical, but they might also be described as backward-looking and quarrelsome. The province as a whole has been described as 'a little England', since the Anglo-Normans certainly played a part in moulding the towns, as did some of the Elizabethan adventurers. However, Cork City is the creation of lively Irish minds; and whether they are Celts or later arrivals, most Corkonians think their city should be the capital rather than Dublin.

There's a sense of separateness about the southwest and this has helped to develop a great mythological tradition, with mother-goddesses figuring prominently in legend and place names. There is Aire of Knockaney in County Limerick, and Aoibhill of Crag Liath, who reappears in the 18th century to preside over the

Please Note
The reader will find that there are occasions when place names vary in spelling from those in this guide book. This is because different translations from the Gaelic exist; there is no completely standardized map to follow. Bartholomews, Ordnance Survey, the RAC and the AA produce very good and detailed maps.

judgement in Brian Merriman's famous vision poem 'Midnight Court'. Anu is mother of the Gods, whose breasts are represented in the Paps Mountains on the Kerry border. Most primitive of all is the ancient Hag of Beare, who spans many centuries; many megalithic monuments are attributed to her activities. She is variously known as Digde, Dige or Duinech, and we are told that she passed through seven periods of youth. She is also supposed to have written the marvellous 9th-century poem 'The Hag of Beare', which is a lament for lost beauty, and the struggle between bodily pleasure and salvation through the Christian way of repentance:

> Yet may this cup of whey
> O! Lord, serve as my ale-feast
> Fathoming its bitterness
> I'll learn that you know best.

Also strong in the mythological tradition is Donn Forinne, the ancestor-God to whom all the Irish will journey after death. His house is believed to be on the summit of Knockfierna Hill in County Limerick.

The history of Ireland has been turbulent, and its telling fraught with prejudice and misunderstanding. But approaching Irish history through its excellent literary tradition is fascinating. Ireland had its Golden Age of learning roughly between the 6th and 11th centuries – Frank O'Connor described it as the civilization of 'the little monasteries'. The monks wrote down the Celtic oral culture, wrote poetry and honoured God in this time, the Dark Ages, when the rest of Europe was in the hands of the barbarians. Ireland also had a strict bardic tradition, in which members of the poets' guild studied for up to 12 years before they qualified. From that disciplined environment came mature poetry as evocative and delicate as a Chinese poem: stirring epics such as 'The Tain', which chronicles the wars of a heroic race, and moving love laments. (Most of us can only read these poems in translation from the Gaelic; luckily, the translations by present-day Irish poets bring them close to us.) The voice of the Gaelic poet describes and bemoans the destruction of the Gaelic ways from the 16th century onwards. From the 18th century, the ability of the Irish to express themselves in the language of the Saxon is apparent from the works of such authors as Jonathan Swift, through to W.B. Yeats and the marvellous poets of today, such as Seamus Heaney. Poetry, theatre and the novel have continued to thrive since the heady days of cultural renaissance and the uprising against the British in 1916.

With your head full of myths, legends and literature, forget sun worship and all its paraphernalia: travel with stout shoes, a warm jersey and an eye turned towards Ireland's beauty and history. There is no such thing as a tiresome, hot journey in the southwest. The climate is good and damp: the rainfall varies between 30 inches in parts to as much as 87 inches in Killarney – but the sunshine, when it comes, intensifies the already beautiful colours of the landscape. Don't rush, for if you do, the charm of the countryside and its people will pass you by.

The largest concentration of houses and cars is in the energetic and attractive city of Cork; its population is around 140,000. It is built along the River Lee and the sheltered waters of Cork Harbour, and stretches up the little hills around. It's a place of exuberant culture and business, and its natives have a great sense of humour about life, as well as a sense of the ridiculous. At the other extreme are the wild and beautiful headlands of west Cork, Kerry and Clare, where you can lose yourself in the mountains and on the long white strands.

Wherever you go in the southwest, you might stay anywhere, from friendly, hospitable farmhouse B&Bs to splendid castles or country houses, where the room proportions and furnishings are reminiscent of a more gracious age. Not only is the food delicious and made from the freshest seafood, local meat, game and vegetables; you will also often find well-chosen wines and, of course, decent whiskey and beer. You'll find the owners and staff of these places keen to help with any request you have, whether it's finding the origins of your great-granny or directing you to the best historical sites, walks, beaches, fishing, golf clubs or craft studios. And the way the Irish speak is another pleasure; you'll find they are a race who can express themselves with great character, humour and exactness.

When you are in Ireland, it is certain that the irritations and annoyances that accompany you through everyday life will disappear, and the desire for a day spent walking in the mountains, doing a spot of fishing and having a good read before a warm fire will become a reality. However, it is important not to stick rigidly to a scheme and become irritated when it has to be delayed for a while, for nothing in Ireland can be planned right down to the last detail. Information can sometimes only be found out on the spot, and Irish opening hours, timetables and other schedules are even more subject to change than in other European countries.

A Guide to the Guide

We hope our inspiring photo essay will set the context for your trip, together with the following selection of the best of southwest Ireland. After this, there is a short and simple section on **History** from pagan times to the present day. This outlines the main events and problems that constitute the complex Ireland of today, and is followed by a brief résumé of the religious background and a selection of the country's most famous saints. Next, you'll find features on the **Old Gods and Heroes**, ancient sites and early architecture (with a glossary of terms in the reference section at the end of the book). The **Topics** section gives brief insights into notable features of Ireland and Irish life. It includes some fascinating pieces on the Fairy People, historic houses, gardens of the southwest, potatoes and the famine, the Burren, and how to trace your ancestors. The **Food and Drink** chapter will provide you with a flavour of the local specialities and the beverages you might want to look out for.

The comprehensive **Travel** section, in conjunction with the **Practical A–Z**, is packed with information that will help you get the best from your visit, including advice on where to stay and eat, sports and leisure activities.

Chapter Divisions

The southwest of Ireland is made up of four counties: **Limerick**, **Kerry**, **Cork** and **Clare**. Each chapter constitutes a gazetteer of a whole county, with lots of local history and anecdotal information, together with descriptions and details of the places of interest. Full, practical lists of transport facilities, festivals, tourist information centres, shopping, leisure activities, places to stay and eat and entertainment possibilities are given in each county section.

At the end of the book, there's an essay on **Language**, a recommended **Further Reading** list and a comprehensive index.

The Best of Southwest Ireland

Ruined Friaries and Churches
Adare, Co. Limerick
Ardfert, Co. Kerry
Oratory of Gallarus, Co. Kerry
Killaloe, Co. Clare
Dysert O'Dea, Co. Clare

Castles
King John's Castle, Co. Limerick
Blarney Castle, Co. Cork
Bunratty Castle, Co. Clare
Newtown Castle, Co. Clare

Fine Houses
Glin Castle, Co. Limerick
Muckross House and Abbey, Co. Kerry
Derrynane House, Co. Kerry
Bantry Bay House, Co. Cork

Gardens
Derreen Woodland, Co. Kerry
Ilnacullin (Garinish Island), Co. Cork
Creagh Gardens, Co. Cork
Anne's Grove, Co. Cork
Timoleague Castle Gardens, Co. Cork

Beaches
Ventry Strand, Co. Kerry
Inch Strand, Co. Kerry
Derrynane Strand, Co. Kerry
White Strand, Co. Kerry

Golf Courses
Adare, Co. Limerick
Ballybunion, Co. Kerry
Tralee, Co. Kerry
Fota Island, Co. Cork
Lahinch, Co. Clare

Museums and Art Galleries
The Hunt Museum, Limerick City
Crawford Municipal Gallery, Cork City

Views
Gap of Dunloe, Co. Kerry
Moll's Gap, Co. Kerry
Mizen Head, Co. Cork
Bantry Bay, Co. Cork
View from Mount Gabriel, near Schull, Co. Cork
Cliffs of Moher, Co. Clare
View from top of Killaloe Cathedral, Co. Clare

Food Markets
The Old English Market, Grand Parade, Cork City

Restaurants
The Park Hotel, Kenmare, Co. Kerry
Packie's, Kenmare, Co. Kerry
Sheen Falls Lodge, Kenmare, Co. Kerry
The Courtyard, Schull, Co. Cork
Ballymaloe House, Shanagarry, Co. Cork
Good Things Café, Durras, Co. Cork
Aherne's Seafood Restaurant, Youghal, Co. Cork
Berry Lodge, Miltown Malbay, Co. Clare

Places to Stay
Adare Manor Hotel, Adare, Co. Limerick
Doyle's Townhouse, Dingle, Co. Kerry
Beaufort House, Beaufort, Killarney, Co. Kerry
Ballyvolane House, Castlelyons, Co. Cork
Ballymaloe House, Shanagarry, Co. Cork
Bantry House, Bantry Bay, Co. Cork
Assolas Country House, Kanturk, Co. Cork
Casey's of Baltimore, Co. Cork
Glanworth Mill, near Fermoy, Co. Cork
Ballinalacken Castle Hotel, Lisdoonvarna, Co. Clare
Berry Lodge, Miltown Malbay, Co. Clare

7

History .

General History 8
Northern Ireland 29
The Republic Today 37
Glossary of Political Parties and Terms 38

02

I found in Munster, unfettered of any
Kings and queens, and poets a many –
Poets well skilled in music and measure,
Prosperous doings, mirth and pleasure.
I found in Connaught the just, redundance
Of riches, milk in lavish abundance;
Hospitality, vigour, fame,
In Cruachan's land of heroic name
I found in Ulster, from hill to glen,
Hardy warriors, resolute men;
Beauty that bloomed when youth was gone,
And strength transmitted from sire to son.
I found in Leinster the smooth and sleek,
From Dublin to Slewmargy's peak;
Flourishing pastures, valour, health,
Long-living worthies, commerce, wealth.

from *Prince Alfrid's Itinerary*
(version by James Clarence Mangan)

If you happen to fall into conversation with an Irishman in a bar, the subjects of religion and politics are bound to arise. With luck you'll have a cool glass of Guinness in your hand, for discussions on Ireland are inevitably emotional. The Irish are good talkers and have very long memories, so it's worth having some idea of their history.

Many of Ireland's troubles have stemmed from her geographical situation; too far from Britain to be assimilated, too near to be allowed to be separate. Queen Elizabeth I poured troops into Ireland because she appreciated the strategic importance of Ireland to her enemies. Over the centuries, Ireland has been offered help in her fight for independence, but it was never disinterested help; whoever paid for arms and fighting men in Ireland wanted to further their own military, political, religious or ideological cause. France in the late 18th century supplied arms to Ireland to distract England from other policies; and in Northern Ireland the IRA were supplied with some guns by foreign powers. Over 30 years of European Union (EU) membership has paid dividends for Ireland. The economic disparity with the UK has narrowed considerably and Ireland has gained in self-confidence as a leading player in a union where the centre of power is not London, but Brussels. The shared economics of EU membership are helping to undermine political and religious differences.

General History

Pre-Celtic Ireland

The hills and river valleys are scattered with ancient monuments dating from the Stone, Bronze and Iron Ages. Most of them suggest some religious significance, though they have been swathed in romance and heroism by the Celtic storytellers or *shanachies* in the cottages and castles. Unfortunately only a few of these survive today as 'memory men'.

The earliest record of man in Ireland is dated between 8,700 and 8,600 years ago, as deduced from fragments found at a camp in **Mount Sandel** near Coleraine. The people of this time lived a nomadic life, hunting and trapping; they could not move around very easily as the countryside was covered by forest, interrupted only by lakes and rivers. They used boats similar to the curraghs used today by fishermen in the west of Ireland, and built lake dwellings, or crannogs. No one is sure where these people came from but they had the island to themselves for 3,000 years. Then came **Neolithic** man, who is perhaps the **Fir Bolg** in Celtic mythology (at this stage everything is very vague). These people were farmers and gradually spread over the whole of Ireland, clearing the forest as best they could with their stone tools. They evidently practised burial rites, for they built chambered tombs of a very sophisticated quality, decorated with spirals and lozenge shapes. (For example, the Great Burial Chamber at Newgrange in the Boyne Valley, County Meath, which dates from between 3500 and 2700 BC, has a chamber large enough to contain thousands of cremated bodies.) These people must have been very well organized, with the energy and wealth to spare for such an ambitious project – similar in its way to the pyramids, and 500 years older.

Around 2400 BC yet another race appeared, who were skilled miners and metal-workers. They were called the **Beaker People**, or the **Tuatha dé Danaan**, as they are known in Irish legend. They opened up copper mines and started to trade with Brittany, the Baltic and the Iberian Peninsula. They had different beliefs about burial: their dead were buried singly in graves lined with stone slabs and covered with a capstone. Other peoples with different burial habits and funeral rituals also arrived at this time, though it is not clear in what order they arrived, or to what extent they intermingled. They are named after objects associated with their culture, hence 'Bowl Food Vessel People', 'Urn People' and 'Vase Food Vessel People'. There are a thousand chambered graves, ring-shaped cairns, standing stones, rows and circles of stones left from these times; they hint at various rituals and, it has been suggested, at observations of the stars.

The Celts

The first arrival of the Celts cannot be precisely dated; a few may have come as early as 900 BC, though the main waves of Celtic invaders occurred between 700 BC and 400 BC. These people had iron weapons and defeated the Beakers, whose legendary magical powers were no defence against the new metal. Known as the **Celts** or **Gaels**, the new invaders had spread from southern Germany, across France, and as far south as Spain. Today everybody in Ireland has pride in the 'Celtic' past: epic tales sing the praises of men and women who were capable of heroic and superhuman deeds, and their beautiful gold jewellery is carefully preserved as proof of their achievements. The Celts brought to Ireland a highly organized social structure, and the La Tène style of decoration (its predominant motif is a spiral or a whorl). Ireland was divided into different clans with three classes: the **free**, who were warriors and owned land and cattle; the **professionals**, such as the jurists, Druids, musicians, storytellers and poets, who could move freely between the petty kingdoms; and, finally, the **slaves**. Every clan had a petty king, who was ruled over by the high king (at Tara in County Meath).

The Gaels made use of many of the customs and mythology that had existed before their arrival, so their Celtic civilization is unique. They were also very fortunate, for although they were probably displaced themselves by the expanding **Roman Empire**, once they got to Ireland they were isolated and protected to some extent by England, which acted as a buffer state. The Romans never extended their ambitions to conquering Ireland, so the Gaels were able to develop their traditions, unlike Celts elsewhere in Europe. They spent most of their time raiding their neighbours for cattle and women, who were used as live currency.

In their religion, the human head was all-important as a symbol of divinity and supernatural power – even when severed from the body, it would still retain its powers. Warriors used to take the heads of slain enemies and display them in front of their houses. The Gaels also believed firmly in an afterlife of the soul: they would lend each other money to be repaid in the next world.

The Arrival of Christianity

Christianity was brought to Ireland in the 5th century AD, according to popular tradition, by **St Patrick**, and quickly became accepted by the kings. **Cormac MacArt**, who ruled in Tara about a century and a half before St Patrick arrived, foresaw great changes and told his court of Druids and nobles that the gods they worshipped were only craven wood. The Druids put a curse on him and soon afterwards he choked to death on a salmon bone. Just before he died he ordered that he was not to be buried in the tomb of Brugh at Newgrange, but on the sunny east point by the River Rosnaree. When St Patrick lit a fire which signalled the end of Druid worship, legend has it that he was looking down from the Hill of Slane on to Rosnaree.

The Christians skilfully reconciled their practices and beliefs with those of the pagans; a famous saying of St Columba was, 'Christ is my Druid'. The early Christians seem to have been very ascetic, building their monasteries in wild and inaccessible places. You can still see their beehive-shaped dwellings on **Skellig Michael** (or Great Skellig), a windswept rocky island off the Kerry coast. The monasteries became universities renowned throughout Europe, which was submerged in the Dark Ages, and produced beautiful manuscripts like the famous *Book of Kells*.

The Viking Invasion

The tranquillity of Ireland, 'land of saints and scholars', was brutally interrupted by the arrival of the **Vikings** or **Norsemen**. They were able to penetrate right into Ireland through their skilful use of the rivers and lakes. They struck for the first time in 795, but this was only the start of a 300-year struggle. Much treasure from the palaces and monasteries was plundered, for the buildings had no defences. The monks used bell towers, known as round towers, in which to store their precious things at the first sign of trouble. Eventually the Norsemen began to settle down; they founded the first city-ports – Dublin, Wexford and Waterford – and started to trade with the Gaels. Military alliances were made between them whenever it helped a particular king in the continuous struggle for the high kingship. After a short period of relative calm another wave of Norsemen invaded and the plundering began again; but **Brian Boru**, who had usurped the high kingship from the O'Neills, defeated the Vikings at Clontarf in 1014 and broke their power permanently. Unfortunately for the Gaelic people, Brian Boru was murdered by some Vikings in his tent just after the victory at Clontarf. Havoc and infighting became a familiar pattern, as the high kingship was fought for by the O'Briens, the O'Loughlins (or O'Loghlens) and the O'Connors. The Gaelic warriors wasted their efforts and their people because no single leader seemed strong enough to rule without opposition. The next invaders saw that their opportunity lay in the disunity of the Irish.

The Norman Invasion and Consolidation

In the mid-12th century the Pope gave his blessing to an expedition of **Anglo-Normans** sent by **Henry II** to Ireland. The Normans were actually invited over by the King of Leinster, **Dermot MacMurragh**, who had made a bitter enemy of **Tiernan O'Rourke** of Breffni by running off with his wife, Devorgilla. He also backed the wrong horse in the high kingship stakes, and the united efforts of the High King **Rory O'Connor** and Tiernan O'Rourke brought about a huge reduction in MacMurragh's kingdom. So he approached Henry II, offering his oath of fealty in exchange for an invasion force of men with names like Fitzhenry, Carew, Fitzgerald and Barry (names you still see in Irish villages). The Normans were adventurers and good warriors: in 1169 several Norman nobles decided to try their luck in Ireland, and found it easy to grab huge tracts of land for themselves. The Gaels had faced so few attacks from outside their country that they were unprepared for battle. Yet, though their weapons were inferior, they had the advantage of greater numbers and a deep knowledge of the countryside. The Normans had a well-equipped cavalry who rode protected by a screen of archers. Once they had launched a successful attack, they consolidated their position by building moats, castles and walled towns.

Strongbow, one of the most powerful of the Norman invaders, married the King of Leinster's daughter and became his heir, but his successes and those of the other Norman barons worried Henry II. In 1171 he arrived in Ireland with 4,000 men and two objectives: to secure the submission of the Irish leaders and to impose his authority on his own barons. He achieved both aims, but the Gaelic lords still went on fighting. In fact, the coming of the Normans began a military struggle which was to continue over four centuries.

The Bruce Invasion

In 1314 **Robert Bruce of Scotland** defeated English forces decisively at Bannockburn, and was in a position to try and fulfil his dream of a united Celtic kingdom by putting his brother **Edward** on the throne in Ireland. At first his invasion was successful, but he left a trail of destruction behind him. The year 1316 was marked by famine and disease exacerbated by the war. His dream brought economic and social disaster to

Ireland, and when Edward Bruce was defeated and killed at Dundalk, few of his allies mourned his death. The Normans' control fluctuated within an area surrounding Dublin known as **the Pale**, and they became rather independent of their English overlord; in some cases, such as the de Burgos (Burkes), they became more Irish than the Irish themselves. The Gaelic lords in the north and west continued to hold their territories. To do so they imported Scottish mercenary soldiers, called **gallowglasses**, who prolonged the life of the independent Gaelic kingdoms for more than two centuries after the defeat of Edward Bruce.

The Nine Years' War: Elizabethan Conquest and Settlement

Since the Norman invasion, Ireland had been ruined by continual fighting. By the late 16th century, **Queen Elizabeth I** was determined to bring the Irish more firmly under English control, especially the Ulster lords who had so far maintained almost total independence. Elizabeth took over the Irish policy of Henry VIII, which had never been fully implemented; her government decided that all the Gaelic lords must surrender their lands to the Crown, whereupon they would be regranted immediately. At this time Ulster, today the stronghold of Protestantism, was the most Gaelic and Catholic part of Ireland, and it was from here that the Earl of Tyrone, **Hugh O'Neill**, and **Red Hugh O'Donnell** launched a last-ditch struggle against Elizabeth.

Initial successes bolstered the rebels' morale. Elizabeth, recognizing the gravity of the situation, sent over her talented favourite soldier, Essex. Most of his troops died from disease and guerrilla attacks, and with no reinforcements he had little alternative other than to make a truce with O'Neill. Disgrace and execution were his reward. In February 1600, Lord Mountjoy arrived in Ireland with 20,000 troops. Risings at Munster were crushed and with them, the aspirations of Connaught and Leinster. The Gaelic chiefs were ruthless in their allegiances. They had hailed O'Neill as Prince of Ireland but now, anticipating defeat, they deserted him. O'Neill's hopes were raised by the long-promised arrival of Spanish troops at Kinsale in 1601, but they only numbered 4,000. When they did do battle against Mountjoy, the Irish were left confused when the Spaniards failed to sally out as arranged.

The Flight of the Earls

O'Neill returned to Ulster on 23 March 1603 and made his submission to Mountjoy, only to learn later in Dublin that Queen Elizabeth had died the very next day. He is said to have wept with rage. Amongst all the nobles, only he might have been able to unite the Irish and beat Elizabeth. O'Neill had his titles and lands returned to him, but the Crown authorities, greedy for his property, began to bait him, taking his land at the slightest excuse and forbidding him from practising Catholicism.

Abandoning hope and his followers, he sailed to Europe with other leading Irish nobles. This '**Flight of the Earls**' took place on 14 September 1607, from the wild and beautiful shores of Lough Swilly in County Donegal. It marked the end of Gaelic leadership and a new period of complete domination by the English. The Irish lords took themselves off to the courts of France and Spain, or into the foreign armies. They had spent most of their energies warring amongst themselves, and their departure paved the way for the settlement of their Ulster lands by new arrivals from Scotland and England.

The Confederation, Cromwell and the Stuarts

By the 1640s Ireland was ready for rebellion again. There were plenty of grievances. **James I**, a staunch Protestant, dispossessed many Gaelic and old English families in Ireland because they would not give up Catholicism, and he began the **'plantation'** of the most vehemently Catholic province, Ulster, with Protestants. When **Charles I** came to the throne, many Catholic families hoped that they might be given some religious freedom and retain their estates, but nothing was legally confirmed. In 1633 **Black Tom**, the Earl of Strafford, arrived with the intention of making Ireland a source of profit rather than loss to the king. In his zeal to do so he succeeded in alienating every element in Irish society. His enemies amongst the Puritans in Ireland and England put pressure on the king to recall him, and he was eventually executed. English politics became dominated by the dissension between the Roundheads and the Cavaliers and the hopeless Irish took note. Their maxim was, 'England's difficulty is Ireland's opportunity'. Charles attempted to deal with the growing unrest in Ireland by giving everybody what they wanted, but he no longer had enough power to see that his laws were carried out. The Gaelic Irish decided to take a chance and rebel; many of them came back from the Continental armies hoping to win back their old lands. In October 1641 a small Gaelic force took over the whole of Ulster and there were widespread uprisings in Leinster. In Ulster, the Gaelic people had been hankering for revenge and the new planted families suffered terribly. (This treatment has never been forgotten by Ulster Protestants.)

The Crown authorities were ineffective in controlling the rebels, who continued to be successful. While the government waited for reinforcements from England, they managed to antagonize the old English because they made the mistake of presuming that they would be disloyal to the Crown, and so viewed them with suspicion. The old English families decided to throw in their lot with the rebels, since they were already considered traitors, but on one condition: a declaration of loyalty from the Gaelic leaders to the Catholic English crown, though Charles I was now seriously threatened in any case by the Puritans.

The Confederation of Kilkenny

By February 1642, two-thirds of Ireland was in rebel hands. The rebels established a provisional government at **Kilkenny** and Charles began to negotiate with them, hoping to gain their support against the Puritans. Things were too good to last. The destructive factors that have ruined many Irish uprisings, before and since, came into play: personal jealousy and religion. The old English were loyal to the king and wanted a swift end to the war; the Gaelic Irish were only interested in retrieving their long-lost lands and were ready to fight to the bitter end. This disunity was exacerbated by the rivalry between the Gaelic commander, **Owen Roe O'Neill**, and the commander of the old English army, **Thomas Preston**. In October 1645, the Papal

Nuncio arrived and the unity of the Confederates was further split: he and O'Neill took an intransigent stand over the position of the Catholic Church, to which Charles I could not agree.

The rebels won a magnificent victory over the Puritan General Munro at Benburb, but O'Neill did not follow it up. The confederates, torn by disunity and rivalry, let opportunities slip past and they lost the initiative. Eventually they decided to support the king and end their Kilkenny government – but by this time Charles I had been beheaded and his son had fled into exile. The Royalists were defeated at Rathmines in 1649 and the way was left clear for the Puritan leader, **Cromwell**, who landed in Dublin soon after.

Cromwell came to Ireland determined to break the Royalists, break the Gaelic Irish, and to avenge the events of 1641 in Ulster. He started his campaign with the **Siege of Drogheda**. There are the most gruesome accounts of his methods: when his troops burst into the town they put all Royalists, women, children and priests to the sword. In all, 3,552 dead were counted, while Cromwell only lost 64 men. The same butchery marked the taking of Wexford. Catholics curse Cromwell to this day. Not surprisingly, he did indeed break the spirit of resistance, and there were widespread defections from the Royalists' side. Owen Roe O'Neill might have been able to rally the Irish, but he died suddenly. Cromwell's campaign lasted only seven months, in which time he took all the towns except Galway and Waterford; these he left to his lieutenants.

By 1652 the whole country was subdued, and Cromwell encouraged all the Irish fighting men to leave by granting them amnesty if they fled overseas. The alternative to exile was, for many families, something that turned out to be even worse: compulsory removal west of the Shannon river, to Connaught and County Clare. Some families had been neutral during all the years of fighting, but that was never taken into account. Cromwell was determined that anyone suspected should go 'to Hell or Connaught'.

The government had lots of land to play around with after that. First, they paid off 'the adventurers', men who had lent them money back in 1642. Next, the Roundhead soldiers, who had not been paid their salaries for years, were granted Irish land in its place. In this manner, the **Cromwellian Settlement** parcelled out even more land to speculators, foreigners and rogues.

Stuart and Orange

After the **Restoration of the Monarchy** in 1660, the Catholics in Ireland hoped for toleration and rewards for their loyalty to the Stuart cause. They felt threatened by the fast-expanding Protestant community, but Charles II did not restore many Catholic estates because he had to keep in with the ex-Cromwellian supporters, though Catholics were given a limited amount of toleration. However, with the succession of Charles's brother, **James**, who was Catholic, things began to look up. In Ireland, the Catholic Earl of Tyrconnell became commander of the army in 1685, and later, chief governor. By 1688 Catholics were dominant in the army, the administration, the judiciary and the town corporations, and by the end of the year Protestant power in Ireland was seriously weakened.

James frightened all those Protestants in England who had benefited from Catholic estates. They began to panic when he introduced sweeping acts of toleration for all religions. His attempts to re-establish the Catholic Church alienated the country to such an extent that the Protestant aristocracy eventually invited **William of Orange** over in November 1688 to relieve his father-in-law of his throne. James fled to France but soon left for Ireland, a natural base for the launch of his counterattack. By the date of his arrival in March 1689, only Enniskillen and Londonderry were in Protestant hands.

The Siege of Londonderry and Battle of the Boyne

The subjugation of the city of Londonderry, in Ulster, was James's first aim. In a famous incident celebrated in Orange songs, a group of apprentice boys shut the city gates to the Jacobite army, and so began the celebrated Siege of Londonderry. The townspeople proved unbreakable, even though food supplies were very low and they were reduced to eating rats and mice, and chewing old bits of leather. Many died of starvation during the 15 weeks of the siege, but just as they were about to give in, the supply ship *Mountjoy* forced its way through a great boom built across the Foyle. This military and psychological victory was of enormous significance in the campaign. When William of Orange himself arrived at Carrickfergus in June 1690, James decided to confront him at the Boyne. William had an army of about 36,000, comprised of English, Scots, Dutch, Danes, Germans and Huguenots, against James' army of about 25,000, made up of Irish and French. William triumphed, and James deserted the battlefield and left Ireland hastily.

At the **Battle of the Boyne**, James seems to have completely lost his nerve. The Jacobite forces had to retreat west of the Shannon to Limerick, and William promptly laid siege to it. So weak were its walls that it is said they could be breached with roasted apples. The defence of Limerick was as heroic as that of Londonderry. Patrick Sarsfield slipped out with a few followers, intercepted William's siege train and destroyed it. William then gave up and left for England, leaving Ginkel in charge. The next year the French King Louis XIV sent over supplies and men to fuel the Jacobite cause, hoping to divert William in Ireland for a little longer. The Jacobite leader St Ruth, who landed with them, proved a disaster for the Irish; Sarsfield would have been a better choice. Ginkel took Athlone and Aughrim in June and July of 1691 after two battles, from which stories of Jacobite courage have inspired patriot poets and musicians. The last hope of the Catholic Irish cause was now Limerick.

The Treaty of Limerick

Sarsfield skilfully gathered together what Jacobite troops were left and got them back to Limerick. (St Ruth had been killed by a cannonball and, rather typically, had appointed no second-in-command.) Ginkel tried to storm the town from both sides, but still Limerick held out, and he began to negotiate with Sarsfield. Honourable terms were made for the Jacobites, and Sarsfield signed the famous **Treaty of Limerick** in October 1691. The next day a French fleet arrived and anchored off the Shannon estuary, but Sarsfield stood by the Treaty, which seemed to guarantee quite a lot: Catholics were to have the same rights as they had had under Charles II and any Catholic estates which had been registered in 1662 were to be handed back; Catholics were to be allowed free access to the bar, bench, army and parliament; and Sarsfield was to be given a safe passage to the Continent with his troops. But the Treaty was not honoured – except for the last clause, which got all the fighting men out of the country. This was one of the dirtiest tricks the English played. To be fair to William of Orange, he wanted the treaty to be enforced, but being new and unsure of his support he complied with the treachery. Eleven thousand Irish Jacobites sailed away to join the French army, forming the Irish Brigade. Over the years, many came to join them from Ireland, and were remembered in their native land as the **Wild Geese**.

The Orange-Stuart war still lives vividly in the imagination of the people today. The Siege of Londonderry has become a sign of Protestant determination: 'no surrender 1690' is scrawled, usually in bright red paint, on the walls and street corners of Loyalist areas in Northern Ireland. The Battle of the Boyne is remembered in a similar way.

The Penal Laws

The defeat of the Catholic cause was followed by more confiscation of land, and the **Penal Laws**. A bargain had been struck with the Protestant planters, who were allowed to keep a complete monopoly of political power and most of the land, in return for acting as a British garrison to keep the peace and prevent the Catholics from gaining any power. To do this, they passed a series of degrading laws, which were briefly as follows. No Catholic could purchase freehold land. Any son of a Catholic, turning Protestant, could turn his parents off their estate. Families who stayed Catholic had their property parcelled out equally amongst their children, so that any large estates soon became uneconomic holdings. All Catholics were made to pay a tithe towards the upkeep of the Anglican Church. All priests were banished; no Catholic schools were allowed, and spies were set among the peasants to report on 'hedge schools', a form of quite sophisticated schooling that had sprung up (priests on the run taught at these schools and celebrated Mass). A Catholic could not hold a commission in the army, enter a profession or even own a horse worth more than £5. Of course, these anti-religious laws had the opposite effect to that intended, and Catholicism took on a new lease of life in Ireland. In addition, **economic laws** were introduced, which put heavy taxes on anything that Ireland produced – cloth, wool, glass and cattle – so Ireland could not compete with England. The trading regulations were particularly disadvantageous to the Nonconformist Ulster Protestants, and many of them left.

Gradually, things began to relax – the Catholics had been well and truly squashed. The Protestants began to build themselves grand and beautiful houses, leaving the damp and draughty tower houses to decay. Irish squires were famous for their hard drinking. (The expression 'to be plastered' comes from the story of a guest who was so well wined and dined at a neighbour's house-warming party that he fell asleep against a newly plastered wall. He woke up next morning to find the plaster had dried, and his scalp and hair were stuck fast into it.)

As the 18th century progressed, however, there were signs of aggression amongst the peasantry. Agrarian secret societies were formed with names like the **White Boys, Hearts of Steel**, and the **Molly Maguires**. They were very brutal and meted out rough justice to tenants and landlords alike. If any peasant paid rent to an unfair landlord, he was likely to be intimidated or have his farm burnt down.

In Ulster, peasant movements were dominated by sectarian land disputes. The Catholics were called the **Defenders** and the Protestant groups the **Peep-O'Day Boys**. In the 1770s, the Penal Laws were relaxed a little; Catholics were allowed to bid for land and they incensed the Protestants by bidding higher. After a particularly bad fight between the two sides in which the Protestants won, the **Orange Order** was founded in 1795. A typical oath of one of the early clubs was, 'To the glorious, pious and immortal memory of the great and good King William, not forgetting Oliver Cromwell, who assisted in redeeming us from popery, slavery, arbitrary power, brass money and wooden shoes.'

When the **American War of Independence** broke out in 1775, Ireland found itself undefended. There were fears of an invasion by France or Spain, and a general feeling that there ought to be some sort of defence force. The **Volunteers** were organized with officers from the Protestant landowning class; but as the fears of invasion receded they turned their considerable muscle to the cause of political reform, and Britain began to fear that they might follow the example of the American colonies. When America sought independence, Irish Protestants and Catholics alike watched with approval, particularly since many of the rebel Americans were of Ulster or Scots blood. The landowners had their own parliament in Dublin, but all important matters were dealt with by London. A group of influential landowners began to think that Ireland would be much better off with an independent Irish parliament. In 1783 the government in London, influenced by the eloquence of the great speaker **Henry Grattan**, acknowledged the right of Ireland to be bound only by laws made by the King and the Irish parliament. Trade, industry and agriculture began to flourish, and the worst of the Penal Laws were repealed or relaxed.

Grattan's Parliament

Grattan's Parliament was really an oligarchy of landowners, but at least they understood the problems of the economy and tried to bring a more liberal spirit into dealings with Catholics and dissenters. Grattan wanted complete Catholic emancipation, but for that the Irish had to wait. Yet Trinity College was made accessible to those of all religious persuasions, although Catholics were forbidden by their bishops to go there. The great Catholic Seminary at Maynooth was founded and endowed with money and land from the Protestant aristocrats, who were worried that the priests educated at Douai might bring back with them some of those frightening ideas of liberty and equality that were floating around France. Dissenters were given equal rights with the Established Church at this time.

Dublin was now a handsome Georgian city, a centre for the arts, science and society. To pay for all this pleasure, landowners began to sublet their estates to land-hungry tenants. In the early 1790s fear and anger swept through Europe in the form of the

French Revolution, and the governments of Europe, whether Catholic or Protestant, drew nearer together in mutual fear. Many who at first were delighted with the revolution in France became disgusted with the brutality of its methods. The Irish government disbanded the Volunteers and got together a militia and part-time force of yeomanry. It was nervous of a French invasion and increasingly of a middle-class organization, the 'United Irishmen', who were tired of a government that only spoke for a tiny proportion of the population.

Wolfe Tone and the United Irishmen

The aim of the **United Irishmen** was to throw open the Irish parliament to all Irishmen, irrespective of their rank or religion. Many United Irishmen were from Ulster Nonconformist backgrounds. Initially the movement was to be non-violent, but when war broke out between England and France, all radical societies were forced to go underground. No liberal ideas could be tolerated during the war effort. **Wolfe Tone** was a Dublin lawyer and a prominent United Irishman. He crossed over to France to try and persuade the French Directory to help.

The Protestant Wind

Wolfe Tone succeeded brilliantly in arguing a case for French intervention and, on the night of 16 December 1796, the last great French invasion force to set sail for the British Isles slipped past the British squadron blockading the port of Brest, and anchored off Bantry Bay five days later. They waited one clear, calm day for the frigate carrying the Commander-in-Chief to arrive – but then the wind changed and blew from the east (remembered in all the songs as a 'Protestant Wind'). The fleet endured a storm for three days, then they cut cable and headed back for France. Only Wolfe Tone and his ship, The Indomitable, remained and, as Tone put it, 'England had not such an escape since the Armada'.

Meanwhile, in the Irish countryside, increasingly brutal attempts were made by the militia and the yeomanry to stamp out sedition. In Ulster, where the United Irishmen were strong, efforts were made to set the United Irishmen against the Orangemen, many of whom had joined the yeomanry. This continual pressure forced the society to plan rebellion. However, government spies had infiltrated its ranks, and two months before the proposed date many of the leaders were arrested. By this time many Irish peasants had joined the United Irishmen, inspired by the heady doctrine of Tom Paine's Rights of Man. The increased power of the Irish parliament had not meant more freedom for them – on the contrary, the heretics and alien landlords now seemed to have more power to persecute them in the forms of tithes and taxes. Yet, the Gaelic-speaking peasants had little in common with the middle-class agitators, and their anger was even more explosive.

The 1798 Rebellion

In May 1798 the rebellion broke out. The United Irish leaders had planned a rebellion believing that they could count on an army of over 250,000. However, the absence of leadership and careful planning resulted in local uprisings with no central support;

even those which achieved some success were quickly crushed. In Ulster there were two main risings, under **McCracken** and **Munro**. The risings both enjoyed brief success during which time the rebels treated any Loyalist prisoners well – a marked contrast to what had happened in other counties. However, the sectarian battles between the Peep-O'Day Boys had already soured the trust of the Catholics, and many of them did not turn up to help the mixed bunch of United Irishmen. Poor Wolfe Tone and others who had started the society with such hopes for affectionate brotherhood saw their ideals drowned in a sea of blood.

Nugent, the commander of the government forces in Ulster, decided to appeal to the rebels who had property to lose, especially those in the rich eastern counties, and he proclaimed a general amnesty if the County Antrim rebels gave up their arms. The rebels of County Down did not get off so humanely: when they had been routed and shot down they were left unburied in the streets for the pigs to eat. McCracken and Munro were executed.

The Races of Castlebar

As the war between France and England became more embittered, Wolfe Tone succeeded in raising another invasion force. On 22 August 1798, **General Humbert** arrived in Killala Bay with 1,000 men and more arms for the rebels, although most of them had dispersed. Humbert captured Ballina and routed 6,000 loyalist troops in a charge called **the Races of Castlebar**. But there were not enough rebels and Humbert had to accept honourable terms of surrender in September. Only a few weeks later, another French expedition arrived with Tone on board and entered Lough Swilly. It was overcome by some British frigates and Wolfe Tone was captured. He appeared before a court martial wearing a French uniform and carrying a cockade. The only favour he asked was the right to be shot, which was refused, whereupon he cut his own throat with a penknife and lingered in agony for seven days.

In the space of three weeks 30,000 people, mostly peasants armed with pitchforks and pikes, women and children, were ruthlessly cut down or shot. The rebellion of 1798 was one of the most tragic and violent events in Irish history, horrifying people to such an extent that they desperately began to search for ways of bringing about change in a non-violent way. Ideas of political and religious equality were totally discredited as a result of the deaths and destruction of property. The British Government found that an independent parliament was an embarrassment to them, especially since the 'Protestant garrison' had not been able to put down the peasant rising without their help.

The Union

William Pitt, the British Prime Minister, decided that union between Great Britain and Ireland was the only answer. First he had to bribe the Protestants to give up their power; many earldoms date from this time. Then the **Act of Union** was passed in 1801, with promises of Catholic emancipation for the majority. Pitt really did want to give them equality, for he saw that it was a necessary move if he wished to make Ireland relatively content.

Unfortunately, Pitt was pushed out of government, and **King George III** lent his considerable influence to those opposed to Catholic emancipation: he claimed that the idea of it drove him mad. The Union did not solve any problems, as the Catholics felt bitterly let down and the temporary Home Rule of Grattan's Parliament was looked back to as an example. Irreconcilable nationalism was still alive and kicking. Union with Great Britain was disadvantageous to Ireland in the areas of industry and trade, and many poorer Protestants were discontented – although from now on the Ulster Nonconformists supported the Union, for many had been disillusioned by the vengeance shown towards Protestants by the Catholic peasantry. The terms of the 1801 Act were never thought of as final in Ireland, although the English failed to understand this.

The Liberator: Daniel O'Connell

Catholics still could not sit in parliament or hold important state offices or senior judicial, military or civil service posts. Finally, the Catholics found a champion among themselves: a Catholic lawyer called **Daniel O'Connell** who believed that 'no political change is worth the shedding of a single drop of human blood'. O'Connell founded the **Catholic Association** which, amongst other things, represented the interests of the tenant farmers. Association membership was a penny a month and brought in a huge fighting fund. Most important of all, the Catholic priests supported him, and soon there were branches of the association everywhere. A turning point for Irish history and the fortunes of Daniel O'Connell came with the Clare election in 1828, when the association showed its strength. O'Connell had an overwhelming victory against the government candidate when all the 40-shilling freeholders voted for him. The whole country was aflame: they wanted Daniel at Westminster. **Wellington**, the Prime Minister of the day, was forced to give in, and the **Emancipation Bill** was passed in April 1829. But this was not a gesture of conciliation, for at the same time he raised the voting qualification from 40 shillings to a massive £10. Protestant fears had been raised by the power of such a mass movement, for tenant farmers had dared to vote in opposition to their landlords, even though voting was public. To English Catholics Daniel was also a 'Liberator'.

For 12 years O'Connell supported the Whig Government and built up a well-disciplined Irish party whose co-operation was essential to any government majority. He was then able to press for some very necessary reforms, and when the viceroy and his secretary were sympathetic, much was achieved. However, with the return of the Conservatives in 1840, O'Connell decided it was time to launch another popular agitation campaign, this time for the repeal of the Union. His mass meetings became 'monster meetings', each attended by well over 100,000 people. The government refused to listen on this issue; British public opinion was firmly against it and in Ulster there was a distinct lack of enthusiasm. Daniel O'Connell arranged to have one of his biggest meetings yet, at Clontarf, where Brian Boru had defeated the Vikings. The Government banned it and O'Connell, unwilling to risk violence, called it off. He himself was arrested for conspiracy and sentenced by just the sort of packed jury he had been trying to abolish. Luckily for him, the House of Lords was less frightened and more just; they set aside his sentence. But by then O'Connell's influence had begun to fade, and some Irish began to look to violence to achieve their aims.

The Young Irelanders

Within the Repeal Association was a group of young men who called themselves the Young Irelanders. They had founded *The Nation* newspaper to help O'Connell, but they soon began to move in a different direction. They believed that culturally and historically Ireland was independent of England and fed their enthusiasm on the painful memories of 1798, composing heroic poetry which they set to old ballad tunes. They were ineffective at practical politics and did not have the support of the clergy. In 1848 they responded to the spontaneous and romantic uprisings in Europe with one of their own. It was a dismal failure and alienated many people who had been in favour of the Repeal of the Union. The movement was not to become respectable again until 1870.

The Great Hunger

The diet of an ordinary Irishman consisted of six pounds of potatoes and a pint of milk a day, and he lived in miserable conditions. The Cromwellian and Williamite plantations, together with the effect of the Penal Laws, left the Catholics with only five per cent of the land. Except in the North, where a thriving linen industry had grown up, the people had to make their living from farming. Absentee landlords became more of a problem after the Union, their agents greedier and their rent demands even higher. From 1845–49 the **potato blight** struck, with tragic results.

The population of Ireland, as in the rest of Europe, began to rise quickly in the late 18th century, perhaps because the potato could feed large families on small plots of land. The most deprived and populated area of Ireland was the west, where the potato was the only crop that would grow. It alone sustained the fragile equilibrium of large families on tiny holdings. The scene was set for agricultural and social catastrophe. As the potato rotted in the ground, people ate cabbage, wild vegetables, turnips and even grass, but these could not supply more than a few meals. Gradually, thousands of people began to die of starvation, typhus fever, relapsing fever and dysentery. Every day corn and cattle were leaving the country; nothing was done that might interfere with the principle of free trade and private enterprise. The government's attitude was rigid, though they allowed maize in, a crop nobody had any vested interest in. Food distribution centres were set up and some relief work was paid for by the government. But this was not very sensible sort of work, mostly digging holes only to fill them in again: something constructive like laying a network of railway lines might have interfered with private enterprise. Out of a population of eight and a half million, about one million died and another million emigrated.

Emigration

The Irish had been emigrating for years, first to escape persecution by fleeing to the Continent and then as seasonal labour for the English harvests. The Ulster Scots had set the first pattern of emigration to America. They had found that Ireland was not the promised land, after being lured over there by grants of land and low rents. Bad harvests, religious discrimination and high rents sent them off at the rate of 4,000 a year. Not many Catholics followed, for there were still restrictions on Catholic emigration. Many Irish went to Australia as convicts or free settlers. But the heaviest years of emigration were just after the famine, especially to the USA. People travelled under appalling conditions in boats called 'coffin ships'. It took six to eight weeks to get to America in those overcrowded and disease-ridden conditions. By 1847 nearly a quarter of a million were emigrating annually.

Irish priests followed their flocks out to America and Australia and founded churches wherever they were needed, so a distinct Irish Catholic Church grew up. Such an influx of starving, diseased Irish Catholics was quite another thing to the steady flow of a few thousand Ulster Scots, and initially a lot of people were prejudiced against them. Most of the emigrants left Ireland loathing the British in Ireland. Their children grew up with the same hatred, and sometimes became more anti-British than the Irish left in Ireland. This bitterness was soon transformed into political activity, aided by the Young Irelanders who had fled to America. Many of the emigrants had come from the west where the Gaelic language and culture existed undisturbed. The rest of Ireland, especially the east, was quite anglicized and became more so with the development of education and transport.

America and Irish Politics

In 1858, **James Stephens** founded a secret movement in Ireland called the **Irish Republican Brotherhood (IRB)**. Shortly afterwards, he and **John O'Mahony**, a comrade from the uprising of 1848 who had fled to America, reorganized the Irish Catholics in America into a twin movement called the **Fenian Brotherhood**. The Fenians called themselves after the legendary Fianna Warriors and were dedicated to the principle of Republicanism. Because of the need for secrecy, the IRB was generally known at this time under the name of the Fenians, the American part of the organization, which was able to function openly. In Ireland, aided by money from America, the Fenians started up a newspaper, *The Irish People*, which was aimed at the urban worker. When the American Civil War was over many Irish-American soldiers came over to help the Fenians in Ireland, although their military operations were always dismal failures. But Fenianism remained a potent force. The execution of Allen, Larkin and O'Brien in 1867, who became known as the Manchester Martyrs, became further powerful propaganda for the Fenian cause. **John Devoy** in America and **Michael Davitt** of the **Irish Land League** were imaginative enough to see that violence was not the only way to fight high rents. They made a loose alliance with **Parnell**, the leader of the **Irish Party** in the House of Commons. John Devoy was head of the *Clan na Gael*, an organization which cloaked Fenianism. In America, through the Fenians, Parnell was able to collect money for the land agitators. John Devoy gave money and moral support to the revolutionaries in their fight for independence. The *Clan* created good propaganda for the Nationalists and, between the death of Parnell and the rise of **Sinn Féin** (the new Nationalist party), did everything it could to drive a wedge between the USA and England, and to keep the States neutral during the First World

War. It even acted as an intermediary between Germany and the IRB who were negotiating for guns.

The Irish-Americans played such an important part in Irish politics that it is worth jumping forward in time for a moment to recount subsequent events. In 1918 **Eamon de Valera**, born in America, was elected by Sinn Féin as head of a provisional government. He came to America with high hopes during the War of Independence in Ireland. He wanted two things: political recognition from the government for the Dáil Eireann – the Irish parliament set up in Dublin in 1919 – and money. He failed in his first aim: he was rebuffed by President Wilson, himself of Ulster Scots blood and very proud of it. However, De Valera got plenty of money, $6 million, in the form of a loan, but he fell out with Devoy. He founded a rival organization called the **American Association for the Recognition of the Irish Republic** (AARIA). When Ireland split over the solution of partition and there was a civil war, the Republicans, who rejected the partition, were supported by the AARIA, whilst the Free Staters had Devoy and *Clan na Gael* behind them. The leading spirit of the AARIA was **Joseph McGarrity**, who later broke with De Valera when he began to act against the IRA. His group and their successors continued to give financial support to the IRA during the Troubles in Northern Ireland.

Now to return to the efforts of the British government to forestall the repeal of the Union, and the efforts of various organizations to bring it about.

Tenants' Rights and the Land War

The Union Government was blamed by many in Ireland for the tragic extent of the famine, but the government was blind to the lessons it should have taught them. The famine had only intensified the land war and the 1829 Act simply enabled the impoverished landlords to sell their estates, which the peasants had no money to buy. So the speculators moved in, seized opportunities for further evictions and increased the rents. Tenant resistance smouldered, stimulated by the horrors of the famine. Michael Davitt organized the resistance into the **National Land League**, with the support of **Charles Stewart Parnell**, the leader of the Irish Party in the House of Commons. In the ensuing **Land War** (1879–82), a new word was added to the English language – 'boycott'. The peasants decided not to help an evicting landlord with his crops and he had to import some loyal Orangemen from Ulster to gather in the harvest. The offending landlord was a Captain Boycott. The tenants wanted the same rights that tenants had in Ulster and fair rent, fixity of tenure and freedom to sell at the market value. They also wanted a more even distribution of the land – at that time three per cent of the population owned 95 per cent of the land.

Behind all the agitation at this time, and all the obstruction the Irish Party caused in parliament, was a desire for the repeal of the Union. But the politicians saw the problem as religion, overpopulation, famine, anything but nationalism. It did not enter English heads that the Irish might not want to be part of Britain – with the Union, in their eyes, Irishmen were on an equal footing with the rest of Great Britain, they were part of the Empire. The Union was also a security against foreign attack and must stay. Only one man said anything sensible on the subject and he was not listened to. **J. S. Mill** said that England was the worst qualified to govern the Irish, because English traditions were not applicable in Ireland. England was firmly *laissez-faire* in her economic policies, but Ireland needed economic interference from the government. This the English politicians had resolutely refused to do during and after the famine. **Gladstone** and other Liberals were aware of the discontent. They tried to take the sting out of Irish nationalism by dealing with the problems individually, believing that then the nationalist grievance would disappear.

Killing Home Rule with Kindness

One of the first things to be dealt with was religion, for it could not be kept out of politics. The Protestant ascendancy still monopolized powerful positions, despite Catholic emancipation. There may have been no legal barriers any more, but there were unofficial ones. The Anglican Church of Ireland remained the Established Church until 1869 and until then the Irish peasant had to pay tithes to it. The Catholic hierarchy wanted a state-supported Catholic education, but the government tried to have inter-denominational schools and universities. This never satisfied the Catholic Church and consequently, much later on, it supported the illegal nationalist organizations. Unfortunately the government was unwilling to establish the Catholic Church in Ireland as they would have had problems with the Protestants in Ulster, so although the Catholic Church had consolidated its position, it was not conciliated.

The distress of the peasant farmers had, by this time, become identified with nationalism, so the government set out to solve the economic problems, thinking that this would shatter the nationalists. But they acted too late. Only in 1881 were the demands of the tenants met. Large amounts of money were made available to tenants to buy up their holdings, and by 1916, 64 per cent of the population owned land. (Many of these new owners had the same surnames as those dispossessed back in the 17th century.) But Britain was remembered not for these Land Acts, generous as they were, but for the Coercion and Crime Acts which **Balfour** brought in to try and control the unrest and anarchy which existed in some parts of the country. The **Land Purchase Acts** took away the individual oppressor and left only the government against whom to focus discontent. The peasants had been given more independence and the landlords were virtually destroyed, therefore the Union became even more precarious. The Nationalists could not be bought off.

Home Rule for Ireland?

Parnell forced the government to listen, often holding a balance of power in the House of Commons, and for a while he managed to rally the whole Nationalist movement behind his aggressive leadership. The bait of universal suffrage was enough for the Fenians to try and overthrow the Union from within the system. The **Secret Ballot Act** in 1872 made this even more attractive than abortive rebellions. But the **Home Rule League** did not succeed, even though Gladstone and the Liberals, who were in opposition at that time, had promised to support it. Parnell's aggressive tactics alienated many Englishmen and his Protestant origins upset some of the Catholic hierarchy, who thought he should have concentrated a little more on pushing the Catholic university they wanted. Also, his affair with Kitty O'Shea and involvement in a divorce case shocked many Victorians and Nonconformists in the Liberal Party. They demanded that Parnell should be dropped from the leadership of the Irish Party, and when the Catholic hierarchy heard this, they also began to openly scold 'the named adulterer' and turned their congregations against him.

Another reason for the failure of the Home Rule Bill was that the predominantly Protestant and industrial North of Ireland had no wish at all to join the South. The North thought that it would be overtaxed to subsidize the relatively backward, agrarian South, and the Protestants were frightened of being swamped by the Catholics. Their fear produced in them a siege mentality; Parnell's divorce case was like a gift from heaven and gave the Protestants a reprieve. English opinion was still against Home Rule, and it was only because the Irish Party had made a deal with the Liberals that there was any hope of their succeeding. With the fall of Parnell, the Irish Party split and lost most of its importance.

Parnell's fall in 1891 and the failure of the 1893 Home Rule Bill initiated a resurgence of revolutionary nationalism. The younger generation was shocked by the way the Catholic Church within Ireland condemned Parnell over the O'Shea case. And, as the moral authority of the Church was cast aside, so was one of the barriers to violence. Parnell's failure to work things out through Parliament seemed to indicate that only violence would work. Young people started to join the Irish Republican Brotherhood (IRB), and even the Church began to show more sympathy because at least nationalism was preferable to the atheistic socialism that was creeping into Dublin.

Gaelic Cultural Renaissance

There was a new mood in Ireland at the end of the 19th century. The people were proud of being Irish and of their cultural achievements. Unfortunately only 14 per cent of the population spoke the Gaelic language (the famine and emigration that followed had seriously weakened its hold); English was taught in schools, knowledge of it led to better jobs and opportunities, and Irish music and poetry were neglected except by a few intellectuals. However, it was in the stories of Ireland's past greatness, her legends and customs, that many diverse groups found a common ground. In 1884 the **Gaelic Athletic Association** (GAA) started to revive the national game of hurling. In 1893 the **Gaelic League** was formed. Its president was **Douglas Hyde**, who campaigned successfully for the return of Gaelic lessons to schools and Gaelic as a qualification for entry to the new universities. He never wanted the League to be a sectarian or political force, but it did provide a link between the conservative Catholic Church and the Fenians and Irish Nationalists. 'The Holy Island of St Patrick' developed an ideal: that of the Catholic, devout, temperate, clean-living Irishman. The Gaelic League and the Gaelic Athletic Association were used by the IRB as sounding boards or recruiting grounds for membership.

The Liberals returned to power in 1906 and things began to look brighter for Home Rule. In 1910 **John Redmond** led the Irish Party and held the balance of power between the Liberals and the Conservatives. In 1914 Asquith's **Home Rule Bill** was passed, although it was suspended for the duration of the First World War. But six years later Ireland was in the middle of a war of independence and the initiative had passed from the British into the hands of the revolutionary nationalists. This happened because the British Government had left Home Rule too late. The time-lag between when it was passed and when it actually might be implemented gave the Irish public time to criticize it and see its limitations. The nationalists began to despair of ever finding a parliamentary solution, for the British could now not force the North into Home Rule and were shutting their eyes to the gunrunning which had been going on since the formation of the Ulster Volunteers.

The Irish people were rather lukewarm about organizations like the IRB and its associated, new **Sinn Féin** Party, founded by Arthur Griffith. In fact, military recruitment, relative prosperity, and the nominal achievement of Home Rule brought Ireland and the rest of Britain closer together. The IRB's military council wanted to do something to stem the fragmentation of their movement. An event on Easter Monday in 1916 meant all was 'changed utterly'. (W.B. Yeats).

Easter Rebellion 1916

Plans for a national rising with German support were made. The support did not arrive but, despite the confusion, the IRB leaders were determined the rising should go ahead in Dublin. It happened very quickly – suddenly the tricolour of a new Irish Republic was flying from the General Post Office in Dublin. Two thousand Irish Nationalist volunteers, led by **Patrick Pearse** of the IRB, stood against the reinforcements sent from England and then surrendered about a week later. People were horrified at first by the waste of life, but then the British played into the hands of Patrick Pearse. All 14 leaders were executed after secret trials. The timing of the uprising was no coincidence. Pearse and the others wanted it to be a blood sacrifice in order to breathe new life into the nationalist cause.

The executions happened before there could be any backbiting as to why the whole thing had been a muddle. Suddenly they were dead, and pity for them grew into open sympathy for what they had been trying to achieve. The Catholic Church was trapped in the emotional wave which advocated revolution. The party that gained from this swing was Sinn Féin; it was pledged to non-violent nationalism and was the public front of the IRB. John Redmond, the leader of the Irish Party at Westminster, had urged everybody to forget their differences with Britain and fight the common enemy, Germany, but the Irish Nationalists, who were negotiating with the Germans, saw things in a very different light. Many Irishmen did go and fight for Britain: some 200,000 men enlisted, but the feeling grew that Redmond was prepared to compromise over Home Rule and shelve it until it suited the British. Sinn Féin, under the influence of American-born Eamon de Valera, set out to mobilize popular support through propaganda and electioneering.

When conscription was extended to Ireland in 1918, even more people decided that **Sinn Féin** was the only party which could speak for them. It won all the Irish seats bar six. Redmond's party was finished. The only problem was that 44 of the Sinn Féin members were in English jails; those that were not met in Mansion House and set up their own Dáil Eireann. Eamon de Valera made an audacious escape from Lincoln prison and was elected the first President of the Irish Republic in 1919. The Irish Volunteers became the **Irish Republican Army** and war was declared on Britain.

The North

Meanwhile, in the North a leader was found to defend the Union in Dublin-born **Edward Carson**. He was a leading barrister in London (he cross-examined Oscar Wilde in that notorious lawsuit), and was openly supported by the Conservatives in England. A solemn **Covenant of Resistance to Home Rule** was signed by hundreds of thousands of Northern Unionists. They would fight using all means possible not to come under an Irish parliament in Dublin. After the Easter rising of 1916, Carson was assured by **Lloyd George** that the six northeastern counties could be permanently excluded from the Home Rule Bill of 1914. When the **War of Independence** broke out in the South, the British offered them partition with their own parliament whilst remaining within Britain. Today they still feel their ties are with a liberal Britain, not the Catholic South. (Remember that, until very recently, in the Republic there was no divorce, limited contraception, mixed marriages were discouraged and the Welfare State is still comparatively undeveloped.)

The War of Independence

The British Government had been caught out by the Dáil's Declaration of Independence. The British were busy trying to negotiate a peace treaty at Versailles and the Americans made it clear that they sympathized with the Irish. Ammunition raids, bombing, burning and shooting began in Ireland, mainly against the Irish Constabulary. The British Government waited until the Versailles Conference had come to an end and then fought back. The **Black and Tans** were sent over to reinforce the police, and Lloyd George tried to play it down as a police situation. Their methods were notoriously brutal and it seemed that their reprisals were more vicious than the IRA incidents that had provoked them. It became a war of retaliation. **Michael Collins** was in charge of military affairs for the IRA; he waged a vicious, well-thought-out campaign against the Black and Tans. By July 1921 a truce was declared because the British public wanted to reach a compromise. In October an Irish delegation, which included Griffith and Collins, went to London to negotiate with Lloyd George. They signed a treaty which approved the setting up of an Irish Free State with Dominion status, similar to Canada. The British were mainly concerned with the security aspect and they made two stipulations; that all Irish legislators should take an oath of allegiance to the Crown and that the British Navy could use certain Irish ports.

Civil War

The Republicans (or anti-treaty side) in the Dáil were furious. They regarded it as a sellout. They did not like the oath, or the acceptance of a divided Ireland. Michael Collins saw it as a chance for 'freedom to achieve freedom' and when it came to the debate on it in the Dáil, the majority voted in favour of the treaty. De Valera was against the treaty and, as head of the Dáil, he resigned; **Arthur Griffith** succeeded him. In June, when the country accepted the treaty, civil war began. The split in the Dáil had produced a corresponding split in the IRA; part of it broke away and began violent raids into the North. The remainder of the IRA was reorganized by Michael Collins into the Free State Army. When he was assassinated, a man just as talented took over, **Kevin O'Higgins**. This period is remembered as the **War of Brothers**, and it was bitter and destructive. Men who had fought together against the Black and Tans now shot each other down. Finally, the Republicans were ready to sue for peace. De Valera, who had not actively taken part in the fighting but had supported the Republicans, now ordered a cease-fire. The bitterness and horror of the Civil War has coloured attitudes to this very day. The differences between the two main parties, **Fine Gael** (pro-treaty) and **Fianna Fáil** (anti-treaty), are historical rather than political, although perhaps in foreign policy Fianna Fáil has taken a more anti-British line. Fine Gael held power for the first 10 years and successfully concentrated on building the 26-county state into something credible and strong. In 1926 De Valera broke with Sinn Féin because they still saw the Dáil and the government in power as usurpers, as bad as the British, and refused to take up their seats. De Valera, the master pragmatist, founded his own party, Fianna Fáil; the new state wanted a change and in 1932 he formed a government. He soon made it clear that Ireland was not going to keep the oath of allegiance or continue to pay the land annuities (the repayment of money lent to help tenants pay for their farms).

De Valera

In 1937 De Valera drew up a new **Constitution** which named the State Éire, or Ireland. It declared Ireland a Republic in all but name and seemed a direct challenge to the Northern Ireland Government. Article 5 stated 'the right of the Parliament and Government established by the Constitution to exercise jurisdiction over the whole of Ireland, its Islands and territorial seas'. Article 44.1.2. recognized 'the special position of the Holy Catholic, Apostolic Roman Church as the guardian of the Faith professed by the great majority of its citizens'. De Valera would not go so far as to 'establish' it, as the Church of Ireland had once been, and as the Catholic hierarchy wanted. (This article was removed from the Constitution in the 1970s). Both parties had trouble with extremists in the 1930s; Fine Gael had to expel General O'Duffy of the Fascist Blue Shirt Movement, and Fianna Fáil were embarrassed by their erstwhile allies in the IRA. De Valera dealt with the situation by setting up a military tribunal and declaring the IRA an illegal organization in 1936. The IRA did not die but went underground and continued to enjoy a curious relationship with the government and the public. When it got too noisy it was stamped on; but the IRA continued to be regarded nervously and with respect for its ideals, and its members' intransigence seemed to be in line with Ireland's dead patriots. In 1939 Éire declared itself neutral during the Second World War which further isolated it from the rest of the British Isles. In 1949, Costello's Interparty Government inaugurated a Republic and broke Commonwealth ties. Relations between the North and the South remained cool until the tentative *rapprochement* in 1965 between Lemass (the Irish Prime Minister, or Taoiseach) and O'Neill (the Prime Minister of Northern Ireland). But relations cooled again rapidly as the Troubles (1968–1970) began and two members of Taoiseach Jack Lynch's Fianna Fáil ministry were implicated in gun-running for the IRA.

Northern Ireland

The North Today

It is very difficult to be impartial about the Troubles in Northern Ireland – they have been tragic and frightening. With the cease-fire holding at the time of writing (albeit under an impasse between the parties, with power-sharing suspended since 2002), the 1998 Good Friday Agreement prepared the ground on which to build a stable society, so there is some hope for the future, albeit cautious.

The basic reason for the start of the Troubles is that the Catholic minority in the North did badly with the division of Ireland in the 1920s: once the Northern Ireland State was set up they were treated as second-class citizens. The series of events that lead up to the present situation is discussed in more detail below. Before you read on, you may find it useful to look at the glossary of Northern Irish political parties and terms at the end of this chapter.

Discontent Amongst Ulster Catholics, 1921–69

The Ulster Protestants made up two-thirds of the population of Northern Ireland, and the Catholics, the rest. Under the leadership of Edward Carson and James Craig, the Ulster Protestants had managed to wrestle their bit of Ulster from the rest of Ireland, and preserve the Union with Britain. They utterly repudiated the idea of a Catholic, Gaelic Republic of Ireland, and held themselves aloof from events in the Free State, later the Republic. No attempt was made to woo the Catholic Nationalists, perhaps because the Protestant leaders, ever-anxious about being turfed out of the Union with Britain and into the Republic of Ireland, directed all their energies into preserving the Union. The **Government of Ireland Act** in 1920 gave Westminster supreme authority over Northern Ireland. The **Ireland Act** of 1949 enshrined the constitutional guarantee that gave the Stormont Parliament the right to decide whether Northern Ireland would remain in the UK or not.

All Catholics were regarded as supporters of the **IRA**, an organization which was indeed a real menace to this shaky state. It was seen as imperative that Catholics should never be allowed into positions of power and influence. **Sir Basil Brooke** (1888–1973) was typical of the type of blinkered cabinet minister who ran the government for years. He, along with **James Craig** (1871–1940), first Prime Minister of Northern Ireland, encouraged Protestants to employ only Protestants, for he, like others, believed that the Catholics were 'out to destroy Ulster with all their power and might'. Brooke became Prime Minister in 1943 and played an active role in linking the Orange Order, of which he was a leading member, with the government of the time. Protestant businesses tended to employ Protestants and Catholics employed Catholics. There were few mixed housing areas or marriages. The Catholic priests fiercely defended their right to run Catholic schools – as they still do.

Government went on at a mainly local level through county and town councils. The Loyalists ensured that they always had a majority on the council through the use of **gerrymandering**. The local voting qualification also favoured Protestants, who were often wealthier, for the franchise was only granted to house owners or tenants, and the number of votes allocated to each person could be as high as six, depending on the value of their property. Because the Protestant rulers controlled housing schemes and jobs, the working-class Protestants were given the lion's share of any existing housing or jobs. Northern Ireland had a much lower standard of living than the rest of the UK, and any advantages were eagerly grasped by these workers, who displayed little feeling of worker solidarity with their fellow Catholics. They never could escape from their religious prejudices to unite against the employers, although the ruling class had feared their alliance during the 1922 riots over unemployment.

The Catholics themselves were ambiguous about the State; most of them in the 1920s were Republicans, and they never gave up hope that the Dublin Government might do something about it. Many believed that the Six Counties could not survive and, in the beginning, Nationalist Republican representatives refused to sit at Stormont. On the other hand, others had watched with horror the bloodshed and bitterness that resulted from the Civil War in the Irish Free State. After being educated, many of the bright ones emigrated rather than fight the system. The IRA attempted over the next 50 years to mount a campaign in the North, but gained little support; a big campaign in 1956–62 that killed 19 people failed miserably. The local Catholics did not back them, and the **B Specials** (Protestant-dominated special police force) zealously pursued the culprits, often at the expense of law-abiding Catholics, who were left resentful and disgruntled. For the time being the Protestant Unionists were able to dominate Catholic Nationalists in elections in a proportion of about four to one. This gave them a feeling of security, which was also bolstered by the gratitude of the British government for their loyalty and help during the Second World War, when Northern Ireland had been a vital bulwark for the rest of the UK.

The Civil Rights Movement – British Troops Move In

Yet things had to change. As young, educated Catholics and Protestants grew up, they began to agitate about the obvious injustices, and the **Civil Rights Association** was formed in 1967. Unfortunately, the marches that drew attention to their aims also attracted men of violence on both sides and, as the marches turned into riots, the Protestant Loyalists, including the **Royal Ulster Constabulary** (RUC) and B Specials, seemed to be in league with the Protestant mobs against the Catholics. At this point the discredited IRA failed to seize their opportunity to woo the Catholics, who were both confused and frightened. The Catholics welcomed the British troops, who were brought in to keep the peace after the Loyalists and police beat up civil rights marchers at Burntollet, and later the inhabitants of the Bogside in Londonderry, in January 1969.

At that time **Terence O'Neill** had taken over from Lord Brookborough as Prime Minister at Stormont. Although of the same Unionist ascendancy stock, he realized that something must be done to placate the Nationalists. The few liberal gestures that he made towards the Catholics and the Republic opened up a Pandora's box of fury and opposition amongst the Protestant Unionists, who found a leader in the **Reverend Ian Paisley**. The reforms O'Neill planned over housing and local government came too late, and he was swept away by the Protestant backlash when he called a General Election in April 1969. The brutality with which the police had broken up the civil rights marches had stirred support for the IRA, and the Summer Marching Season was marked by even more violence.

The IRA Exploit Events

The IRA organized itself to exploit the situation. It split into two after an internal struggle, and the murders and bombings that dominated events after this time are mainly the work of the Provisional IRA, commonly called the IRA. The British Army lost the confidence of the Catholic community it had come to protect through heavy-handed enforcement of security measures. Besides, the IRA posed as the natural guardians of the Catholics, so there were cheers amongst the Catholic Nationalists when the IRA killed the first British soldier in October 1970. The IRA aimed to break down law and order; to them any method was legitimate, and any member of the army or police a legitimate target.

The Stormont Government hastened to pass some much-needed reforms between 1969 and 1972. The RUC was overhauled, and the B Specials abolished. A new part-time security force was set up within the British Army and called the **Ulster Defence Regiment** (UDR). In 1971 a new Housing Executive was set up to allocate houses fairly, irrespective of religious beliefs. The IRA managed to conduct a destructive bombing campaign in the cities – innocent civilians were killed or injured and buildings destroyed. British soldiers responded to rioting in the Bogside in January 1972 by killing 13 people on what has become known as Bloody Sunday. A cycle of violence begetting violence began to spiral, and society divided along even more sectarian lines than before. The legacy of psychological distress and bitterness from this time is still terrible to contemplate.

UK Attempts to Solve the Problem

In 1972 the Stormont Government and Parliament were suspended by the British Government, which had always retained full powers of sovereignty over it, and Direct Rule from Westminster was imposed. There is a **Secretary of State for Northern Ireland**, who is appointed by the Prime Minister of the United Kingdom and sits in the UK Cabinet, and takes forward Government policy. Members of Parliament from the constituencies of Northern Ireland are elected from various parties and sit in Westminster, where they try to bring local issues to the attention of the House.

Internment was introduced in 1971, where large numbers of terrorist suspects were imprisoned without trial. This hardened Catholic opinion against British justice, and the practice was gradually phased out after a couple of years. Subsequently, the **Diplock court** system was introduced, where alleged terrorists are tried by a single judge with no jury. This was justified by the amount of intimidation to which the jury could be subjected. Various power-sharing initiatives between the largely Protestant

Unionist parties and the Catholic and Nationalist SDLP did not get off the ground, so Direct Rule continued. The suspension of the Stormont Parliament removed the constitutional guarantee of the 1949 Act but it was renewed in the 1973 **Constitution Act**, which established the principle that any change in the status of Northern Ireland would have to have majority consent.

The Sunningdale Agreement

In December 1973 the leaders of the Northern Irish parties, a new Executive, and Ministers from the United Kingdom and, for the first time, the Republic of Ireland, met together at Sunningdale. They agreed to set up a **Council of Ireland** which would work for co-operation between Northern Ireland and the Republic. The Agreement provided for a new type of Executive in Northern Ireland, in which power was to be shared as far as possible between representatives of the two communities in a joint government. It was the dawn of new hope for the province, but the Unionist masses and the Republican terrorists did not want this new co-operation to work. Faced with a general strike called by the Ulster Workers' Council which paralysed the province, the government did not use the army to break the strike, but allowed intimidation by 'Loyalist' paramilitary organizations to win the day. The Unionist members of the Executive resigned, and Direct Rule had to be resumed. Many people believe that if the Sunningdale Agreement had been implemented, much suffering could have been avoided sooner.

The Victims of the Troubles

The province suffered sectarian killings, bombings, and the powerful propaganda of the hunger strike campaign by IRA prisoners in the early 1980s. The economy was struggling, and well-educated members of society, both Protestant and Catholic, left in droves. However, since the first cease-fire in 1994, things have improved, the economy has picked up and foreign investors are looking again at Northern Ireland. The Ulster people have suffered the gradual erosion of their society through violence, intimidation, and the subtler psychological effects that violence induces. On the positive side, the spirit and bravery of the Ulster people remains unbroken, and manufacturing businesses continue to thrive and to compete in international markets. But the statistics in such a small population are grim. Between 1969 and 1994, 3,168 people lost their lives and around 3,300 people were injured and maimed, of whom around 2,200 were civilians. Feelings of despair, fear and outrage in both communities led to extreme attitudes in the 1980s. The Reverend Ian Paisley and his colleagues had a huge following, whilst support for Sinn Féin increased considerably at the expense of the Constitutional Nationalists and the SDLP.

The Anglo-Irish Agreement

In 1985, after initial efforts by **Garrett Fitzgerald**, the leader of the Fine Gael Party in the Republic, and **Margaret Thatcher**, the British Prime Minister, the **New Ireland Forum** met in Dublin. It was agreed that Northern Ireland would remain in the United

Kingdom as long as the majority so desired, and that the Dublin Government should have an institutionalized consultative status in relation to Northern Irish affairs.

The effect of the Agreement was largely positive, although gradual. Both governments made progress in the complicated area of extradition and cross-border security, especially after the general revulsion in the Republic against the IRA bomb attack in Enniskillen in 1987. The British Government grasped the nettle of injustice over the conviction of the 'Guildford Four' and the 'Birmingham Six', prisoners convicted of bombings on mainland Britain. The reopening of these cases and the subsequent acquittal of these prisoners dissipated much bad feeling in the Republic of Ireland where there is great scepticism about British justice in relation to the Irish. One of the most important achievements of the Agreement was that the Irish Government formally accepted 'the principle of consent' by the people of Northern Ireland. Any change in the Constitution Act of 1973 had to have majority consent. The Unionists were not mollified by this, for it was enshrined in the Constitution of the Republic that the Irish Republic claimed the whole island, and this claim had not been given up. The Agreement made the world realize that the 'Brits out' solution would mean forcibly transferring a million-strong Protestant population into a united Ireland that did not really want them, and the probability of bloody civil war.

The strong emotional link between the rest of the UK and the Ulster Unionists has changed since the beginning of the 20th century. The Union was no longer regarded as a cause in itself; many English, Welsh and Scots know little about Northern Ireland and questioned the lives lost and money spent maintaining the Union. The Unionists understood this very clearly and felt increasingly threatened. The Nationalists had not rejected the IRA, who continued to work for the destruction of the six-county state through murder and bombing campaigns in Ulster. In Britain and Europe, the IRA followed a campaign of bombing 'soft' British military targets, and assassinating British politicians and industrialists in order to turn British public opinion against the Union with Northern Ireland.

1990–1993

Inter-party talks began in Northern Ireland and, before they broke down, some progress was made in defining the three complicated relationships between the North and the UK, the North and the Republic, and the Republic and the UK. This meant there was a set of negotiating mechanisms for the peace process to be furthered. British policy continued to try and find the middle ground between opposing parties in the North, and it was hoped that the politics of the extremists would wither away. In 1992 and 1993, the IRA carried out bombing attacks in the financial heart of London and elsewhere. One such attack in a shopping centre in Warrington killed two children; there was worldwide revulsion, and a peace movement was launched in Dublin. The IRA could continue their campaign of violence indefinitely, but there were signs that key elements in the IRA wanted to try and change things through political action. In April 1993, **John Hume** of the SDLP started a dialogue with **Gerry Adams** of Sinn Féin. Both the British and the Irish Governments reacted furiously to this, but popular nationalist support for the dialogue, in both the North and South, forced the governments to rethink their policy. The British Prime Minister, **John Major** and his Irish counterpart, **Albert Reynolds**, began a new policy of trying to draw the extremists into the political process and to aim at all-party talks for a lasting constitutional settlement which would bring peace. In October 1993, the IRA planted a bomb in a Belfast fish and chip shop killing ten people; a terrible revenge was exacted by extremist loyalists who shot 14 people in a public house in Greysteel. Both acts horrified the people of Northern Ireland.

The Downing Street Declaration

On 15th December 1993, the Irish and British Prime Ministers presented a **Joint Declaration** which successfully managed to address the competing claims of the Nationalists and the Unionists. The British Government declared in the document that Britain 'had no selfish strategic or economic interest in Northern Ireland' and recognized the right of the people of Ireland, North and South, to self-determination. Both governments affirmed that the status of Northern Ireland could only be changed with the consent of 'a great number of its people'. In the event of an overall political settlement, the Irish Government declared it would drop its claim to the Six Counties contained in articles 2 and 3 of the Irish Constitution. The Irish Government would establish a forum for peace and reconciliation at some later date. Both governments offered a place at the negotiating table to the extremists on both sides if they renounced violence.

Cease-fire

After a disappointing reaction to the Declaration and prevarication for several months, the IRA eventually announced 'a complete cessation of military operations' on 31st August 1994. In the following weeks the extremist Unionist forces of the UFF, the UVF and the Red Hand of Ulster announced a cease-fire, conditional upon the IRA's continuing cease-fire. This cease-fire brought great opportunities for eventual peace, and the people of the North became increasingly convinced that they must find politicians who were prepared to find new ways of settling their differences. An end to the day-to-day killing was a huge relief to everybody who lived there. Unfortunately, the main protagonists still disagreed over major issues such as the release of prisoners, the withdrawal of the British Army, decommissioning of arms amongst terrorist groups, the future of community policing in Northern Ireland, and the role of the Southern Irish Government in the future of the province.

The British and Irish Governments produced two important framework documents in 1995. These sought to provide a basis for discussion in a **Northern Irish Forum** with elected delegates from all the different parties. The framework documents proposed a new assembly elected by proportional representation, a new relationship between North and South and between all the countries surrounding the Irish Sea. However, the discussions met stalemate over the **decommissioning of arms**. The IRA and Sinn Féin wanted the British Army to withdraw first and all political prisoners to be released before they gave up any of their weapons. The Unionists wanted the IRA to give up their arms first as a sign of their good intentions. In February 1996, the IRA declared their part in the cease-fire over with a bomb attack on Canary Wharf in London, which killed two people. The talks continued without Sinn Féin, little progress was made, and things looked very gloomy.

In the UK, the Conservative Government under John Major was replaced in May 1997 by a Labour Government with a huge majority. The new Prime Minister, **Tony Blair**, was no longer reliant on the Unionist vote in the House of Commons which gave him a freer hand all round. The Official Unionists, under the leadership of **David Trimble**, were breaking out of their reactionary 'Ulster Says No' mould, and it seemed as if the influence of Ian Paisley and his DUP was on the wane.

In the British elections, Sinn Féin's **Gerry Adams** and **Martin McGuinness** were voted into Westminster, although they did not take up their seats. In the Irish Republic, a general election brought a victory for Fianna Fáil, and their leader, **Bertie Ahern**, said he was willing to talk to Sinn Féin about a new cease-fire. The new Northern Ireland Secretary of State, **Dr Mo Mowlam**, also promised to admit Sinn Féin to the talks if they called a new cease-fire. The American senator **George Mitchell**, who had been given the delicate task of brokering all-party talks, suggested that the talks on the decommissioning of arms should take place at the same time, but separately from the talks on the future of the province.

Sectarian tension was heightened in the mid-1990s, when Orange marchers insisted on taking their traditional routes, which often lay in Catholic areas. In July 1997, at Drumcree in Portadown, violence flared up and spread throughout the province when an Orange Order march planned to march down the Garvaghy Road on its way from Drumcree Church. The reaction within the Nationalist community was intense in the face of what they saw as sectarian intimidation. The head of the Orange Order Lodges decided to cancel and reroute some of the potentially violent 12th July marches. Tension in the province was running high, after events at Drumcree, but this gesture from the Orange Order helped. Horrible sectarian murders added to the tension but the restoration of the IRA's cease-fire in August improved matters considerably. In September 1997 the leaders of Sinn Féin joined the all-party talks. The Official Unionist Party dropped their demand that the decommissioning issue must be settled before any negotiations could begin. Instead, an independent commission on illegal arms decommissioning was set up.

At last, negotiations between all the concerned parties could begin; both the Irish and British Prime Ministers emphasized that there was now a clear agenda and timescale, and that the talks must not get lost in prevarication. The talks consisted of three interlocking and interdependent strands: the internal settlement of the province; North-South relations; and Anglo-Irish relations.

The Good Friday Agreement

On **Good Friday, 11th April 1998**, after many vicissitudes, the world was told that there had been a historic agreement. It mapped out radical new arrangements for a devolved Ulster Assembly, a council of ministers linking Northern Ireland and the Republic, and limited cross-border bodies who would work things through together. A new Council of the Islands would be set up which would link all the devolved assemblies in the UK, and the governments in Dublin and London. The Irish Government promised to amend Articles 2 and 3 of its Constitution which lay claim to the Six Counties. In return, the British Government stated that it would replace the Government of Ireland Act.

The people of Ireland from both sides of the border voted their approval of the Good Friday Agreement in a **Referendum** in 1998. However, the slow progress towards implementation of its terms was frustrating and has suffered some discouraging setbacks. Many Unionists were against it, and their vote was split. The new Assembly requires representatives to classify themselves as either Unionist, Nationalist or 'Other', and certain legislation requires the consent of all three groups. The various Unionist parties make up the largest group in the Assembly. The SDLP is the dominant Nationalist Party, followed by Sinn Féin. The principal 'other' party is the Alliance who polled badly. **David Trimble**, at the time leader of the UUP, was appointed the Assembly's First Minister with Seamus Mallon of the SDLP as deputy, with executive authority in the hands of 12 ministers who, along with 98 others, make up the Northern Ireland Assembly. The Assembly decides on the internal affairs of state, while security, justice, and taxation remain the province of the Secretary of State and government in Westminster. (At the time of writing, the Assembly remains in suspension following claims of IRA intelligence gathering at Stormont in 2002. David Trimble has stepped down as UUP leader after a disastrous UK election result in which the party lost four of their five seats in Westminster, including Trimble's own, to the DUP and Sinn Féin.)

Slowly, new structures and organizations have been created to fulfil Strand One of the Good Friday Agreement. The Unionists are aware that over the next 25 years or so, the population will become more balanced, and thus their negotiating position will weaken. The Nationalists, too, are weary of the Troubles, and have seen their status within the province improve significantly over the years, while Sinn Féin and other Republican groups are experiencing the many dividends of joining the democratic process. However, there are major issues over arms (*see* opposite, above) and the resolution of the issue of the Drumcree parade, which is frequently rerouted by the Parades Commission.

The future of community policing in Northern Ireland is also problematic. The IRA has been policing Catholic West Belfast for years, to protect their financial empire and to control lawless youths. Historically, there has always been Catholic hostility towards the RUC and few Catholic recruits joined the force because of their fear of the IRA. In order to create a more representative force, in 2001 the RUC was reformed and renamed the **Police Service of Northern Ireland** (PSNI), with a new uniform and oath of allegiance. This was necessary for the law to be reimposed on criminal activities and extortion rackets. Punishment beatings and sectarian beatings have not ceased, however.

The **Omagh bombing** on August 15th 1998 was horrific in terms of civilian deaths, with 28 people killed and hundreds injured. This was perpetrated by the **Real IRA**, a splinter group of the Provisional IRA, which has emerged since Sinn Féin agreed terms on the cease-fire and the Good Friday Agreement.

Since 1998, both Nationalists and Unionists have benefited greatly from the relative peace and stability that the agreement has brought. At the same time, the difficulty of implementing its terms fully has contributed to a polarization of politics. The anti-agreement DUP has become the largest Unionist party, while Sinn Féin has overtaken the moderate SDLP as the largest Nationalist party. Peace appears to have fed the extremes.

The implications of these developments for the peace process are as yet unclear. On the positive side, neither Sinn Féin nor the DUP appears to want to repudiate the agreement. Indeed, in December 2004, a deal on weapons decommissioning between them was almost brokered, although it ultimately foundered on the largely symbolic issue of photographic evidence. On the negative side, the agreement has yet to foster real trust between the political leaders or their respective supporters. Northern Ireland remains a deeply divided society. Suspended between war and peace, the politics of transition may continue for some time yet.

The Republic Today

The Irish Republic has a titular Head of State, a **President** who is elected for seven years by the vote of the people. The President is empowered on the recommendation of the Dáil to appoint the Prime Minister or **Taoiseach** (pronounced 'tee-shookh', which means literally, 'leader'), sign laws and invoke the judgement of the Supreme Court on the legality of Bills. He/she is also supreme commander of the armed forces. The Irish Parliament consists of the President and two Houses: the Dáil and the Senate. The Dáil is made up of 166 members (**TDs**) elected by adult suffrage through proportional representation. The Senate is made up of 60 members: 11 are nominated by the Taoiseach; 49 are elected by the Dáil and county councils from panels representative of the universities, labour, industry, education and social services. The average length of an Irish government is three years.

In the 1970s and 1980s each Irish government has had to face unemployment, growing emigration and a huge national debt. In 1988, incomes measured by GDP per head were just 63 per cent of those in the UK. By 1998, the Republic had overtaken the UK, and now its GDP is one of the best in the European Union. The forecast for the future is that the Republic's economy could grow annually by over five per cent a year. European investment in technology, food processing, pharmaceuticals and the marketing industries has benefitted Ireland enormously. This is partly because of its young, well-educated population and skilled workforce. Emigration has almost halted. Growing numbers of economic migrants, particularly from Eastern Europe, are entering the country, causing a worrying upsurge in racism. Yet statistics from the 2002 Census revealed that, in the preceding six years, Irish-born people returning to Ireland actually outnumbered non-Irish entrants to the country. Even more positive, a recent US survey of 22 countries found that Ireland was overall top for feelings of national pride while another large scale survey of 111 countries worldwide deemed the country offers the best 'quality of life'.

The Republic is a major supporter of the **EU** and has been famously described as 'Europe's best pupil'. Ireland has done very well economically from EU funding, but it is now becoming a net contributor to the EU after years of being a net recipient.

The principle of neutrality so long adhered to in foreign affairs is no longer certain. Developments within the EU may see a watering down of Irish neutrality, as they include a commitment by all members to a common security policy and involvement in the 60,000-strong Rapid Reaction Force. The traditional lines of Irish parties are also changing from the pro- and anti-treaty (of 1921) stances. **Mary Robinson** when President of Ireland (1990–97) brought a new flexibility and dynamism into Irish politics. Her policies have continued with the election of **Mary McAleese** to the post in 1997, the first Irish President to come from Northern Ireland.

Irish Political Parties

The origins of the two major Irish political parties, Fianna Fáil and Fine Gael, hark back to the violent differences between those against the Free State Treaty and those for it in the turbulent 1920s.

Fianna Fáil has established itself as the dominant ruling party.

Fine Gael is the second largest party in the country. It is close to other Christian Democrat parties in Europe, and has strong European inclinations.

The Labour Party has found it difficult to gain support as people have tended to be very conservative and voted as their family do – either Fine Gael or Fianna Fáil. This is changing as Labour has increased its power base in the last 15 years in Dublin and Cork and formed coalition governments either with Fianna Fáil or Fine Gael. Growth has also been fed by its incorporation in 1999 of the small Democratic Left Party.

Sinn Féin is the political arm of the Official IRA (a banned organization), but does not command much support in the Republic. However, in the mid-1980s Sinn Féin dropped its absenteeist policy and has for the first time accepted the seat it won in the last general election (the last time it won a seat was in 1957 and the last time a Sinn Féin member took one up was in 1922).

Other Parties in the Dáil

The Progressive Democrats were founded in 1985 by former members of Fianna Fáil after a split in that party. It is currently in a coalition partnership with Fianna Fáil.

The Green Party is allied to Greens in 28 other countries.

Glossary of Political Parties and Terms

These labels and identities crop up constantly in discussions on Northern Ireland:

Catholic: approximately 605,639 people belong to the Roman Catholic Church in Northern Ireland.

Protestant: refers to Church of Ireland members, Presbyterians and other non-Catholic denominations. The Church of Ireland number around 279,280 people, and Presbyterians number some 336,891.

Unionist: refers to supporters of the Union with Great Britain, who have no wish to share an Irish nationality with the Republic of Ireland. There are two main Unionist parties in Northern Ireland. The Official Unionists (UUP) were the original party and are, on the surface, more willing to discuss options to try and solve the crisis in the State. The Democratic Unionist Party (DUP), led by Ian Paisley, is more radical and Protestant. It is very anti any co-operation with the Irish Republic, and anti the pope.

Alliance: a label used for a party composed of moderate Unionists, both Protestant and Catholic, but it loses out to the more extreme parties.

Loyalist: refers to a Protestant who is prepared to use violence to prevent a United Ireland and to maintain the Union with the UK.

Nationalist: refers to anyone who supports a united Ireland. In Northern Ireland, the Socialist Democratic and Labour Party (SDLP), formed in 1970, is committed to achieving a United Ireland through peaceful and democratic means. It is not linked, except through its aims, to Sinn Féin, the political wing of the IRA, which is less choosy about its methods.

Taig: an offensive term used by Loyalists to describe Catholics.

Fenian: a term for a Catholic that suggests he/she is a Republican.

Republican: a supporter of United Ireland. Used as a synonym for an IRA supporter.

Republican Movement: this covers both Sinn Féin and the IRA.

IRA: the label used to describe the Irish Republican Army, which did not disband after the Civil War in Ireland ended (1920–21). The IRA is outlawed in the Republic of Ireland and the United Kingdom. The objective of its members is to fight by the gun and bomb until the whole of Ireland is free of the British, and the Six Counties reunited with the rest of Ireland. In 1969, with the start of civil disturbances, the IRA was reinvigorated. Firstly it reorganized itself and split into two. The Marxist Socialist-inspired members call themselves the Official IRA (OIRA), whereas the traditionalists call themselves the Provisional IRA (PIRA) after the 'Provisional' government of Ireland set up in the GPO after the Easter Rising of 1916. The ideals of the 'Provos' are straightforward: a United Republic of Ireland, whatever the cost in terms of violence. The Provisionals are generally referred to as the IRA, since the Officials have dropped out of the action, and declared a cease-fire in 1972. A further splinter from the PIRA, formed after the Good Friday Agreement, is the Real IRA.

UVF and **UDA**: The Ulster Volunteer Force and the Ulster Defence Association are illegal Protestant terrorist organizations that recruit from the working class. They're usually involved in revenge sectarian killings and assassinations of IRA members.

UFF and **LVF**: The Ulster Freedom Fighters and Loyalist Volunteer Force are illegal Protestant paramilitary organizations that engage in violent sectarian and Republican killings.

RUC: (Reformed in 2001 as the Police Service of Northern Ireland, *see* p.36.) The Royal Ulster Constabulary managed much of the security of Northern Ireland in co-operation with the British Army. The Catholic Nationalists in Northern Ireland traditionally regarded it with dislike and suspicion, believing it to be biased by its largely Protestant Unionist membership. Catholics who joined it were singled out for death by the IRA, but it still managed to have eight per cent (mainly English) Catholics.

The B Specials: a special, part-time reserve force within the RUC with special powers to search out IRA members, operating from the 1920s until the 1970s. Catholics maintain that they beat up alleged members and intimidated ordinary Catholics.

UDR (Ulster Defence Regiment): once a regiment of the British Army. Many of its soldiers were part-time and drawn from the Protestant population in Ulster. Over 250 UDR soldiers were killed, more often while off-duty than in uniform.

The Orange Order: a sectarian and largely working-class organization that originated as a secret Protestant working-class agrarian society known as the Peep-O'Day Boys. William of Orange (William III of England) became their hero, and the society changed its name to the Orange Order in 1795. Its members have a traditional fear of the Catholic majority in Ireland and are Unionist in politics. Orange Lodges are still active in Northern Ireland.

The Summer Marching Season: the Orange and Hibernian marches during July and August. Each side commemorates opposing events in the history of Ireland. In the past, drums and equipment were lent between the two sides, but the present conflict has distilled into bitterness and hatred, and this has ceased. The Orange marchers in particular frequently take provocative routes through Catholic areas.

Gerrymandering: refers to the policy of concentrating large numbers of Catholics with Republican views in unusually big electoral districts, whilst Protestant Unionists were in smaller districts. This meant that the Protestant Unionists were always certain to win a larger number of representatives, district by district. Gerrymandering gradually became the norm from the late 1920s until the electoral reforms at the beginning of the 1970s.

Civil Rights Movement: begun in the 1960s, inspired by the American Civil Rights campaigner Martin Luther King. The Civil Rights Association, founded in 1967, called for jobs, houses and 'one man, one vote' in council elections. It was supported by both Catholics and Protestants; the leadership of the Association has been described as 'middle-aged, middle-class and middle-of-the-road'. The Civil Rights Movement was hijacked by a more Republican and Socialist element and the mob violence that attended the Civil Rights marches. It eventually lost out to the IRA.

Direct Rule: The Government of the United Kingdom of Great Britain and Northern Ireland has so far (and during the suspension of power-sharing at the time of writing) retained full powers of sovereignty on all matters over the Northern Ireland Government at Stormont. Thus, when the riots and bloodshed began to get out of control, and the Stormont Government seemed unable to implement reforms or control the police, Direct Rule was imposed in 1972. It was ended in 1998 with the creation of a new Northern Ireland Assembly. However, the process of devolution stalled in 2002 and at the time of writing has not yet been restored.

Religion

03

Despite a small decline in the last few years, Ireland still has the largest number of regular churchgoers in Western Europe, and although many of the social factors which generally undermine religion are present, they do not seem to be having a huge effect yet.

The reminders and symbols of a religious faith and deep love of God are to be seen everywhere throughout the country. The images that fill my mind are a child in white, showing off her dress after her first Holy Communion; rags caught in brambles around a holy well; cars parked up a country lane, everybody piling out for Mass, umbrellas held high and skirts fluttering. The people of Ireland invoke and refer to the Virgin Mary and to Jesus often in their everyday talk. Roadside shrines to the Virgin are decorated with shells and fresh flowers, and some people still stop what they are doing to say the Angelus at noon and at sunset. Grey neogothic churches dominate the small country towns, while in the smaller villages the chapel or church is a simpler building, planted around with dark yews and beeches above which the ceaseless cawing of the rooks can be heard.

In Ireland most people will want to know what religion you are – whether Catholic, Presbyterian, Church of Ireland, Baptist, Methodist or Quaker. If your religion is still a mystery, they will very soon find out, not by a direct question, but in a very round-about way of conversation and enquiry. There has long been a strong, although small, Jewish community in Ireland; and recently an increase in Islam and Buddhism. In the past, the Christian clergy would have encouraged their congregation to feel sorry for these 'poor heathens', and the greatest pity was reserved for those who did not believe in a God at all. This huge Catholic complacency is less obvious as Ireland develops into a more liberal and democratic society. The history of Ireland has had much to do with this feeling of religious identity, and, unfortunately, in the North this mix of politics and religion has produced individuals whose extreme Catholic or Presbyterian attitudes are reminiscent of 17th-century Europe. The bigotry that characterizes such attitudes has been a major factor in the political situation in the North today. Great efforts are made by some of the clergy to organize ecumenical meetings but mostly their congregations ignore them. The challenges to the clergy in the North are enormous because, in this welcome period of peace, they must try to work together against sectarianism, and to promote reconciliation between the different Christian traditions.

Church leaders in Ireland realize that for the present position of religion in Ireland to continue, they will have to adapt to the many social trends that are changing Christian Ireland. Among the factors driving the trends are prosperity and an increase in materialism, a young, well-educated population, and a rise in the feeling that the individual should decide for himself on many of the moral issues on which the churches used to pronounce. This is especially true in matters of sex, marriage and family life. Under pressure from many groups, and a national referendum, the Republic has brought in divorce, and birth control measures are widely available. The respect usually accorded to those in religious life has been shaken by a number of church scandals, and many people feel that the churches must become more open and accountable.

Pre-Christian Ireland

The Irish have been religious for five thousand years, and there are plenty of chambered cairns to prove it. The Celts who arrived in waves mostly between 500 BC and 300 BC seem to have been very religious, and had a religious hierarchy organized by Druids. These people worshipped a large number of gods, and central to their beliefs was the cult of the human head. They believed that the head was the centre of man's powers and thoughts. Their stonemasons carved two-headed gods, and the style of their work has a continuity which can be traced up to the 19th century. There are heads in the Lough Erne district which are difficult to date. They could be pagan, early Christian or comparatively modern.

The origins of the earlier Tuatha Dé Danaan are lost in legend: they may have been pre-Celtic gods or a race of invaders, themselves vanquished by the Celts. They are believed to have had magical powers and heroic qualities. Today they are remembered as the 'wee folk' who live in the raths and stone forts. Here they make fairy music which is so beautiful that it bewitches any human who hears it. The wee folk play all kinds of tricks on country people, from souring their milk to stealing their children, and so a multitude of charms have been devised to guard against these fairy pranks. I can remember being told about the fairies who used to dance in magic rings in the fields; the trouble was that if you tried to go up to them they would turn into yellow ragwort dancing in the wind.

Early Christian Ireland

Christianity is believed to have come to Ireland from Rome in the 4th century, although St Patrick is credited with the major conversion of the Irish in the 5th century. The Irish seem to have taken to Christianity like ducks to water, although much of our knowledge of early Christianity comes through the medieval accounts of scholarly (but possibly biased) clerics. One explanation for the ease with which Christianity took over is that the Christians didn't try to change things too fast and incorporated elements of the Druidic religion into their practices. An example of this assimilation by the Christians is the continuing religious significance of the holy wells. Ash and rowan trees, both sacred to the Druids, are frequently found near the wells, and Christian pilgrims still leave offerings of rags on the trees as a sign to the Devil that he has no more power over them. *Patterns* (pilgrimages) and games used to be held at the wells, although they often shocked the priest, who would put the well out of bounds and declare that its healing powers had been destroyed. There are many everyday signs that the spiritual life of the Irish people harks back to pagan times. In cottages you might see a strange swastika sign made out of rushes. This is a St Brigid's cross, hung above the door or window to keep the evil spirits away. Fairy or sacred trees are still left standing in the field even though it is uneconomic to plough round them – bad luck invariably follows the person who cuts one down.

Monasteries in Early Christian Ireland

The first Christian churches were built of mud and wattle, and later of oak wood; the larger ones were painted inside with frescoes and decorated linen hangings.

The need for chalices, altar vessals, bells and bible covers stimulated craftsmen to produce filigree and enamel work and carvings. By the end of the 5th century, a monasticism of the kind associated with the communities of the Desert Fathers in the Near East and Eastern Europe came to Ireland, and many place names with *disert* in them are indicative of this type. Larger, more relaxed monasteries flourished, and became the most important centres in the region. Each followed the rule established by its founder. The episcopal organization set up by St Patrick was replaced by one in which the abbots were the more effective leaders in the Church; the position of abbot became hereditary, whether or not the next-of-kin was an ordained priest.

By the end of the 6th century the Church was firmly monastic, with great monasteries such as Clonmacnoise in County Offaly and Clonfert in County Galway. These centres were responsible for big strides in agricultural development and were important for trade; they also became places where learning and artistry of all sorts were admired and emulated. The Ireland of 'Saints and Scholars' reached its peak in the 7th century. The monks sought an ascetic and holy way of life, although this was pursued in a warlike manner. The ultimate self-sacrifice was self-imposed exile, and so they founded monasteries in Scotland, England, France, Italy and Germany. The abbots, by the 8th century, had become all-powerful in Irish politics; many were tied by kinship to petty kings, and so were involved in their territorial disputes. Missionaries continued to leave Ireland and contribute to the revival of Christianity in Europe, and there was a blossoming of the arts with wonderful metalwork and painted manuscripts. By the 9th century, the monasteries were commissioning intricately carved stone high crosses, such as you can see at Ahenny in County Tipperary.

Religious Discrimination

Religious discrimination is long-established in Ireland. Over the centuries Catholics and Protestants have suffered by not conforming to the established church, although Catholics have undoubtedly received the greatest share of discrimination and persecution. The Huguenots, who were skilled workers and established the important linen industry, arrived when Louis XIV revoked the Edict of Nantes in 1686. The biggest group of dissenters were the Presbyterians: most of them were Scots who settled in Ulster during the 17th century. They had been persecuted in Scotland because of their religious beliefs and now they found that Ireland was no better; the Presbyterians were as poor as the native Irish, and many found life so hard that they emigrated to America. Quakers, Palatines (German Protestants), Moravians, Baptists and Methodists also settled in Ireland, but their numbers have declined through emigration and intermarriage.

Religion in Ireland Today

The 1991 population census reveals that, overall, 75.1 per cent of Irish are Catholic, 14 per cent are Protestant, while the rest of the percentage is made up of people who either were not inclined to state their religion, or who did not have any religion at all.

In the Republic, the Catholic majority of 91.6 per cent is obviously the controlling force in political and social life and the Protestant minority has bowed out gracefully.

The Protestants used to represent almost 10 per cent of the population but this figure has declined to 3.1 per cent through mixed marriages and emigration.

In theory the modern state does not tolerate religious discrimination, and it is true that both Jews and Protestants have reached positions of importance and wealth in industry and banking. However, the Protestant classes had it so good during the hundreds of years of British rule that it is not surprising that for a short time there was a legacy of antipathy towards anyone connected with the mainly Protestant ascendancy. Happily, the antipathy has nearly disappeared now. The Church is still very powerful; the bishops' exhortations on divorce, contraception, AIDS etc. are listened to with great earnestness by the politicians, and the sanctity of the family is held to be of the greatest importance. Of course, in Northern Ireland, the laws of the land are quite secular, being laid down by the British government, but divorce is still quite unusual there, too, and the principal UK legislation on abortion, the 1967 Abortion Act, has not been extended to the province.

The parish priest is of great importance in Irish society and is usually very approachable. You might meet him in the village bar having a drink and a chat. Nearly every family has a close relative who is a priest or a nun, and they leave in great numbers to serve overseas, taking their particular brand of conservative Catholicism with them. Schooling is mostly in the hands of the Church (incidentally, Ireland has a very high standard of literacy and general education), and thankfully the days of the cane and the cruel sarcasm of the priest-teachers described by so many Irish writers has disappeared. The people in the top positions in Ireland today mostly went to Christian Brother Schools (look in the Irish *Who's Who*). So did many county councillors and petty officials who organize Ireland's huge bureaucracy. The old-boy network still gets favours done, grants approved and planning permission granted.

In Northern Ireland, there is a divided system – although all schools are eligible for 100 per cent state funding, most Catholics attend Catholic 'maintained' schools and more Protestant children attend state 'controlled' schools. There's a small but growing number of mixed religion primary and secondary schools, attended by around two per cent of children. Irish people practise their religion faithfully in rural areas. The churches are full on Sundays, and visits to Knock, Croagh Patrick and Lough Derg are made many times in a person's lifetime. Holy wells are still visited, and Stations of the Cross go on even in ruined churches and friaries. But in the cities more and more young people and other disillusioned individuals have moved away from the church, and some religious orders are forced to advertise for their priests. The numbing censoriousness of Catholicism and Protestantism in Ireland has become part of the island's image, just like the green hills and constant rain, but it is a theme which has been overplayed. Great community involvement and care comes directly from the churches, and the social events are great fun. The Irish are among the most generous when it comes to raising money for world disasters, and this charity work is usually channelled through the Church.

Death and weddings are always occasions for a bit of craic, and there is also a party whenever the priest blesses a new house. Irish couples spend more on their engagement rings and weddings than their English counterparts; it is a really big occasion. The Irish wake has lost many of its pagan rituals – mourning with keening and games involving disguise, mock weddings, jokes and singing. Nowadays, the dead person is laid out in another room and people come to pay their last respects, and then spend the rest of the evening drinking, eating and reminiscing.

Irish Saints

Every locality in Ireland has its particular saint. The stories that surround him or her belong to myth and legend, not usually to historical fact. One theory is that all these obscure, miraculous figures are in fact Celtic gods and goddesses who survived under the mantle of sainthood. Included below is a short account of the lives of some of the most famous saints, about whom a few facts are known.

Brendan (c. 486–575), Abbot and Navigator

This holy man is remembered for his scholastic foundations, and for the extraordinary journey he made in search of Hy-Brasil, believed to be an island of paradise, which he had seen as a mirage whilst looking out on the Atlantic from the Kerry Mountains. His journey is recounted in the *Navigato Brendan*, a treasure of every European library during the Middle Ages. The oldest copies are in Latin and date from the 11th century. The account describes a sea voyage that took Brendan and 12 monks to the Orkneys, Wales, Iceland, and to a land where tropical fruits and flowers grew. Descriptions of his voyage have convinced some scholars that he sailed down the east coast of America to Florida. Tim Severin, a modern-day explorer, and 12 others recreated this epic voyage between May 1976 and June 1977. In their leather and wood boat, they proved that the Irish monks could have been the first Europeans to land in America (the boat is at the Lough Gur Interpretative Centre, County Limerick; *see* p.139). Christopher Columbus probably read the *Navigato*, and in Galway there is a strong tradition that he came to the west coast in 1492 to search out traditions about St Brendan. The saint's main foundation was at Clonfert, which became a great scholastic centre. One of his monks built the first beehive-shaped cells on Skellig Michael, the rocky island off County Kerry. Other foundations were at Annaghdown in County Galway, and Inisglora in County Mayo. Brendan is buried in Clonfert Cathedral, and he is honoured in St Brendan's Cathedral in Loughrea, County Galway, where the beautiful mosaic floor in the sanctuary depicts his ship and voyage.

St Brigid (died c. 525), Abbess of Kildare

Brigid, also known as Briget, Bride and Brigit, is the most beloved saint in Ireland and is often called Mary of the Gael. Devotion to her spread to Scotland, England and the Continent. Traditions and stories surrounding her describe her generous and warm-hearted acts to the poor, her ability to counsel the rulers of the day, and her great holiness. Her father was a pagan from Leinster and she was fostered by a Druid. (This custom of fosterage in Ireland existed right up to the 19th century.) She decided not to marry and founded a religious order with seven other girls. They were the first formal community of nuns and wore simple white dresses. St Brigid has her feast day on 1 February, which is also the date of the pagan festival Imbolg, marking the beginning of spring. She is the patron of poets, scholars, blacksmiths and healers, and is also inevitably linked with Brigid, the pagan goddess of fire and song. There is a tradition that St Brigid's Abbey in Kildare contained a sanctuary with a perpetual fire, tended only by virgins, whose high priestess was regarded as an incarnation and successor of the goddess. The two women are further linked by the fact that Kildare in Irish means 'church of oak', and St Brigid's church was built from a tree held sacred to the Druids. There's a theory that Brigid and her companions accepted the Christian faith, and then transformed the pagan sanctuary into a Christian shrine.

Kildare was a great monastic centre after Brigid's death, and produced the now lost masterpiece, the *Kildare Gospels*. Tradition says that the designs were so beautiful that an angel helped to create them. The St Brigid's nuns kept alight the perpetual fire until the suppression of the religious houses during the Reformation. Brigid was buried in Kildare Church, but in 835 her remains were moved to Downpatrick in County Down, because of the raids by the Norsemen. She is supposed to share a grave with St Patrick and St Colmcille, but there is no proof of this. In 1283 it is recorded that three Irish knights set out to the Holy Land with her head; they died en route in Lamiar in Portugal, and in the church there the precious relic of her head is enshrined in a chapel to St Brigid. The word 'bride' derives from St Brigid. It is supposed to originate from the Knights of Chivalry, whose patroness she was. They called the girls they married their brides, after her, and hence the word came into general usage.

St Colmcille (*c.* 521–97), Missionary Abbot

Along with St Patrick and St Brigid, Colmcille, also known as Columba and Columcille, is probably the most famous of the Irish saints, a charismatic personality who was a scholar, poet and ruler. He spread the gospel to Iona and hence to Scotland. St Colmcille was a prince of Tyrconnell (County Donegal), and a great-great-grandson of Niall of the Nine Hostages, who had been High King of Ireland. On his mother's side he was descended from the Leinster kings. He was educated by St Finian of Movilla, in County Down, and also by Finian of Clonard and Mobhi of Glasnevin. He studied music and poetry at the Bardic School of Leinster, and the poems he wrote which have survived are delightful. A few are preserved in the Bodleian Library, Oxford. He chose to be a monk, and never to receive episcopal rank. He wrote of his devotion: 'The fire of God's love stays in my heart as a jewel set in gold in a silver vessel.' In 545 he built his first church in Derry, the place he loved most. Then he founded Durrow and later Kells, which became very important in the 9th century when the Columban monks of Iona fled from the Vikings and made it their headquarters. In all, Colmcille founded 37 monastic churches in Ireland; he also produced the *Cathach*, a manuscript of the Psalms. At the age of 42 he set out with 12 companions to be an exile for Christ. They sailed to the island of Iona, off the west coast of Scotland, which was part of the Kingdom of Dalriada ruled over by the Irish King Aidan. He converted Brude, King of the Picts, founded two churches in Inverness, and helped to keep the peace between the Picts and the Irish colony. The legend that he left Ireland because of a dispute over the copy he made of a psalter of St Finian is very dubious. Apparently the dispute caused a great battle, although the high king of the time, King Diarmuid, tried to settle the dispute and had ruled against Colmcille, saying: 'to every cow its calf, to every book its copy'. The saint is supposed to have punished himself for the deaths he caused by going into exile. Colmcille was famous for his austerity, fasting and vigils; his bed and pillow were of stone. He died at Iona, and his relics were taken to Dunkeld (Scotland) in 849.

St Columban (died 615), Missionary Abbot

Columban, also known as Columbanus, is famous as the great missionary saint. He was born in Leinster and educated at Bangor in County Down under St Comgall, who was famed for his scholarship and piety. Columban set off for Europe with 12 other religious men to preach the gospel and convert the pagans in Gaul (France) and Germany. He founded a monastery at the present-day Annegray, in Burgundy, in 575, and his rule of austerity attracted many. Luxeuil, the largest monastery, and Fontaines were both established within a few miles of Annegray. When Columban was exiled by the local king, he and his followers founded Bobbio in the Apennines, between Piacenza and Genoa. Bobbio became a great centre of culture and orthodoxy from which monasticism spread. Its great glory was its library, and its books are scattered all over Europe and regarded as treasures.

St Enda of Aran (died c. 535), Abbot

Famous as the patriarch of monasticism, he's described as a warrior who left the secular world in middle life. He had succeeded to the kingdom of Oriel, but decided to study for the priesthood. Granted the Aran Islands by his brother-in-law, Aengus, King of Cashel, he is said to have lived a life of great severity, and never had a fire in winter, as he believed that 'hearts so glowing with the love of God' could not feel the cold. He reputedly taught 127 other saints, who are buried close to him on the islands.

St Kevin of Glendalough (died c. 618), Abbot

Many stories surround St Kevin, but we know he was one of the many Irish abbots who chose to remain a priest. He lived a solitary, contemplative life in the Glendalough Valley. He played the harp, and the Rule for his monks was in verse. He is supposed to have prayed for so long that a blackbird had time to lay an egg and hatch it on his outstretched hand. His monastery flourished until the 11th century. In the 12th century St Lawrence O'Toole came to Glendalough and modelled his life on St Kevin's, bringing fresh fame to his memory. The foundation was finally destroyed in the 16th century.

St Kieran (c. 512–49), Abbot

St Kieran, also known as Ciaran, is remembered for his great foundation of Clonmacnoise, where the ancient chariot road through Ireland crosses the Shannon River. Unlike many Irish abbots he was not of aristocratic blood, for his father was a chariot-maker from County Antrim, and his mother from Kerry. St Kieran attracted craftsmen to his order, and Clonmacnoise grew to be a great monastic school, where, unusually for Ireland, the position of abbot did not become hereditary. Kieran died within a short time of founding the school. Many kings are buried alongside him, for it was believed that he would bring their souls safely to heaven.

St Malachy (1094–1148), Archbishop of Armagh

Malachy is famous as the great reformer of the Irish Church. He persuaded the Pope, Eugenius III, to establish the Archbishops of Ireland separately from those of England. He also ensured that it was no longer possible for important ecclesiastical positions to be held by certain families as a hereditary right. For example, he was appointed Bishop of Armagh, although the See of Armagh was held in lay succession by one family. It was an achievement to separate the family from this post without splitting the Irish Church.

The saint was educated in Armagh and Lismore, County Waterford, and desired only to be an itinerant preacher. His great talents took him instead to be Bishop of Down and Connor, and in 1125 he became Abbot-Bishop of Armagh. He travelled to France, where he made a lasting friendship with Bernard of Clairvaux, the reforming Cistercian. The Pope appointed him papal legate in Ireland, and whilst abroad he made some famous prophecies; one was that there will be the peace of Christ over all Ireland when the palm and the shamrock meet. This is supposed to mean when St Patrick's Day (17 March) occurs on Palm Sunday.

St Patrick (c. 390–461), Bishop and Patron Saint of Ireland

St Patrick was born somewhere between the Severn and the Clyde on the west coast of Britain. As a youth he was captured by Irish slave-traders and taken to the Antrim coast to work as a farm labourer. Controversy surrounds the details of Patrick's life. Popular tradition credits him with converting the whole of Ireland, but nearly all that can be truly known of him comes from his *Confessio* or autobiography, and other writings. Through these, he is revealed as a simple, sincere and humble man who was full of care for his people; an unlearned man, once a fugitive, who came to trust God completely. Tradition states that after six years of slavery, voices told him he would soon return to his own land, and he escaped. Later, other voices called to him from Ireland, entreating him 'to come and walk once more amongst us'.

It is believed that he spent some time in Gaul (France) and became a priest; perhaps he had some mission conferred on him by the Pope to go and continue the work of Palladius, another missionary bishop who worked among the Christian Irish. It is believed that some confusion has arisen over the achievements of Palladius and Patrick. Patrick, when he returned to Ireland, seems to have been most active in the north, whilst Palladius worked in the south. He made Armagh his primary see, and it has remained the centre of Christianity in Ireland. He organized the church on the lines of territorial sees, and encouraged the laity to become monks or nuns. He was very concerned with abolishing paganism, idolatry and sun-worship, and he preached to the highest and the lowest in the land. Tradition credits him with expelling the snakes from Ireland, and explaining the Trinity by pointing to a shamrock. One of the most famous episodes handed down by popular belief is that of his confrontation with King Laoghaire at Tara, known as the seat of the high kings of Ireland, and the capital of Meath. It was supposedly on Easter Saturday in 432, which that year coincided with a great Druid festival at Tara. No new fire was allowed to be lit until the lighting of the sacred pagan fire by the Druids. St Patrick was camped on the Hill of Slane which looks onto Tara, and his campfire was burning brightly. The Druids warned King Laoghaire that if it was not put out, it would never be extinguished. When Patrick was brought before Laoghaire, his holiness melted the king's hostility and he was invited to stay. Although Laoghaire did not become a Christian, his brother Conal, a prince of the North, became his protector and ally.

Certain places in Ireland are traditionally closely associated with St Patrick, such as Croagh Patrick in County Mayo, where there is an annual pilgrimage to the top of the 2,510ft (765m) mountain on the last Sunday of July; and Downpatrick and Saul in County Down. The cult of St Patrick spread from Ireland to many Irish monasteries in Europe, and in more modern times to North America and Australia, where large communities of Irish emigrants live. The annual procession in New York on 17 March, St Patrick's Day, has become a massive event, where everybody sports a shamrock and drinks green beer. However, quite a few Irish believe St Colmcille should be the patron saint of Ireland, not this mild and humble British missionary.

Oliver Plunkett (1625–81), Archbishop of Armagh and Martyr
This gentle and holy man lived in frightening and turbulent times, when to be a practising Catholic in Ireland was to court trouble. He was born into a noble and wealthy family whose lands extended throughout the Pale. He was sent to study in Rome and was a brilliant theology and law scholar. He became a priest in 1654 and in 1669 was appointed Archbishop of Armagh. Oliver was one of only two bishops in Ireland at that time, and the whole of the laity was in disorder and neglect. Apart from the hostility of the Protestants, the Catholics themselves were divided by internal squabbles. Oliver confirmed thousands of people, and held a provincial synod. He did much to maintain discipline amongst the clergy, to improve education by founding the Jesuit College in Drogheda, and to promulgate the decrees of the Council of Trent. Oliver managed to remain on good terms with many of the Protestant gentry and clergy, but was eventually outlawed by the British government. The panic caused by the false allegations made by Titus Oates in England about a popish plot was used by Plunkett's enemies, and he was arrested in 1678. He was absurdly charged with plotting to bring in 20,000 French troops, and levying a charge on his clergy to support an army. No jury could be found to convict him in Ireland, so he was brought to England, where he was convicted of treason for setting up 'a false religion which was the most dishonourable and derogatory to God of all religions and that a greater crime could not be committed against God than for a man to endeavour to propagate that religion'. He was hanged, drawn and quartered at Tyburn in July 1681. His head is in the Oliver Plunkett Church in Drogheda, County Louth, and his body lies at Downside Abbey, Somerset.

Stone Circles
and What Followed

04

Ireland is fascinatingly rich in monuments, and you cannot fail to be struck by the number and variety of archaeological remains all over the country. They crown the tops of hills or stand out, grey and mysterious, in the green fields. Myths and stories surround them, handed down by word of mouth. Archaeologists too have their theories, often as varied and unprovable as the myths.

Man is known to have lived in this country since middle Stone Age times (roughly from about 6000 BC). There are no structures left from these times but, after the coming of Neolithic or New Stone Age peoples, some of the most spectacular of the Irish monuments were built.

Here is a brief description of the types to be seen, in order of age. (*See* the Glossary, pp.253–6, for a complete list of archaeological, architectural and associated terms.)

Stone Circles

Stone circles served as temples and date back to early Bronze Age times. Impressive examples may be seen at Lough Gur, County Limerick, and on Beltany Hill, near Lifford, County Donegal. **Earthen circles** probably served a similar purpose: for example, the Giant's Ring at Drumbo near Belfast surrounds a megalith. They have been variously interpreted as ritual sites and astronomical calendars and are mainly found in the southwest and the north of Ireland. Standing stones are associated with them.

Megalithic Tombs

Neolithic colonizers with a knowledge of agriculture came to Ireland between 3000 and 2000 BC and erected the earliest megalithic chambered tombs. They are called the **court cairns** because the tombs are made up of a covered gallery for burial, with one or more unroofed courts or forecourts for ritual purposes. Examples of their pottery have been found in these tombs. Court cairns are mainly found in the northern part of the country – north of a line between Clew Bay in the west and Dundalk Bay in the east.

Linked to the court cairns is the simple and imposing type of megalith – the **dolmen** or portal dolmen. This consists of a large, sometimes enormous, capstone and three or more supporting uprights. The distribution of dolmens is more widespread but tends to be eastern. Another variety of megalith is the **wedge-shaped gallery**. There are numbers of such tombs in the Burren area in County Clare, where they are built from the limestone slabs so common in the region. Most excavated wedges belong to the early Bronze Age: 2000 to 1500 BC. They are now largely bare of the cairns or mounds that covered them. The people who built them advanced from being hunters to growing crops and keeping domestic animals.

The most spectacular of the great stone tombs are the **passage graves**. The best known is Newgrange, one of a group on the River Boyne, west of Drogheda, County Louth. Its construction and the carvings on the stones put it amongst the most important megalithic tombs in Europe. The graves belong to a great family of structures found from eastern Spain to southern Scandinavia. The decorative carving that covers many of the stones consists of spirals, lozenges and other motifs, and is thought to have some religious significance. **Unchambered burial mounds** also occur throughout the country. They date largely from the Bronze Age, but earlier and later examples are known.

Standing Stones

These are also known as *gallauns*, single pillar stones with a ritual significance, which occasionally mark grave sites. Other standing stones carry inscriptions in ogham characters.

Ring Forts

The most numerous type of monument to be seen in Ireland is the ring fort, known also as **rath, lios, dun, caher** and **cashel**. There are about 30,000 throughout the country. These originated as early as the Bronze Age and continued to be built until the Norman invasion. The circular ramparts, varying in number from one to four, enclosed a homestead with houses of wood, wattle-and-daub or partly stone construction. Well-preserved examples of stone forts are those at Staigue, County Kerry, and the cashels of the Aran Islands, off the coast of County Clare. Collections of earthworks identify the royal seats at Tara in County Meath, and Navan Fort in County Armagh, where earthen banks are now the only reminders of the timber halls of kings. Like Tara in County Meath, they lie at the centre of a complex tangle of myth and tradition in the ancient Celtic sagas.

Hill forts

Larger and more defensive in purpose are the hill forts, whose ramparts follow contour lines to encircle hill tops. To this class belongs the large green enclosure at Emain Macha known as Navan Fort, County Armagh.

Crannogs

Crannogs (from *crann*, tree), or lake dwellings, are defensive dwelling sites used by farmers, with even earlier origins than the forts, that continued in use sometimes until the 17th century. The Craggaunowen Living Past centre in County Clare (*see* p.240) has a very good example.

Early Irish Architecture

Before the Norman invasion, most buildings in Ireland were of wood. None of these have survived. In the treeless west, however, tiny corbelled stone buildings shaped like beehives, called **clochans**, were constructed. They were used as oratories by holy men. Some, possibly dating from the 7th century, still exist. Clochans are particularly common in County Kerry: there are many in the Dingle Peninsula and some very well-preserved examples in the early monastic settlement on Great Skellig, off the Kerry coast. Also in Kerry is the best-preserved example of an early boat-shaped oratory, at Gallarus (*see* p.174).

Most of the early **mortared churches** were modelled on wooden prototypes. They were very small and were already built with stylistic features characteristic of Irish buildings: steeply pitched roofs and inclined jambs to door and window openings.

Many of these small churches would have been roofed with wood, tiles or thatch, but some were roofed with stone. The problem of providing a pitched roof of stone over a rectangular structure was solved by inserting a relieving semicircular arch below the roof. (The small space over the arch forms a croft.) These buildings lack features by which they can be accurately dated, but a conservative dating would be from the beginning of the 9th century onwards.

Round Towers

Contemporary with these early Irish churches, and very characteristically Irish, are round towers, of which about 120 are known to have existed in Ireland. They are tall, gracefully tapering buildings of stone, with conical stone roofs, which were built as monastic belfries, with the door approximately 12ft (3.5m) from the ground. This is a clue to their use as places of refuge or watchtowers during the period of Viking raids between the 9th and 11th centuries. Food, precious objects and manuscripts were stored in them. The ladder could then be drawn up. There are about 70 surviving examples in varying degrees of preservation.

The monk who wrote these beautiful lines expresses the tensions of those days:

Bitter the wind tonight,
Combing the sea's hair white:
From the North, no need to fear
the proud sea-coursing warrior.
version by John Montague

High Crosses

These carved stone crosses, usually in the typical 'Celtic' ringed form, contain a great variety of biblical scenes and ornament. They are found in most parts of the country in early monastic sites. The earliest type are simple crosses carved on standing stones. They are most common in the west and on the Dingle Peninsula in County Kerry. The development of **low-relief carving** began in the 7th century, gradually becoming more complex.

The **ringed high cross** first appears at a later date, and the earliest high crosses, dating from the 8th century, are in southern Kilkenny and Tipperary. Impressive examples are at Ahenny, County Tipperary, and at Kilkieran, County Kilkenny. In this group the cross-shafts and heads are magnificently carved in sandstone with spirals and other decorative forms derived from metalwork, with figure-carvings on the bases. To the north, in the Barrow valley, is another group that are later in date and more roughly carved in granite. **The Barrow group** has an interesting innovation: the faces of the shafts and heads are divided into panels, in which a scene, usually biblical, is portrayed.

Sandstone was used again for these crosses in the 10th century and they still grace monastic ruins scattered across the Central Plain of Ireland. The West Cross and Muiredach's Cross at Monasterboice in County Louth are the best examples of this. (In each case the east and west faces of the crosses are carved with scriptural scenes while the north and south faces have spirals, vine-scrolls, and other decorations.) Favourite subjects for the carver were the Crucifixion, the Last Judgement, Adam and Eve, Cain and Abel, and the arrest of Christ.

By the end of the 11th century the cross was changed: the ring was often left off, and the whole length of the shaft was taken up with a single figure of the **crucified Christ**. Ecclesiastical figures often appear on the opposite face and on the base, and the decoration of the north and south faces usually consists of animal-interlacing. Crosses of this style were carved until the mid-12th century.

Romanesque Architecture

Characteristics of this decorative style appear in Irish buildings of the 12th century. While remaining structurally simple, the Irish churches of the period have carved doorways, chancel arches or windows, with ornament in an Irish variation of the style. The most impressive example of the style is the arcaded and richly carved Cormac's Chapel on the Rock of Cashel, County Tipperary, which was consecrated in 1134. The use of **rib-vaulting** over the chancel here is very early, not only for Ireland, but for the rest of Europe. Many of the characteristic features of the early churches, such as antae and sloping jambs, were kept throughout the Romanesque period. The use of the **chevron**, an ornamental moulding, is common in Irish-Romanesque work, and it is nearly always combined with rows of beading. This style is also referred to as Hiberno-Romanesque.

Transitional Architecture

When the Romanesque style was popular, at the same time another, plainer type of church building was being introduced by the Cistercian order, whose first church in Ireland, Mellifont Abbey in County Louth, was designed after churches of the **Continental** type with simple carved decoration.

Gothic Architecture

With the coming of the Normans and the changes they wrought, the native tradition in building declined, and Gothic architecture was introduced in the 13th century. The Irish Gothic **cathedrals** were on a smaller scale than their English and Continental counterparts, and the grouping of lancets in the east window and south choir wall are typical of the Irish buildings. Gothic parish churches in the plain early English style were built only in the anglicized parts of the country.

Because of the turbulent times during the 14th century, there was very little building done in Ireland. But this changed in the 15th and 16th centuries and a native Gothic style began to emerge, particularly in the western counties. It is best seen in the **Franciscan friaries** and the rebuilt **Cistercian abbeys** of the period. A good example of the Franciscan style, with narrow church, a tall tapering tower, carved cloister and small window openings, can be seen at the well-preserved ruin at **Quin** in County Clare. (The Cistercian style, with a larger church, a huge square tower topped by stepped battlements, and a carved cloister, can be seen at Kilcooly and Holycross, County Tipperary.)

Castles

Although the Normans had built many castles before they came to Ireland, in the first years of the invasion they built fortifications of wood, usually taking over the sites of ancient Irish forts. The remains of these can be seen all over the eastern half of the country in the form of **motte-and-baileys**.

At the end of the 12th century, the construction of **stone fortifications** on a large scale began. An early example of Norman building skill is at Trim, County Meath. It has a great square keep in a large bailey, defended by a high embattled wall, with turrets and barbicans. A particularly attractive feature of the Irish countryside is the ruined 15th- or 16th-century **tower house**, which became common from about 1420. These fortified farms consisted of a tall, square tower which usually had a small, walled *bawn*, or courtyard. In most cases the *bawn* has disappeared.

The Old Gods and Heroes

The Old Gods and Heroes

05

The Celts

Nobody knows exactly when the first Celts arrived in Ireland; it was some time before 1000 BC, with the last wave of people coming around the 3rd century BC. The Greek chroniclers were the first to name these people, calling them *Keltori*. Celt means 'act of concealment', and it has been suggested that they were called 'hidden people' because of their reluctance to commit their great store of scholarship and knowledge to written records. 'Kilt', the short male skirt of traditional Celtic dress, may also come from this word.

The Celtic civilization was quite sophisticated, and much of the road-building attributed to the Romans has been found to have been started by the Celts. The Romans frequently built on their foundations. In Ireland, ancient roads are often discovered when bog is cleared.

Ireland's ancient and rich epic story tradition was strictly oral until the Christian era. Even then, it was well into the 7th century before the bulk of it was written down by scribes, who often added to or changed the story to make some moral Christian interpretation. The reluctance of the Celts to commit their knowledge to writing is directly related to the Druids and their power, because the Druidic religion was the cornerstone of the Celtic world, which stretched from Ireland to the Continent and as far south as Turkey. Irish mythology is therefore concerned with the rest of that Celtic world, and there are relationships with the gods and heroes of Wales, Scotland, Spain and middle Europe.

The *Book of the Dun Cow* and the *Book of Leinster*, the main surviving manuscript sources, date from the late 11th century. Many earlier books were destroyed by the Viking raids, and entire libraries lost. The various sagas and romances that survived have been categorized by scholars into four cycles. First, the **mythological cycle**: the stories that tell of the various invasions of Ireland, from Cesair to the Sons of Milesius. These are largely concerned with the activities of the Túatha Dé Danaan, the pagan gods of Ireland. Next there is the **Ulster Cycle**, or deeds of the Red Branch Knights, which include the tales of Cú Chulainn and the *Táin Bó Cuailgne*. Then there is the **Cycle of Kings**, mainly stories about semimythical rulers; and finally the **Fenian Cycle**, which relates the adventures of Fionn MacCumhail (Finn MacCool) and the warriors of the Fianna. Only qualified storytellers could recite these sagas and tales under Brehon (Celtic) laws, and they were held in great respect. Several qualities emerge from these sagas and tell us a great deal about the society of Iron Age Ireland, and indeed Europe. The stories are always optimistic, and the Celts had evolved a doctrine of immortality of the soul.

The heroes and gods were interchangeable – there were no hard and fast divisions between gods and mortals. Both had the ability to change shape, and often reappear after the most gruesome deaths. The gods of the Dé Danaan were tall, beautiful and fair, although, later, in the popular imagination, they became fairies or the 'little people'. They were intellectual as well as beautiful, but as gullible as mortals, with all our virtues and vices. They loved pleasure, art, nature, games, feasting and heroic single combat. It is difficult to know whether they are heroes and heroines made into gods by their descendants or otherwise. In the 11th century, Cú Chulainn was the most admired hero, particularly by the élite of society. Then Fionn MacCumhail took over. He and his band of warriors became very popular with the ordinary people right up to the early 20th century. The English conquests in the 17th century and the resulting destruction and exile of the Irish intelligentsia meant that much knowledge was lost, though the peasantry kept it alive in folklore recited by the *seanachie* or village storyteller. Then, with the famines and vast emigration of the 19th century, the Irish language came under great threat and, with it, the folklore.

The stories were anglicized by antiquarians and scholars, at the end of the 18th century and later in the 19th century, who did much to record and translate the Irish epic stories into English and to preserve the Gaelic; many were Ulster Presbyterians. Other names that should be remembered with honour are William Carleton, Lady Wilde, T. Crofton-Croker, Standish James O'Grady, Lady Gregory and Douglas Hyde. Their writings and records of Irish peasant culture have become standard works.

The question of where Irish myth ends and history begins is impossible to answer. Historical accounts are shot through with allegory, supernatural happenings and fantasy. Nothing at all has changed, as a similar mythical process is applied to modern Irish history.

Directory of the Gods

Amergin: a Son of Milesius. The first Druid of Ireland. There are three poems credited to him in *The Book of Invasions*.

Aonghus Óg: the god of Love, son of Dagda. His palace was by the River Boyne at Newgrange. Also known as Aengus.

Ard Rí: the title of High King.

Badhbha or Badh: goddess of battles.

Balor: a god of death, and one of the most formidable Fomorii. His one eye destroyed everything it gazed on. Destroyed by his own grandson, Lugh.

Banba, Fotla and Eire Dé Danaan: sister goddesses who represent the spirit of Ireland, particularly in Irish literature and poetry. It is from the goddess Eire that Ireland takes its modern name.

Bilé: god of life and death. He appears as Cymbeline in Shakespeare's play.

Bran: 'Voyage of Bran' is the earliest voyage poem, which describes through beautiful imagery the Island of Joy and the Island of Women. Also, the hound of Fionn MacCumhail.

Brigid: goddess of healing, fertility and poetry. Her festival is one of the four great festivals of the Celtic world. Also a Christian saint who has become confused in popular folklore with the goddess.

Caílte: cousin of Fionn MacCumhail. One of the chief Warriors of the Fianna, and a poet. A Christian addition to his story has returned him from the Otherworld to recount to St Patrick the adventures of the Fianna.

Conall Cearnach: son of Amergin, a warrior of the Red Branch, and foster brother and blood cousin of Cú Chulainn. He avenged Cú Chulainn's death by slaying his killers.

Conchobhar MacNessa: king of Ulster during the Red Branch Cycle. He fell in love with Deidre (*see* below) and died from a magic 'brain ball' which had been lodged in his head seven years before by the Connaught warrior, Cet.

Conn: one of the Sons of Lir, the ocean god, changed into a swan by his jealous stepmother Aoife. Also, Conn of the hundred battles, High King from AD 177 to 212.

Cormac MacArt: High King from AD 254 to 277 and patron of the Fianna, he reigned during the period of Fionn MacCumhail and his adventures. His daughter was betrothed to Fionn MacCumhail but eloped with one of Fionn's warriors, Diarmuid. His son succeeded him and destroyed the Fianna.

Cú Chulainn: the hound of Culann, also called the Hound of Ulster. He has similarities with the Greek hero, Achilles. He was actually called Sétanta until he killed the hound belonging to Culann, a smith god from the Otherworld. He promised to take its place and guarded his fortress at night. He became a great warrior whose battle frenzy was incredible. Women were always falling in love with him, but Emer, his wife, managed to keep him. He is chiefly famous for his single-handed defence of Ulster during the War of the Tain (Bull of Cuailgne) when Ailill and Medb of Connacht invaded (*see* Medb). He was acknowledged as champion of all Ireland, and forced to slay his best friend, Ferdia, during a combat at a crucial ford. Later Cú Chulainn rejected the love of the goddess of battles, Mórrigan, and his doom was sealed; his enemies finally slew him. During the fatal fight he strapped his body to a pillar stone because he was too weak to stand. But such was his reputation that no one dared to come near him until Mórrigan, in the form of a crow, perched on his shoulder, and finally an otter drank his blood.

Dagha: father of the gods and patron god of the Druids.

Diarmuid: foster son of the love god, Aonghus Óg, and a member of the Fianna. The goddess of youth put her love spot on him, so that no woman could resist loving him. He eloped with Grainne, who was betrothed to Fionn MacCumhail, and the Fianna pursued them for 16 years. Eventually the couple made an uneasy peace with Fionn, who went out hunting with Diarmuid on Ben Bulben, where Diarmuid was gored by an enchanted boar who was also his own stepbrother. Fionn had the power to heal him with some enchanted water, but he let it slip through his fingers. Aonghus Óg, the god of love, took Diarmuid's body to his palace and, although he did not restore him to life, sent a soul into his body so that he could talk to him each day.

Deidre: Deidre of the Sorrows was the daughter of an Ulster chieftain. When she was born it was forecast by a Druid that she would be the most beautiful woman in the land, but that, because of her, Ulster would suffer great ruin and death. Her father wanted to put her to death at once but Conchobhar, the Ulster King, took pity on her and said he would marry her when she grew up. When the time came she did not want to marry such an old man, particularly as she had fallen in love with Naoise, a hero of the Red Branch. They eloped to Scotland. Conchobhar lured them back with false promises, and Naoise and his brothers were killed by Eoghan MacDuracht. Deidre was forced to become Conchobhar's wife. She did not smile for a year, which infuriated her husband. When he asked her who she hated most in the world, she replied, 'you and Eoghan MacDuracht'. The furious Conchobhar then said she must be Eoghan's wife for a year. When she was put in Eoghan's chariot with her hands bound, she somehow managed to fling herself out and dash her head against a rock. A pine tree grew from her grave and touched another pine growing from Naoise's grave, and the two intertwined.

Donn: king of the Otherworld, where the dead go.

Emain Macha: the capital of the kings of Ulster for six centuries, which attained great glory during the time of King Conchobhar and the Red Branch Knights.

Emer: wife of Cú Chulainn. She had the six gifts of womanhood: beauty, chastity, eloquence, needlework, sweet voice and wisdom.

Female champions: in ancient Irish society women had equal rights with men. They could be elected to any office, inherit wealth and hold full ownership under law. Cú Chulainn was instructed in the martial arts by Scáthach, and there was another female warrior in the Fianna called Creidue. Battlefields were always presided over by goddesses of war. Nessa, Queen of Ulster, and Queen Medb of Connacht were great warriors and leaders. Boadicea of Britain was a Celtic warrior queen who died in AD 62, and this tradition survived into the 16th century with Grace O'Malley of County Mayo.

Ferdia: the best friend of Cú Chulainn, killed by him in a great and tragic combat in the battle over the Brown Bull of Cuailgne (or Cooley).

Fergus MacRoth: stepfather of Conchobhar, used by him to deceive Deidre and Naoise and his brothers. He went into voluntary exile to Connacht in a great fury with the King, and fought against Conchobhar and the Red Branch. But he refused to fight against Cú Chulainn, which meant the ultimate defeat of Queen Medb and her armies.

The Fianna: known as the **Fenians**. A band of warriors guarding the high king of Ireland. Said to have been founded in about 300 BC, they were perhaps a caste of the military élite. Fionn MacCumhail was their greatest leader. In the time of Oscar, his grandson, they destroyed themselves through a conflict between the clans Bascna and Morna. In the 19th century the term was revived as a synonym for Irish Republican Brotherhood, and today it is used as the title for one of the main Irish political parties, Fianna Fail, which means 'Soldiers of Destiny'.

Fintan: the husband of Cesair, the first invader of Ireland. He abandoned her and survived the Great Deluge of the Bible story by turning into a salmon. Also, the Salmon of Knowledge who ate the Nuts of Knowledge before swimming to a pool in the River Boyne, where he was caught by the Druid Finegas. He was given to Fionn MacCumhail to cook. Fionn burnt his finger on the flesh of the fish as he was turning the spit, sucked his thumb, and acquired the knowledge for himself.

Fionn MacCumhail: anglicized as Finn MacCool. He was brought up by two wise women, then sent to study under Finegas the Druid. After acquiring the Knowledge of the Salmon, Fintan, he became known as Fionn, the Fair One (his childhood name had been Deimne). He was appointed head of the Fianna by Cormac MacArt, the High King at the time, in place of Goll MacMorna who had killed his father. His exploits are many and magical. His two famous hunting hounds were Bran and Sceolan, who were actually his own nephews, the children of his bewitched sister. His son, Oísín, was the child of the goddess Sadb, but he suffered unrequited love for Grainne. In the story of the Battle of Ventry, Fionn overcomes Daire Donn, the King of the World. He is said not to be dead, but sleeping in a cave, waiting for the call to help Ireland in her hour of need.

Dé Fionnbharr and Oonagh: gods of the Dé Danaan who have degenerated into the King and Queen of the Fairies in folklore.

Fionnuala: the daughter of Lir. She and her brothers were transformed into swans by her jealous stepmother, Aoife. The spell was broken with the coming of Christianity, but they were old and senile by then.

Fir Bolg: 'Bagmen'. A race who came to Ireland before the Dé Danaan. They do not take much part in the myths.

Fomorii: a misshapen and violent people, who are the evil gods of Irish myth. Their headquarters seems to have been Tory Island, off the coast of County Donegal. Their leaders include Balor of the Evil Eye, and their power was broken for ever by the Dé Danaan at the second Battle of Moytura, in County Sligo.

Gaul: Celt. Gaulish territory extended over France, Belgium, parts of Switzerland, Bohemia, parts of modern Turkey and parts of Spain.

Geis: a taboo or bond which was usually used by Druids and placed on someone to compel them to obey. Grainne put one on Diarmuid.

Goibhnin: smith god, and god of handicraft and artistry.

Goll MacMorna: leader of the Fianna before Fionn MacCumhail.

Grainne: anglicized as Grania. Daughter of Cormac MacArt, the high king. She was betrothed to Fionn MacCumhail but thought him very old, so she put a *geis* on Diarmuid to compel him to elope with her. Eventually he fell in love with her (*see* under 'Diarmuid'). After Diarmuid's death, although she had sworn vengeance on Fionn, she allowed herself to be wooed by him and became his wife. The Fianna despised her for this.

Laeg: charioteer to Cú Chulainn.

Lir: ocean god.

Lugh: sun god who slew his grandfather, Balor, and the father of Cú Chulainn by a mortal woman. His godly status was diminished into that of a fairy craftsman, Lugh Chromain, a leprechaun.

Macha: a woman who put a curse called *cest nóiden* on all Ulstermen, so that they would suffer from the pangs of childbirth for five days and four nights in times of Ulster's greatest need. This curse would last nine times nine generations. She did this because her husband boasted to King Conchobhar that she could beat the king's horses in a race, even though she was pregnant. She died in agony as a result.

Medb: anglicized as Maeve. Queen of Connacht, and wife of Ailill. She was famous for her role in the epic tale of the cattle raid of Cuailgne (Cooley), which she started when she found that her possessions were not as great as her husband's. She wanted the Brown Bull of Cuailgne which was in Ulster, to outdo her husband's bull, the White-Horned Bull of Connacht. This had actually started off as a calf in her herd, but had declined to stay in the herd of a woman. She persuaded her husband to join her in the great battle that resulted. The men of the Red Branch were hit by the curse of the *nóiden* (*see* Macha), and none could fight except Cú Chulainn, who was free of the weakness the curse induced and single-handedly fought the Connacht champions. Mebh was killed by Forbai, son of Conchobhar, while bathing in a lake. The bulls over which the great battle had been fought eventually tore each other to pieces.

Milesians: the last group of invaders of Ireland before the historical period. Milesius, a Spanish soldier, was their leader but his sons actually carried out the Conquest of Ireland.

Nessa: mother of Conchobhar. A strong-minded and powerful woman who secured the throne of Ulster for her son.

Niall of the Nine Hostages: High King from AD 379 to 405, and progenitor of the Uí Neill dynasty. There is a confusion of myth and history surrounding him.

Niamh: known as Niamh of the Golden Hair. A daughter of the sea god Manannán Mac Lir. She asked Oísín to accompany her to the Land of Promise and live there as her lover. After three weeks, he discovered three hundred years had passed.

Nuada of the Silver Hand: the leader of the Dé Danaan gods, who had his hand cut off in the great battle with the Fomorii. It was replaced by the god of healing.

Ogma: god of eloquence and literature, from whom ogham stones were named. These are upright pillars carved with incised lines that read as an alphabet from the bottom upwards. They probably date from AD 300.

Oísín: son of Fionn and Sadh, the daughter of a god, and leading champion of the Fianna. He refused to help his father exact vengeance on Grainne (to whom Fionn was betrothed) and Diarmuid (with whom Grainne eloped), and went with Niamh of the Golden Hair to the Land of Promise. Oísín longed to go back to Ireland, so Niamh gave him a magic horse on which to return, but warned him not to set foot on land, as three hundred years had passed since he was there. He fell from his horse by accident and turned into an old, blind man. A Christian embellishment is that he met St Patrick and told him the stories of the Fianna, and they had long debates about the merits of Christianity. Oísín refused to agree that his Ireland was better off for it. His mood comes through in this anonymous verse from a 16th-century poem translated by Frank O'Connor.

Patrick you chatter too loud
And lift your crozier too high
Your stick would be kindling soon
If my son Osgar stood by.

Oscar or Osgar: son of Oísín. He also refused to help Fionn, his grandfather, against Diarmuid and Grainne. The high king of the time wished to weaken the Fianna and allowed the two clans in it, Morna and Bascna, to quarrel. They fought at the battle of Gabhra. Oscar was killed and the Fianna destroyed.

Partholón: the leader of the third mythical invasion of Ireland. He is supposed to have introduced agriculture to Ireland.

Red Branch: a body of warriors who were the guardians of Ulster during the reign of Conchobhar MacNessa. Their headquarters were at Emain (*Eamhain*) Macha. The Red Branch cycle of tales has been compared to the Iliad in theme. The main stories are made up of the *Táin Bó Cuailgne* (the Brown Bull of Cuailgne or Cooley). Scholars accept that the cycle of stories must have been transmitted orally for nearly a thousand years, providing wonderful descriptions of the remote past.

Topics

The People

The people are thus inclined: religious, frank, amorous, sufferable of infinite paines, verie glorious, manie sorcerers, excellent horsemen, delighted with wars, great alms-givers, passing in hospitality.
Holinshed's *Chronicles*, 1577

This description so aptly fits the Irish today that it is only necessary to add a few superficial remarks on the subject. Conditions have changed radically. For a start, almost half of the population lives in the spreading cities. Still, compared to its neighbour, England, and to many other European countries, Ireland is a very rural place and even city-dwellers have close links with their country background. Regardless of where they live, Irish people have a healthy disdain for time and the hustle and bustle of business. Remember the old Irish saying as you travel around: 'When God made time he made plenty of it.' You will gain a great sense of shared identity and neighbourly feeling, particularly towards those in trouble, or the very old.

The traits peculiar to the Irish people, which always reassert themselves wherever they are in the world, are numerous. Among them are a delight in words and wordplay (reading anything by Flann O'Brien or James Joyce will give you a taste of it); a love of parties and craic (a good time), lively music, dancing and witty talk; a ready kindness that never fails; warm hospitality; and a keen interest in your affairs which is never mere inquisitiveness, but a charming device to put you at your ease.

They are an untidy race – in their houses and in the countryside. This, mixed in with a certain sloppiness, leads to the phenomenon of rusty cars dumped in lonely glens, litter in any old place and general mess. Not for the Irish the freshly painted doors and gateways of the Anglo-Saxon. There is a lot of ignorance and indifference in matters aesthetic. Old buildings go to rack and ruin, and vile ribbon development chokes the towns and the countryside around them.

An Irish person never forgets an insult or a wrong, and this memory will go back for generations. It might have been a quarrel over land or the meanness of the local gentry. Oliver Cromwell is still remembered with hatred for his savage campaign in the 1650s. The Irish have a quarrelsome spirit which is quickly roused in the face of bland priggishness. Each province and county of Ireland produces more individual traits. For example, the northerners have a reputation for directness of speech and a fighting spirit. The Munster people are held in respect for their poetry. A Dubliner might be considered by others as a bit of a know-all. The people of Connacht are famous for their great hospitality and strength.

Finally, one last word in this briefest of outlines: the Irish still have a great sense of the spiritual. The Catholic Church is very strong (despite recent sex scandals, the secularization of the schools and the introduction of divorce) but so is the faith of Church of Ireland members, and of the Presbyterians, to judge by the large numbers who attend their churches on Sundays. Religion is the great anchor, that pervades all aspects of living. This perhaps partially explains the paradox that in Ireland there is little thought for the future, and life is lived for the moment.

The Fairy People

The Fairy People, or *Daoine Sidhe*, are a rich part of Irish folklore. According to peasant belief, they are fallen angels who are not good enough to be saved and not bad enough to languish in Hell. Perhaps they are the gods of the Earth, as it is written in the *Book of Armagh*; or the pagan gods of Ireland, the Túatha Dé Danaan, who may also have been a race of invaders whose origins are lost in the mists of time. Antiquarians have different theories but, whatever they surmise, these fairy people persist in the popular imagination; they and their characteristics have been kept alive in tradition and myth.

The Fairy People are quickly offended, and must always be referred to as the 'Gentry' or the 'Good People'. They are also easily pleased, and will keep misfortune from your door if you leave them a generous bowl of milk on the windowsill overnight. Their evil is mostly without malice, and their chief occupations are feasting, fighting, making love and playing or listening to beautiful music. The only hard-working person among the Fairy People is the leprechaun, who is kept busy making the shoes they wear out for their dancing.

It is said that many of the beautiful tunes of Ireland are theirs, remembered by mortal eavesdroppers. The story is that Carolan, the last of the great Irish bards, slept on a rath which, like the many prehistoric standing stones in Ireland, had become a fairy place in folk tradition, and forever after the fairy music ran in his head and made him the great musician he was. Some of the individual fairy types are not very pleasant; here are brief descriptions of a few.

The banshee, from *bean sidhe*, is a woman fairy or attendant spirit who follows the old families and wails before a death. The keen, the funeral cry of the peasantry, is said to be an imitation of her cry. An omen that sometimes accompanies the old woman is an immense black coach, carrying a coffin and drawn by headless riders.

The leprechaun, or fairy shoemaker, is solitary, old, and bad-tempered; the practical joker amongst the 'Good People'. He is very rich because of his trade and buries his pots of gold at the end of rainbows. He also takes many treasure crocks, buried in times of war, for his own. Many believe he is the Dé Danaan god Lugh, the god of arts and crafts, who degenerated in popular lore into the leprechaun.

The leanhaun shee, or fairy mistress, longs for the love of mortal men. If they refuse, she must be their slave; if they consent, they are hers, and can only escape by finding another to take their place. The fairy lives on their life, and they waste away, but death is no escape. She has become identified in political song and verse with the Gaelic Muse, for she gives inspiration to those whom she persecutes.

The Pook seems to be an animal spirit. Some authorities have linked it with a he-goat from *púca* or *poc*, the Gaelic for goat. Others maintain it is a forefather of Shakespeare's Puck in *A Midsummer Night's Dream*. It lives in solitary mountain places and old ruins, and is of a nightmarish aspect. It is a November spirit, and often assumes the form of a stallion. The horse comes out of the water and is easy to tame if you can only keep him from the sight of water. If you cannot, he will plunge in with his rider and tear him to pieces at the bottom.

Boglands

Ireland is literally rich in boglands, formed over many hundreds of years. In the past, boglands were despised except as a source of fuel, but now we know how rich they are in flora and fauna. A vast quantity of folklore has grown up around them, beautifully described in *Irish Folk Ways* by E. Estyn Evans. In many fairy stories the human is lured off the path into the bog by strange lights at night. Walking on bogs can be very mucky and sometimes dangerous, so keep to the few paths and try to go with a local to guide you. Many writers describe the great peace and wellbeing to be had from a day out on the bogs cutting turf. Even now, a Dubliner clings to his cutting rights on a piece of Wicklow hill, for there is something eminently satisfying about cutting the sods of rich blackness, and then, later, during the bitter cold winter nights, heaping it onto the open fire. Underneath the bog, well-preserved bodies, jewelled crosiers for bishops, golden cups, giant elks' antlers and brittle pots of butter have all been revealed as the turf is cut away.

About 14 per cent of Ireland's land surface is bog. The brooding immutability of the bog, the drizzling rain and winds which sweep it, have surely contributed towards the Irish philosophy of fatality. There are two types of bogs – blanket and raised. The latter are mainly to be found in the midlands. In Ireland, wetness is a key factor in the formation of the peat which begins to grow on lakes and ponds as plants invade the water. Sphagnum moss is the vital plant because it holds water like a sponge and has a great capacity for trapping nutrients. Peat builds up because it releases acid that inhibits the breakdown of dead plants.

The Irish economy has been bolstered by the boglands. The Government-owned turf company, *Bord na Mona*, was set up in 1946 and has drained vast areas of peat, cutting it by machine and using the fuel to generate electricity. The sphagnum in the upper layers is baled as horticultural peat and sold for use in gardens all over Great Britain.

But the draining of the bogs has consequences for rivers and for those living near them in valleys, for the bogs act like huge natural sponges that soak up rainfall and release it very slowly. Thus, if the bog is stripped away there is danger of flooding. The stripping of the bog is also very costly ecologically, as gully erosion results. Some hand-cut bogs, when left, show signs of being colonized and healed by the bog-forming plants themselves. But this is unlikely to happen in machine-cut bogs. Sheep-grazing and burning also do damage. A balance must be found between economic needs and conservation needs, because at the rate the machines can cut the turf, the bogs will disappear in a matter of years. All the insects, birds and animals that find a home in the bog will go if nothing is done. We will lose the flight of the golden plover, the special mosses and flowers.

Recently, the tourist and environmental interest of the boglands has been evaluated and there is potential for wildlife conservation in 'cutaway' bogs – the bogs that are exhausted of peat. If you are interested, there is a bogland Nature Centre on the Bog of Allan at Lullymore, near Rathangan, County Kildare (*t (045) 860133*). In County Kerry, the Bog Village museum near Glenbeigh is a replica of the kind of dwellings which were usual in Ireland in the early 1800s, and describes how people made use of the bog for fuel and dug out the remains of ancient timber which the bog had preserved.

For more information contact the Peatland Conservation Council at the Bog of Allan Nature Centre (details above, *www.ipcc.ie*).

Music

Traditional Irish music is played everywhere throughout the island, in the cities and the countryside. Government sponsorship helped to revive it, especially through *Radio an Gaeltachta* (Irish-language radio) in the west. Nowadays there is great enthusiasm for it amongst everyone: a nine-year-old will sing a lover's lament about seduction and desertion, without batting an eyelid, to a grandfather whose generation scarcely remembered the Gaelic songs at all.

Traditional music has strengthened its hold on the cultural life of the country, rather than declining as it has sadly done in England. It continues to be a vibrant and relaxed medium that draws all generations of families and friends together. The 1845–49 famine silenced the music and dancing for a while, but today Ireland has one of the most vigorous music traditions in Europe and this is a big pull for many visitors. Irish ballads are sung the world over; each emigrant considers himself an exile still, and the commercial record industry churns out ballads. Most record covers tend to be decorated with grinning leprechauns and a few shamrocks for good measure.

Serious traditional music is not in this sweet folksy style of the easy listening variety. Listening to it can induce a state of exultant melancholy, or infectious merriment; whatever way, it goes straight to your heart. The lyrics deal with the ups and downs of love; failed rebellions, especially that of 1798; soldiering; dead heroes; religion; and homesick love for the beauty of the countryside. Comparatively few deal with occupations or work! The bard in pre-Christian society was held in honour and great awe, for his learning and the mischievous satire in his poetry and music. After the Cromwellian and Williamite wars, he lost his status altogether; music and poetry were kept alive by the country people who cheered themselves up during the dark winter evenings with stories and music.

The harp is, sadly, scarcely used nowadays, except when it is dragged out for the benefit of tourists at medieval banquets in Bunratty Castle, etc. The main traditional instruments used are the uilleann pipes, more sophisticated than the Scottish bagpipes, the fiddle (violin) and the tin whistle. The beat and rhythm is provided by a handheld drum made from stretched goat hide, called the bodhrán. The accordion, flute, guitar and piano are used by some groups as well, and these can be played singly or together.

The airs, laments, slip jigs and reels all vary enormously from region to region, and you might easily hear a Cork man or a Clare fiddler discussing with heated emotion the interpretation of a certain piece. These are constantly improvised on and seldom written down; inevitably some of the traditional content of a piece gets changed from generation to generation. A form of singing that had almost died out by the 1940s is the *Sean-Nós*, 'fully adorned', which is sung in Gaelic and unaccompanied by instruments. In more recent times, the *Sean-Nós* section in music festivals has been overflowing with entrants.

You will have no difficulty in hearing traditional ballads or folk music performed in the local bars or hotels; players usually advertise in the local newspaper or by sticking up a notice in the window. The group of musicians seem only too happy to let you join in, and as the atmosphere warms up the music really takes off. In 1951 *Comhaltas Ceoltoírí Eireann* was set up for the promotion of traditional music, song and dance. It now has two hundred branches all over the country, and their members have regular sessions (*seisiúns*) that are open to all. Ask at the local tourist office or write to *Comhaltas Ceoltoírí Eireann* (*32 Belgrave Square, Monkstown, County Dublin,* **t** *(01) 280 0295, www.comhaltas.com*). A popular feature of the traditional music scene are the *seisiúns* – these are informal sessions of music, ceilidhs and traditional cabaret.

For information on local musical happenings, contact the local tourist office – there is bound to be a *fleadh* going on somewhere near you. The local Radio Kerry (96–98FM) is a mine of information on music festivals, *seisiún* and theatre. The All-Ireland *Fleadh* is held at the end of August in a different town every year. There are smaller festivals around the southwest each year. At these you can hear music of an incredible standard spilling into the streets from every hall, bar, hotel and private house. It takes a great deal of stamina and several jars to see the whole thing through. Do not expect a formal concert-hall environment, as music and craic thrive best in small intimate gatherings, which are often unplanned sessions in the local bar.

In Kerry, Father Pat Ahearn has got together a National Folk Theatre (*Siamsa Tire*) which has performances in song, mime and the dance of ordinary life, set in rural Ireland years ago. It was founded in 1974 to promote Irish folk culture through the medium of music, with heavy emphasis on traditional Irish dancing and singing. The theatre is based in two thatched cottages, in Finuge and at Carraig on the western tip of the Dingle Peninsula. Each cottage is known as *Teach Saimsa*, which means the house of musical entertainment. *Siamsa Tire* (**t** *(066) 712 3055, www.siamsatire.com*) offers nightly performances in the summer.

Today Ireland is producing some good musicians of a completely different type from the folk groups. The local bands that perform in the bars play jazz, blues and a rhythmical and melodious version of pop played on traditional instruments. Look in the local newspaper of any big town or ask in a record shop; they will know what gigs are on and will probably be able to sell you a ticket as well. Some of the top names on the rock and pop scene come from Ireland, for instance, Van Morrison, U2 and the Corrs. The phenomenal success of *Riverdance*, which has toured the world and sold out in every venue, has given traditional music and dance the glamour of Broadway.

Tracing Your Ancestors

If you have any Irish blood in you at all, you will have a passion for genealogy; the Irish seem to like looking backwards. When they had nothing left – no land, no Brehon laws, no religious freedom – they managed to hold on to their pride and their genealogy. Waving these before the eyes of French and Spanish rulers ensured that they got posts at court or commissions in the army. There is no such thing as class envy in Ireland: the next man is as good as you, and everybody is descended from some prince or hero from the Irish past. It is the descendants of the Cromwellian parvenus who had to bolster up their images with portraits and fine furniture. Now the planter families have the Irish obsession with their ancestors too.

Information and sources for research are rather fragmented. It would be best to write to the Genealogical Office in the National Library in Dublin before you come to

Important Sources of Information in Ireland

General Civil Registration of Births, Marriages and Deaths, General Register Office, Convent Road, Roscommon, t 090 663 2900, or t 1890 252076, www.groireland.ie. Marriages of non-Catholics were recorded from 1845. Registration of everybody began in 1864. Will supply copies of certificates on request. *Open Mon–Fri 9.30–12.30 and 2.15–4.30.*

Genealogical Office, at the National Library, 2 Kildare Street, Dublin 2, t (01) 603 0200, www.nli.ie. Consultations by appointment. Enquiries into heraldry, genealogy and family history; searches for a small fee. List of research agencies in the Republic. *Open Mon–Fri 10–4.45, Sat 10–12.30.*

Registry of Deeds, Henrietta Street, Dublin 7, t (01) 670 7500, www.landregistry.ie. Records of land matters from 1708 onwards. *Open Mon–Fri 10–4.30.*

National Library, Kildare Street, Dublin 2, t (01) 603 0200, www.nli.ie. *Open Mon 10–9; Tues and Wed 2–9, Thurs and Fri 10–5.* Many sources: books, papers and manuscripts.

National Archives, Bishop Street, Dublin 8, t (01) 407 2300, www.nationalarchives.ie. The Public Record Office was burnt in 1922 and many Church of Ireland registers were lost, but not all. Important genealogical sources: Griffith's Primary Valuation of Ireland, 1848–63, records names of land/property owners and occupiers. *Open Mon–Fri 10–5.*

Ulster Historical Foundation, Balmoral Buildings, 12 College Square East, Belfast, t (028) 9033 2288, www.ancestryireland. co.uk. Undertakes searches and published *Ulster Libraries, Archives, Museums and Ancestral Heritage Centres – A Visitor's Guide.* Local records from 1864 held at county level. Church records vary widely in age, and are an essential primary source. Parochial registers kept by parish priests and Church of Ireland rectors nationwide. Enthusiastic historical or heritage societies and priests have indexed the county parish records.

Irish Family History Foundation, Pat Stafford, Yola Farmhouse, Tagoat, Co. Wexford, t (053) 32610, www.irishroots.net. Cross-border umbrella organization for local genealogical and historical societies. Centres provide computerized information on Irish families have opened up all over Ireland. All parish and appropriate civil records are being collected and filed. All centres can be accessed through www.irish-roots.net.

Irish Genealogy Ltd, www.irishgenealogy.ie. Coordinates the Irish Genealogical Project for researchers.

Association of Professional Genealogists, c/o 30 Harlech Crescent, Clonskeagh, Dublin 14. A regulating body for genealogists with a list of members at indigo.ie/%7Eapgi/.

Clare Heritage Centre and Genealogical Society, Church St, Corofin, t (065) 683 7955, clare.irish-roots.net. *Open Mon–Fri 9–5.30.*

Cobh Heritage Centre, Co. Cork, t (021) 481 3591, www.cobhheritage.com

Ireland, and ask their advice. For Ulster families, try the Ulster Historical Foundation (*see* boxed addresses). Before approaching these organizations, you must have found out as much as possible from family papers, old relatives, and the records of the Church and State in your own country; your local historical or genealogical society might be able to help. Find out the full name of your emigrant ancestor and the background of his or her family, whether rich or poor, merchants or farmers, Catholic or Protestant. The family tradition of remembering the name of the parish or townland is a great help.

In America, immigrant records have been published by Baltimore Genealogical Publishing Company in seven volumes, and list the arrival of people into New York between 1846 and 1851. In Canada, the Department of Irish Studies, St Mary's University, Halifax is very helpful. In Australia, the Civil Records are very good: try the National Library, Canberra, the Mitchell Library, Sydney, and the Society of Australian Genealogists, Richmond Villa, 120 Kent Street, Sydney.

Historic Houses

If you want to try and understand the Anglo-Irish, who have a very muddled status amongst most shades of opinion, it's best to look around one of their houses.

The expression 'Anglo-Irish' has political, social and religious connotations. It is used to describe the waves of English settlers and their descendants who became so powerful in the land after the success of the campaigns of Elizabeth I of England. An optimistic view is held by some that Anglo-Irish is a tag that should only be applied to literature, and indeed it does seem ridiculous that after three hundred years of living in a place these landowning families are not counted as truly Irish. On the one hand, it is a fact that the sons of the Ascendancy were educated in England and served the British Empire as soldiers or civil servants, and that they beheld themselves as different from the native Irish. However, on the other hand, many of these people felt a great and patriotic love for Ireland, led revolts and uprisings against British rule and, starting with the Normans, became, in the very apt, anonymous and undated Latin saying, 'more Irish than the Irish'.

Ireland's big houses were built by families who would be most offended if you called them English, although, as far as the Gaelic Irish are concerned, that is exactly what they are. 'The Big House' is another very Irish expression and it is applied to a landowner's house regardless of its size or grandeur. In fact, if you look through Burke's *Guide to Irish Country Houses* and the rather depressing, but fascinating, *Vanishing Houses of Ireland* (published by the Irish Architectural Archive and the Irish Georgian Society), you will get a very good idea of the variety and huge number of houses that belonged to the gentry.

The English monarchs always financed their Irish wars by paying their soldiers with grants of land in Ireland and, as the country was so unruly, the settlers lived in fortified or semi-fortified houses during the 17th century. There are only a very few examples of Tudor domestic architecture, the most famous being Ormonde Castle,

Carrick on Suir, County Tipperary. Look out for the early 17th-century plasterwork if you visit Bunratty Castle, County Clare.

The victory of William of Orange over James II was complete when the Jacobites surrendered at the Treaty of Limerick in 1696. Within a few years the Penal Laws were introduced, which severely restricted the freedom of both Catholics and Nonconformists. The majority of big houses were built in the hundred years following the 1690s, when the Protestant landowners settled down to enjoy their gains. The civil and domestic architecture that survives from these times is both elegant and splendid, and is to be found in every county. The chief centre of this 18th-century architecture was, of course, Dublin. Before the unfortunate Union of Ireland with England in 1801, it was a confident, learned and artistic capital and today, in spite of the building developers, it has held on to its gracious heritage.

The big house usually consists of a square, grey stone block, sometimes with wings, set amongst gardens and parkland with stables at the back, and a walled garden. Sometimes it is called a castle, although the only attribute of a castle it may have is a deep fosse. A lingering insecurity must often have remained, for many are almost as tall as they are wide, with up to four storeys, rather like a Georgian version of the 16th-century tower house. The buildings are completely different in atmosphere here from their counterparts in England. They have not undergone Victorian 'improvements' or gradually assumed an air of comfortable mellowness over the centuries. It was an act of bravado on the part of the Anglo-Irish to build them at all, because they always had to be on the alert against the disaffected natives, who readily formed aggressive, agrarian groups such as the White Boys. They never had enough money to add on layer after layer in the newest architectural fashion; their houses remained as Palladian splendours or Gothick fantasies built during the Georgian age, when the fortified house could at last be exchanged for something more comfortable.

The big houses that remain are full of beautiful furniture, pictures, *objets d'art* and the paraphernalia of generations who appreciated beauty, good horses, hard drinking and eating, and were generous and slapdash by nature. It is against this background of grey, stately houses looking onto sylvan scenes and cosseted by sweeping trees that one should read Maria Edgeworth, supplying some details yourself on the Penal Laws, the famine, the foreignness of the landlords and their loyalties. The literature on the big house is huge, and if you read Thackeray, Trollope, Charles Lever, Somerville and Ross and more Maria Edgeworth on the subject, you will be not only entertained but well informed. The big house, courthouse, jail and military barracks were all symbols of oppression, and not surprisingly many of them got burnt out in the 1920s; but the rooms of these houses echo with the voices of talented and liberal people – the wit of Sheridan and Wilde, the conversations of Mrs Delany, the gleeful humour of Somerville and Ross – as you wander around.

In England there is a whole network of organizations and legislation to protect the historic house. In the Republic of Ireland there is no equivalent of the National Trust (although the Department of the Environment, Heritage and Local Government aims to conserve historic sites and gardens). This means there are few grants for repairs to

Selected Architects

Francis Johnston (1760–1829). Originally from Armagh, where he was responsible for many fine buildings such as the Observatory, he moved to Dublin in 1793. He did a lot of quality work in Dublin and made a huge contribution to founding the Royal Hibernian Academy of Painting, Sculpture and Architecture in 1823; he was its president for many years. He also designed some 'Gothick' castles such as Charleville Forest in County Cork.

Sir Richard Morrison (1767–1849). Regency architect from west Cork who designed the neoclassical Fota House in County Cork where the estate buildings, including a huntsman's lodge, are scaled-down versions of the house.

James and George Richard Pain. Pupils of the famous English architect John Nash, who designed grand houses all over Ireland, the Pain brothers came to Ireland around 1818. James went to Limerick and George Richard built up his practice in Cork where he constructed many fine buildings. One example is St Patrick's Church in Lower Glanmire Road, built in 1836, which has a fine Corinthian portico.

Davis Ducart. A Sardinian who moved to Ireland in the 18th century, he designed two notable buildings: the Limerick Custom House between 1765–69, and the Mayoralty House (now the Mercy Hospital) in Prospect Row, Cork, between 1765–1773. He also designed Riverstown House at Glanmire.

Thomas and Kearns Deane. These brothers left their mark on Cork: Kearns Deane designed and built St Mary's Dominican Church on Pope's Quay between 1832–39; Thomas Deane produced University College in Tudor Gothic collegiate style, modelled on the Oxford colleges, between 1845–1849.

buildings, and relatively less effective legislation to protect them from dereliction or neglect. Even now the big house is persistently regarded by the powers that be as tainted with the memories of colonialism and an oppressive age. They are labelled as 'not Irish', although the craftsmen who built and carved the wonderful details of cornicing, stuccowork and dovetailing, elegant staircases and splendid decoration were as Irish as could be. There are many desolate shells to glimpse on your travels, though it is still possible to go around quite a selection of well cared-for properties.

The National Heritage Council (now known as the The Heritage Council) is allocated a little money to help a few architecturally important buildings each year. It was set up by Charles Haughey and has helped to change official attitudes, but it is the Irish Georgian Society which so far has done most to secure the future of the big house. Founded in 1958 to work for the preservation of Ireland's architectural heritage, the society has carried out numerous rescue and restoration works on historic houses. The Irish Georgian Society is based at 74 Merrion Square, Dublin 2, **t** (01) 676 7053, *www.irish-architecture.com.*

If these gracious buildings and their gardens and parkland interest you, book into the country-house hotels such as Ballymaloe House in County Cork. For more details of country-house lodgings, see 'Where to Stay' in **Practical A–Z**, p.119, and individual entries in each county chapter.

There is a growing demand to stay in or rent an Irish castle and some of them are quite reasonably priced. Elegant Ireland is a company that will organize the most specialized of requests and holiday schedules. They have a range of very exclusive, attractive country houses where you can stay as the guest of friendly, interesting hosts, and where you can be sure of good food. They will also organize rented self-catering properties, from a castle to a thatched cottage. For details contact Elegant Ireland, 15 Harcourt Street, Dublin 2, t (01) 475 1632, *www.elegant.ie*. Luxurious tours can also be arranged.

'Hidden Ireland' is the collective name for a number of privately owned historic houses throughout Ireland offering accommodation and often dinner. To view their wide range of properties, obtain a brochure by contacting P. O. Box 31, Westport, County Mayo, t (01) 662 7166, *www.hidden-ireland.com*.

You could also combine classical music and architecture if you followed the Music in Great Irish Houses festival, which takes place in June each year. Many of the houses chosen as venues are not usually open to the public, which makes the occasion very special. For 10 days in June music-lovers can travel over a large part of Ireland to listen to top-class performers in Ireland's beautiful stately houses. Ask for details from the Irish Tourist Board (*Bord Fáilte*) or contact Music in Great Irish Houses, 65 Sandymount Road, Sandymount, Dublin 4, t (01) 664 2822, *www.musicirishhouses.com*.

Later Architectural Forms

Palladian

The term used to describe a pseudo-classical architectural style taken from the 16th-century Italian architect Palladio. Sir Edward Lovett Pearce introduced the Palladian style to Ireland, and it was continued by his pupil Richard Cassels, also known as Castle.

Neoclassical

A style of building which is similar to that of Palladio, but was more directly inspired by the civilization of Ancient Rome. Neoclassical became popular in the 1750s and remained so until the Gothic Revival.

Gothick

An amusing and romantic style which was popular in the late 18th century. It is spelled with a 'k' to distinguish it from the serious, and later, Gothic Revival. Gothick castles were built by Francis Johnston and the English Pain brothers, who came over to Ireland with John Nash during the 1780s. Details like towers and battlements were added to more severe classical houses.

Gothic Revival

From the 1830s onwards, many houses and churches were built in a style harking back to the Tudor and perpendicular forms; the popularity of these gradually gave way to the more severe style of the early English and Decorated Gothic. The English church architect Augustus Pugin (1812–52) equated Gothic with Christian and classicism with pagan. He designed some churches and cathedrals in Ireland including St Mary's Cathedral in Killarney. J.J. McCarthy (1817–82), an Irish architect, was very strongly influenced by Pugin.

Hibernio-Romanesque

A style which was popular in church architecture from the 1850s onwards. It fitted in with growing national feelings to lay claim to an 'Irish style' that existed before the Anglo-Norman invasion.

Irish Rococo Plasterwork

The great period of rococo plasterwork in Ireland began with the Swiss Italian brothers Paul and Philip Francini, who came to Ireland in 1734 to decorate the ceiling at Carton, Maynooth, for the Earl of Kildare. They were great stuccadores, and modelled plaster figures, trophies, fruit and flowers in magnificent combinations.

The Irish craftsmen quickly learned the technique, and between 1740 and 1760 many beautiful ceilings were created. These craftsmen tended to leave out figures, concentrating instead on birds, flowers and musical instruments. The ceilings are graceful, yet full of life, with a swirling gaiety which make Adam ceilings, which later became the fashion, seem stilted.

Gardens and Parklands of the Southwest

Gaelic Ireland does not have a long horticultural tradition. It began when the Anglo-Normans and later settlers introduced the idea of a pleasure garden, with its flowers and fruits. The unsettled state of Ireland, with its many hundreds of years of internal fighting and conquest, left little time for gardening until the 18th century. By then the country was calmer, and the new 'Ascendancy' began to build themselves comfortable houses, formal gardens and parklands. They planted their estates with fine oak and beech woods, and it is usually fairly obvious today where the lands around you formed part of a demesne because of the trees. Inevitably, these parks and gardens were regarded as symbols of conquest and were often attacked by the landless peasants. An attitude still prevails in Ireland which does not value trees, except as firewood, and very few are left to grow on the lands of the small farmer.

That said, one of the most attractive features of the Irish landscape is the way your eye is drawn to the top of ancient raths or ring forts which are crowned by graceful trees. These grow undisturbed because of their association with the fairies, especially the hawthorn tree. Many landlords planted beeches, oaks and yews around these ring forts and on small hillocks in the 19th century, and they contribute greatly to the beauty of the landscape.

Cork and Kerry have some of the finest and most inspiring gardens in Ireland. The climate is especially favourable, mild and damp, with magnificent scenery to offset the artful designs and grand schemes of plants and trees, water and stone.

Gardens of Southwest Ireland

This is only a skeleton list of gardens to give you an idea of those you can visit. Always make an appointment and check the opening times, as many of them are not regularly open.

Clanaboy, Woodleigh Park, Model Farm Road, County Cork, t (021) 454 1560.

Lakemount, Barnavara Hill, Glanmire, County Cork, t (021) 482 1052.

Fota Arboretum, Fota Island, County Cork, t (021) 481 2728, www.heritageireland.ie.

Anne's Grove, Castletownroche, County Cork, t (022) 26145, www.irishlandmark.com.

Hillside, Annmount, Glounthane, County Cork, t (021) 435 3119.

Lismore Castle, just inside the border of County Waterford, t (058) 54424, www.lismorecastle.com.

Timoleague Castle Gardens, Bandon, County Cork, t (023) 46116.

Bantry House, Bantry, County Cork, t (027) 50047, www.bantryhouse.ie.

Creagh, Skibbereen, West Cork, t (028) 22121.

Ilnacullin, Garinish Island, Glengarriff, County Cork, t (027) 63040, www.heritageireland.ie.

Derreen, Lauragh, Kenmare, County Kerry, t (064) 83103.

Dunloe Castle Gardens, Beaufort, County Kerry, t (064) 44111.

Muckross House Gardens, Killarney, t (064) 31440, www.muckross-house.ie.

Glin Castle Gardens, t (068) 34173, www.glincastle.com.

The gardeners and creators of these magical places have had the benefit of the climate, but also the talent to make something very beautiful to the eye and to the spirit. County Clare has its own natural garden in the Burren, where you can spend hours gazing at the cracks and fissures in the limestone pavements where the varied plant life arranges itself beautifully. County Limerick has one magnificent garden, at Glin, which is open to the public.

Cork City has many small suburban gardens, each a jewel of imagination in this city of little hills. It is possible to see quite a few by appointment, particularly if you time your visit during the Cork Garden Festival in May, but be aware that it is not held every year. It is also instructive and fun to join a gardening seminar at the Allen's Ballymaloe Cookery School in Shanagarry, t (021) 464 6785, www.cookingisfun.ie. They have created a wonderful kitchen garden with a colourful parterre of herbs, which is well worth a visit.

The mid 18th century saw the fashion for naturalized parkland take over from formal gardening. In the 19th century William Robertson, who started life as an Irish garden boy in County Laois, led the revolution against bedding plants and artifice and became the advocate of wild gardens, where the plant was suited to the situation and the garden to the nature of the ground. Anne's Grove grounds in County Cork are a fine example of his style. This 39-acre garden is set on sloping ground which leads down to a river. The garden consists of many parts – mature parkland, an ornamental walled garden divided by box hedges, and a rock garden – but its most stunning feature is the wild rhododendron woodland within the glen which leads to the water gardens and gorge. A winding path leads you on to pass magnolias and rhododendrons of every type, some with flaking cinnamon bark, and huge leaves arranged around blossoms of subtle yellows, whites and reds. The water garden in the gorge is bright with yellow primulas and day lilies while rodgersias, astilbes, bamboo, gunnera and other plants fill in the scene with varying shades of green lushness. A rustic bridge, a weir, rapids and an island add more interest, while above the river rise limestone cliffs where a totally different vegetation thrives. Anne's Grove is lucky enough to have both acid-loving and limestone-loving plants. The garden was started in 1906 by Richard Grove Annesley who realized the possibilities in the area of acidic soil and gathered seeds of species of rhododendrons from plant-hunters working in China and the Himalayas. The Annesley family still live in the pretty 18th-century house at the centre of the garden. It is open to the public most of the year.

Potatoes and the Famine

Potatoes were the main food of peasants in the 19th century. The whole family would sit around a *rishawn* (willow basket) placed on the three-legged iron pot in which they had been boiled. The summer months were known as the hungry months, as the old crop of potatoes was finished. The last Sunday in July, or the first Sunday in August, was the ancient feast of Lughnasa (Lammas), a celebration of the start of the new harvest. Sometimes a delicious mixture of new potatoes, cabbage, milk, onion, spices and melted butter would be eaten from the first digging of the new potatoes. This is known as colcannon (*cál ceannann*, literally, white-headed cabbage).

The potato crop enabled large families to live on tiny, subdivided holdings on the poorest land. The spuds were grown in lazy beds, the farmers using spades to build up ridges of soil on these stony hillside farms. You can still see the traces of lazy beds in hillside parts of Munster. Today they are no longer cultivated; many were abandoned in the famine times.

The potato blight, a fungal disease that struck between 1845–1849, had fatal consequences for the peasants living on this subsistence economy, especially in the west and southwest of the country. Huge suffering, death and disease followed, and the departure of millions of folk for Britain, Australia, Canada and America. The consequences of the famine and emigration were enormous, and still affect Ireland today. The population of Irish-speaking small farmers declined dramatically by 1847; nearly a quarter of a million emigrated every year. The landscape was emptied of people, villages were deserted, and the more prosperous farmers increased their land holdings. Very often all but the eldest son in a family emigrated; he was left to carry on with the farm, and he did not marry until very late in life, usually when his parents were dead. The wandering labourer who had an important place in society gradually died out as a class after the famine. These wandering labourers went to hiring-fairs all over the provinces to be taken on by 'strong' or 'comfortable' farmers, as the better-off were called. Many were poets and storytellers and helped to keep the ancient oral tradition alive. The spade was the essential tool that each labourer carried with him, and every region in Ireland had its own variation of spade made by the blacksmith to suit local conditions. A Munster spade is typically a very long, narrow blade with fishtail ends.

'Clonakilty God help us' is an expression that originates from the time when that area westwards through Rosscarbery and Skibbereen suffered terribly. At Knockfierna, in west County Limerick, is a very well preserved famine village. At the time of the famine, about one thousand people lived on the hill overlooking the Golden Vale. After the famine, only three hundred remained. These people lived in terrible conditions, doing backbreaking work to survive. Today there is no one left; only the derelict huts remain. The Knockfierna Heritage and Folklore Group has developed a National Famine Commemoration Park with restored famine dwellings on their original sites, around which you can still see the potato ridges. The group has also compiled much local history of the time. It is a fascinating place, and provokes sombre reflection as well as admiration for the resilience of these poor people. You can walk up there at any time; make sure you are wearing stout shoes. Ask for directions in Ballingarry. The Rambling House is sometimes open for traditional music sessions in the summer.

Wren Boys

Ireland of past times was a place of fascinating customs that fitted around a calendar of feast days and penance days. Many of the traditions predated Christianity, but were absorbed by the Christian calendar. One custom which is still alive is 'hunting the wren' on St Stephen's Day, the day after Christmas. In the past, groups of young boys caught a wren (or more if they could). The tiny bird was hung on a small holly bush decorated with ribbons which was then carried triumphantly from house to house. The first group to reach a house would be given money as their arrival signalled good luck for the coming year. Each region had slight variations of this practice, although the rhyme the boys chanted as they went on their rounds was fairly universal and went something like this:

The wren, the wren, the king of birds,
On St Stephen's Day was caught in the furze,
Although he is little, his family is great,
Put your hand in your pocket and give us a treat.
Sing holly, sing ivy, sing ivy, sing holly,
A drop just to drink it would drown melancholy.

The money collected would be spent on drink and food. Some folk did not approve of these goings on and refused to open their doors, so the wren boys would avenge themselves by burying the wren opposite the offending house, which was supposed to bring bad luck.

In the Dingle Peninsula the custom has continued and, on St Stephen's Day in Dingle, groups of wren boys converge on the town, and there is much fun and entertainment. The ceremony was always more complicated in these parts and involved mock battles, the use of masks and disguises, the fife and drum and the *lair Ohan* ('white mare') – a hobby horse, which in olden days could turn quite nasty and threaten any folk who did not pay up. Nowadays, besides the straw and tinsel decorations, all sorts of wigs, masks, and other disguises are used by the wren boys.

They dance and sing and a band of fife and drum musicians march around the town. The tradition of using fife and drum in Dingle exists perhaps because it used to be a garrison town in the days of English rule. The pubs are full and the streets crowded, and although Dingle is a town devoted to the tourist in summer, this is one custom that does not need cultivation by the tourist board to survive. If you happen to be in Dingle on St Stephen's Day, it is a riot of colour and fun; if you are not, try and catch the Listowel Harvest Festival and Races in mid-September when there is an all-Ireland wren boys competition, and plenty of traditional music and dancing.

The Burren

The Burren is an area of about 150 square miles (380sq km) of rock, a wild desolate place, but a fascinating place too, especially for archaeologists and plant-lovers, which is best sought out on foot. The most useful maps to have with you are the folding landscape series by Tim Robinson, and you will need strong shoes, for it is rough country. You can get some small sense of its beauty from the car if you follow some of the tiny country roads around Ballyvaughan, Kilfenora and Turlough.

This is a classic limestone karst landscape overlaid in its southern parts by shale and clay, which is being very gradually worn away. The processes that formed it are very complicated, but a much simplified explanation is this: about 270 million years ago, the plateau which is now the Aran Islands and the Burren lay under a shallow sea. Movements in the earth's crust thrust it up, and subsequent movements caused the limestone to crack and fracture into blocks and rectangular slabs. That it did not fracture even more dramatically is probably due to the granite underlying it. Glaciation made further changes, gouging out turloughs or hollows which now form temporary lakes, breaking off chunks of stone which were then left in the train of the glacier, where today they make striking shapes against the skyline.

The Burren has no outstanding mountains; the hills are not much more than 1,000ft (305m), weathered to a flaky silver, and the valleys are filled with hazel scrub and more stones. These stones are known as pavements, slashed as they are with fissures and holes where colonies of beautiful plants can grow. Feral goats roam the valleys, and you might be lucky and spot a pine marten. One of the glories of the Burren are the colonies of bloody cranesbill. Other plants that delight the eye are the spring gentian, the hoary rock rose, spring sandwort, mountain avens and orchids. Often plants of alpine and arctic origin grow near species of Mediterranean origin. They are sheltered in the grikes (fissures) and in the clints (small hollows) in the limestone where rain and soil gather. The grikes are sometimes up to six feet or more deep and in the shadowy, wet atmosphere ferns and other plants flourish. Very little surface water lies on the Burren; any rainwater quickly runs into the fissures, holes and subterranean passages that pierce the limestone.

All the rivers in the Burren (except for the Caher River) flow mostly underground. Where streams re-emerge as springs or turloughs (lakes that rise or fall according to the water table), it is usual to find a green patch of flowering herbs and grazing.

The Burren Display Centre at Kilfenora contains a lot of information on various aspects of the Burren, a scale model and a number of excellent audiovisual displays. The Burren is threatened by modern farming methods. The small cattle farms barely bring in a living, and the obvious way to make the pastureland more profitable is to use the EU grants to spray the hillsides, which of course kills the unique flora. Some of the ancient settlements and ring forts are in danger of being destroyed: many of them have never even been listed because of lack of funds. There are excellent local guides who will show you the Burren and its wealth of plant life and prehistoric settlements. Enquire at the Burren Centre (*t (065) 708 8030*).

Courting at Lisdoonvarna

This breezy spa town on the edge of the Burren has had a reputation for respectable matchmaking ever since people came to take the sulphur-tasting waters in the late 18th century. Comfortable farming families came to socialize, settle deals and match their sons and daughters in advantageous marriages. Lisdoonvarna adapted itself very well to aiding these deals, traditionally with the help of a matchmaker.

Nowadays it is a resort town all year round, although September is the liveliest month, as most people came to the spa after the harvest. The tradition of matchmaking and courting is assiduously promoted by the hoteliers, and various festivals attract those on the lookout for a romance. There are two official matchmakers now, and people do end up marrying the stranger they met in Lisdoonvarna. They may meet first in the attractive pump room, drinking a glass of the healthy mineral waters. Their acquaintance will be furthered in the Ballrooms of Romance where waltzes, country music and Irish jigs melt the reserve of the mainly rather elderly bachelor boys and girls. There is a younger element there for the craic and the booze. Lisdoonvarna is an amusing place to visit and a good base from which to explore the Burren and the dramatic Clare coastline.

Naomhogs

These are canoes made of tarred canvas stretched on a frame, similar to the curraghs of Connacht. They are still used for fishing off the coast of County Kerry, although they are now rare in comparison to the motorized wooden boats. The main difference between the *naomhogs* and the curragh is that the *naomhog* is driven by bladeless oars that swivel between two tholepins; the curragh has only a single tholepin by which the oar is hinged through a hole. J.M. Synge (1871–1909) spent some time on the Blasket Islands and he described a conversation about the canoes that he had with Maurice O'Sullivan, who wrote a wonderful account of his youth on the Blasket Islands called *Twenty Years a Growin'*. 'They are no better than boats,' said Maurice, 'but they are more useful. Before you get a heavy boat swimming you are up to your waist, and then you will be sitting the whole night like that; but a canoe will swim in a handful of water, so that you can get in dry and keep warm and dry the whole night. Then there will be seven men in a big boat and seven shares of fish, but in a canoe there will be three men only and three shares of fish, though the nets are the same in the two.'

Puck Fair (*Aonach an Phuic*, the Goat Fair)

This fair, also known as 'the Gathering', is held in Killorglin, County Kerry, between 10 and 12th of August. It is a very old tradition, although the first written historical reference to it is not until 1617 when Jenkin Conway was granted a patent to 'hold a fair on Lammas day and the day after'. The fair still attracts thousands of people from all over the country. On the evening of the first day, a billy goat, ribbons flowing from his horns, is hoisted onto a platform in the Market Square where, for the next two days, he presides as a pampered king over crowds of people and a busy livestock market. Much drinking and enjoyment is in order, especially on the third day, when shops and business premises stay open all day and long into the night. There are various theories as to the origins of this ritual. Some believe it is a custom dating from pagan times and the worship of the Celtic God, Lugh. This idea was reinforced when a stampede of goats warned the town of the impending arrival of the British forces – it was seen as a pagan warning. It was previously held at Lughnasa (Lammas) on 1st August, when many fairs were held all over Ireland. Sadly, few genuine fairs besides the Gathering have survived.

The Munster Cloak

The Munster Cloak is a black hooded cloak that country women used to wear. Although it is an image of bygone times, old women in County Cork wore this garment, derived from the great mantle of ancient Ireland, right up to the 1970s. It is made of heavy lined wool and in the past could be scarlet, blue or grey as well as black. Today a few Irish designers have revived this romantic and warm cloak. Try Cleo in Kenmare (2 *Shelbourne Street,* *t* *(064) 41410*).

Michael Collins (1890–1922): Revolutionary Leader

Michael Collins is to many the popular hero of the War of Independence, and a martyr of the Civil War. He is affectionately referred to as 'the Big Fellow'. He was born at Woodfield, on a small farm near Sam's Cross between Clonakilty and Rosscarbery. His dark good looks, daring and formidable intelligence have become the stuff of legend. He went to London at the age of sixteen and worked as a clerk; while he was there he joined the IRB (Irish Republican Brotherhood). He returned to Ireland to fight in the Easter Rising of 1916. He was imprisoned for nine months and after his release became one of the leaders of the Sinn Féin and Volunteer movements. After the Sinn Féin victory in the 1918 General Election and the establishment of the Irish

Parliament, he became Minister of Home Affairs and later Minister of Finance. War was declared on Britain (*see* **History** p.27); during this time he escaped capture by the Black and Tans and the British Army many times, through clever disguises and concealments. He organized jail breaks for Republican prisoners, including Eamon de Valera. Collins also directed the Volunteers' organization and intelligence system and soon kept the Republican side well informed of British plans. He was quite ruthless in his use of ambush and guerrilla warfare to intimidate and wear down the British Army and the RIC. His strong charismatic personality and quick temper made him many friends and a few sworn enemies among the leaders of Sinn Féin.

By 1921 he had come to accept that negotiations with Britain must begin, as did De Valera, who insisted that Collins be a member of the delegation that negotiated the Anglo-Irish Treaty of December 1921, which partitioned Ireland. De Valera knew that Collins would have to make concessions at the negotiating table, which he as President of the Irish Republic could not. It was useful to set Collins and Griffith up as scapegoats and remain true to his principles in Dublin. After the Treaty was signed in London, an initial wave of general relief was felt by the people but once it became clear that Cathal Brugha and Austin Stack, along with De Valera, did not accept the treaty, the nation began to divide. Michael Collins became the Chairman of the Provisional Government which had to persuade the anti-partitioners that the Treaty was the best compromise. He was now hated by many of his former colleagues. After the Civil War in Ireland began in June 1922, he became Commander-in-Chief of the Government forces. In Ireland this war is called 'the Uncivil War' or 'the War of Brothers': it was a terrible period and Collins knew that it was only a matter of time before the assassin's bullet would find him. On August 22, 1922, the last day of his life, he returned to visit the remains of his old home, burned down a year previously in a revenge attack for an IRA raid; later that day he was ambushed and murdered on the road to Bandon. He was two months short of his thirty-second birthday. His shooting and the trauma of the Civil War are still a raw subject in Ireland and it is only recently that an official re-evaluation has begun. The 1996 film about the Big Fellow, starring Liam Neeson, has done much to raise his profile.

Blow-ins

Ireland, and in particular the southwest, has been attracting increasing numbers of Europeans and North Americans over the years, attracted by the beautiful landscape and relaxed way of life. The positive side of this is that many tumbledown stone cottages and some dilapidated grander houses have been restored in a sympathetic way. The local communities have benefited from the introduction of delicious cheeses, a great variety of vegetables, some great restaurants, and a cross-fertilization of artistic and cultural ideas. The economic situation of these refugees from urban life varies; many are trying to practise self-sufficiency on smallholdings and become very involved with their community, others are rich tax exiles, or part-timers with other homes. As the number of incomers or 'blow-ins' (as they are called) increases, the natural resentment which accompanies any large influx into a closely knit community is growing too. This has led to a small minority calling for Ireland for the Irish, especially where land developers are buying up tracts of land in local beauty spots and covering them with holidays houses and chalets. Land and house prices have risen steeply, making it difficult for locals to buy their first homes. The planning laws in Ireland are notoriously insufficient and easy to sidestep. Local people have found to their cost that issues such as the provision of sewage facilities and water supplies are often inadequately addressed, and the closure of traditional rights of way remains contentious. It is not by any means only the 'blow-ins' from other countries who are resented by some – the city folk from Dublin and Cork, and the inevitable local entrepreneur who is hellbent on building holiday homes all over the place, also come in for sharp criticism. The coastal landscapes of Ireland are still stunning and largely unspoilt, and the majority of local people are delighted to see visitors from all over the world, but there is a growing awareness that the uncontrolled building of holiday homes will kill the very thing that most visitors to Ireland come for – unspoilt country life and landscapes.

Gaelic Games

Hurling (or hurley) and Gaelic football are uniquely Irish games, played widely in the counties of southwest Ireland. Both games are extremely fast and demand expert coordination, quick thinking, brawn, bravery and sure-footedness. It is probably fair to say that hurling requires the most skill and practice – Dr Johnson described it as 'hockey without the rules'. Hurling has been played all over the world wherever Irish migrants have settled. In Scotland it is called shinty, and was introduced by Irish missionaries along with Christianity. Gaelic football, which uses the same pitch as hurling, is often described as a mixture of soccer and rugby, although it is much older than either of these games.

The first recognized version of hurling was recorded in County Meath in 1670. However, hurling has existed in Ireland since pre-Christian times: the hero Cú Chulainn (the 'hound of Cullen') was named thus after killing a ferocious guard dog by driving a hurling ball down his throat. Skill on the hurling field in these ancient times was equated with one's ability on the battlefield. By the 17th and 18th centuries, the games were sometimes wild and violent, the rules were not set, and many regional variations existed.

To watch a hurling game at one of the grounds in Cork City, Killarney, Ennis, Thurles or Tralee will give you a huge buzz and some insight into Irish culture. Matches are advertised in the local newspapers, or you can get details from the local tourist office. They are organized under the auspices of the GAA, the Gaelic Athletic Association (*www.gaa.ie*.), which has been described as the 'greatest single bonding force in the Gaelic nation'. The GAA was founded in 1884 by Michael Cusack and Maurice Davin in a hotel meeting in Thurles. The Association standardized the rules in order to preserve the traditions of the games, in particular hurling, which was in danger of being gentrified and becoming a variant of hockey. Rugby was also becoming the accepted alternative to Gaelic football, especially amongst the middle classes. After the horrors of the Great Famine, many Irish customs and pastimes had fallen into decline, yet hurling was still very popular in much of southwest Ireland. The founding of the GAA was part of a general movement within Ireland, initiated by largely middle-class intellectuals, which sought to promote and esteem all things Irish. The literary revival and the language movement were part and parcel of this, but they did not achieve the mass following that grew up around the GAA, which was built on rural and Catholic support. Influential patrons of the GAA in its infancy were Dr Croke, the Archbishop of Cashel and Emly, Charles Stewart Parnell and Michael Davitt. The GAA organizes the two sports on a parish, county and provincial level. Among the most famous of the many different leagues and championships are the All Ireland Club Championship, the finals of which are played in Croke Park in Dublin on St Patrick's Day; the Railway Cup in early spring; and the Sam Macguire Cup. At a Gaelic football match between Tipperary and Dublin held at Croke Park during the War of Independence, Auxiliaries opened fire on the crowds and killed thirteen spectators and the Tipperary goalkeeper. This is known as Bloody Sunday, unfortunately not the only one.

Hurling is played with a *camán* or curved stick, variously known as a *cambuc*, *camack*, *camac*, *crabsowl*, *shinney*, shinty, *hockie*, hockey or *hawkey* throughout the Celtic fringes of Britain. The Galway Statutes of 1527 include it as one of the prohibited games, describing it as 'the horlinge of the litill balle with hockie stickes or staves'. The Irish hurling stick is short with a wide blade and is used to hit the ball in the air, to bounce it along on the stick or balance it there whilst running and being tackled aggressively. The stick is also used to hit the ball along the ground, although the breadth of the Irish stick means that the players cannot be as dextrous as their Scottish neighbours across the water, who play with a narrower stick. The Ireland versus Scotland matches at Croke Park are legendary, the strengths and shortcomings of each method of hurling adding up to a match of equals.

Cork and Tipperary have a famous rivalry that has built up over the years and makes matches between them especially electric. Christy Ring of Cloyne, County Cork, and Nicholas English, who played brilliantly for Tipperary, spring to mind as hurling heroes, and heroes are what the players are in the minds of their parish, county and province. People line the roads and streets to welcome home their teams and bonfires are lit to celebrate great victories. All the players are unpaid, and play just for the game and the glory. Cork and Tipperary are the main hurling winners; Limerick is becoming increasingly skilful and Kilkenny is famous for its craft or style. County Kerry is undoubtedly the champion of Gaelic football, having won many of the All-Ireland matches.

The ball in Gaelic football and hurling can be dribbled, punched, or kicked and carried in the hand for not more than four steps, after which it must be either bounced or 'solo-ed'. This means dropping the ball on to the foot or stick and kicking or throwing it back into the hand. In hurling you are not allowed to catch the ball more than twice. The goalposts for both games are the same shape as for rugby, although the crossbar is lower than on a rugby post. The ball used in Gaelic football is smaller than a soccer ball, while in hurling it is hard and leather-covered, like a hockey ball with raised ridges.

The growing popularity of soccer all over Ireland is seen as something of a threat to hurling and Gaelic football, as both need commitment and training from an early age. The willing involvement of the religious orders, who used to run many of the educational establishments and helped train players after school, has not been replaced within the more secular organization. The dominance of Munster and the modern cult of counting success above everything is discouraging those clubs throughout Ireland that have never been very successful. However, the Irish government gave the GAA a grant of €40 million in 2004 towards the refurbishment of Croke Park, which was completed in early 2005.

Food and Drink

07

Beyond the Potato

Eating out in the southwest of Ireland can be a memorable experience if the chef gets it right. The basic ingredients are the best in the world: succulent **beef**, **lamb**, **salmon**, **seafood**, **ham**, **butter**, **cream**, **eggs** and wonderful country **breads** – which are often home-made. Breads vary from crumbly, nutty-tasting **wheaten bread** to moist, white **soda bread**, crispy **scones**, **potato bread** and **barmbrack**, a rich fruity loaf which is traditionally eaten at Hallowe'en tea. Irish potatoes are light and floury and best when just off the stalk, and crispy carrots and cabbages are sold in every grocery shop, often bought in from the local farms. If you stay in a rustic country-house hotel, the walled garden will probably produce abundant rare and exotic vegetables and succulent fruit.

The history of Ireland has quite a lot to do with the downside of cooking: overcooked food, few vegetables and too many synthetic cakes. The landless peasants had little to survive off except potatoes, milk and the occasional bit of bacon, so there is little traditional 'cuisine'. **Fish** was until recently regarded as religious 'penance food', to be eaten only on Fridays. Some Irish people talk with amusement of those who eat oysters or mussels, and much of the fine seafood harvested from the seaweed-fringed loughs and the open sea goes straight to France, where it appears on the starched linen tablecloths of the best restaurants. But do not despair if you love **fat oysters**, **fresh salmon**, **juicy mussels** or **langoustines**, because they can always be got, either in the bars, the newer restaurants (which are really excellent) or straight from the fishermen. Fish of all sorts is also becoming more and more readily available.

Having got over the trauma of the famine, and since the relative prosperity of the 1960s, many people in Ireland like to eat meat: you cannot fail to notice the number of butchers or 'fleshers' in every town. **Steak** appears on every menu, and if you are staying in a simple farmhouse, huge **lamb chops** with a minty sauce, **Irish stew** made from the best end of mutton neck, onions and potatoes, and **bacon and cabbage casserole** baked in the oven are delicious possibilities.

One of the greatest success stories recently in Irish food exports has been **Irish cheese**: the Irish cheese market is now worth millions of euros, with the largest recent growth in the sector of farmhouse and traditional cheeses made by small craft producers. Munster cheeses you should come across include: **Carrigaline** (sweet and buttery, made by the O'Farrells in Carrigaline); **Burren Gold** (similar to Gouda, from Aillwee Cave); **Coolea** (also like Gouda; made by Dick Willems of Coolea); **Ardrahan** (semi-soft and nutty, from Ardrahan House, Kanturk); **Ballintubber** (a hard vintage cheese blended with chives, from Cahill's of Newcastle West); the award-winning **Durrus** (semi-soft and creamy, from near Bantry); **Gubbeen** (semi-soft, rich and savoury, from Gubbeen House near Schull); **St Tola** goat's cheeses (from Inagh, County Clare); **Milleens** (floral and firm to creamy, made on the Beara Peninsula at Eyeries); **Mount Callan** (hard, rich and tangy when mature, from near Ennistymon); **Desmond** and **Gabriel** (both hard, piquant and aromatic, from Schull).

Remember, everything in Ireland works on a personal basis. Start your enquiries for any sort of regional delicacy at the local post office, grocer or butcher, or in the pub.

Barmbrack (*Bairín Breac*) Recipe

This delicious moist currant bread was traditionally eaten at Hallowe'en. The name comes from the Irish for speckled cakes. Nowadays bakers sell a poor version of it. Another version uses baking powder instead of yeast and is referred to as 'tea brack'.

75g (3oz) fresh yeast or 35g (1½oz) dried yeast
140g (5½oz) sugar
2 tablespoons butter
450g (1lb) sifted flour
1 egg, beaten
half a level teaspoon ground ginger
quarter level teaspoon ground nutmeg
225g (8oz) sultanas
100g (4oz) currants
50g (2oz) chopped peel
pinch of salt

Cream the yeast with half a tablespoon of sugar and one tablespoon of tepid water; it should froth. Rub the butter into the sifted flour, add 75g (3oz) sugar, the beaten egg, ginger and nutmeg; mix well. Make a well in the middle and pour in the yeast mixture. Beat with a wooden spoon for 10–15 minutes, until the dough clings to the spoon. Work in the dried fruit and peel and finally add the salt; mix and turn into a warmed bowl. Cover and leave to rise in a warm place for about an hour until it doubles in size. Turn out and knead gently. Lightly grease two 17.5-cm (7-inch) cake tins and distribute the mixture equally between them. Leave to rise again for 30 minutes. Bake in a hot preheated oven at 220°C, 425°F or gas mark 7 for 7 minutes, then reduce to 190°C, 375°F, gas mark 5 and bake for 45 minutes. When the cake is ready, dissolve the remaining two tablespoons of sugar in a tablespoon of boiling water and glaze the cake with the mixture. Put back in the oven for a few minutes to dry, then cool on a wire rack.

Literature

Historic Hotels of Europe issues a booklet every year, *Ireland's Blue Book,* which includes some of the best hotels in the southwest (see *www.irelands-blue-book.ie*). Possibly the best food guide is Bridgestone's *Irish Food Guide*, which contains a directory of good restaurants and sources, compiled by Sally and John McKenna.

Legal and Illicit Liquids

'The only cure for drinking is to drink more', so goes the Irish proverb. Organizations such as the Pioneers exist to wean the masses off 'the drink' – alcohol costs an arm and a leg, what with the taxes and the publican's cut; yet, nevertheless, an Irish bar can be one of the most convivial places in the world. The delicious liquor, the cosy snugs and the general hubbub of excited conversation, which in the evening might easily spark into a piece of impromptu singing, makes the business of taking a drink very pleasant. Pubs can also be as quiet as a grave, especially in the late afternoon when a few men nod over their pint, and an air of contemplation pervades. Murphy's, Smithwick's ale and Harp lager are three very good legal brews made in Ireland.

You are bound to have been lured into trying **Guinness** by the adverts you see all over Europe, for the export trade is thriving; but the place to get a real taste of the creamy dark liquor is in an Irish bar. The quality of taste once it has left the brewery in Dublin depends on how well the publican looks after it and cleans the pipe from the barrel, so it varies greatly from bar to bar. Note that Guinness should be served chilled, and, if it's obvious that you are a tourist, your Guinness might be decorated with a shamrock drawn on its frothy head. If you are feeling adventurous, try something called Black Velvet – an interesting cocktail comprised of Guinness and champagne.

Whiskey has been drunk in Ireland for more than five hundred years and the word itself is derived from *uisge beatha*, the Irish for 'water of life'. It is made from malted barley with a small proportion of wheat, oats and occasionally a pinch of rye. There are several brands, but Jameson's and Paddy, made in the south, and Bushmills, made in the North, are the best.

Irish coffee is a wonderful combination of contrasts: hot and cold, black and white, and very intoxicating. It was first dreamed up in County Limerick in the early 20th century. It's made with a double measure of Irish whiskey, one tablespoon of double cream, one cup of strong, hot black coffee, and a heaped tablespoon of sugar. To make it, first warm a stemmed whiskey glass. Put in the sugar and enough hot coffee to dissolve the sugar. Stir well. Add the Irish whiskey and fill the glass and pour the cream slowly over a spoon. Do not stir the cream into the coffee; it should float on top. The hot whiskey-laced coffee is drunk through the cold cream.

Poitín (pronounced 'pot-cheen') is illicit whiskey, traditionally made from grain or potatoes, although nowadays it is only made from grain. Tucked away in the countryside are stills which no longer bubble over a turf fire, but on a Calor gas stove. Poitín is pretty disgusting stuff unless you get a very good brew – and it probably kills off a lot of brain cells, so you're much better off sticking to the legal liquid.

If you happen to stay in that wonderful country house, Longueville, near Mallow, you must order a bottle of dry, fruity white **wine** produced from its vineyard, one of the first in Ireland. It is delicious and rare, because of the fierceness of the frost and uncertainty of the sunshine.

The old-fashioned, serious drinking **bar** or pub, with high counters and engraved glass windows, frosted so the outside world cannot intrude, is gradually disappearing. It used to be a male preserve, where farmers on a trip into town could be heard bewailing the weather or recounting the latest in cattle and land prices or gossip. What the inns have lost in character they compensate for, to a degree, with comfort. The bar of the local hotel is the best place to find the priest when he is off duty. My favourite drinking establishment is the grocery shop, also a bar, where you ask for a taxi/plumber/undertaker, only to find that the publican or his brother combines all these talents with great panache.

Do take note that in 2004 the Irish government introduced a blanket **ban on smoking** in any public workplace, which includes all bars, nightclubs and restaurants.

Travel

08

Getting There

By Air from the UK and Europe

British Airways, British Midland, Air Wales, FlyBE, Air France, Ryanair, TAP Air Portugal, Swiss Air, SAS (Scandinavian Airlines), **Lufthansa** and **Iberia** run regular scheduled flights from European capitals and major cities. The Irish national airline, **Aer Lingus**, also handles an enormous number of flights from European destinations, and, if you're going to immerse yourself in all things Irish, you might as well start with this airline and its hostesses, all dressed in green.

There are direct flights to **Cork**, **Shannon** and **Dublin** from the four main London airports (Heathrow, Gatwick, Luton and Stansted) and additional flights to certain cities from other British regional airports. **Ryanair**, for example, has regular flights to Dublin from Aberdeen, Blackpool, Bournemouth, Birmingham, Bristol, Cardiff, Doncaster (Sheffield), Durham Tees Valley, Edinburgh, Glasgow Prestwick, Leeds Bradford, Liverpool, London Gatwick, London Luton, London Stansted, Manchester, Newcastle and Nottingham East Midlands Airport. **British European** (Flybe) fly from Birmingham to Shannon and from Southampton and Exeter to Dublin.

Prices are always in flux but are reasonable by European standards.

Student and Youth Discounts

If you can produce an **International Student Identity Card** (ISIC), you can expect to get discounts of at least 10% on standard passenger rates for travel. There are student or 'under 26' rates for flights between Britain and Ireland, and similar concessions for transatlantic flights. Contact **USIT** (Union of Students International Travel) in Limerick at Central Buildings, O'Connell Street, **t** (064) 602 1904, *www.usit.ie*. Agencies specializing in student and youth travel can help you apply for the correct ID cards, as well as filling you in on the best deals (*see* box, below).

Airline Carriers

UK

Aer Arann, t 0800 587 2324, *www.aerarann.ie*. Birmingham, Bristol, Edinburgh and Southampton to Cork.

Aer Lingus, t 0845 084 4444, *www.aerlingus.ie*. Birmingham, Edinburgh, Glasgow, London Heathrow and Manchester to Dublin. Heathrow to Cork and Shannon.

Air France, t 0870 142 4243, *www.airfrance.co.uk*. London City to Dublin.

Air Southwest, t 0870 241 8202, *www.airsouthwest.com*. Bristol and Newquay to Dublin.

Air Wales, t 0870 777 3131, *www.airwales.com*. Plymouth to Cork.

British Airways (BA), t 0870 850 9850, *www.ba.com*. London Gatwick to Dublin, Manchester to Cork.

British Midland (BMI), t 0870 607 0555, *www.flybmi.com*. London Heathrow to Dublin.

BMIBaby, t 0870 264 2229, *www.bmibaby.com*. Nottingham to Dublin; Birmingham, Cardiff, Leeds Bradford, Manchester, Teeside to Cork.

EasyJet, t 0905 821 0905 (65p/min), *www.easyjet.com*. Gatwick to Cork and Shannon.

EU Jet, t 0870 414 1414, *www.eujet.com*. Kent International to Shannon.

FlyBE, t 0871 700 0123, *www.flybe.com*. Birmingham to Shannon.

Luxair, t 0800 389 9443, *www.luxair.lu*. Manchester to Dublin.

Ryanair, t 0871 246 0000 (10p/min), *www.ryanair.com*. Probably your best bet; Ireland's fastest-growing airline flies from most UK regional airports to Cork/Shannon.

Thomsonfly, t 0800 000 747, *www.thomsonfly.com*. Coventry to Cork and Shannon.

USA and Canada

Aer Lingus, t 1 800 IRISH AIR, *www.aerlingus.com*.

American Airlines, t 800 433 7300, t 800 543 1586 (TDD), *www.aa.com*.

British Airways, t 800 AIRWAYS, *www.ba.com*.

Air Canada, t 1 888 567 4160 (Canada), t 800 268 0024 (USA), *www.aircanada.ca*.

Continental, USA and Canada t 800 231 0856, *www.continental.com*.

Delta, USA and Canada t 800 241 4141, t 800 831 4488 (TDD), *www.delta.com*.

Northwest Airlines, t 800 447 4747 (24hr), *www.nwa.com*

By Air from the USA and Canada

The main airports for transatlantic flights are **Shannon** and **Dublin,** which are served by direct scheduled flights from Atlanta, Boston, Chicago and New York. There are also direct flights to Dublin on Air Canada. Many other airlines also fly to European destinations, where you can pick up connecting flights.

Since **prices** are constantly changing and there are numerous kinds of deals on offer, the first thing to do is find yourself a travel agent who is capable of laying the current options before you. The time of year you choose can make a great difference to the price and availability of tickets. Expect to pay more and to have to book earlier if you want to travel between June and August. Apex and SuperApex are the most reliable and flexible of the cheap fares. New York to Shannon or Dublin return on an Apex fare ranges from about US$350–1,000. A number of companies offer cheaper **charter flights** to Ireland – look in the Sunday travel section of

The New York Times. Remember to read all the small print as there are often catches, such as big cancellation penalties and restrictions about changing the dates of your flights. Sometimes charter contracts include provisions that allow charter companies to cancel your flight, change the dates of travel and add fuel surcharges after you have paid your fare. If you're considering travelling to Cork or Shannon via Dublin, it is cheaper to buy a ticket that includes the additional flight with the transatlantic flight, rather than paying for the second stage of the journey separately.

The **flight time** from New York to Dublin is about 5 hours, 30 minutes. From Los Angeles it is about 10 hours, 30 minutes. Flying time from Toronto is approximately 8 hours and from Vancouver, 10 hours, 30 minutes.

Shannon Airport is a free port offering a huge variety of duty-free goods for non-EU residents, plus a selection of Irish specialities: cut crystal glass, Connemara rugs and marble, Donegal tweed, smoked salmon, etc. If you do not want to get burdened with

United Airlines, t 800 538 2929, t 800 323 0170 (TDD), *www.united.com.*

Charters, Discounts and Special Deals

UK
Trailfinders, 215 Kensington High St, London W8, t 0845 058 58 58, *www.trailfinders.co.uk.* Also: *www.cheapflights.co.uk* *www.expedia.co.uk* *www.lastminute.com* *www.travelocity.com*

USA and Canada
Air Brokers International, 685 Market St, Suite 400, San Francisco, CA 94105, t 1 800 883 3273, *www.airbrokers.com.*
Travel Avenue, USA t 1 800 333 3335, *www.travelavenue.com*
Last Minute Travel Club, USA and Canada, t 1 800 442 0568, *www.lastminutetravel.com.*
New Frontiers, 5757 West Country Bld, Suite 656, Los Angeles, CA 90045, t 1 800 677 0720, *www.newfrontiers.com.*

Student Discounts

UK and Ireland
Europe Student Travel, 6 Campden Street, London W8, t (020) 7727 7647
STA Travel, 86 Old Brompton Rd, London SW7, t (020) 7361 6145, *www.statravel.com.* Also many other branches in the UK, particularly at universities.
Usit Campus, 52 Grosvenor Gardens, London SW1, t 0870 240 1010, *www.usit campus.co.uk* Also branches at most UK universities.
Usit, Aston Quay, Dublin 2, t (01) 602 1600, *www.usit.ie.*

USA and Canada
Airhitch, t 877 247 4482, *www.airhitch.org.*
STA, t 800 781 4040, *www.statravel.com*, with branches across North America.
Travel Avenue, t 800 333 3335, *www.travel avenue.com.*
Travel Cuts, 187 College St, Toronto, Ontario M5T, t 1 866 246 9762, *www.travelcuts.com.*

lots of presents and packages during your stay in Ireland, you can get everything here at the last minute. Goods bought in the duty-free area just before takeoff can be taken on the plane without any extra weight charges. Information on transport and accommodation is available at the tourist offices at all the major airports, which are open all year.

Students can get a range of discounted flights; *see* box, p.93. Trawl the small ads in newspaper travel pages (for example, *San Francisco Chronicle*, *New York Times*, *Chicago Tribune* and *Toronto Globe and Mail*). Numerous travel clubs and agencies also specialize in discount fares, but they may require you to pay an annual membership fee.

Check **websites**, including: *www.justfares. com* (t 800 766 3601); *www.flyaow.com* (discounted tickets on 500 worldwide airlines, also discount car rental and hotels), *www. air-fare.com*; *www.cheapflights.com*; *www. expedia.us*; *www.travelocity.com*; *www.orbitz. com*; *www.priceline.com* (bid for low-cost airline tickets); *www.travellersweb.ws* (t 1 866 888 2192); *www.smartertravel.com*. Airlines update their online databases late at night, so check for deals after midnight, before they've been advertised in the morning newspapers.

There are various programmes available for US students to combine working or studying with travelling in Ireland. Try **The Irish American Cultural Institute**, 1 Lackawanna Place, Morristown, NJ 07960, t 973 605 1991, *www.irishaci.org*.

Transport from the Airports

Airport shuttle buses run between the main airports and city centres. They're comfortable, frequent and economical; taxi drivers, by contrast, tend to ask high prices for a ride into the city – around €18 from Dublin Airport to the city centre. Dublin Bus runs an **Airlink 747** service between Dublin Airport and the Central Bus Station (*Busáras*) every 10–15 minutes, see *www.dublin-airport.com* for detailed information. *Bus Eireann* runs a similar and very frequent reasonably priced service between **Cork Airport** and Cork City (*see* p.184 and *www.buseirann.ie*), and from **Shannon Airport**

to Limerick, the nearest city, 15 miles (25km) away, and Ennis (*see* p.232).

By Boat

Gone are the days when you could cross the Atlantic by liner. The only regular scheduled sea crossings to Ireland these days come from Great Britain and continental Europe.

The only way to get directly to southwest Ireland by **ferry** is from **Swansea** in Wales to **Cork**. The ferries from the British west coast tend to cross the Irish Sea in the shortest distance possible, from the points along the coasts of Wales and Scotland that stretch out farthest towards the east coast of Ireland.

Which port and crossing you choose will depend on where you are starting from and where you wish to go to in Ireland – which is not as obvious a statement as it may seem. The main crossings are as follows: **Fishguard** and **Pembroke** in south Wales serve **Rosslare Harbour** (near Wexford) and southeast Ireland. **Holyhead**, off Anglesey in north Wales, takes passengers to **Dublin** and the neighbouring port of **Dun Laoghaire**, in the centre of the east coast. The route is also served by a high-speed catamaran which crosses the Irish Sea in under 2 hours. There is also a seasonal service to the **Isle of Man** from **Dublin**.

All the Irish ferry ports are well connected to bus and rail transport termini, and all the ferries have drive-on/drive-off facilities for car drivers.

Prices depend very much on the time of year and the length of the crossing. Price structures also relate to how long you intend to stay in Ireland and, if you are taking your car, the number of passengers in the car, the length of the car and so forth. Consult individual ferry companies about combination tickets, which enable you to enter Ireland through one port and leave by another. To give you some idea of costs, here are a few examples. On the **Swansea–Cork** ferry, the return fare for 5 adults and a car costs UK£69–279 (€100–408); on Stena's **Fishguard–Rosslare** route, foot passengers pay from UK£30 (€44) for a 5-day return, while 2 adults and a car pay from

Ferry Services

From Great Britain

Swansea Cork Ferries, Swansea, **t** (01792) 456 116; Cork **t** (021) 427 1166, *www.swansea corkferries.com*.
Swansea–Cork, 1 sailing every or every other day in each direction, during summer, 10hrs (overnight crossing from Swansea).

Irish Ferries, Dublin, **t** 0818 300 400; London, **t** 0870 517 1717; Liverpool, **t** 08705 171717, *www.irishferries.com*
Holyhead–Dublin, 2 sailings daily, all year, 3¼hrs; 3 catamaran sailings daily, all year, less than 2hrs.
Pembroke–Rosslare, 2 sailings daily, all year, 3½hrs.

Stena Line, Ashford, Kent, **t** 08705 707070; Dublin, **t** (01) 204 7777, *www.stenaline.co.uk*
Holyhead–Dun Laoghaire, 4 sailings daily,
all year, 3½hrs, plus 2 catamarans, 1½hrs.
Fishguard–Rosslare, 3–6 sailings daily all year, 3½hrs, catamaran 1½hrs.

Isle of Man Steam Packet Co., **t** 08705 523523, *www.steam-packet.com*
Isle of Man–Dublin, mid-May–mid-Sept, 4½hrs (contact operators for schedule); Sea Cat, 2hrs 40mins.

From France

Irish Ferries, Dublin **t** (01) 661 0511; Cherbourg **t** +33 44 28 96, *www.irishferries.ie*
Roscoff–Rosslare, 1–2 sailings per week April–Sept, 16hrs.
Cherbourg–Rosslare, 2–3 sailings per week, all year, 18hrs.

Britanny Ferries, Cork **t** (021) 277801; Roscoff **t** +33 29 28 00, *www.brittany-ferries.com*
Roscoff–Cork, 1 sailing per week, Mar–Oct only, 14hrs.

UK£145–279 (€212–408) (5 day return); travelling by Express Ferry costs approximately UK£30 (€44) more. Passenger fares for children are half the adult fare or less. Crossings from France are more expensive. **Cherbourg to Rosslare** with Irish Ferries, one-way, costs €59 for foot passengers, €282 for 1 adult and a car, and €579 for 4 adults and a car.

By Rail

All the car ferries crossing back and forth between England and Ireland are scheduled to link up with the UK railways' **boat trains**, which go frequently and speedily from London to Fishguard, Liverpool and Holyhead. You can buy your **ticket** at any railway station or booking office, or credit card bookings can be made by phone on **t** 08457 484950, or at *www.nationalrail.co.uk*. There are **free seat reservations** on all direct train services to and from the ports. You can get couchettes on the night trains, but when it's quiet you should be able to have a comfortable snooze by stretching out in your seat. For well researched and exhaustively up-to-date details of all train and ferry routes to Dublin and Cork, see the excellent independent website *www.seat61.com/ ireland.htm*.

London (Paddington) to Cork via Swansea takes 11 hours, **London (Euston) to Dublin** via Liverpool–Dun Laoghaire and Holyhead–Dun Laoghaire takes 8 hours. Adult return **fares** for London to Cork are UK£78–93 (€115–136), and between London and Dublin UK£32–58 (€47–85), depending on how far you book in advance (the cheapest book-ahead fares are currently available from Virgin Trains, **t** 0845 722 2333, *www.virgintrains.co.uk*).

If you intend to travel extensively in Europe, an **Inter-Rail pass** (for EU citizens who have been resident in the EU for at least six months) may be worth considering. A Zone A card covering the UK and Republic of Ireland offers one month's unlimited travel and costs UK£159 (under 26) or UK£223 (over 26).

The equivalent North American **Eurail Pass** takes in first class travel through 17 countries. Passes are valid for 15, 21, 30, 60 or 90 days (**prices** range from $588-$1,654 for adults travelling 1st class or from $382-$1,075 for under 26s travelling 2nd class). Bear in mind that cards are not valid for travel on trains in the UK; however, all fares include discounted fares on Eurostar plus free or discounted travel on selected ferries, lake steamers, boats and buses.

Rail passes for UK and EU citizens who have been resident in the EU for a minimum of 6 months:

www.raileurope.co.uk/railpasses; rail passes enquiry line, **t** 08707 30 44 95; travel centre located at 178 Piccadilly, London W1.

www.railchoice.co.uk.

www.seat61.com/Railpass.htm; extensive information on every kind of rail pass.

Rail passes for US and Canadian residents only:

www.raileurope.com, US **t** 1 877 257 2887; Canada **t** 1 800 361 RAIL.

www.europeonrail.com, **t** 201 255 2898; rail passes, rail-and-drive, car rental, timetables.

www.railconnection.com, **t** 1 888 RAILPASS; rail passes for all ages.

www.eurorailways.com, **t** 1 866 768 8927; rail passes, rail-and-drive passes, senior and youth passes, car rental, air tickets.

www.railpass.com, **t** 800 722 7151; passes, also vacation tours.

www.europrail.net, **t** 1 888 667.

By Bus

Travelling by bus and ferry to the southwest of Ireland is an endurance test, because the journey seems endless, with lots of stops through England and Ireland to pick up other travellers. The main advantage is that it's cheap and gets you straight to destinations in the provinces, so you don't have to catch onward buses, trains and taxis on arrival in Ireland. The small coaches to-ing and fro-ing across the Irish Sea are flourishing private enterprises in the hands of local individuals. They leave all parts of Ireland for the chief cities of England, Scotland and Wales, full to the brim with Irish people returning to work or coming home on leave. You will not find details of the smaller companies at your travel agent; look at the weekly newspapers for the Irish in Britain, such as the *Irish Post* (*www.irishpost.co.uk*) and *The Irish World* (*www.theirishworld.com*).

Bus Eireann and **Eurolines** run regular services between all parts of Ireland and Great Britain. Eurolines buses leave London from Victoria Coach Station. Discount passes for those under 26, over 50 and families can be bought from coach stations and travel agents for National Express/Eurolines (details given below).

As a guide to **prices**, London to Cork via Swansea takes around 15 hours and costs around UK£55 (€80) return. London to Dublin via Holyhead takes around 11 hours and costs UK£39–52 (€57–76), depending on how far in advance you book and how flexible you want to be.

Eurolines/National Express, **t** 0870 580 8080, *www.eurolines.co.uk.*

Bus Eireann, Dublin, **t** (01) 836 6111, *www.bus eireann.ie.*

Entry Formalities

Passports and Visas

Citizens of the UK, EU, US, Canada, Australia and New Zealand **all need a passport** to enter the country, but visas and return tickets are not required. Further information on Irish consulates/embassies and visas is available at *www.foreignaffairs.gov.ie.*

Customs

Duty-free allowances have been abolished in the EU. If you're travelling between two EU countries, you won't have to declare locally bought spirits, wine, beer and cigarettes etc.

In theory, you can buy as much as you like, provided you can prove the purchase is for your own use and not for other purposes (e.g. selling on to friends). In practice, customs will be more likely to ask questions if you buy in bulk, e.g. more than 3,200 cigarettes or 400 cigarillos, 200 cigars or 3kg of tobacco; plus 10 litres of spirits, 90 litres of wine and 110 litres of beer. Travellers caught exporting any of the above for resale will have their goods seized along with the vehicle they travelled in, and could face imprisonment for up to seven years. For residents of Britain and other EU countries, the usual EU regulations apply regarding what you can bring into your home country. Note that you **cannot** bring fresh meat or meat products, vegetables, plants or plant bulbs, hay or straw (or articles packed with these materials) into the UK. For more information see *www.revenue.ie.*

Non-EU visitors can claim back the 17.36% **Value Added Tax** (VAT) on goods purchased in Ireland and exported by you within three months of purchase. You will need a **Cashback voucher** stamped by the shop and customs before you leave Ireland. You can present the stamped vouchers at the Cashback desk at Shannon or Dublin airports, or claim the refund by post after your return.

Pets can be brought to Ireland, provided that they come directly from Britain, the Channel Islands or the Isle of Man and have lived there for at least six months. For further details contact the **Pets Travel Scheme**, t 08703 665 333.

Getting Around

By Air

It's feasible to fly from one city to another in Ireland; but this is a small island and the main destinations are adequately covered by rail and bus, so internal air travel is mainly for the traveller under pressure. **Aer Lingus** and **Ryanair** run flights from Cork, Kerry, Galway, Sligo, Donegal and Shannon to Dublin.

By Rail

Irish Rail services, Dublin t 1 850 444 2222, *www.irishrail.ie*.

Domestic train routes are operated by the Irish Rail arm of **CIE** (*Coras Iopair Eireann*), the national transport company, which also runs a bus network to most parts of the Republic. The system is rather like the British system of 40 years ago, with the old signal boxes that still need humans to operate them and keep an eye on things.

People are always friendly on trains, and the ticket inspectors are far from officious. Services are reliable, if not comprehensive, and fares are reasonable. It is cheaper to buy a return ticket than two singles. Best value of all, however, are railcards, allowing unlimited travel over a given period of time.

Special Rail Tickets

There are a number of ways to take good advantage of Ireland's public transport systems through specially priced rail tickets. For student fares, *see* p.93.

Irish Explorer for Rail and Bus: Allows you to travel 8 days out of 15. This ticket costs €194.

Irish Explorer for Rail Only: 5 days' travel over 15 days; costs €127.

Irish Rover: An all-Ireland ticket, which allows you up to 5 days' travel over 15 days, and costs €157.50.

Emerald Card: 15 days' travel over 30 days on bus/rail for €375.

Children's tickets are all half-price.

Ireland is now part of the **Eurail Pass** network (*see* p.95) allowing unlimited rail travel on European railways including the Republic of Ireland, but excluding the UK and Northern Ireland. To obtain a pass you must be a resident of a non-European country and buy your pass outside Europe. There are special rates for anyone up to 26 years old. With a Eurail Pass you can go from France to Ireland free on the ferry, provided you do not pass through Britain.

It takes 2hrs 45mins by train from Dublin to Limerick and 2hrs 40mins from Dublin to Cork. If you're travelling extensively by rail, it may be worth investing in the comprehensive *Rail Map of Great Britain & Ireland* (Thomas Cook, £7.95/€11.85).

By Bus

The **bus service** throughout Ireland is efficient and goes to the most remote places. The main company in the Republic is *Bus Eireann* (Irish Bus), t (01) 836 6111, *www.bus eireann.ie*, run by CIE. Freelance operators also run many tours. The main routes are covered by **Expressway** bus services. Prices are reasonable.

You can pick up a **Provincial Bus and Expressway Timetable** at CIE or tourist offices and at some newspaper stands. Note that bus destinations posted on the front of the bus are often written in Irish. If in doubt, ask.

Special Bus Tickets

Irish Rambler Bus Only: valid in the Irish Republic only, the Irish Rambler allows 3 days out of 8 consecutive days' travel for €53.

For concessionary tickets applying to both bus and rail, see the 'Special Rail Tickets' section, above.

By Car

To explore the southwest of Ireland with minimum effort and maximum freedom, bring a car. If you fill it up with people who share the ferry and petrol costs it won't be too expensive.

Buy a detailed **road map** and, if you have time, choose the minor roads and just meander. It is along these little lanes that the secret life of Southwest Ireland continues undisturbed. The black-and-red cows still chew by the wayside, while the herdsman, usually an old man or a child, salutes you with an upward nod. Nearby is the farmstead, cluttered with bits of old machinery and a cheerful sense of the makeshift, where everything is kept to be used again. An old front door will stop a gap in the hedge, old baths serve as cattle troughs, clucking hens roost on the old haycart; next year, the cart might be bought by the tinkers, who will varnish it up to adorn some suburban garden. You will come upon castles and the ruins of small, circular buildings called clochans, still breathing with memories, tumbled even further by the local farmer in search of stone. There are views of those many hills that have never reached the pages of any guidebook.

One of the best things about driving in Ireland is the lack of other cars and the absence of ugly (if useful) motorways with their obligatory motor inns and petrol stations (although on the outskirts of Dublin these are very much present).

Look out for the country driver who tends to drive right in the middle of the road, never looks in his mirror to see if anyone is behind, and is unlikely to indicate if he suddenly decides to turn left or right. Beware particularly of drivers wearing an old tweed cap – they are usually the worst offenders. You'll also get drivers from the other extreme, doing crazy speeds on narrow roads. Cars will frequently pull out of a side road in front of you and, just as you are getting up enough steam to pass, suddenly decide to turn off down another side road again.

Don't be alarmed by the sheepdogs that appear from every cottage door to chase your car – they are well skilled at avoiding you.

If your car **breaks down** you will always be able to find a mechanic to give you a hand; whether it's late at night or on a Sunday, just ask someone. He or she will sweep you up in a wave of sympathy and send messengers off in all directions to find someone with a reputation for mechanical genius. If it is some small and common part that has let you down, he will either have it or do something that will get you by until you come to a proper garage. One thing you will notice is that the Irish have a completely different attitude to machinery from most nationalities. In England, if you break down, it is an occasion for embarrassment; everybody rushes by hardly noticing you or pretending not to. In Ireland, if your car has broken down the next passing car will probably stop, and the problem will be taken on and discussed with great enjoyment. The Irish can laugh at the occasional failure of mechanical objects.

Facts and Formalities for Car Drivers

In Ireland you **drive on the left** – that is, when you are not driving in the middle of the road. **Petrol** stations stay open until around 8pm, and the village ones are open after Mass on Sundays. If you are desperate for petrol and every station seems closed, you can usually knock on the door and ask somebody to start the pumps for you. The **speed limit**, which is in kilometers per hour from 2005, is 62mph (99kph) on the open road, 30mph or 40mph (48kph or 64kph) through villages, towns and built-up areas, and 70mph (110kph) on motorways.

Drivers and front-seat passengers must always wear a **seat belt** – it is illegal not to. Children under 12 should travel in the back. There are **strict drink-driving laws** and the police will make you take a breathalyser test if they suspect that you are driving under the influence of alcohol.

There are some excellent **motoring maps**: Bartholomew's ¼-inch, obtainable from the British AA (Automobile Association) and Bord Fáilte, gives good details of minor roads. The **road numbering** system uses **N** to denote national, or main roads, and **R** for regional roads. Scenic routes are signposted and marked on the Bord Fáilte map.

Place names on signposts in the Republic are usually given in English and in Irish; in the Gaeltacht areas, where Irish only is used, a good map will come in handy. (We have tried to give Irish Gaelic place names where possible in the touring chapters – but be aware that spellings are not standard and you may have to be creative.) The old white signposts give distances in miles; the new green ones give distances in kilometres. All other traffic signs are more or less the same as the standard European ones.

Car parking in Cork city centre is controlled by a disc system. Parking discs can be bought, usually in books of ten, at shops and garages near car parks. Unexpired time on a parking disc can be used at another parking place.

Car Hire

Local firms can offer better deals than the big ones listed below. That said, renting a car

> ### Car Hire Firms
>
> These are only some of the bigger firms who will meet you at the airports and the ferry ports.
>
> **Avis**, Shannon **t** (061) 715600; Cork **t** (021) 428 1171; Cork Airport **t** (021) 432 7460; Dublin **t** (01) 605 7500; *www.avis.ie*.
>
> **Budget**, Shannon **t** (061) 471361; Cork **t** (021) 314000; Dublin **t** (01) 837 9611; *www.budget.ie*.
>
> **Dan Dooley Rent-a-Car**, central reservations **t** (062) 53103, *www.dandooley.com*
>
> **Hertz**, Dublin **t** (01) 844 5466; *www.hertz.ie*.
>
> **National Car Rental**, Shannon **t** (061) 472633; Cork **t** (021) 431 8623; Dublin **t** (01) 844 4162, *www.nationalcar.com*
>
> For further details contact the **Car Rental Council**, 5 Upper Pembroke St, Dublin 2, **t** (01) 676 1690, *www.carrentalcouncil.ie*.
>
> ### Motoring Organizations
>
> **American Automobile Association**, **t** 1 800 AAA HELP, *www.aaa.com*
>
> **British Automobile Association**, **t** 0870 600 0371, *www.theaa.com*.
>
> **Irish Automobile Association**, Dublin **t** (01) 617 9540, Cork **t** (021) 52444, *www.aaireland.ie*

in Ireland is never cheap. Prices start at around €154 per week, but you might be able to bargain if business is slack. Look out also for the fly-drive or rail-sail-drive packages offered by some of the airlines, holiday and ferry companies: these usually represent major savings.

Note that to hire a car you should normally be over 23, and should be in possession of a licence which you have held for at least two years without endorsement. The car hire company will organize insurance, but do check this. If you do not take extra collision-damage waiver insurance you can be liable for damage up to €1,700. For more info contact the **Car Rental Council**, 5 Upper Pembroke Street, Dublin 2, **t** (01) 676 1690, *www.car rentalcouncil.ie*.

By Bike

The southwest of Ireland is one of the most pleasant places to cycle around. The roads are uncrowded, there are still lots of birds and animals that live around the hedgerows, and there is no pollution to spoil the impression of rural Ireland: only the occasional strong manure smells that come in between the delicious whiffs of gorse or honeysuckle.

The majority of airlines will carry your bike for free, as part of your baggage allowance, but do check individual company regulations first. You can bring your own bike free on the ferry, or you can rent one. There is a **Raleigh Rent-a-Bike** network (**t** (01) 465 9659, *www.raleigh.ie/rent-a-bike.htm*), with centres throughout the southwest. Prices begin at about €20 per day, €80 per week, with a deposit of €80. Tandems, racing bikes and ordinary touring bikes are available.

Information about **Irish Cycling Safaris** is available at *www.cyclingsafaris.com*.

Bikes can easily be taken on trains and buses for a small fee per journey. However, space is obviously more limited on a bus and not to be relied upon. For further information, get the Cycling Ireland leaflet from the nearest Bord Fáilte office. This gives details of the main hire companies, lists Irish cycling holiday specialists, and also suggests a number of routes.

Specialist Tour Operators

There are literally hundreds of tour companies offering all manner of enticing holidays. *Bord Fáilte* has lists of the main operators in their brochures. Alternatively, contact your travel agent.

Special Interest Holidays

Travellers who want holidays with a special focus – ancestor-hunting, angling, bird-watching, farm and country, gastronomy, gardens, golf, horse-riding, sailing, a mixture of these or none of them – are particularly well catered for in Ireland. The main specialist holiday companies are listed in the tourist board brochures. *Bord Fáilte* also has a *Learning for Leisure* brochure which gives details of organizations offering holidays 'designed to enable participants to acquire new leisure skills – sports, gardening, cookery, arts and crafts, etc. in a relaxed and green environment'. *See also* 'Summer Schools' in **Practical A–Z**, p.117, and listings under the headings 'Sports and Activities', in each of the touring chapters.

Based in Ireland

Emerald Star Line Ltd, The Marina, Carrick-on-Shannon, Co. Leitrim, **t** (071) 962 7633, *www.emeraldstar.ie*. Cruising holidays on the River Shannon. Impressive onshore facilities and variety of boats.

Go Ireland, Killorglin, Co. Kerry, **t** 800 3698 7412 (Ireland), **t** 0800 783 8359 (UK), *www.goireland.ie*. Guided and independent walking and cycling holidays in Co. Kerry.

Irish Country Holidays, Old Church, Mill St, Borrisokane, Co. Tipperary, **t** (067) 27789, *www.country-holidays.ie*. Opportunity to live as part of a small, rural community. You can spend your week in Ballyhoura, Co. Limerick,

the Barrow/Nore area, Lough Corrib country, and west Cork. Each community has something special to offer in the way of landscape, customs and amenities.

Irish Cycling Safaris Ltd, Bike Shop, UCD, Dublin 4, **t** (01) 260 0749, *www.cyclingsafaris.com*. Leisurely, one-week cycling holidays around Co. Cork and Co. Kerry.

John Nicholas Colclough, Colclough Tours, 71 Waterloo Road, Dublin 4, **t** (01) 660 7975, *www.tourismresources.ie*. Runs tours anywhere in Ireland. He'll tailor an itinerary to suit you, organize a car with a guide/driver, and arrange accommodation ranging from the traditional farmhouse to the grandest castle. As well as sites of historical importance, the tours accommodate a varied range of interests from gardens, genealogy and ghosts to gourmet meals.

Based in the USA

Backroads, 801 Cedar St, Berkeley, CA 94710-1800, **t** 1 800 GO-ACTIVE, or 462 2848, *www.backroads.com*. Multi-sport – golf, hike and bike – packages in Co. Kerry and Co. Cork.

CIE Tours International Inc, 100 Hanover Ave, PO Box 501, Cedar Knolls, NJ 07927-0501, **t** 1 800 CIE-TOUR, or 973 292 3438, *www.cietours.com*. Escorted coach, self-drive or independent holidays, including 'Irish Pub and Folk' and 'Irish Legends' tours through the southwestern counties.

Classic Adventures, PO Box 143, Hamlin, New York, NY 14464-0144, **t** 1 800 777 8090, *www.classicadventures.com*. Guided biking holidays in the southwest.

Golf International Inc, 14 E 38th Street, New York, NY 10016, **t** 1 800 833 1389, *www.golfinternational.com*. Great variety of golf courses to sample from Kenmare to Ballybunion on these customized or escorted tours.

Hitchhiking

We would of course recommend you exercise caution and common sense if you choose to hitchhike when visiting any country. Women travellers, single or not, are advised

not to do it at all – if you're on a budget, stick to public transport, or hire a bicycle over shorter distances. Even if you do decide to hitch, you'll see more cows and sheep wandering along minor roads than cars.

Practical A–Z

09

Before You Go

A little preparation will help you get much more out of your holiday. Check the list of festivals at the beginning of each county chapter to help you decide where you want to be and when, and book accommodation early. If you plan to base yourself in one area, write ahead to the **local tourist offices** listed in the touring chapters for complete lists of self-catering accommodation, hotels and camp sites in their areas, or else contact an agency in the UK or USA (*see* p.100). For more general information, get in touch with an Irish national tourist office.

Children

If you are travelling with children you will find that most B&Bs will welcome them. Many have family rooms with four or five beds, and charge a reduced price for children. Most supply cots and highchairs, and offer a baby-sitting service, but always check beforehand. Some farms and country houses keep a donkey or pony, and have swings and a play area set up for children.

Irish people love children, and happily tolerate seeing and hearing them in bars and

eating places during the daytime. They will offer children's menus at a cheaper price and generally be helpful. That said, they will be slightly less pleased if you turn up with them for dinner at night. If you are contemplating staying in some of the smart country-house hotels which are full of precious antiques and fine furnishings, please check in advance that it is a suitable place for children.

The many national monuments, heritage centres, gardens and parks usually charge much less for children or offer a family ticket that will save you money.

Climate and When to Go

Ireland lies on the path of the North Atlantic cyclones, which makes the climate mild, equable and moist. In the southwest, rainfall is heaviest in the coastal areas, where it averages over 80 inches (203cm) a year.

Rain is the country's blessing, yet from the reputation it has in its own country and abroad you might imagine it was a curse. It keeps the fields and trees that famous lush green, and the high level of water vapour in the air gives it a sleepy quality and softens the colours of the landscape. The winds from the east increase the haziness and mute the colours, but these are nearly always followed by winds from the northwest which bring clearer air and sunshine. So the clouds begin to drift and shafts of changing light touch the land. Nearly every drizzly day has this gleam of sunshine, which is why the Irish are always very optimistic about the weather.

Average Maximum Temperatures in °C/°F

	Jan	April	July	Oct
Cork	5/41	8/46	15/59	10/50
Killarney	7/45	10/50	16/61	13/55

Average Monthly Rainfall in mm

	Jan	April	July	Oct
Cork	125	67	68	106
Killarney	165	80	85	135

The Gulf Stream in the Atlantic means there are never extremes of cold or hot weather. Snow is not common, but when it does fall it is seldom severe.

Spring tends to be relatively dry, especially after the blustery winds of March, and the crisp colours and freshness of autumn only degenerate into the cold and damp of winter in late December.

You can hope for at least six hours of sunshine a day over most of the country from May to August.

Disabled Travellers

Bord Fáilte produces useful booklets advising travellers with disabilities; they also publish a list of accessible accommodation in their annual guides, available from tourist offices. In Dublin, the National Rehabilitation Board offer a county-by-county factsheet detailing information on accessible accommodation. See below for a list of specialist organizations who should be able to provide information and advice.

Specialist Organizations for Disabled Travellers

In Ireland

Comhairle, 44 North Great George's Street, Dublin 1, t (01) 874 7503, *www.comhairle.ie.*.

Irish Wheelchair Association, Blackheath Drive, Clontarf, Dublin 3, t (01) 818 6400, *www.iwa.ie.* Services for disabled travellers; also guides for disabled holiday-makers.

National Disability Authority, Dublin 4, t (01) 608 0400, *www.nda.ie.*

National Rehabilitation Board, Access Department, 25 Clyde Road, Dublin 4.

In the UK

Access Ability, *www.access-ability.co.uk.* Information on travel agencies catering specifically for disabled people.

Emerging Horizons, *www.emerginghorizons. com.* International on-line travel newsletter.

Holiday Care Service, Imperial Building, Victoria Rd, Horley, Surrey, RH6 7PZ, t (01293) 774 535, Minicom t (01293) 776 943, *www. holidaycare.org.uk.* Up-to-date info on destinations, transport and tour operators.

RADAR (Royal Association for Disability and Rehabilitation), 12 City Forum, 250 City Road, London EC1V 8AF, t (020) 7250 3222, Minicom t (020) 7250 4119, *www.radar. org.uk.* Information and books on travel.

RNIB (Royal National Institute of the Blind), 105 Judd St, London WC1H 9NE, t (020) 7388 1266, *www.rnib.org.uk.*

In the USA

American Foundation for the Blind, 11 Penn Plaza, Suite 300, New York, NY 10001, t (212) 502 7600, or t 800 AFB LINE, *www.afb.org.* The best source of information in the USA for visually impaired travellers.

Mobility International USA, PO Box 10767, Eugene, OR 97440, t (541) 343 1284, *www. miusa.org.* Information on international educational exchange programmes and volunteer service overseas.

SATH (Society for Accessible Travel and Hospitality), 347 5th Avenue, Suite 610, New York, NY 10016, t (212) 447 7284, *www.sath.org.* Travel and access information; also details other access resources on the web.

Eating Out and Drinking

The standard of **restaurants** in Ireland is improving. This is especially true of those that are run by people from the rest of Europe, many of whom set up here because of the beauty of the country and the excellence of the fresh ingredients. There are Irish cooks, too, who combine the local specialities and traditional recipes with ingredients and cooking methods from other cultures. The excellent **Ballymaloe Restaurant** (*see* p.219) and the **Good Things Café** (*see* p.205), both in County Cork, are examples that spring immediately to mind.

Still, eating out can be disappointing. Too many restaurants are still serving up musty, watery vegetables, overcooked meat, frozen fish, and salads of the limp iceberg lettuce and coleslaw variety. Also, eating out is not cheap, unless you opt for a pub or café lunch. Some restaurants offer a tourist menu, but on the whole these establishments offer good value rather than good cooking. To avoid a bad experience during your stay, it's probably an idea to stick to establishments recommended in this guide.

To get around the serious problem of eating cheaply, however, fill up at breakfast time. In B&Bs, if the lady or gentleman of the house offers high tea or supper for guests, take advantage of that as well. The food they produce is usually home-made, delicious and very good value. Irish people love their food, and are generous with it: huge portions are normal in the home and often in restaurants. It is a sign of inhospitality to give a poor meal. ''Twas but a daisy in a bull's mouth', they'll say.

Bakeries usually offer tea, coffee and soft drinks along with sandwiches, fresh apple pie, doughnuts, cakes and sausage rolls. **Roadside cafés** will serve the usual menu of cooked breakfast, burgers, hot dogs or chicken and chips. Bigger towns and cities will have Chinese restaurants, pizza places and fish and chips.

Vegetarians will find that an increasing number of restaurants cater for their needs. Certainly, vegetarians will find that even where no special menu exists, people are generally happy to provide suitable fare. If you are staying in a country house, you should telephone in advance to let them know you are vegetarian.

You can sample the many delicious **Irish cheeses** (see **Food and Drink**, p.88, for a run-down of cheeses you'll encounter in the southwest) by finding a good deli or health food shop, buying some bread and salad and taking yourself off to eat a picnic in some wonderfully scenic place. If it is drizzling, warm yourself up afterwards with a glass of Irish coffee in the local pub.

Most **restaurants** serve lunch and dinner, but do check before you go. A few do only dinner and Sunday lunches. Some country places only open only for the weekend during the winter months; some only open Tuesday to Saturday, even in summer. Cafés and snack places are not usually open in the evening for meals.

You will normally find the service friendly and helpful, and a **service charge** is included in the bill at all restaurants (*see also* 'Tipping', p.108). Some places might not accept **credit cards**, so check what payment methods they accept before you order your meal.

If there is no liquor licence of any sort, the manager is usually quite happy to let you bring in your own (**BYO**) wine or beer, if you ask. (Publicans in Ireland have a monopoly on licences, and many restaurants are not able to obtain them without having to fulfil ludicrous requirements for space-planning).

Restaurant Categories

A variety of good eating places are listed in each touring chapter. In the various culinary deserts which exist, those listed are the best of an indifferent lot. Places are categorized in cost brackets (*see* box, above left). Do bear in mind that proprietors and places may change; telephone in advance if your venue of choice is somewhere that requires a special journey.

Luxury

These restaurants include creative and delicious cooking from fine ingredients. They are often in the dining rooms of country houses or castles, where the silver and crystal sparkle and you are surrounded by fine pictures and furniture. Or they may be smart, fashionable hotels or restaurants in towns, in the city, or on the coast.

Expensive

Restaurants in this category are similar to those in the luxury bracket, with an emphasis on well-cooked vegetables and traditional ingredients. Again, many country-house hotels come under this category, as do seafood restaurants around the coast and city establishments. **Lunch** in expensive places is often a very reasonably priced set meal, so ask about the lunch specials if you're looking for a cheaper meal.

Moderate

The quality of the food may be as good as the more expensive places, but the atmosphere is informal and perhaps a little less stylish.

Inexpensive

This category includes bar food, lunch-time places and cafés. You can usually be sure of good home-made soup, snacks and at least one simple main course.

Drink

Public houses are open Mon–Sat 10am–11.30pm (unofficially, they may stay open into the early hours of the morning). In winter they close half an hour earlier. On Sundays and St Patrick's Day they open from 12.30pm–10pm, and they are closed on Christmas Day and Good Friday. Children are often allowed to sit in the lounge bar with packets of crisps and fizzy orange to keep them happy.

If you do get into a conversation in a bar, a certain etiquette is followed: men always buy everybody in your group a drink, taking it in turn to buy a round; women will find they are seldom allowed to. Both sexes offer cigarettes around when having one (though only outside bars these days, *see* p.90). If there

are ten people in your group you are likely to find yourself drunk from social necessity and out of pocket as well.

For further information about eating and drinking in the southwest of Ireland, *see also* **Food and Drink**, pp.87–90.

Electricity

The current is 220 volts AC, so you should bring an adaptor if you have any North American appliances. Wall sockets take the standard British-style three-pin (flat) fused plugs, or two-pin (round) plugs.

If you are worried, there are good travellers' adaptors on the market which can usually cope with most socket-and-plug combinations.

Embassies

Australian Embassy, Fitzwilton House, Wilton Terrace, Dublin 2, **t** (01) 664 5300, *www.australianembassy.ie.*
British Embassy, 31 Merrion Road, Dublin 4, **t** (01) 269 5211, *www.britishembassy.ie.*
Canadian Embassy, 65 St Stephen's Green, Dublin 2, **t** (01) 417 4100.
US Embassy, 42 Elgin Road, Dublin 4, **t** (01) 668 8777, *http://dublin.usembassy.gov/.*

Emergencies and Hazards

Emergencies

Ambulance, fire brigade and police **t** *999.*

If you do find yourself in trouble, there will be no shortage of sympathetic help. If you fall ill, have an accident, or are the victim of some crime, people will rush to your aid. Whether they bring quite the help you need is another matter. If in doubt, get the advice of your hotel, the local tourist office, or call the police.

In serious cases (medical or legal), contact your embassy (see above) or consulate. Try not to panic: in the case of medical treatment, take your insurance documents, inform the people treating you of your insurance cover, and make sure you keep all receipts (or at least get someone reliable to do this for you).

Beasts

If you decide to have a picnic in some inviting green field, check that there is not a bull in it first. High-spirited bullocks can be just as alarming; they come rushing up to have a good look and playfully knock you over in the process.

Fairies

There is one hazard which you might only have dreamt about: the mischievous fairies might put a spell on you so that you never want to return to your own country. It's not a joke, for Ireland is an enchanting country and difficult to leave. As a rule it is no use enquiring about charms against this enchantment, or any other; the answer is always the same: 'There used to be a lot of them in the old days, but the priests put them down.' (You get that answer about poitín too.) Beneath, there is a sort of sneaking belief in fairies; for why, in a perfectly modern housing estate outside Sligo, is there a ragged mound which escaped the bulldozer and cement? Perhaps because it is a fairy rath?

And one last word on fairies: have you ever heard how they came into existence? Padraic Colum found out from a blind man whom he met in the west, who believed in them as firmly as in the Gospels. When the Angel Lucifer rebelled against God, Hell was made in a minute, and down to it God swept Lucifer and thousands of his followers, until the Angel Gabriel said, 'O God Almighty, Heaven will be swept clean.' God agreed and compromised, saying, 'Them that are in Heaven let them remain so, them that are in Hell, let them remain in Hell; and them that are between Heaven and Hell, let them remain in the air.' And the angels that remained between Heaven and Hell are the fairies.

Midges

Toads and adders are said to have fled from Ireland at the sound of St Patrick's bell tolling from the top of Croagh Patrick Mountain in County Mayo. Unfortunately, the voracious midges of the west coast did not take their cue. They are very persistent on warm summer evenings, so remember to arm yourself with some sort of insect repellent.

There is plenty of choice in the chemists. Wasps, hornets and horseflies also emerge in summer to irritate.

Sea Bathing

A major hazard can be strong currents in the sea. One beach may be perfectly safe for bathing, and the one beside it positively dangerous. Always check with locals before you swim. There are lifeguards on most of the resort beaches.

Theft from Cars

Although it hardly seems necessary in some of the more isolated spots in the southwest, it is always safer to lock your car, or if you're in a city, to leave it in an authorized car park. Cars do get stolen, so take sensible precautions. Don't leave luggage or valuables in your car.

Walking

Walkers who intend to go through bog and mountainous country – be warned that, even though it looks dry enough on the road, once into the heather and moss you will soon sink into waterlogged ground. Wear stout walking boots, and bring at least one extra jersey and a waterproof coat. Sudden mists and rain can descend, and you can get very cold.

Experienced mountain rescue teams are non-existent here, so if you do go off into a mountain range, leave word locally as to where you plan to go, or put a note on your car. During the **shooting season** (grouse and snipe from August to 3 January, duck from September to 31 January, and pheasant from 1 November to 1 January), be careful of wandering into stray shot on the hilly slopes or in marshy places.

Health and Insurance

Medical Treatment

If you need medical or dental treatment in the Republic, you will be expected to pay for the treatment then claim back the costs from your insurance company.

For all kinds of **medical care**, citizens of EU countries can benefit from the mutual agreements that exist between EU member countries. British citizens travelling to the Republic can make use of any GP who has an agreement with the Health Board, but to benefit from this you should take **Form E111** with you (available from UK post offices and health centres, in advance of your departure; make sure it is stamped).

In extremis, the international emergency services offered by companies such as Europ Assistance or Travel Assistance International, which are often incorporated into travel insurance packages, demonstrate their blessings.

Travel Insurance

Regarding travel **insurance**, the best advice is to always insure your holiday as soon as you book your ticket. Standard travel insurance packages issued by the major insurance companies cover a broad range of risks, including cancellation due to unforeseen circumstances, transport delays caused by strikes or foul weather, loss or theft of baggage, medical insurance (make a note of a 24hr medical emergency number) and compensation for injury or death. The cost of insurance may seem substantial, but it is negligible when compared to almost any claim, should misfortune befall you. It's also worth checking to see whether any of your existing insurance schemes cover travel risks: certain British household insurance schemes, for example, include limited travel cover. Be aware that accidents resulting from sports are rarely covered by ordinary insurance.

To make a **claim** for loss or theft of your belongings, you will need evidence that you have reported it to the police. Check your insurance details for the documentation required by the insurance company in such circumstances. It is, by the way, useful to have more than one copy of your insurance policy – if your baggage is stolen, the document may go with it.

Heritage and Interpretative Centres

In the last ten years there has been a huge growth in these centres all over Ireland. The larger ones incorporate local history, flora and fauna, using audiovisual aids, life-size models or actors dressed in period costume, producing an 'experience' to remember. The Office of Public Works have purpose-built a few Interpretative Centres in places of great natural beauty and fragile ecology. Controversy was provoked by the planned siting of one such centre in the middle of the Burren. It's inevitable that such places will destroy a part of the beauty and peace with huge car parks, WCs, craft centres etc., however sympathetic the architecture and landscaping may be.

Many of the small heritage centres double as **genealogical centres** and are situated in fine old buildings (mainly in towns and cities), which have been restored by the strenuous efforts and enthusiasm of the local people. These centres are listed in the touring chapters under 'Sports and Activities'.

Internet

The Internet contains a wealth of information to help you prepare all the practical details for your holiday, such as accommodation, especially in the busy summer months when festivals make beds hard to come by in the smallest of towns. The Internet can also enhance your knowledge of Ireland's history, politics and culture before you leave home.

It is also an invaluable tool for keeping in touch with home once you're abroad, and access sites, such as Internet cafés, are blossoming in southwest Ireland. Airports and libraries usually provide public access points and local tourist offices should be able to direct you to the nearest Internet café.

Maps

Ordnance Survey produces Ireland Holiday Maps (1:250,000), which cover the different regions and provide good, all-round, tourist information. For general touring, a **Michelin** road map (1:400,000) is fine and the **OS Discovery Series** (1:50,000) gives greater detail for walkers. The maps distributed by local tourist offices are often the best for pinpointing places of interest, beaches etc.

Note that in the **Gaeltacht** areas in Cork and Kerry you'll find the signposts are **in Irish Gaelic only**; we have done our best to give both anglicized and Irish place names where possible in the touring chapters, but be aware that spellings may vary slightly.

If in London, visit **Stanfords**, 12 Long Acre, WC2, **t** (020) 7836 1321, *www.stanfords.co.uk*, for the biggest specialized selection of maps and travel books.

Money

Currency

The official currency of the Republic of Ireland is the **euro** (€). Euro notes come in denominations of 5, 10, 20, 50, 100, 200 and 500, with coins for €1 and €2. Each single euro consists of 100 **cents**; coins are used for 1, 2, 5, 10, 20 and 50 cents.

As everywhere, the best exchange rates are available at banks, and the worst at hotels. Rates will also be less good at bureaux de change, though these are useful when banks are closed.

You can obtain cash in local currencies from bank ATMs, usually sited in airports as well as towns and cities. Check with your bank or building society as to whether charges will be applied to your withdrawals, and which ATMs you may use. Leading credit and debit cards (Visa, Mastercard/Access, American Express and Diner's Club) are widely accepted in major hotels, restaurants and shops.

The main brands of traveller's cheques (American Express, Visa and Thomas Cook) are accepted by banks throughout the Republic of Ireland and Northern Ireland.

Banks

Small towns have at least one bank. The banks are open Mon–Fri 10–12.30 and 1.30–4 and until 5.30pm on Thursday. Banks in the larger towns will usually have one day each week – normally market day – when they will stay open until 5pm.

The bank usually occupies the grandest house in town – the various banking groups seem to have some sort of conscience about historical buildings, which is very rare in Ireland. The moving of money is accompanied by massive security, which looks very out of keeping with the happy-go-lucky attitude in Ireland, but is necessary because bank raids have been so common.

Tipping

Tipping is not really a general habit except in taxis and in eating places where there is table service. Taxi drivers will expect to be tipped at a rate of about 10% of the fare; porters and doormen a few cents or so. There is no tipping in pubs, but in hotel bars where you are served by a waiter it is usual to leave a small tip.

A **service charge** of 12% (sometimes 15%) is usually raised automatically on hotel and restaurant bills. Where this is not the case, a tip of this magnitude would be in order, if the service merits it.

Newspapers

For a spot of pre-reading before you go, take a look at the list of links to Irish newspapers online at *www.bl.uk/collections/ irish.html*.

In the US, good sources of information include *www.irishamericannews.com* in Chicago and the Irish American Partnership in Boston, *www.irishap.org*.

The best newspaper to read when you're in Ireland is the *Irish Times* (*www.ireland.com*), followed closely by the *Irish Independent* (*www.unison.ie/irish_independent*) and the *Cork Examiner*. The *Irish Times* on Saturdays lists what's on – exhibitions, festivals, concerts, etc. around the country.

Image (*www.image.ie*) is a glossy magazine along the lines of *Harpers & Queen*, and has information on fashion, interior decoration and restaurants. *Phoenix* (*www.phoenix-magazine.com*) is the Irish equivalent of *Private Eye*.

Packing

Whatever you do, come expecting rain – wellies or walking boots, umbrellas, coats and waterproofs are essential. Once you get out into the rain, though, it's never as bad as it looks, and the clouds will start to clear eventually. Bring warm **jerseys**, **trousers**, **woolly socks**, and **gloves** for autumn, winter and early spring. The best thing to do is to expect the cold and wet and then get a pleasant surprise if it's sunny and hot – so don't forget to sneak in a few **T-shirts** just in case. Sometimes the sun shines furiously in March and April.

If you like walking, bring a pair of fairly stout **walking shoes** or **boots** – trainers end up bedraggled and let the water in. **Fishing rods** and **swimsuits** are worth packing, if you think you may have cause to regret leaving them behind. Bring a **sleeping bag** if you plan to stay at youth hostels. If you plan to stay in B&B accommodation you might want to bring your own **towel**, as those supplied could be on the mean side.

You will be amazed at what the village shop sells, from pots and pans to fine wines, and maybe some fresh salmon trout if you are lucky. In the Republic you can be sure of finding a shop open until 10pm in the evening and on Sundays as well. Chemists are also well stocked so that headache pills, camera films and contraceptives are easily obtainable.

Post Offices and Telephones

Postal Services

Letterboxes in the Republic of Ireland are green. If you don't have a fixed address, letters can be sent Poste Restante (General Delivery) to any post office and picked up with proof of your identity. If after three months they are gathering dust in the corner, they will be returned to the sender. There is a post office in every village, which is usually the telephone exchange as well and a hive of activity. You can send telemessages from the post office but you need to book in advance. The post office should be open Mon–Fri 9–5 and Sat 9–1, Sun and public holidays closed. Sub-post offices close at 1pm one day a week.

Telephones

To call the Irish Republic from the UK, dial **t 00 353** followed by the area code, **minus** the first zero. It is more expensive to phone in Ireland during office hours than outside them.

Note that if you phone from your hotel you are liable to be charged much more than the standard rate. Phonecards, sold by most newsagents, are a much cheaper, more convenient option, especially in remote areas where public phones may be hard to find.

Mobile (cell) phone numbers in the Republic of Ireland are 10 digits long, and begin with **t 085, t 086, t 087** or **t 089**. You must dial all 10 digits when making a call within the country.

Ireland shares the same **time zone** as Great Britain and follows the same seasonal clock adjustment in the summer (i.e. GMT +1 hour from the end of March to the end of October).

Shopping

Shopping in Ireland is a relaxing pastime because nobody ever makes you feel that you have to buy anything, so you can browse to your heart's content. Good design and high-quality craftsmanship make for goods which will last a lifetime, and delight the senses. Irish linen, handloomed tweed, Aran sweaters, pottery, glass and modern Irish silver can be found easily in the craft centres which have been set up all over the country.

The **Craft Council of Ireland** (The Cattle Yard, Kilkenny, **t** (056) 776 3754, *www.ccoi.ie*) is a relatively new body that has given a great boost to the many talented craft workers, and helped them to market their wares and join forces in studios and workshops, usually in IDA (Industrial Development Authority) parks. If you see something you like at any of the craft shops and centres, buy it there and then because you are not likely to see it again in another shop. Craft items are not cheap because of the artistry and labour involved, but you can find bargains at china, crystal and linen factory shops if you seek them out.

The main goodies to take home with you are described in detail below. Fleeting pleasures, which you can share with your friends back home, are smoked salmon, cheese, wheaten bread, home-cured bacon, and whiskey. These are available at Shannon and Dublin Airport shops. Grinning leprechauns, colleen dolls, Guinness slogan T-shirts and shamrock mugs are stacked high in most gift shops if you want something cheap and cheerful, but don't ignore the real products from Ireland.

Shop Opening Hours

Shops are open 9.30–5.30, Mon–Sat. Craft shops in scenic areas are usually open on Sundays as well, especially if they have tearooms. In some towns there is an **early closing** day when businesses close at 1pm. This is normally a Wednesday, although it may be a different day in some areas. You can be sure that if one town has shut down, its neighbour will be open for business.

Large shopping centres which operate on the outskirts of town are unaffected by early closing. **Dunnes Stores** can usually be found in these shopping centres. It is the equivalent of the UK-based retailer Marks & Spencer, and sells cheap clothing.

Irish Specialities

Irish lace: one of the lightest and most precious of all the specialities you can pack in your suitcase, can be found in Kenmare, County Kerry, and in Limerick City. In Limerick the lace is worked completely in thread on the finest Brussels net.

Tweed: a wonderful fabric that not only keeps you warm in winter, but also lets your skin 'breathe'. It is useful most of the year if you live in northern climes and are not addicted to central heating. It is hand-woven from sheep's wool, and the Irish have got not only the texture and tension of the cloth right, but also the speckled, natural colours of the countryside (*see* the Blarney Woollen Mills' website at *www.blarney.com*). Donegal tweed is particularly attractive, in all its subtle shades.

Hand-knitted sweaters: make sure you buy one which has the hand-knitted label on it; it makes the whole difference when you are buying an **Aran** sweater. These are made out of tough wool, lightly coated in animal oils, so they are water-resistant and keep you as warm as toast. You can get them in natural white or various colours, and the pattern differs quite a bit. In the past, the wives of the fishermen used to have a family pattern so that they could identify anyone who had drowned. These knits come in a variety of styles; they stretch after being worn a while and last for years. It is possible to buy original and attractive hand-knitted clothing in

Public Holidays

New Year's Day 1 January
St Patrick's Day 17 March
Good Friday (widely observed as a holiday, but not an official one)
Easter Monday
May Day 1 May
June Holiday First Monday in June
August Holiday First Monday in August
October Holiday Last Monday in October
Christmas Day 25 December
Boxing Day 26 December

craft shops all over the southwest. Elegant stoles and generous shawls, woven bedspreads and car rugs are some other excellent buys.

Linen: Irish linen is another item to look out for: tea cloths, sheets and hand-embroidered tablecloths and handkerchiefs.

Glass: Waterford Crystal is world-famous for its quality and design. You can buy it in good quality stores all over the southwest, but remember it can also be purchased as you leave the country at Shannon Airport's duty-free shop, although the selection is small. All the stores will pack and mail glass overseas for you. It is still possible to buy old Waterford glass, which has a blackish tint to it, in antique shops – but it is very costly. Attractive crystal glass can be bought in the Cork factory. As you travel through the southwest you may well discover other original glass-blowers, as small craft industries are flourishing all over the country.

Pottery and china: talented potters work in rural communities all over Ireland, and one of the best places to find their work for sale is at IDA centres. Craft shops also usually carry the local potters' work.

Jewellery, silver and antiques: amongst all the other trinkets and souvenirs available, Claddagh rings still remain the nicest of all love tokens and are very evocative of the southwest of Ireland.

Woven products: all over Ireland you can buy items made of willow or rush: bread baskets, turfholders, place mats and St Brigid Crosses (charms against evil).

Books: *see* the Irish Bookstore on-line at *www.kennys.ie*.

Traditional musical instruments: from fiddles and violins to uilleann pipes (*see www.uilleannobsession.com*), which will make a wonderful present if you have a musical friend.

Food and drink: soda, wheaten and potato bread are found all over the southwest. When you are leaving the country, McCambridge's brown bread is available at the airport shops. Smoked salmon is sold all over the southwest and at the airport shops. Farmhouse cheese in every shape, size and texture is available from the producer and from wholefood shops and delicatessens. Irish whiskey (note the 'e', which is the Irish way of spelling it) is slightly sweeter than Scotch. Try Bushmills, Black Bush, Paddy's, Powers and Jamesons. All these brands are available in off-licences throughout the southwest. Cork gin is considered to have a delicious tang of juniper, far superior to the English brand of Gordon's. Popular liqueurs are Irish Mist, containing whiskey and honey; Tullamore Dew; and Bailey's Irish Cream.

Sports and Activities

Adventure Sports

The Association for Adventure Sports (AFAS) can give you information and contact telephone numbers and addresses for hang-gliding, mountaineering, canoeing, sub-aqua, board-sailing, surfing – in fact, almost any sport that you can think of. Contact **AFAS**, Carrowcashel, Ramelton, County Donegal, **t** (074) 915 2800, *www. adventuresports.ie*, to obtain a list of what is available in the southwest.

Bird-watching

Bird sanctuaries abound in the southwest and if you walk along rocky shores there are some spectacular cliffs dripping with hundreds of birds. For details write to the National Parks and Wildlife Service, 7 Ely Place, Dublin 2, **t** (01) 647 2300. Field trips are organized by local branches of the Irish Wild Bird Conservancy, and there are details in the

quarterly newsletter. Write to **BirdWatch Ireland**, Rockingham House, Newcastle, County Wicklow, Ireland, **t** (01) 281 9878, *www.birdwatchireland.ie*.

The Bowl Game

Pronounced to rhyme with 'owl', this is only traditionally played in County Cork and County Armagh, along country lanes. The ball is made of very heavy iron, and the object of the game is to cover the greatest possible distance with a given number of bowls. The best players are strong and skilful, and the ball is a dangerous missile. It is illegal to play on public roads, but this did not stop it happening in the past; small children were stationed along the roads to warn competitors of oncoming traffic and the police. Today, the game has been saved from extinction and accommodated into the tourist calendar.

Canoeing

This is an exciting and compelling sport with smooth-flowing stretches of beautiful rivers, rapids and weirs. The principal rivers are the Shannon, Suir and Blackwater. You can always camp by the waterside as long as you get permission from the owner. For details of the many rivers and waterways, sea canoeing and tuition, contact **AFAS**, Carrowcashel, Ramelton, County Donegal, **t** (074) 915 2800, *www.adventuresports.ie*.

Caving

This activity has become more organized recently with the establishment of the Speleological Union of Ireland. For information, contact AFAS (address above) or the **Speleological Union of Ireland**, House of Sport, Long Mile Road, Walkinstown, Dublin 12, *www.cavingireland.org*.

Cruising the Inland Waterways

This is an unforgettable and exciting way to travel around. The River Shannon is the main area in the southwest, and it is navigable from Lough Key to Killaloe. Along the waterways you pass tumbledown castles, abbeys, beautiful flowers, birds and peaceful, lush scenery. In the evening you can moor up your boat for a meal and a jar and listen to some good, traditional music. There are festivals and

Weights and Measures

1 kilogram	2.205 lb	1 lb	0.45 kilograms
1 litre	1.76 Imperial pints	1 Imperial pint	0.56 litres
1 litre	2.11 US pints	1 US pint	0.47 litres
1 centimetre	0.39 inches	1 Imperial gallon	4.54 litres
1 metre	39.37 inches / 3.28 feet	1 US gallon	3.78 litres
1 kilometre	0.621 miles	1 foot	0.305 metres
1 hectare	2.47 acres	1 mile	1.609 kilometres
		1 acre	0.404 hectares

boat rallies, but they only happen for a couple of days a year, so if it's peace and quiet you want, don't worry.

On the **Shannon** several companies offer luxury cabin cruisers for self-drive hire, ranging from two to eight berths. All are fitted with fridges, gas cookers, hot water and showers; most have central heating. A dinghy, charts, binoculars and safety equipment are included on the river and lough routes. Groceries and stores can be ordered in advance and collected when you arrive. You have to be over 21 to be skipper, and the controls must be understood by at least two people, but no licence is necessary. You get an hour of tuition, or more if you need it. Ask for details from your travel agent, or the nearest Irish tourist office, or contact the following companies direct:

Emerald Star Line, Carrick-on-Shannon, County Leitrim, **t** (071) 962 7633, *www. emeraldstar.ie*

Derg Marine Cruisers, Killaloe, County Clare, **t** (061) 376364.

Day trips and pleasure cruises are also available on the Shannon. Some of the companies listed above also operate river cruises. It is possible to take the *Killarney Waterbus* through the famous lakes for a trip of 1½ hours, **t** (064) 32638.

A useful reading book is *The Shell Guide to the Shannon*.

Fishing

We are grateful to Antony Luke for the following personal account. Antony has been returning on holiday to Ireland since 1963. He acts as a consultant on fishing matters to the corporate entertainment company Country and Highland, gives fly-fishing instruction, and organizes salmon-fishing parties. He has a cottage on one of the northern isles of Orkney where he keeps a lobster boat, and from where he runs a successful business exporting fish and shellfish. Thanks also to Peter O'Reilly for his help with the updating of this section.

Whatever the catch, one always returns from Ireland with a story and happy memories. The sport is excellent, and all visitors are treated with great hospitality and charm. Tackle shops are very helpful, and *Bord Fáilte* issues a wealth of information, including dates of angling competitions, and an excellent brochure entitled *Angling in Ireland*.

Fishing in the southwest is readily available to the general public. You can fish on any day including Sundays. Unlike the UK, there is no closed season for coarse fishing. Seasons for other types of fishing vary and some rivers have their own seasons. Costs are also comparatively low.

For the purposes of **licensing**, fishing in the Republic can be divided into four categories: **game**, for salmon and sea trout (migratory); **trout** (non-migratory); **coarse**, for perch, roach, rudd, bream, tench etc., and pike; and **sea-fishing**. Visitors require a licence for the first. It is possible to purchase individual or composite licences from *Bord Fáilte* offices in your country of residence. They can be bought from any Fisheries Board office in the southwest (**t** (026) 41221 for County Cork and County Kerry), from all government-run fisheries, and from many tackle shops.

One of the finest aspects of the sport in Ireland is the variety of different fishing **techniques** that are to be found in quite small areas. It is possible to fish a lake system – either dapping or wet-fly – and a river on the same day. In the UK, this is only possible in a few places on the west coast of Scotland, and to some extent in the

Hebrides. A ghillied boat is often necessary if you wish to fish on the lakes. Irish ghillies have a great knowledge of the shoals and bays where fish lie. They are also highly entertaining.

Coarse fishing is immensely popular, particularly with visitors from the UK, where there is a closed season from mid-March to mid-June, and pike-fishing here is amongst the best in Europe.

It would take a book much longer than this one to list all the **rivers and loughs** for visiting game-fishers. On the whole, salmon-fishing is privately owned, but good association water is available for the general public. In the southwest the River Blackwater has early runs of salmon, and grilse later, and there are a number of rivers and lake systems, notably Lough Currane at Waterville, and the Maine and Laune including the Killarney Lakes. Fishing on the mighty River Shannon was adversely affected by the introduction of the hydroelectric scheme in 1929, but the Castleconnell beats are still worth a visit.

Sea trout have been in sad decline over the years and a number of well-known sea-trout fisheries have suffered badly due to 'Sea Lice' (which many claim is due to salmon farming). Considerable research is now being done by the Salmon Research Trust at Newport and things have shown a slight improvement. By contrast, runs of salmon and grilse have held up well in recent years.

Sea-angling is becoming increasingly popular with the more hardy fisherman. The Central Fisheries Board issues a comprehensive booklet. More boats are available for hire than ever before, although they can be expensive for the individual; it is best to organize a group of four or more. Kinsale is one of the main centres for sea-angling. Here, when the sea warms a degree or so, odd species of tropical fish arrive. Out of Kinsale there is also good shark-fishing, and many other species such as conger, skate and, for the less selective, huge bags of large pollack, can be caught. Other main sea-fishing stations are Youghal, Ballycotton and Baltimore in County Cork, and Cahirciveen and the Dingle Peninsula in County Kerry. As a rule,

all stations will be able to supply boats for hire, rods, tackle etc.

Golf

We are grateful to Bruce Critchley for this expert guide to Ireland's golf courses. Bruce is one of television's golf commentators, following a successful amateur international career in the 1960s. Now a consultant to golf-course developers, he also, in association with his wife's company, Critchley Pursuits, arranges tours of British, Irish and Continental courses for both English and American enthusiasts.

With the possible exception of Scotland, Ireland can boast more courses per head of population than any other country in the world. As with Scotland, quality is in no way diminished by quantity and, in common with the rest of the British Isles, the greatest courses are usually situated at the seaside.

Should the visitor be anxious to get going after flying into Shannon, he could almost walk to the **Shannon Golf Club** from the airport terminal building. A modern course, inland in character, there is good use of water and lovely views down to the River Shannon. But the real treasures lie on the other side. **Ballybunion** has long stood beside the very best, and recently a second 18 has been added of almost equal quality. Some 20 miles (32km) to the south, Arnold Palmer has laid out an outstanding course on Kerry's coastline at **Tralee**.

The beautiful Ring of Kerry offers two widely differing courses, the **Dooks** at **Glenbeigh** and the mighty links of **Waterville**. Glenbeigh, only 5,750 yards (5,260m) in length, is supposedly the third-oldest course in the country and follows the naturally undulating dunes, as courses only could in the 19th century. Waterville is of much more recent construction and, with the ocean on three sides, the coastal wind is an ever-present factor.

Just inland are a pair of courses on the shores of **Killarney**. Can there be any more beautiful setting for golf anywhere in the world? Perhaps the courses don't quite match up to the view, but then very few would. Nevertheless, it is a joy to play here.

Finally, and even though a little off the beaten track, no trip to this neck of the woods should miss the little nine-hole gem at **Bantry**, overlooking the famous bay with its stunning views. To the north, **Lahinch**, traditionally the home of the South of Ireland Championships, is another good course with nothing but the Atlantic between it and Boston.

Away from the pounding of the Atlantic Ocean, the courses don't have the sand dunes out of which links courses are traditionally carved. Nonetheless, the natural beauty of the countryside lends a great backdrop wherever courses are constructed. And on the scenic front, the little nine-holer at **Doneraile** should not be passed up.

Cork has a couple of courses of which **Little Island** is the most spectacular. Holes alternate between the edge of a massive quarry on one side and views over the estuary on the other. Southwest of the city, **Bandon Golf Course**, set in the grounds of Castle Bernard Castle, is well worth a visit, as is **Midleton** to the east.

So wherever you go in the southwest, golf courses abound, and whatever your standard you'll find something to enjoy. With facilities getting ever more crowded around the major cities of the world, here is golf as it used to be – the ability to get on a course in the hours of daylight, and green fees that are not going to break the bank.

Lastly, a couple of words of advice. If you are thinking of a golfing holiday, some of the courses do get busy in summer and it is always advisable to check with clubs in advance and, where necessary, get a confirmed tee time.

Also, every travelling golfer should carry a handicap certificate as proof of competence. Trolleys will be for hire at most clubs and quite a few will be able to lay on caddies if ordered in advance. Golf carts are not a feature of Irish golf and are not encouraged. One or two courses will permit their use with a medical certificate, but you will have to provide the cart.

Bord Fáilte publishes a couple of good guides on golfing and there is a useful website on Irish golf at *www.globalgolf.com/Ireland/index.html*. Clubs and courses in the southwest are listed in each touring chapter, under 'Sports and Activities'.

Hang-gliding

Ireland is a hang-glider's paradise: shaped like a saucer with a mountainous rim. The wind blows from the sea or from the flat central plains. Most of the hills are bare of power lines and trees, and the famous turf provides soft landings. Flying is controlled by the **Irish Hang-Gliding Association**, 5 Avondale Crescent, Dublin Rd, Arklow, County Wicklow, *www.ihpa.ie*.

Horse-racing

Irish people are wild about horses; they breed very good ones, and they race them brilliantly. Limerick and Mallow are well known provincial courses in the southwest and holiday meetings are held at Killarney (mid-July), Tralee (end of August), and Listowel (late September).

Most hunts organize point-to-point meetings – 3-mile (4.8km) chases over fences for amateur riders – between January and May. Point-to-points are usually freezing cold but great fun; the background and form of each horse is known and discussed with great enthusiasm. A speciality of Irish National Hunt racing are 'Bumpers' which are two-mile (3.2km) flat races confined to amateur riders, riding novice jumpers.

The weekly *Irish Field* and daily *Racing Post* and *Sporting Life* publish form, venues and times of all race meetings and point-to-points. The Irish Tourist Board (*Bord Fáilte*) Calendar of Events lists racing fixtures at the back.

Hunting

This is another popular sport in Ireland. Any visitors are welcomed by the various hunts, and it is not very expensive. Ask the Irish Tourist Board (*Bord Fáilte*) for a list, or the local riding centre for details.

Altogether there are 85 recognized packs, and although some are stag hounds and harriers, in the main they are foxhounds. The hunting **season** starts in October and ends in March, with meets starting in the mid-morning. Stables for the hire of a horse for the day's hunting can usually be found through the local hunt secretary (although you must be experienced).

Hurling

Munster men are famed for their prowess at this game which is similar to hockey but much more vigorous, and played with a larger, broad-bladed stick (also known as a *camán* or a hurley) and a hide-covered ball. There are fifteen to a side, and the ball may only be picked up to be tossed into the air and struck. It may also be caught on the flat of the stick and carried like this while the player runs. This is to the Irish what cricket is to the English.

Hurling is promoted by the **Gaelic Athletic Association** (GAA); when it is played well it can be beautiful to watch, and occasionally extremely dangerous. Money earned is put back into national programmes; the GAA is still closely connected with Nationalist objectives. Look in local newspapers for details of matches. *See* also **Topics**, p.84.

Mountaineering and Hill-walking

The mountains and hill areas are not high (few peaks are over 3,000ft/915m), but they are rugged, varied, beautiful and unspoilt. There are quartz peaks, ridges of sandstone, bog-covered domes, and cliff-edged limestone plateaux.

Excellent walking trails have been or are in the process of being developed. General advice, information and a list of hill-walking and rock-climbing clubs can be obtained from the **Mountaineering Council of Ireland**, Sport HQ, 13 Joyce Way, Parkwest Business Park, Dublin 12, **t** (01) 625 1115, *www.mountaineering.ie*. They can also send you a full list of guides. *Bord Fáilte* tourist offices in the southwest also stock hill-walking information sheets for individual areas.

The Ordnance Survey ½-inch-to-1-mile maps and a compass are essentials for serious walkers. Please remember there are very few tracks on the mountains, and always let your hotel know where you are climbing or walking, or leave a note in your car, just in case you have an accident. Mountain rescue in the main mountain areas is co-ordinated by the *Garda* (police).

Riding Holidays

There are many new residential schools and companies offering pony-trekking holidays. The Irish are putting their natural love of horses to good use, and the areas of beauty where you can ride include empty beaches that stretch for miles, heathery valleys, forests, empty country roads and loughside tracks. Accommodation and food are arranged for you. Full details from *Bord Fáilte*, Upper O'Connell Street, Dublin 1, **t** (01) 284 4768, *www.ireland.ie*, or from the following equestrian centres:

Clonshire Equestrian Centre, Adare, County Limerick, **t** (061) 396770, *www.clonshire.com*.
Dunraven Arms Hotel, Adare, County Limerick, **t** (061) 396633, *www.dunravenhotel.com*.
El Rancho Farmhouse and Riding Stables, Ballyard, Tralee, County Kerry, **t** (066) 712 1840.

Sailing

The coastline is uniquely beautiful, with diverse conditions and landscapes. The waters are never crowded, and the shoreline is completely unspoilt. On one of those sublimely beautiful evenings when the light touches each hill and field with an exquisite clarity, you will think yourself amongst the most privileged in the world. And if you want a bit of craic, there are splendid bars and restaurants to be visited in the sheltered harbours.

But the peace and calm of the sky, land and sea in the many inlets is deceptive, for the open seas in the northwest can be rough and treacherous, exposed as they are to the North Atlantic. So a journey around the whole coastline should only be attempted by experienced sailors.

If you do not have your own yacht, it is possible to charter a variety of craft; if it is your ambition to learn to sail, there are several small and friendly schools.

Ireland has a long sailing tradition, with many yacht and sailing clubs on the southwest coast. The Royal Cork Yacht Club at Crosshaven is the oldest in the world, and was founded in 1720 as the Water Club of the Harbour of Cork. Cork Harbour is a very large and sheltered expanse of water with several pleasant marinas, notably East Ferry. Many of these clubs preserve their original clubhouses, and emanate a feeling of tradition and comfort. Visitors are made very welcome, and are encouraged to use the club facilities. Those who wish to eat on board can buy wonderful bread, cheese and other high-quality groceries from the local shops. Seafood can be bought from the trawlers fishing the waters around you. And it is possible to find good food and entertainment in local bars and restaurants, especially in the Cork and Kerry area.

Where to Sail

The coastline bordering the counties of Cork and Kerry is a favourite with sailors, and it has a good selection of charter companies, sailing schools and windsurfing facilities. The harbours are charming, and the peninsulas and islands around which you can sail are magnificent. You will also find sites of historical interest that are close to the harbours of Crosshaven, Kinsale, Rosscarbery, Glendore, Schull, Rosbrin, Castletownbere, Kenmare, Caherdaniel, Dingle, Kilrush and Tralee.

If you want to sail around Ireland, further west, in County Galway and County Mayo, there is exciting sailing around the Aran Islands, Clifden, Renville and Clew Bay, and the many deserted islands with hauntingly beautiful names such as Inisgloria and Iniskea.

Just north of Dublin there are several excellent sailing centres which still retain the charm of fishing villages. Inland is the huge freshwater Lough Derg in the River Shannon system, where you can anchor in a sheltered bay or in one of the charming canal harbours.

Galway Hookers

The most traditional form of sailing boat is the Galway hooker, with its black sails. Galway hookers used to be a familiar sight, transporting turf and other goods between the islands, but by the 1970s they had almost disappeared. Happily, a few sailors discovered what great sport can be had with hooker-racing – you can see these races at summer regattas in the west of Ireland – and the craft of making the hooker is slowly reviving. Try asking around in Ballyvaughan, or contacting *An Ceathrue*, t (091) 595349.

Bringing Your Own Yacht

There is no tax or duty if you bring in your own yacht for a holiday; a special sticker is issued by customs officials on arrival. Mariners should apply to the harbour master of all ports in which they wish to anchor. On arrival at the first port of entry, the flag 'Q' should be shown. Contact should then be made with the local customs official or with a *garda* (civil guard) who will be pleased to assist. Fees are very reasonable in marinas and harbours. Note that it is illegal to land any animals without a special licence from the Department of Agriculture, but this does not apply to pet dogs which come from Great Britain.

Yacht Charter

The main centres for charter are on the southwest coastline. Private charter can be arranged at leading sailing centres elsewhere. Bare-boat and crewed charters are available on boats ranging from four- to seven-berth.

For a complete list of yacht charter companies, contact **Bord Fáilte**, Upper O'Connell Street, Dublin 1, t (01) 284 4768, *www.ireland.ie*. One of the biggest charter companies in the Cork area is **Sail Ireland Charters**, t (021) 477 2927.

Sailing Schools

Most of the schools are residential and located in areas of scenic beauty. Many offer other outdoor sports such as boardsailing (windsurfing), canoeing and sub-aqua. A full list of schools is available from *Bord Fáilte* in Dublin (*see* above) and you can gain advice from the **Irish Sailing Association**.

Sailing Organizations

Irish Sailing Association, 3 Park Road, Dun Laoghaire, County Dublin, t (01) 280 0239, *www.sailing.ie*.

Irish Cruising Club (ICC), 8 Heidelberg, Ardilea, Dublin 14, t (01) 288 4733.

Useful Media

The Irish Cruising Club (*www.irishcruisingclub.com*) publishes *Sailing Directions* which covers the entire coast of Ireland, including details of the coast, sketch plans of harbours, information about tides and port facilities.

The *Directions* come in two volumes – one for the south and west, and one for the north and east. Available from most Irish booksellers, and from Read Newsagents, 24 Nassau St, Dublin, t (01) 679 6011. Also recommended: *Sailing Around Ireland* by Wallace Clark (Batsford), and *Islands of Ireland* by D. McCormick (Osprey, 1977). The BBC issues gale warnings and shipping forecasts on Radio 4.

Seaweed Baths

On the less frequented northern shores of County Kerry, Ballybunion is a seaside resort popular with the Irish themselves for many good reasons. Best of all are the seaweed baths, which are barely mentioned in the tourist literature. The bathhouse is a simple building right on the beach; a glistening light plays on the sea and promontory where the ancient Fitzmaurice Castle casts a sharp silhouette, a perfect place to walk afterwards. You are provided with a small towel and ushered into one of the bathrooms where hot sea water pours on to a mound of black serrated wrack. Once in the bath, the seaweed floats around, releasing a thin glutinous jelly, so that the water becomes a hot silky gel. The benefits of seaweed for the skin are well documented, and powdered seaweed is incorporated into many expensive body creams. In this sea-encircled country, wrack is used in cooking, chewed like gum, spread on the land to fertilize the soil, and used for make-up products, but having a bath in it is definitely an experience worth making a special trip for. *See also* **County Kerry**, p.178.

Steeplechase

In County Cork in 1752, a group of sporting gentlemen rode their horses hell for leather from the steeple of Buttevant's Protestant Church to the Spire of St Leger's Church at Doneraile, about 4 miles (7km). The wager was to see who was the fastest. No obstacle was too great and they urged their horses over hedges, walls, streams. Thus the steeplechase was born.

Sub-aqua

Ireland's oceans are surprisingly warm and clear because they are right in the path of the Gulf Stream, so it would be very difficult to

find a better place for underwater swimming or diving. The underwater flora and fauna is vast and varied, and you are always bumping into shoals of fish. *Subsea* is the official journal of the Irish Underwater Council, which publishes information about the affiliated clubs, articles on diving, etc. Write to the Hon. Secretary, **Irish Underwater Council**, 78a Patrick St, Dun Laoghaire, t (01) 284 4601, *www.scubaireland.com*. There are centres for experienced divers and equipment hire in County Kerry and County Clare. Ask for the relevant fact sheet in any tourist office. By the way, it is illegal to take shellfish from the sea.

Surfing

Owing to Ireland's geographical position, great swells endlessly pound the southwest coast, producing waves comparable to those in California. Many of the beaches in County Kerry and County Clare are first-rate for breakers. As hire centres are not numerous, it is best to bring your own board and wetsuit; although you can occasionally hire them from hotels and adventure sports centres.

All those interested in the huge Atlantic swell should contact Mr Roc Allan, Chairman of the **Irish Surfing Association**, Easkey Surf and Information Centre, Easkey, County Sligo, Ireland, t (096) 49428. They will send out details of beaches and surfing centres.

Swimming and Beaches

There are lovely beaches (also called strands) wherever the sea meets the land. If you wish to go sea-bathing (it can be surprisingly warm because of the Gulf Stream), bear in mind that swimming is not a regulated sport, and that there are lifeguards only on the most popular beaches, if at all. Be aware of the possibility of a strong undertow or current, and ask locally about the safety of beaches.

Summer Schools

The phrase 'Ireland, land of saints and scholars' is delightfully apt when it comes to the tradition of learning. You can study some fascinating subjects in a beautiful environment, and still feel as if you are on

Specialist Summer Schools

Art/Painting
Burren College of Art, Ballyvaughan, County Clare, t (065) 707 7200, *www.burrencollege. com*. Photography/painting/sculpture.
Crawford School of Art and Gallery, Emmet Place, Cork, t (021) 427 3377, *www.crawford artgallery.com*.
Diseart, Dingle, County Kerry, t (066) 915 2476, *www.diseart.ie*.

Cookery
Ballymaloe Cookery School, Kinoith House, Shanagarry, Midleton, t (021) 464 6785, *www.cookingisfun.ie*. Run by Darina and Tim Allen. Courses vary from one day to three months.

Irish Studies and Music
Faculty of Celtic Studies, University College, Cork, t (021) 490 2607, *www.ucc.ie/ faculties/celtic*.
Willie Clancy Summer School, Miltown Malbay, t (065) 708 4281, *www.setdancing news.net/wcss*. Lectures and workshops in traditional Irish music and dance.

holiday. The Irish Tourist Board will send you a free up-to-date list of programmes and prices if you write and ask for the *Live and Learn* booklet, from the **Group and Education Department**, *Bord Fáilte*, Upper O'Connell Street, Dublin 1, t (01) 284 4768, *www.ireland.ie*.

The courses range from the seriously intellectual to activity holidays. You can study for a month, two weeks, a few days: the variety is tremendous. Some are run by Ireland's own universities which offer courses on literature, politics, history, Gaelic and archaeology. Private companies run arts and crafts courses, landscape painting and English language courses. There are courses in environmental studies in beautiful places such as the Burren, and classes in traditional music and dancing.

Activity holidays include windsurfing, hill-walking, riding, canoeing, fishing, cycling, golfing and dinghy-sailing. Some cater for all ages from toddlers upwards; in particular the adventure centres which are mainly on the west coast. *See* 'Specialist Tour Operators' in **Travel**, p.120.

Opposite in the box is a selection of others that are on offer.

Toilets

Public loos – labelled in Irish *Fir* (men) and *Mna* (women) – are usually in a pretty bad way. Nobody minds if you slip into a lounge bar or hotel to go to the loo, though it's a good excuse to stop for a drink as well.

Tourist Information and Guides

The people who work for *Bord Fáilte*, the Irish tourist board, would get you to the moon if they could – should you ask for it. They will do anything to help and organize whatever is practicable; and if they do not know the answer to something, they can always refer you to someone who does. They can supply you with a wealth of beautifully presented maps and leaflets; most of which are free, although they also publish fuller booklets on, for example, accommodation, for which there are modest charges. They can book your hotel or B&B and help you to find one which is in your price range.

There are tourist information offices scattered all around the southwest; many of them open only during the summer season. The following, however, are open throughout the year. (A full list of tourist information offices can be obtained from *Bord Fáilte* or the Irish Tourist Board in London. *See* 'Before You Go', p.102.)
Irish Tourist Board: *Bord Fáilte*, Upper O'Connell Street, Dublin 1, t (01) 284 4768, *www.ireland.ie*.

Offices in Counties Cork and Kerry
www.corkkerry.ie
Clonakilty: Ashe Street, Clonakilty, County Cork, t (023) 33226.
Cork City: Grand Parade, Cork City, t (021) 425 5100.
Kinsale: Pier Road, Kinsale, County Cork, t (021) 477 2234.
Skibbereen: *Oifig Fáilte*, Town Hall, Skibbereen, County Cork, t (028) 21766.

Dingle: The Quay, Dingle, County Kerry, t (066) 915 1188.

Killarney: *Áras Fáilte*, Beech Road, Killarney, County Kerry, t (064) 31633.

Tralee: Ashe Memorial Hall, Tralee, County Kerry, t (066) 712 1288.

Offices in Counties Limerick and Clare

www.shannonregiontourism.ie

Limerick City: Arthurs Quay, Limerick, t (061) 317522, *touristofficelimerick@shannondev.ie.*

Ennis: Arthur's Row, Ennis, County Clare, t (065) 682 8366, *touristofficeennis@ shannondev.ie.*

Shannon Airport: Arrivals Hall, Shannon Airport, County Clare, t (061) 471664, *touristofficeshannon@shannondev.ie.*

Tour Guides

In most areas of the southwest you can obtain the services of a **guide**. Guides love their country and their famous facility with words can make touring with one an unforgettable pleasure. Local tourist offices should be able to put you in touch, or you can try **Beatrice Healy**, a well-respected freelance guide, on t (01) 454 5943; or **OLGA (Official Local Guiding Association) Cork**, Cork City, t (021) 488 5405, who organize tours all over the southwest.

Where to Stay

Whether you are a traveller with plenty of loot to spend, or one who is intent on lodging as cheaply as possible, the southwest offers plenty of choice. Places to stay range from romantic castles, graceful country mansions, cosy farmhouses and smart city hotels to hostels which, although spartan, are clean and well-run. Many of these hostels have double or family rooms, are independently owned, and require no membership cards: they welcome young and old.

In each county chapter there are lists of recommended accommodation, divided into price categories which are explained overleaf. With this as a guide, it is possible to avoid the many modern and ugly hotels where bland comfort is doled out for huge prices, and the shabby motels and the musty bed-and-breakfast establishments (B&Bs) which are very uncomfortable. Farmhouse accommodation is usually a safe bet. One thing you can be sure of is that the Irish are amongst the friendliest people in Europe, and when they open their doors to visitors, they give a great welcome. The many unexpected kindnesses and the personal service that you will experience will contribute immeasurably to your visit. The countryside is beautiful, and there are many sights to see, but what adds enjoyment and richness is the pleasant conversation and humour of the people.

Accommodation Prices

Bord Fáilte register and grade hotels and guest houses, and they divide the many B&B businesses into Farmhouses, Town Houses and Country Houses. All of this is very useful, but apart from indicating the variety of services available and the cost, you really do not get much idea of the atmosphere and style of the place. The establishments listed in this book are described and categorized according to price, and include a variety of lodgings ranging from a luxurious castle to a simple farmhouse – all have something very special to offer a visitor. This may be the architecture, the garden, the food, the atmosphere and the chat, or simply the beauty of the countryside. The most expensive offer high standards of luxury, and the cheapest ones are clean and comfortable. Most are family-owned, with a few bedrooms, and none fits into a uniform classification, but they are all welcoming and unique places to stay. The price categories are of necessity quite loosely based, and some of the more expensive establishments do weekend deals which are very good value. Please, always check prices (rates are quoted in euros) and terms when making a booking.

Luxury

You can expect top-quality lodgings with style and opulence. Furnishings will include priceless antiques, whilst the facilities and service provide every modern convenience you could wish for.

Expensive

All the bedrooms have their own bathroom, direct-dial telephone, central heating, TV and the other paraphernalia of modern living, but they have something else as well – charm, eccentricity, and a feeling of mellow comfort. They are places where you might sleep in a graceful four-poster hung with rich cloth, and wake up to the sort of hospitality where the smell of coffee is just a prelude to a delicious cooked breakfast, and the sharp, sweet taste of home-made jam on Irish wheaten bread.

Moderate

Although not as luxurious, most of these places have private bathrooms and an extremely high standard of cooking and service. They have a wonderful atmosphere combined with attractive décor which is sometimes more atmospheric for its touch of age.

Inexpensive

Pretty whitewashed farmhouses, Georgian manses, rectories, old manor houses, modern bungalows and fine town houses come under this heading. They are very good value, good craic, and you will get marvellous plain cooking. Only some of the bedrooms will have *en suite* facilities, and some will not have central heating, but there will be perfectly good bathrooms close by and washbasins in the room. And if you are travelling in the late spring/summer, you do not need heating anyway!

Reservations

Bord Fáilte can be of immense help when you are making a reservation or trying to decide where to stay. You can make a reservation direct with the premises, or use the Irish Tourist Board offices in Great Britain who operate an enquiry and booking service. Offices in other countries operate an enquiry service only. *Bord Fáilte* offices throughout the southwest will make you a reservation for the

price of a telephone call. They will only book you into registered and approved lodgings, and a 10% deposit is payable.

Make sure that you book early for the peak months of June, July and August. At other times of the year it is usually quite all right to book on the morning of the day you wish to stay; this gives you great flexibility. However, the excellent lodgings soon get known by word of mouth, so they are always more likely to be booked up in advance.

Literature

The *Bord Fáilte* tourist offices keep plenty of booklets on various types of accommodation: the most comprehensive list, covering the whole of Ireland, is the *Accommodation Guide*; others include an *Illustrated Hotels and Guesthouses Guide*; an *Illustrated Farmhouse Guide*, an *Illustrated Town and Country Guide*, and a *Caravan and Camping Guide*. There is also the *Self-catering Guide*, *The Blue Book*, which lists Irish country houses and restaurants, *The Hidden Ireland Guide*, *Friendly Homes of Ireland*, and *Elegant Ireland*. See 'Historic Houses' in **Topics**, p.72.

Hotels

Bord Fáilte register and grade hotels into five categories: **A* grade** stands for the most luxuriously equipped bedrooms and public rooms with night service, a very high standard of food and plenty of choice. Most bedrooms have their own bath and suites are available – the sort of place where delicious snacks are automatically served with your cocktails. This grading includes baronial mansions set in exquisite grounds or the rather plush anonymity of some of the city and town hotels. **A grade** stands for a luxury hotel which doesn't have quite so many items on the *table d'hôte*, nor does it have night service; but the food is just as good and the atmosphere less restrained. **B* grade** stands for well-furnished and comfortable; some rooms have a bath, cooking is good and plain. **B and C grades** are clean, comfortable but limited, **B** offering more in the line of bathrooms and food.

All *Bord Fáilte* graded hotels have heating and hot and cold water in the bedrooms. If you come across a hotel that is ungraded, it is because its grading is under review or because

Accommodation Price Ranges

Note: Prices listed here and elsewhere in the book are for B&B per person.

Luxury	over €114
Expensive	over €76
Moderate	€38–76
Inexpensive	€13–38

Websites for Accommodation
Irish Tourist Board:
   www.ireland.ie/accommodation.asp
The Blue Book: www.irelands-blue-book.ie
Friendly Homes of Ireland: www.tourism
   resources.ie
The Hidden Ireland: www.hidden-ireland.com
Independent Holiday Hostels: www.hostels-
   ireland.com
Irish Hotels Federation: www.beourguest.ie.

it has just opened, or does not comply with *Bord Fáilte* requirements. The prices of hotels vary enormously, no matter what grade they are, and the grading takes no account of atmosphere and charm. Many of the most delightful and hospitable country houses come under grades B or C, while some of the grade A hotels are very dull. All graded hotels and guest houses are listed in the *Bord Fáilte Guest Accommodation* booklet and in the *Be Our Guest* booklet.

Guesthouses

These are usually houses which have become too large and expensive to maintain as private houses. The minimum number of bedrooms is five. The grade **A** houses are just as good as their hotel equivalent, as are those graded lower down the scale, although the atmosphere is different. In fact, guesthouses are some of the best places to stay.

If you decide to vary your accommodation from guesthouse to town and country house or farmhouse, you will discover one of the principles of Irish life: that everything in Ireland works on a personal basis. If you are on holiday to avoid people, a guesthouse is the last place you should book into. It is impossible not to be drawn into a friendly chat, whether about fishing or politics.

You will get a large, thoroughly uncontinental breakfast, and delicious evening meals with a choice within a set meal. Dinner is always very punctual, at 8pm, after everyone has sat around by the fire over very large drinks. Lunch or a packed lunch can be arranged. All grades of guesthouse have hot and cold water, and heating in the bedrooms. Grade **A** guesthouses have some rooms with private bathrooms, but their reputation is based on scrumptious food and comfortable surroundings. As a general guide, a comfortable, even luxurious night's sleep will cost €20–40, although the more basic guesthouses cost no more than a farmhouse B&B. A delicious meal ranges from €14–25. Sometimes the owners provide high tea, or the only meal they may do is breakfast. Our selection of guesthouses is included in the list of places to stay in each county section.

Farmhouses, Town Houses and Country Houses

Often these family homes make your stay in this country, for you meet Irish people who are kind, generous and intelligent. This is also the most economical way to stay in Ireland if you don't want to stay in a tent or in a youth hostel. If you are not going to a place that is recommended, it is largely a matter of luck whether you hit an attractive or a mediocre setup, but always watch out for the shamrock sign, the *Bord Fáilte* sign of approval. Wherever you go, you should get a comfortable bed (if you are tall, make sure it is long enough, as sometimes Irish beds can be on the small side), and an enormous breakfast: orange juice, cereal, two eggs, bacon, sausages, toast and marmalade, and a huge pot of tea or coffee. If you get rather tired of this fry-up, ask your hostess the night before for something different and she will be happy to oblige. Another thing – the coffee is invariably weak and tasteless; it's much safer to stick to tea. Nevertheless, breakfast is still a very satisfying meal, which means you don't feel hungry again until the evening.

B&B per person ranges between €20–35 if you are sharing a bedroom (a single room is sometimes more expensive). You can get much cheaper weekly rates, with partial or full board. Very often you can eat your evening meal in the dining room of the B&B. Again, there will be masses to eat and piping hot food – and it might better than local restaurants and cafés. Breakfast and other meal times are flexible: they happen when it suits you, but you should give notice before 12 noon if you want dinner.

Some houses serve dinner for €15–20, and some 'high tea', which is less costly.

'High tea' is a very sensible meal which has evolved for the working man who begins to feel hungry at about 6pm. You get a plate of something hot, perhaps chicken and chips, followed by fresh soda bread, jam and cakes and a pot of tea. Sometimes you get a salad. This leaves you with plenty of time to go out and explore in the evenings – whether to the pubs or the countryside. Some houses provide tea and biscuits as a snack for late-night nibblers.

More and more establishments today have *en suite* bathrooms with a loo, basin and bath or shower. You usually pay a little extra for this. If there is only a communal bathroom you will be charged a trivial amount for the hot bath – if you are even charged at all. Ask the woman of the house for a towel or, better still, carry your own, as those you are given are usually the size of a tea towel. Take your bath whenever you want; your hostess will ask you how many you had at the end of your stay. The bathroom is shared by everybody, family and guests, and it should be immaculately clean.

For people hitching or using public transport, the town houses are the easiest to get to and find, but my favourites are farmhouses, followed closely by country houses. The farms concentrate on dairy, sheep, crop farming or beef cattle and often a mixture of everything. Tucked away in lovely countryside, they may be traditional or modern. The farmer's wife, helped by her children, makes life very comfortable and is always ready to have a chat, and advise you on the local beauty spots, and good places to hear traditional music or go to a ceilidh. Some of the town and country houses are on fairly main roads, but they are generally not too noisy as there is so little traffic about. The type of house you might stay in ranges from the Georgian to the chalet-style bungalow, from a semi-detached to a 1950s dolls' house. There are a bewildering number of architectural styles in the new houses beginning to radiate out from small villages.

It is wise to book maybe a night or two ahead during July and August, though it is rarely necessary. This means that you do not have to be tied, and can dawdle in a place as much as you want.

Renting a House or Cottage

Every regional office of *Bord Fáilte* has a list of houses and apartments to let; there is also a short list of self-catering houses at the back of the *Guest Accommodation* booklet. Places to rent range from converted stable blocks or modern bungalows to stone-built cottages.

There is a very popular 'Rent an Irish Cottage' scheme (*see* below), with centres in County Limerick and County Clare. On the outside the cottages are thatched, whitewashed and traditional; inside they are well-designed with an electric cooker, fridge and kettle – all the mod cons you could want. There are built-in cupboards, comfy beds, and linen. Simple, comfortable Irish-made furniture and fittings make it a happy blend of tradition and modern convenience. The cottages vary in size: some take eight, others five. Easter and May, June, July and August are the most expensive times with prices around €300–600 a week, but in October, sometimes the nicest month weather-wise, a cottage for six is very reasonable at around €275 per week. The local people take a great interest in you because they are all shareholders in the scheme and so do their best to make you content. Write to *Bord Fáilte* for details of the scheme and other self-catering cottages. **Rent an Irish Cottage**, 51 O'Connell Street, Limerick, **t** (061) 411109, *www.rent acottage.ie*.

Youth Hostels

The Irish YHA is called *An Oige* and has a number of hostels in the southwest. They are often in wild and remote places, so that they are doubly attractive to the enterprising traveller. Members of the International Youth Hostel Federation can use any of these. If you haven't got a card, you can join; there is no age limit. All you have to do is buy something called an International Guest Card, by purchasing six welcome stamps. The stamps may be bought one at a time at six different hostels.

The youth hostels are often the most superb houses, and they range from cottages to castles, old coastguard stations to old military barracks. They are great centres for climbers, walkers and fishers, and not too spartan; many have a comfortable laxity when it comes to the rules. You must provide your own sheet and sleeping bag. A flap or pocket to cover the pillows can be bought at the *An Oige* office, and the hostel provides blankets. Bring your own knives, forks, spoons, tea towels, bath towel, soap and food. All the hostels have fully equipped self-catering kitchens, and most also provide breakfast, packed lunches and an evening meal on request.

Charges vary according to age, month and location; during July and August it is slightly more expensive, and it is vital to book. This applies also to weekends. All *An Oige* hostels may be booked from one hostel to another, or centrally by contacting the head office (*see* below). Most hostels are open all year round. It's quite a good idea to combine hostelling with staying at B&Bs (*see* 'Farmhouses, Town and Country Houses', opposite.)

There are several rail/cycling holidays on offer to hostel members. An essential handbook and an excellent map can be got from the *An Oige* Office, 61 Mountjoy Street, Dublin 1, **t** (01) 830 4555, *www.irelandyha.org*.

Independent Holiday Hostels of Ireland (IHH) is a completely separate organisation from YHA. It is a co-operative society of hostels ranging from Georgian houses to restored mills. They are friendly, open to everyone (children are welcome in most hostels), and most have double and family rooms. All hostels will rent you sheets and all hostels provide duvets and blankets. The average price for a dormitory bed in high season is €13. Send off for a list of hostels to IHH Office, 57 Lower Gardiner Street, Dublin 1, **t** (01) 836 4700, *www.hostels-ireland.com*.

Many other organizations such as the YWCA, ISSACS and colleges of further education offer cheap and comfortable accommodation. Some of them have excellent eating facilities attached; call the local tourist office for a list.

Camping and Caravanning

The camping and caravan parks which meet the standards set by *Bord Fáilte* are listed in a booklet available from the tourist offices, or you can order it direct from Irish Camping and Caravanning Holidays, 2 Offington Court, Sutton, Dublin 13. There is also a selection in the *Guest Accommodation Guide* republished every year by *Bord Fáilte*; in County Cork you could try the Tent Shop, 7 Parnell Place, Cork City, **t** (021) 278833. Sites are graded according to amenities and many of them are in beautiful areas, often on the coast. Laundry rooms, hot showers and loos, shops, restaurants, indoor games rooms and TV make camping easy and also more civilized, especially if you have children. It is sometimes possible to **hire** tents and equipment, caravans and motor homes (RVs). For full details check the *Caravan and Camping* booklet or consult *www.camping-ireland.ie*.

Overnight **charges** on camp sites are about €7–12 per night, with a small charge per person at some parks, and fees for electrical linkup, hot showers and laundry facilities. If you are bringing your own caravan or camping equipment to Ireland and have Calor **gas appliances**, the only ones on sale in Ireland which are compatible are those supplied by Gaz. Some caravan parks accept dogs if they are on a leash. Note that some sites are **reserved** for caravans and motor homes only.

Farmers can be very tolerant of people turning up and asking if they can camp or park their caravan in a field. You must ask their permission first, and tell them how long you want to stay. Be polite, do not get in the way and you will find that they will give you drinking water, lots of chat, and perhaps even vegetables from their gardens.

Women Travellers

Irish men have an attitude towards women which is as infuriating as it is attractive. They are a grand old muddle of male chauvinism, with a dash of admiration and fear for their mothers, sisters and wives. Irish women have a sharp wit which makes them more than a match for 'your man' in an argument, but at the same time they work their hearts out.

If you are a lone female travelling around, you will find an Irish man will always help you with your luggage or your flat tyre and stand you for a meal or a drink, without any question of you buying him a round (though of course you should use your common sense in this situation). If one tries to chat you up in a bar, or at a dance, it is usually a bit of craic, not to be taken seriously, and the game is abandoned at once if you get tired of it. They probably think that you ought to be travelling with somebody else, but it's only the women who will say so, saying, with a smile, that it must be a bit lonesome. If you walk into an obviously male preserve, such as a serious drinking pub, don't expect to feel welcome, because you won't be unless everybody is drunk and by that time you would need to scarper. A bit of advice, which does not apply just to women, was pithily put by an Irish politician: 'The great difference between England and Ireland is that in England you can say what you like, so long as you do the right thing. In Ireland you can do what you like, so long as you say the right thing.' If you are hitchhiking on your own, or with another girl, you will get plenty of offers to take you out dancing that night (again, exercise caution and use your common sense).

Women travellers are advised against hitchhiking, whether travelling alone or in a group (see also p.100).

County Limerick

10

County Limerick

pp. 230–1

CLARE

Newmarket on Fergus

Shannon Airport ✈ N19 •Shannon

Bunratty

Killadysert

Killimer

River Shannon

Pallaskenry

Kilcornan

Dromore Castle

Foynes

Tarbert

Glin

N69

Askeaton

R. Deel

Franciscan friary

❸

Adare•

R. Galey

p.142

Castle Matrix

Rathkeale

Ardagh

L I M E R I C K

Athea

R. Feale

Newcastle West

Ballingary

❹
Knockfierna Hill

K E R R Y

Abbeyfeale

N21

Broadford

Mullaghareirk Mountains

N21

pp.182–3 C O R K

Liscarroll

Highlights

1 St Mary's Cathedral in Limerick City
2 The Hunt Museum in Limerick City
3 The fine ecclesiastical ruins of Adare
4 A walk up Knockfierna Hill, near Croom
5 Lough Gur Stone Age Interpretative Centre

pp. 230–1

10 km
5 miles

N

Clonlara
Castleconnell
LIMERICK
N18
Annacotty
Clonkeen
N69
Clarina
Murroe
Slievefelim
Mountains
Clare Glens
T
I
P
P
E
R
A
R
Y
R. Mulkear
N21
Ballyneety
R. Dead
N24
Croom
R. Camoge
Lough
Gur
R. Maigue
N20
Limerick Junction
Tipperary
Bruree
Kilmallock
Duntryleague
Hill
Galbally
Kilfinane
Galtymore
Mountain
Galty Mountains
Ardpatrick
Castle Oliver
Ballyhoura Mountains

pp.182–3

A limerick is a nonsense verse, and Limerick is also a lovely county in Ireland. The county existed long before the five-line stanza, but since Edward Lear popularized them in his nonsense book, limericks have become world-famous. The origin of these poems is intriguing and open to debate, but it is claimed that in the 18th century a group of poets known as the Poets of Maigue, who lived near Croom, wrote these witty verses in good-natured sparring and as drinking songs. James Clarence Mangan, himself a great poet, translated them into English in the 1840s and they became popular in England.

One of the poets, a tavern-keeper named Sean O'Tuama, wrote:

I sell the best brandy and sherry
To make my good customer merry
But at times their finances
Run short as it chances
And then I feel very sad, very.

One of his customers, Andy MacCraith, replied:

O Tuomy! you boast yourself handy,
At selling good ale and bright brandy,
The fact is your liquor
Makes everyone sicker,
I tell you that – I, your friend, Andy.

County Limerick itself is a quiet farming community, dotted with the ruins of hundreds of castles and bounded on the north by the wide River Shannon, which flows into the sea. On its other sides lie a fringe of hills and mountains: the peaks of the Galtees in the southeast, the wild Mullaghareirk Mountains in the southwest and the rich Golden Vale in the east. There are lovely forest walks in all these places and good sailing on the Shannon. The visitor will be fascinated by Lough Gur, with its wealth of archaeological remains, and the many ruined Norman castles and monasteries that survive among the green fields and old farmhouses, lying snugly in the valleys. The best dairy cattle come from County Limerick, and it is also famous for its horse-breeding, due largely to the county's fertile pastures.

Limerick likes to call itself the 'Birthplace of the Celtic Tiger'. When Taoiseach Sean Lemass liberalized Ireland's economic policies in the 1950s, the county was one of the first to take advantage. The Shannon Development and the Free Trade Zone still provide a lot of jobs. Limerick City has a reputation for its vibrant cultural life; a good university, excellent museums, art galleries and classical music concerts.

History

Not surprisingly in such fertile countryside, the monks founded important monasteries here. That they were rich is proved by the bejewelled Ardagh Chalice, discovered in a ring fort in 1868 and now in the National Museum in Dublin. The Vikings, in search of new territory and loot, sought them out up the Shannon Estuary and destroyed many centres of learning. They founded a colony here, which was to become the City of Limerick later on.

Next came the Anglo-Normans, also attracted by the rich lands. Among the principal families were the Fitzgeralds, the de Burgos, the de Lacys and the Fitzgibbons. But the Earls of Desmond, the heads of the Fitzgeralds, owned the most; they ruled like independent princes, and eventually quarrelled with their Tudor overlords in England. (They and their supporters are known as the Geraldines.) The Tudors tried to centralize their authority in the 16th century, and consequently the Geraldines, who by now were completely Gaelicized, started a revolt in 1571 and

Arrival and Getting Around

By Air

Shannon Airport (*www.shannonairport.com*) lies about 15 miles north of Limerick City in County Clare, off the N19. A regular **airport bus** runs to and from Limerick City bus station (45mins; at least one per hour 7am–midnight, fewer on Sun; €7). There's also a 24-hour **taxi desk** in the Arrivals hall (fares around €30).

By Train and Bus

Limerick City's train and bus stations sit together on Parnell Street. **Bus** services (**t** (061) 313333) go to Cork, Ennis, Tipperary, Dublin and Waterford; **train** services run to Dublin, Cork and Clonmel/Waterford/Rosslare.

By Bike

Emerald Alpine, 1 Patrick Street, Limerick, t (061) 416983. Hire bikes from here.

By Car

Traffic is one of Limerick City's biggest problems. Parking isn't easy either, and most of the centre is a disc parking zone.

Shannon Car Ferry

See **County Clare**, p.232, for information on the Tarbert–Killimer car ferry.

Festivals

Dates of festivals vary and some towns have one-off festivals – check at the tourist office.

January

UnFringed: alternative theatre, dance, cabaret, comedy and arts festival, held in Limerick.

February

Kate O'Brien Weekend: annual festival for Limerick's famous author.

March

Limerick Spring Festival (weekend closest to 17th): including the huge **St Patrick's Day Parade**, with marching bands and street entertainers; **Limerick International Band Recital Competition**, with jazz ensembles, concert bands and orchestras; and the **International Marching Band Parade and Competition**, where Irish and international bands compete on the streets.
EV+A – Exhibition of Visual + Art: Irish and international contemporary art in Limerick, selected by a leading curator (March–May).

April

Fresh Film Festival: young people's film festival in Limerick; *www.freshfilmfestival.net*.
Ballyhoura Walking Festival: near Kilfinane. 3-day event with graded walks.

May

Fleadh by the Feale (May Bank Holiday weekend): traditional music, song and dance in Abbeyfeale. There's even a bones-playing competition; *www.fleadhbythefeale.com*.

July

Irish Coffee Festival: celebrates – you guessed it – Irish coffee, invented by local Foynes Airport chef Joe Sheridan in 1942; *www.irishcoffeefestival.com*.
Shannon International Music Festival: 5 days of classical music in Limerick, with acclaimed guests – in 2005 it includes soprano Emma Kirkby; *www.icorch.com*.

August

Limerick Agricultural Show: showjumping, horticulture, craft exhibitions and family entertainment; *www.limerickshow.com*.
Galbally Garden Fete: pipe bands, carnival, fun and games, and music from a top Irish band.

September

Eigse Michael Hartnett Literary Festival: Irish and international poets and writers, singing and lectures in Newcastle West.

October

Lough Gur Storytelling Festival: storytelling, drama, music and singing, held in Bruff.
Limerick International Poetry Festival: poetry slams, readings and book launches in Cuisle.
Castleconnell Craft Fair: Irish-made crafts.

November

Sionna Festival of Dance and Music: 3 weeks of traditional music and dance in Limerick.

maintained a constant guerrilla war against the crown and its agents. This ended in savage wars, repression and ruin for their house.

Throughout the following centuries up to the present, Limerick has played a significant role in uprisings against English rule. In 1650 there was the 12-month siege of Limerick by Cromwell, which ended in capitulation. The Jacobite-Williamite war (1689–91) saw two more sieges in which the heroic General Patrick Sarsfield played his role (see p.131). William Smith O'Brien, a Limerick man, was one of the leaders of the abortive 1848 Rebellion, and three of the leaders of the 1916 Rising in Dublin were from the county. Edward Daly and Con Colbert were executed, but Eamon de Valera escaped that fate because of his American birth. Later, he was one of the leaders of the War of Independence (1919–1921) and President of Ireland from 1959 to 1973.

Limerick City

Limerick City at first sight has something rather drab about it. The novelist Kate O'Brien came from the respectable middle class that moulded this city in the 19th century, and she described it as having 'the grave, grey look of Commerce'. It is largely Georgian in character: a grid pattern of streets was superimposed onto the older town, which followed the curve of the River Shannon.

Limerick is doing its best to forget the hard times of the 1940s–60s, and has recently been given a substantial facelift. It has a reputation for smart clothes shops, and the Art School here has produced some talented fashion designers. Also it has the much-lauded Hunt Collection of art treasures, which is worth making the journey for alone. For a city of its size (pop. 87,000), Limerick also has a buzzy nightlife. Previously high levels of unemployment and emigration have decreased significantly as new industries have been set up, and its cultural life is healthy. The city is very proud of its musical heritage, with a strong choral tradition, chamber music and marching bands. Mezzo-soprano Suzanne Murphy was born here, the 1990s saw local band 'The Cranberries' gain international stardom and there's an Irish World Music Centre (see p.133). The people of Limerick are not so proud, however, of Frank McCourt's descriptions of their city in Angela's Ashes (a memoir of his childhood), even though a walking and bus tour (see p.132) points out some of the places mentioned in his grim, exuberant and funny portrait of life in 1930s–40s Limerick.

History

Like Londonderry, Limerick is a symbolic city full of memories, and there is lots to see that reveals Limerick's more ancient past. It was founded in AD 922 by the Norsemen, and has always been an important fording place on the River Shannon; in 1997 the city celebrated the 800th anniversary of its royal charter. More concrete evidence of the past is the massive round tower of King John's Castle, built in 1200, which sits on the river guarding Thomond Bridge and is one of the best examples of fortified Norman architecture in the country. The motto of the city is Urbs antiqua fuit studiisque asperrima belli, 'An ancient city inured to the arts of war'.

The history of the city is certainly stirring. In the wars of 1691 it was eventually surrendered to the Williamite Commander Ginkel after a fierce battering from his guns. The siege that preceded the surrender is stored away in the psyche of Irishmen. During the 1690s there were three struggles going on: the struggle of Britain and her Protestant allies to oppose the ascendancy in Europe of Catholic France, the struggle of Britain to subdue Ireland, and the struggle between the Protestant planter families and the Catholic Irish for the leadership of Ireland. The French supplied money and commanders to help Catholic James II wrest his crown back from the Protestant William of Orange. The majority of the Catholic Irish supported the Jacobite cause and many joined up.

It is part of Irish folk memory that the French commander St Ruth and King James were asses, and that the Irish commander Patrick Sarsfield was intelligent, daring and brave. The Irish army had been beaten at the Boyne under St Ruth and had retreated to Limerick, where the walls were said to be paper thin. William began a siege while he waited for the arrival of big guns, but Patrick Sarsfield led a daring raid on the siege train from Dublin and destroyed it. Sarsfield rode through the night with 600 horses into the Clare Hills, forded the Shannon and continued on through the Slievefelim Mountains. Finally, he swooped down on William III's huge consignment of guns and blew them skywards. His action saved Limerick from destruction for a time, when the siege was abandoned. When William did break through Limerick's walls he sent in 10,000 men to wreak havoc, but the women and children of the city fought alongside their men and beat them back.

The second siege began the following year and this time heavy losses were inflicted when the Williamite leader, Ginkel, gained control of Thomond Bridge. The promised help never came, and there was nothing to do but negotiate an honourable treaty. This Sarsfield did, and he agreed to take himself and 10,000 Irish troops off to France, in what became known as 'The Flight of the Wild Geese'. But the terms of the treaty were not carried out. The stone beside Thomond Bridge, where it was supposed to have been signed, is known as 'The Stone of the Violated Treaty'. In the Catholic Cathedral of St John is the Sarsfield Monument by sculptor John Lawlor (1820–1901).

The City Centre

The old Viking town of Limerick sits on an island formed by the Shannon and the Abbey River (a branch of the Shannon). Known as **English Town**, it's one of the most interesting parts of Limerick to wander in, along with its Irish counterpart across the water. The Vikings and later the Normans tried to keep the native Irish from living and trading in the city area, so the Irish settled on the other side – in **Irish Town**. A short circular walk will take you around the main places of interest.

In the centre is the tourist office and Arthur's Quay Park, between the Shannon and the city's sparkling new shopping district. From here, cross the river by Sarsfield Bridge, then turn right up Clancy's Strand, which gives you a good view of the city.

This passes the **Limerick Treaty Stone** (*see* **History**, p.15) and leads to Thomond Bridge and the Old Town. You also pass **King John's Castle** (*open daily, April–Oct 9.30–6; Nov–Mar 10.30–4.30, last adm 1hr before close; adm;* **t** *(061) 360788*), which has a two-floor interpretative centre that explains the castle's history through displays and an audiovisual show. Outside, you can explore the battlement views, excavations of pre-Norman buildings and a reconstruction of the courtyard as it might have looked in medieval times. The **Limerick Museum**, next door in Castle Lane (*open Tues–Sat 10–1 and 2.15–7, closed public hols; adm; t (061) 417826*), houses an impressive collection of items from the Neolithic, Bronze and Iron Ages, as well as the city's mace and sword. Other civic treasures include the famous 'Nail': a pedestal that was formerly in the Exchange (once in Nicholas Street; only a fragment of the façade

Tourist Information

Limerick City: Arthur's Quay, **t** (061) 317522, *touristofficelimerick@shannondev.ie, www.shannonregiontourism.ie*; open all year.
Shannon Airport: **t** (061) 471664, *touristoffice shannon@shannondev.ie*; open all year.

Tours

An *Angela's Ashes* **Walking Tour** takes you around scenes from Frank McCourt's memoir (daily at 2.30 from St Mary's Action Centre, 44 Nicholas Street, **t** (061) 318106). The **Great Limerick Tour** travels in an open-top bus (mid-June–mid-Aug daily at 11am and 2.30pm; **t** (061) 313333).

Shopping

The best **shopping streets** in Limerick are Cruises Street, Arthur's Quay, Patrick Street, William Street and O'Connell Street. The daily **Milk Market** sits on the corner of Ellen Street and Wickham Street; on Fridays stalls sell arts and crafts, and on Saturday mornings it becomes a busy farmers' market.
Irish Handcrafts, 26 Patrick Street, Limerick. Woollens and tweeds.
Greenacres Deli, Carr Street, Milk Market, Limerick. Worth visiting for picnic items; sells a feast of Mediterranean and local food.
Niamh Hynes, Newgarden Road, Lisnagry, **t** 377331. Hand-thrown porcelain decorated with colourful creatures.

Sports and Activities

Golf

Limerick Golf Club, Ballyclough, **t** (061) 415146, *www.limerickgc.com*.

Limerick Golf and Country Club, Ballyneety, **t** (061) 351881, *www.limerickcounty.com*. Championship-quality course.
Rathbane Golf Club, off the R512 Lough Gur road, **t** (061) 313655, *www.rathbanegolf.com*.

Horse Racing

Limerick Racecourse, Patrickswell, **t** (061) 320000, *www.limerick-racecourse.com*.

Where to Stay

Limerick City **t** (061–)

Radisson SAS Hotel, Ennis Road, **t** 326666, *www.radissonsas.ie (luxury–expensive)*. Plush but not completely bland, this modern hotel has landscaped gardens and many facilities (pool, sauna, solarium, gym, tennis courts and beauty salon, and a spa opening in 2006). Expansive hot or cold buffet breakfast and a good dinner menu.
Castletroy Park Hotel, Dublin Road, **t** 335566, *www.castletroy-park.ie (expensive)*. Modern four-star hotel with an uninspiring exterior, but has suprisingly good accommodation and a reputation for good food.
Kilmurry Lodge Hotel, Castleroy, **t** 331133, *www.kilmurrylodge.com (expensive–moderate)*. Looks inviting, with vine-clad exterior and 4-acre gardens, comfortable rooms and a particularly nice restaurant where fresh, local food is cooked by award-winning chefs.
Hanratty's Hotel, 5 Glentworth Street, **t** 410999 *(moderate)*. Old hotel established in 1796, with atmosphere and good facilities.
Railway Hotel, Parnell Street, **t** 413653, *www.railwayhotel.ie (moderate)*. Old-fashioned and very comfortable family-run hotel.
Woodfield House Hotel, Ennis Road, **t** 453022, *www.woodfieldhousehotel.com (moderate)*.

remains) where the merchants of Limerick used to pay their debts. (Most trading centres in England had one of these, hence the expression 'to pay on the nail'.)

Walk down Nicholas Street to **St Mary's Cathedral**, the only ancient church building left in the city, built in 1172 by Donal Mor O'Brien, King of Munster. Inside, it has plenty of atmosphere, monuments and impressive furnishings, including some superb 15th-century oak misericords carved into the shapes of fantastic beasts, such as the cockatrice and griffin. They are known as 'mercy seats' because, although it looked as if the singers were standing, they could instead use them to half-sit or lean on. The

Within walking distance of the centre; cosy hotel with a steakhouse restaurant.

Alexandra Guest House, 5–6 O'Connell Avenue, t 318472 (*inexpensive*). Attractive Victorian house with *en suite* rooms, only 5mins walk from the city centre.

Mount Gerard B&B, O'Connell Avenue, t 314981 (*inexpensive*). Family B&B in a lovely Victorian house. Convenient for the centre.

Eating Out

Moll Darby's, 8 George's Quay, t 411511 (*moderate*). Right in front of King John's Castle, in an atmospheric original stone building. Hearty food, including steaks and seafood. *Open daily 5.30–11pm.*

Quenelle's Restaurant, Steamboat Quay, Limerick, t 411111 (*moderate*). Gourmet dining in crisp surroundings with a view over the quays. Fine meat, fish, game and vegetarian dishes. *Open for lunch Thurs–Fri 12.30–2.30, dinner Mon–Sat 6.30–10pm.*

The Parlour Restaurant, inside Thady O'Neills, Ennis Road, t 322777 (*moderate*). Finely decorated with a cosy atmosphere, and classic, creative dishes.

Ducarts, in the Hunt Museum, Rutland St, t 312662 (*moderate–inexpensive*). Pleasant lunch spot where you can have a meal or just a snack on the terrace, with a view over the Shannon. *Open Mon–Sat 10–5, Sun 2–5.*

Greene's Café-Bistro, 63 William Street, t 314022 (*inexpensive*). Central carvery-bistro, with beautiful stained glass and wholesome Irish dishes. *Open Mon–Sat 8am–6pm.*

Green Onion Cafè, inside Limerick's, Ellen Street (*inexpensive*). Popular café serving veggie options and good Italian coffee.

Matt the Thresher, Birdhill, t 379227 (*inexpensive*). On the road into Limerick

(and technically in Tipperary), a delightful country pub serving excellent food and home-made bread, with views across the Shannon.

Ruben's Café and Wine Bar, 17 Denmark Street, t 312599 (*inexpensive*). Great for wholesome food and vegetarian dishes, and set in a pleasant renovated stone building. *Open Mon–Sat 10–5.30*

The Wild Onion Bakeshop and Café, High St, *www.wildonioncafe.com* (*inexpensive*). Scrumptious breakfasts and lunches, including home-made vegeburgers, cakes and breads. *Open Tues–Fri 8–4, Sat 9–3.*

Entertainment and Nightlife

Pubs and Clubs

The Old Quarter, Little Ellen Street. Relaxed Art Deco-style bar, with outdoor seating and regular jazz ensembles.

Schooners, Steamboat Quay, t 328147. On the banks of the Shannon; popular for its live local bands. *Open Mon–Wed 10am–11.30pm, Thurs–Sat to 12.30am, Sun to 11pm.*

Traditional Music

Belltable Arts Centre, 69 O'Connell Street, t 319866, *www.belltable.ie*. Great arts centre, with especially good events during festivals.

Dolan's, 3–4 Dock Road, t 314483, *www.dolans-pub.ie*. Lively venue in the old docklands area, with music played by accomplished musicians. Good for food too.

Irish World Music Centre, University of Limerick, t 202917, *www.iwmc.ie*. Lunchtime concerts on Tues and Thurs.

The Locke, George's Quay, t 413733. Bar dating back to 1724; very relaxed atmosphere.

acclaimed **cathedral choir** can be heard here regularly (*Sept–July, most Suns at 11.15am and at evensong, first Sun of month 7pm*). The oak for the misericords and barrel-vaulted roof came from the Cratloe Woods in County Clare. The cathedral was vandalized by Cromwell's soldiers, although it still has its pre-Reformation limestone high altar. Note the spectacular chandeliers. The Hiberno-Romanesque doorway on the west side is splendid, and the graveyard and garden surrounding the cathedral are charming. In summer there's a **son et lumière** show about Limerick (*nightly, 9.15pm*).

A few minutes' walk down Bridge Street and over the little Abbey River brings you to the best thing in Limerick: the Old Custom House in Rutland Street. This restored 18th-century building is now home to the **Hunt Museum** (*open Mon–Sat 10–5, Sun 2–5; t (061) 312833, www.huntmuseum.com*) and is a rare example of architecture by Davis Ducart. John Hunt was a noted art historian and Celtic archaeologist who died in the 1970s. He and his wife Gertrude gathered together a remarkable European collection of over 2,000 objects, part of which comprises a hoard of archaeological finds that are considered the second most important in Ireland today. There's also 18th-century silver; jewels, including early Christian brooches; paintings (one by Picasso); and Egyptian, Roman, Greek and medieval carved statues and artefacts, including the 9th-century bronze **Cashel Bell**, the largest in Ireland, found near Cashel town in 1849. As self-portraits go, the one by Robert Fagin with his half-naked wife is rather stunning; so, in a different way, is the bronze horse by Leonardo da Vinci.

After the 1760s, when the city walls were dismantled, English and Irish Town merged and Georgian streets and squares were built. St John's Square has the lofty spire of the Victorian Gothic **St John's Cathedral**, as well as a number of lovely old buildings of the mid-18th century. From here, a walk up Brennan's Row and a right on Sean Heuson Place brings you to the **Milk Market** (*see* 'Shopping', p.132).

More fine Georgian streets can be found on the southern edge of the city centre, around the **Crescent**, a development of the early 1800s at the southern end of O'Connell Street, and around **People's Park**. Close to the entrance of the park, off Pery Square, the **Limerick City Gallery of Art** (*open Mon–Fri 10–6, Thurs to 7, Sat 10–1; adm free; t (061) 310633, www.limerickcity.ie*) has a collection of modern Irish paintings, and holds some very interesting exhibitions of contemporary art.

The **Belltable Arts Centre** (*69 O'Connell St, t (061) 319866, www.belltable.ie*) is situated to the southwest; various travelling theatre companies stop off here and it's well worth seeing what's on. There is also a small gallery that shows the work of many local artists and is part of the international EV+A festival (*see* p.129). The University of Limerick, on the edge of the city off the main Dublin road (N7), houses several art collections; the **National Self-Portrait Collection** (*open Mon–Fri 9–5; t (061) 333644, www.ul.ie/campuslife/arts/arts.html*) is the most worthwhile. The university is also home to the Irish Chamber Orchestra (*www.icorch.com*) and has a fine concert hall. Classical, traditional and world music concerts take place here regularly, especially during the International Festival of Music (*see* p.129).

Limerick is the great bastion of rugby in Ireland, and one of the many local clubs wins the All-Ireland League almost every year. Hurling is also a very popular and successful sport in Limerick, in which local clubs have their own style of playing.

Around County Limerick

Down the Shannon to Glin

From Limerick City, the N69 follows the Shannon Estuary. Sitting between the road and the Shannon are two very prominent landmarks: the crumbling 15th-century **Carrigogunnell Castle** at Clarina, superbly set on a volcanic rock with a commanding view of the river, and, four miles farther west, the romantic silhouette of **Dromore Castle** (*private*), designed by E.W. Godwin for the Earl of Limerick in 1870.

In the vicinity of Kilcornan is the gutted ruin of **Curragh Chase**, which burnt down in 1942. The minor Victorian poet Aubrey de Vere lived most of his long life here, and was often visited by Tennyson. One visit produced the poem 'Lady Vere de Vere'. Aubrey de Vere did many good works during the famine and he is buried in Askeaton. The ruin is in a very romantic setting; the demesne is now **Curragh Chase Forest Park** (*open daily; www.coillte.ie*) and footpaths are laid out in the arboretum and around the reed-filled lake. Also in Kilcornan you'll find the **Celtic Park and Gardens** (*open Mar–Oct, 9–6; adm adults €5, under 12s free; t (061) 394243*), a fascinating collection of original and recreated Celtic structures, such as a dolmen, a lake dwelling, a stone templar church and extensive, well-planned gardens. Just west, **Askeaton Friary** is a preserved 14th-century complex endowed by the Earls of Desmond, with fine ancient stone carvings.

At **Foynes**, Limerick's little port, a very interesting hour can be spent at the **Flying Boat Museum** (*open April–Oct daily 10–6; adm adults €5, 5–14s €2.50; t (069) 65416, www.flyingboatmuseum.com*). Between 1939 and 1945 Foynes was famous as a base for seaplanes crossing the Atlantic. The radio and weather room with original transmitters, receivers and Morse code is fascinating. Many high-ranking British and American officers passed through Foynes during the Second World War and Irish coffee was concocted then, by the restaurant's chef (*see* 'Festivals', p.129). **Boyce's Garden** (*open May–Sept 10–6; t (069) 65302*), at Mount Trenchard, is a superb one-acre garden overlooking the Shannon, with herbaceous borders, rock garden and pergola.

At **Glin**, a lovely village on the Shannon, you can visit **Glin Castle** (*see* 'Where to Stay', p.136), which is still the ancestral home of the Knights of Glin, part of the Fitzgerald tribe. The present Knight is an art historian and stalwart campaigner on behalf of Ireland's historic buildings, which are so often left to decay. The castle is Georgian Gothic with castellations, and noted for its flying staircase, plasterwork and 18th-century furniture, portraits and landscape paintings. The gardens (*visitors welcome by arrangement*) are beautifully planned and tended, and are a fitting extension to this romantic house. Exotic plants and the dark-leaved myrtle with its creamy, scented flowers love the mild climate; the walled garden is large and sloping and filled with fruit, herbs and vegetables for the house. The hens have Gothic-style quarters and a headless Ariadne stands in a rustic temple. By the castle gates is the **Glin Heritage and Genealogical Research Centre** (*open June–Sept Tues–Sun 10–6; t (068) 34001*). Tarbert, west of Glin in County Kerry, is the site of the **car ferry** across the Shannon, which makes a very useful short cut into County Clare (*see* p.232).

Tourist Information

Adare: Adare Heritage Centre, Main Street,
t (061) 396255; *open Feb–Dec*.

Shopping

Lucy Erridge Crafts, Main Street, Adare, t (061)
396898. Knitwear and unusual crafts.
Orchard Pottery, Castleconnell, t (061) 377181.
Stoneware with colourful Celtic designs.

Sports and Activities

Golf

Adare Manor Golf Club, Adare, t (061) 396566,
www.adaremanor.ie. See hotel listing, right.
Newcastle West Golf Club, Rathgoonan,
Ardagh, t (069) 76500.
Abbeyfeale Golf Centre, Dromtrasna Collins,
Abbeyfeale, t (068) 32033.

Pony Trekking

Clonshire Equestrian Centre, Adare, t (061)
396770.
Yerville Stables, Pallasgreen, t (061) 351547.

Where to Stay

Adare Manor Hotel and Golf Resort, Adare,
t (061) 396566, *www.adaremanor.ie* (*luxury*).
Original house of the Earls of Dunraven. A
mix of Victorian, Gothic and Tudor Revival
fantasy, with beautiful grounds, horse-
riding, shooting and an 18-hole golf course.
Dunraven Arms Hotel, Adare, t (061) 396633,
www.dunravenhotel.com (*luxury*). Old-world,
with appealing interiors, friendly staff, a pool
and garden. The **Maigue Restaurant** serves
top rate food, and the **Inn Between** is more
informal, within a thatched cottage.
Glin Castle, Glin, due west of Adare by the
Shannon, t (068) 34173, *www.glincastle.com*
(*luxury*). Home to the Knight of Glin and his
wife, with 15 exclusively decorated rooms,
plus a sitting room, library, drawing room
and gardens. The **dining room** offers Irish
country house cuisine, with organic fruit and
vegetables picked from their walled garden.
See also p.77 and p.135. *Open March–Nov*.
The Mustard Seed, Ballingarry, t (069) 68508,
www.mustardseed.ie (*expensive*). 19th-
century house on a hill with characterful
rooms, a great dining room (*see* opposite)
and pretty, lovingly-kept gardens.
Ash Hill House, Kilmallock, t (063) 98035,
www.ashhill.com (*moderate*). Crenellated,
turreted Georgian house with 3 large,
comfortable rooms and a 2-bedroom
apartment, fascinating plasterwork ceilings
and shades of Anglo-Irish splendour. Also a
stud and working farm; dogs are welcome.
Castle Oaks House, Castleconnell, t (061)
377666, *www.castleoaks.ie* (*moderate*).
Converted Georgian house by the Shannon,
convenient for golf and angling. The award-
winning **Acorn Restaurant** has a good menu.

Following the border with Kerry, southwards from Glin, you come to **Athea**, a centre for traditional music and a pretty place. All around are lovely hill walks and drives. **Abbeyfeale**, on the N21 south of Athea, surrounded by rolling hills, is another centre of traditional music, song and dance. It is also the gateway to Killarney and Tralee. To the east are the **Mullaghareirk Mountains**, which are forested mainly with the uniform evergreens so beloved of the Forestry Commission.

Adare and the Maigue Valley

About 10 miles (16km) from Limerick, going southwest on the N20/N21, **Adare** (*Ath Dara*: ford of the oak) is set in richly timbered land through which the little River Maigue flows. This village has attracted visitors for many years. There is only one wide street, Main Street, set on both sides with pretty thatched cottages, many of which

Courtenay Lodge, Newcastle West, t (069) 62244, *www.courtenaylodgehotel.com* (*moderate*). Comfortable but standard; close to some of Ireland's best golf courses.

Millbank House, Murroe, t (061) 386115, *www. millbankhouse.com* (*moderate*). Guests are made very welcome at this Georgian house on a farm. Fish for trout and salmon on the Mulcair River, which flows through it.

Ivy House, Craigue, Adare, t (061) 396270 (*inexpensive*). 3 rooms in an ivy-covered 18th-century house on the N21. *Open Mar–Oct.*

O'Driscolls B&B, Glin, t (061) 386115, *www.odriscolls-accommodation.com* (*inexpensive*). In the village; 4 homely rooms, with views onto a flower-filled garden and a lounge with open fire in winter.

Reens House, near Rathkeale, Ardagh, t (069) 64276 (*inexpensive*). 17th-century Jacobean house on a dairy farm. Open April–Oct.

Self-catering

Ballyteigue House, Rockhill, Bruree, t (063) 90575, *www.ballyteigue.com*. Gracious Georgian house for 9 with country-style interiors, plus a beautiful cottage for 6.

Finniterstown House, Adare, t (061) 396232, *www.tourismresources.ie/cht/finn.htm*. Early 19th-century home of the O'Grady Clan, in farmland with tennis courts. Sleeps 10.

Springfield Castle, Drumcollogher, t (063) 83162, *www.springfieldcastle.com*. Fabulous historic home for holiday lets; sleeps 14 plus 4 in a cottage in the grounds.

Eating Out

See also the hotel listings, above.

The Wild Geese Restaurant, Main Street, Adare, t (061) 396451, *www.thewild-geese.com* (*luxury*). Heady mix of classic French and modern Irish cooking at this award-winning restaurant. The table d'hôte dinner menu is slightly cheaper (€30 for 2 courses, €36 for 3).

The Mustard Seed, Echo Lodge, Ballingarry, t (069) 68508, *www.mustardseed.ie* (*expensive*). Delicious and imaginative food from organic sources; the smoked salmon with walnut oil is memorable.

M. J. Finnegan's, Dublin Road, Annacotty, just east of Limerick, t (061) 337338 (*moderate*). Excellent 18th-century pub food, with a rose garden and ceilidh music at weekends.

Worrall's Inn, Castleconnell, t (061) 377148 (*moderate*). Popular family-run restaurant with an extensive menu and wine list.

The Blue Door Restaurant, Adare, t (061) 396481 (*inexpensive*). Simple, good modern Irish food, with a daily menu.

Pubs

Duggan's, Bridge Street, Newcastle West. A fine selection of pints.

The Gables, Colbert Street, Athea. Enjoy traditional music here.

Paddy the Farmers, Annacotty. Cosy pub with lots of energy, once voted Pub of Distinction.

The Ramble Inn, Church Street, Abbeyfeale. Also good for Irish music.

are antique shops, craft shops or restaurants (one of them is the local tourist office). The village is noted for its fine ecclesiastical ruins, but first notice the restored village washing pool opposite the Trinitarian Abbey, just off Main Street. You can imagine the stories and scandal exchanged here as the village women washed their clothes.

The finest ruin is the **Franciscan Friary** (*in the grounds of Adare Manor Golf Club; ask at the entrance for permission to visit*) founded in 1464 by Thomas, Earl of Kildare and his wife. (The village belonged to the Kildare branch of the Fitzgeralds, or Geraldines.) The friary was attacked and burned by Parliamentary forces in 1539 and 1581, but its ruins are beautifully proportioned, and can be seen from the long narrow **bridge** of 14 arches (*c.* 1400) on the outskirts of the village (on the N20 going north). The modern village has grown up around the rest of the ecclesiastical buildings. The **Augustinian Priory**, now the Church of Ireland Church, was founded in 1315 by the Earl of Kildare. It was restored in 1807 by the first Earl of Dunraven. He and his family did much to protect the old buildings, and built the thatched cottages in Main Street in the 1820s.

His family used to own the Gothic Tudor Revival-style **Adare Manor** (now a luxury hotel, *see* p.136), whose lush parklands surround the village with elegant formal gardens. The **church** has some interesting carvings of animals and human heads, and gives a good idea of what an Irish medieval church must have looked like.

The ruined **Desmond Castle**, on the banks of the Maigue beside the bridge, was built in the 13th century on the site of an earlier ring fort. It is a fine example of feudal architecture with its square keep, curtain walls, two halls, kitchen, gallery and stables.

The area around Adare is known as the Palatine because of the number of Lutherans (refugees from southern Germany) who settled here in the 18th century under the patronage of Lord Southwell. The British Government encouraged them to come and paid their rents for a number of years. **Rathkeale**, 17 miles (27km) west of Adare, has a small **Irish Palatine Heritage Centre** (*open mid-May–mid-Sept Tues–Fri 10–12 and 2–5, Sun 2–5; adm €4; t (069) 64397, www.irishpalatines.org*) devoted to their history. The Palatines are credited with introducing crop rotation, and their descendants, bearing such names as Ruttle, Shier, Teskey and Switzer, are still numerous in the area. Rathkeale is one of the largest towns in County Limerick and is in the centre of the dairy farming region. It is notable for its fine, early 19th-century courthouse and doorways in the main street.

Castle Matrix (pronounced 'mattrix') (*open June–Aug daily 11–4; adm; t (069) 64284*), about a mile to the southwest, is a fine Geraldine tower house built in about 1410. The poet-Earl of Desmond, whose style epitomized the courtly love genre, lived here in the 1440s. The castle has been restored and houses a unique collection of documents relating to the Wild Geese, Irish soldiers who served so nobly in the Continental armies of the 17th and 18th centuries. Castle Matrix has the reputation for being the first place in Ireland where the potato was grown (though of course Youghal makes that claim too). According to local history, the poet Edmund Spenser met Walter Raleigh here in 1580, and they became great friends. When Raleigh returned from his successful voyage to America he presented some potatoes to their host, Lord Southwell, who cultivated them with some success. The Methodist movement in North America was initiated at Castle Matrix: Palatine refugees on the estate were converted by John Wesley, and in 1760 Philip Embury and Barbara Ruttle Heck sailed to New York and founded a church there.

A short distance southwest is **Ardagh**, famous for the chalice, brooches and bronze cup discovered in an ancient ring fort (now in the National Museum in Dublin). The chalice is wrought of gold, silver and bronze, and ornamented with enamel, amber and crystal. The 15th-century medieval **Desmond Hall** (*open mid-June–mid-Sept daily 9.30–6.30; adm adults €2, children €1; guided tours; t (069) 77408, www.heritage ireland.ie*), in the Square, is where the Earls of Desmond would once have held banquets. The hall has a fine oak musician's gallery and limestone hooded hearth, with a vaulted lower chamber and tower.

Croom, right in the middle of County Limerick and in a charming position on the River Maigue, is celebrated as the meeting place of the 18th-century Gaelic poets of the Maigue. Here the light verse of the limerick was first popularized and later taken up by Edward Lear. (Their poetry is available in translation; it is unforgettable for its wit and feeling.) An old Geraldine **castle** is hidden behind a wall on the southern approach to the village. Croom was frequently attacked by the O'Briens whose territory it bordered. Their battle cry was 'The strong hand forever!' (*'Lamh laid ir abu!'*) and it was always met by the rallying cry of the Geraldines, 'Croom forever!' (*'Cromadh abu!'*). The old grain mill at **Croom Mills** (*open April–Oct daily 10–5; café and craft shop open all year; t (061) 397130, www.croommills.com*), with its 16ft water wheel, has been restored as a working mill and heritage centre.

Knockfierna Hill, 6 miles (10km) southwest of Croom, is a fine place for a walk. It is held sacred to the *Dé Danaan*, King of the Other World, or Death, *Donn Forinne*, and translates as 'the hill of truth'. From the summit you can see a great expanse of blue mountains and the pale Shannon Estuary. This area was badly affected in the famine and you can see restored cottages at the **Famine Park** near Ballingarry (*see* p.79).

Lough Gur

Lough Gur, 11 miles (17km) south of Limerick City, is guarded by the remains of two **castles** built by the Earls of Desmond. Legend holds that the last of the Desmonds is doomed to hold court under Lough Gur and to emerge, fully armed, at daybreak on every morning of the seventh year in a routine that must be repeated until the silver shoes of his horse are worn away. As if to echo the story, the lake is horseshoe-shaped. Lough Gur is rich in field-antiquities, revealed when the water level was lowered by drainage in the 19th century. Man has been here since 3000 BC and you can see **stone circles**, wedge-shaped **graves**, a **crannog**, a **ring fort** and **Neolithic house sites**. The impressive **Interpretative Centre** (*open May–Sept daily 10–6; guided tours; adm; t (061) 385186, www.shannonheritage.com*), built as two Neolithic dwellings with steeply pitched, thatched roofs and wattle fences, has an excellent audiovisual exhibition explaining the history of the Lough Gur area from the Stone Age.

Kilmallock, about 11 miles (17km) south of Lough Gur on the R512, is in the rich land of the Golden Vale. It was founded by St Mocheallog, and received a charter in the time of Edward III, during which period it was heavily fortified. Built by the Geraldines (Fitzgeralds), it was a centre of Desmond power between the 14th and 16th centuries, and was partially destroyed during the Desmond Rebellion. It was also used in the Cromwellian and Williamite wars, when its fortifications were destroyed. The 15th-century **King's Castle** still stands in the centre of town; it has the appearance of a tower house, but as well as being a citadel it has been used as an arsenal, a school and a blacksmith's. **Blossom's Gateway** is a surviving remnant of the town's medieval walls, and is one of the best examples of its kind in Ireland. **Kilmallock Museum** (*open daily 1.30–5; guided tours of the town available; t (063) 91300*), near the castle, has a small collection of relics from the town's past and models of medieval Kilmallock and its Stone-Age counterpart, recently excavated nearby. There is a beautiful ruined 13th-century **Dominican Priory** (known locally as 'the abbey') across the river, dating from the 13th century. A pillar in the aisle arcade shows a ball flower ornament, which is very rare in Ireland though it was common in England during the 14th century.

To the south of Kilmallock are the **Ballyhoura Mountains**, which straddle the border with County Cork, pleasant farming country with opportunities for pony trekking and walking. The slight remains of a **round tower** can be seen beside a **holy well** at **Ardpatrick**. Two miles south of Ardpatrick, in the demesne of Castle Oliver, Marie Gilbert was born in 1818. She rose to become Lola Montez, the mistress of King Ludwig I of Bavaria.

Approximately 12 miles (18km) to the east, outside the village of Galbally, a lovely walk may be made up **Duntryleague Hill** where you can explore a megalithic **passage tomb** and the remains of a **stone circle**.

Bruree, 4 miles (7km) to the west of Kilmallock on the R518, is the place where Eamon de Valera grew up. His mother came from here; his father was a Spaniard. De Valera was born in Manhattan, but when his father died his mother sent him back here at the age of two to be reared by his grandmother. The school he went to is now the **De Valera Museum and Bruree Heritage Centre** (*open Mon–Fri 10–5, Sat–Sun 2–5; adm adults €5, children €2.50; t (063) 90900*). He became a maths teacher and joined the Gaelic League, beginning his lifelong championship of the Irish language. He is referred to affectionately in Ireland as 'Dev'. An old corn mill with a huge **millwheel**, the second largest in Ireland, is a striking view as you enter the village from the west.

East of Limerick

Castleconnell, 6 miles (9km) from Limerick, is a pretty Georgian spa town on the Shannon. **Murroe** (also spelt Moroe) and the Clare Glens are on the northeastern borders of Limerick, about 10 miles (16km) from Limerick City on the R506. Murroe lies under the foothills of the **Slievefelim Mountains**, and is dominated by the 19th-century mansion of **Glenstal**, which was built by the Barrington family as a massive Norman Revival castle. The Barringtons left it in 1921 after Winifred, a daughter of the house, was shot dead in an ambush while travelling with an army officer and a District Inspector of the RIC. Now a Benedictine monastery, **Glenstal Abbey** (*www.glenstal.org*) is the only Benedictine boys' school in Ireland, and is a centre for the promotion of ecumenicalism. It has a remarkable collection of Russian icons, and the church is open to the general public for Mass and Benediction. The monks will always make you welcome; they sell beautiful hand-turned wooden bowls, books by Glenstal monks and others, and music in their shop. The wooded grounds are very beautiful in May and June when the rhododendrons are out.

The Barringtons donated the **Clare Glens** to the County Councils of Limerick and North Tipperary for the pleasure of the public. The Glens, 3 miles (5km) north of Murroe, are not so much glens as a scenic gorge with sparkling waterfalls. There is a nature trail which leads you through this beautiful wooded place.

A further 4 miles or so west, at **Clonkeen**, is a small rectangular church, about 12th-century, with a richly decorated Irish Romanesque doorway and north wall window.

County Kerry

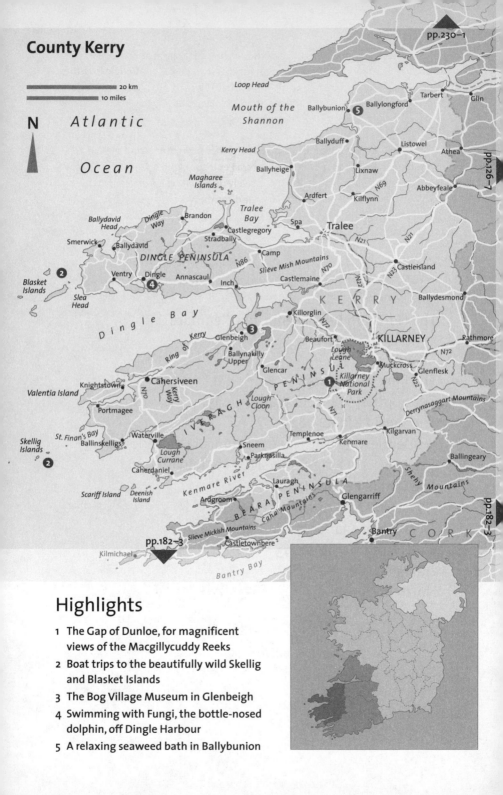

County Kerry

20 km
10 miles

N

Atlantic

Ocean

pp.230–1
pp.126–7
pp.182–3

Loop Head

Mouth of the Shannon

Ballybunion ⑤ Ballylongford   Tarbert   Glin

Kerry Head   Ballyduff   Listowel   Athea

Ballyheige   Lixnaw   N69   Abbeyfeale

Magharee Islands   Ardfert   Kilflynn

Tralee Bay   Spa   **Tralee**

Ballydavid Head   Dingle Way   Brandon   Castlegregory   N21   N21

Smerwick   Ballydavid   Stradbally   Camp   Castleisland   N23

DINGLE PENINSULA   N86   *Slieve Mish Mountains*   N70

Blasket Islands ②   Ventry   Dingle ④   Annascaul   Inch   Castlemaine   N22   K E R R Y   Ballydesmond

Slea Head   Killorglin   N72   **KILLARNEY**   Rathmore

Dingle Bay   Glenbeigh ③   Beaufort   Lough Leane   Muckross   N72   Glenflesk

Ring of   Kerry   Ballynakilly Upper   Glencar   *Killarney National Park*   N22

Knightstown   **Cahersiveen**   Kerry Way   N70   P E N I N S U L A   *Derrynasaggart Mountains*

Valentia Island   Portmagee   I V E R A G H   Lough Cloon   N71

Skellig Islands ②   St. Finan's Bay   Ballinskelligs   Waterville   Lough Currane   Sneem   Templenoe   Kilgarvan   Ballingeary

Scariff Island   Deenish Island   Caherdaniel   Parknasilla   Kenmare   *Shehy Mountains*

Kenmare River   Lauragh   P E N I N S U L A   Glengarriff

Ardgroom   B E A R A   *Caha Mountains*   C O R K

Kilmichael   *Slieve Mickish Mountains*   Castletownbere   **Bantry**

Bantry Bay

Highlights

1 The Gap of Dunloe, for magnificent views of the Macgillycuddy Reeks
2 Boat trips to the beautifully wild Skellig and Blasket Islands
3 The Bog Village Museum in Glenbeigh
4 Swimming with Fungi, the bottle-nosed dolphin, off Dingle Harbour
5 A relaxing seaweed bath in Ballybunion

Kerry (*Ciarraí*, Ciar's people) is packed with some of the most beautiful scenery in Ireland and the friendliest folk. It is a kingdom all of its own, whose people love to use words with skill, flamboyance and humour. An irregularly shaped county with long fingers of land reaching into the sea, it boasts the opulent lakes of Killarney at its centre, set amongst the wooded slopes of the Macgillycuddy's Reeks, the grandest mountain range in the land. To the west are the peninsulas of Iveragh and Dingle, dear to every traveller who sees their splendour, where mountains and sea are jumbled together in a glory of colour. The Beara Peninsula, which Kerry shares with County Cork, has an equal beauty but is relatively unexplored. Every year small farmers create a pattern of golden hay ricks and cornfields, and wild flowers grow in the hawthorn hedges and handkerchief fields where the black Kerry cow grazes – when she's not creating a jam in the narrow country lanes. One exotic plant which has colonized the southwest to its advantage is the scarlet-blossomed fuchsia; other subtropical plants thrive too, due to of the warming effects of the Gulf Stream.

Off the coast are some fascinating islands that it is possible to visit with some perseverance. On the Skellig Rocks, the word of God has been praised and celebrated for six hundred years. Valentia is a soft, easy island by comparison, connected to the mainland by a causeway. The Blaskets, three miles out to sea, are beautiful but deserted: the community of subsistence farmers and fishing folk that the islanders recorded in a couple of lyrical biographies, sadly, is gone.

The possibilities for enjoying yourself in County Kerry are numerous. If you're motoring around the narrow country lanes you'll see the most superb views of seascape, hill and valley. (But don't try to do too much driving in one day, for the roads are very twisty and each bend holds more alluring beauty – you can end up driving too much and exploring too quickly.) County Kerry's hotels and restaurants are generally of a very high standard, and the seafood and salmon are all that could be desired. Sailing, deep-sea fishing, diving and water skiing are all easy to arrange, as are golf, game fishing, horse-riding and walking in the heathery mountains. For those who most like to wander among gardens and around historic buildings, there are several properties open to the public. (One of the most famous is Derrynane House, the house of Daniel O'Connell, 'the Great Liberator'.) For those interested in the ancient past, Kerry is scattered with ogham stones, standing stones, forts and the beehive-shaped cells called clochans, the stone huts of holy men. Interpretative centres have opened up to educate those interested in local history and to cater for the coach tours.

You should expect some rainy weather and cloud, for County Kerry is notoriously wet and warm.

History

A brief historical outline must start, as always, back in the time of the Bronze Age, some 4,500 years ago. Miners from Spain and Portugal were attracted by the precious metals to be found in the mountains, and it is still possible to find traces of their mines and their assembly places, which are marked with stone circles, rock carvings and wedge tombs. From the wealth of legend that remains of the later Bronze Age

Getting There and Around

By Air

Kerry airport is about 12 miles north of Killarney on the N23. There is no shuttle bus service from the airport. A **taxi** to Killarney city centre will cost approximately €20. **Kerry Airport, t** (066) 976 4644, *www.kerryairport.ie*.

By Bus or Train

The rail and bus **stations** are located next to each other, by the Great Southern Hotel on Park Road, which is a few minutes from the town centre.

Kerry is linked to Dublin by a good **train** line from Killarney (**t** (064) 31067).

Bus Eireann (**t** (064) 30011) provides a good **bus service** to many parts of the county. In July and August they run daily **coach tours** round the Ring of Kerry and the peninsula from Killarney and Tralee, *see* p.157.

By Ferry

If you're driving from Shannon Airport you can save yourself some time by avoiding Limerick City and taking the **Killimer–Tarbert car ferry**, *see* **County Clare** p.232.

By Bike

Killarney Rent-a-Bike, Old Market Lane, Main Street, Killarney, **t** (064) 32578. Gives out a free map with rentals.

O'Sullivan's Bike Shop, Bishop's Lane, New Street, **t** (064) 31282.

Trailways Outdoor Centre, College Street, **t** (064) 39929. Also arranges tours and accommodation.

Car Hire

National, Kerry Airport, **t** (021) 432 0755, *www.carhire.ie*.

Randles Irish Car Rental, Kerry Airport, **t** (064) 31232, *www.irishcarrentals.com*.

Getting to Islands off Kerry

Bring something to eat and drink with you, as well as some all-weather gear. Note that all trips are weather-dependent.

Blasket Islands

The **Blasket Island Boatmen** sail from Dunquin Pier every half-hour from 10am in summer, **t** (066) 915 6422.

The *Peig Sayers* sails from Dingle, **t** (066) 915 1344, *www.greatblasketisland.com*; her owners offer an overnight package including dinner, B&B and the return trip to the islands (€70pp).

Skellig Islands

The fragile environment on Great Skellig means a limit is set on how many people can visit, so reservations are essential in high season. Fares cost around €32 and average journey time is 50mins.

Ballinskelligs Watersports go from Ballinskelligs Pier (**t** (066) 947 9182).

Michael O'Sullivan does the trip from Waterville (**t** (066) 947 4255).

Boats also sail from Portmagee or Valentia: **Pat and Des Lavelle**, **t** (066) 947 6124, *indigo.ie/~lavelles*. Husband-and-wife team who are both experts on the Skelligs .

A **water bus tour** is available from the Skellig Experience Heritage Centre on Valentia Island, **t** (066) 947 6306.

and early Iron Age (500 BC), it is possible to build up a picture of society as it was then: hierarchical, aristocratic and warlike. There were no towns, and cattle-raising and raiding dominated everything. Farmers lived in ring forts and on crannogs for defensive reasons. Writing was confined to an archaic form of Irish, which you can see on the ogham stones scattered around the county. Kerry beaches were the landing places for many of the legendary invasions, voyages and battles of Ireland's past. The miners who sailed into the bays from Spain are recorded in legend, as are the other waves of settlers.

Christianity came in the 5th century and great changes began. The old tribal centres went into decline, and powerful new kingdoms emerged, often with an abbot-prince

Valentia Island

You can get here over the **bridge** at Portmagee, or a **car ferry** runs in season between Reenard Point and Knightstown (cars €4 return, pedestrians €3; journey 5mins; t (066) 947 6141).

Festivals

March
St Patrick's Week, including a **Great Parade** (17th), and **Roaring 1920s Festival**.

April
Samhlaíocht **Easter Arts Festival**, Tralee. Programme of music, dancing and street entertainment; www.samhlaiocht.com.

May
Killarney Races, Killarney Racecourse, t (064) 31125.
Féile na Bealtaine, May Day festivals in Dingle and Ballyferriter; www.feilenabealtaine.ie.
Listowel Writers' Week, a literary festival; www.writersweek.ie
Walking Festival, Kenmare (late May–early June); www.kenmarewalking.com.
Siamsa Tíre, National Folk Theatre of Ireland, Tralee. Music, folklore and dance (May–Sept); www.siamsatire.com.

June
International Bachelor Festival, Ballybunion.
Kerry Festival of Music, Kenmare, traditional music.
Tralee Races, Ballybeggan, t (066) 712 6490, www.traleehorseracing.com.

July
Killarney Races, Killarney, t (064) 31125.
Cahirsiveen Festival of Music and the Arts, www.celticmusicfestival.com.
Castlegregory Summer Festival (mid-July).
Féile Lughnasa, Cloghane and Brandon, includes a pilgrimage to Mount Brandon; www.irishcelticfest.com.

August
Rose of Tralee Competition, Tralee, www.roseoftralee.ie. Major festival and beauty contest.
Puck Fair, Killorglin (10–12th), www.puckfair.ie.
Races and Regatta, Dingle.
Tralee Races, Ballybeggan, t (066) 712 6490, www.traleehorseracing.com.
Fleadh Cheoil na hEireann, Clonmel. Celebration of Irish culture, music, song and dance; www.clonmelfleadh.com.
Blessing of the Boats, Dingle Pier (one Sunday in late Aug or early Sept).

September
Listowel Harvest Festival and Races, includes the Harvest Queen competition, street entertainment, races and marching bands. Very popular with the farming community.

October
Patrick O'Keeffe Traditional Music Festival, Castleisland.

December
Wren Boys' Festival, Dingle and Listowel (26th), parades, music and fireworks in an ancient tradition.

at their heads. A strong monastic structure grew up and some monasteries became great centres of learning. The monks learnt the art of writing and recorded the sagas and legends. Many of these centres were in inhospitable locations – the 'dysart' of some place names. In Kerry there is the wonderfully preserved 7th-century foundation on Skellig Michael.

In the upheavals and faction-fighting of the 11th and 12th centuries, three ruling families emerged in Kerry as definite clans: the MacCarthys south of Killarney; the O'Donoghues around Killarney; and the O'Sullivans around the Kenmare Rivers. These are names that crop up again and again in Kerry's history, right up to today. In the 13th century, with the arrival of the Anglo-Normans, the Fitzgeralds and other closely related fighting men established strongholds throughout the region. They became the Palatine Earls of Desmond (*Deas Munhan*, West Munster) and brought with them many tenants and fighting men who introduced the common Kerry names of Walsh, Browne, Chute, Landers, Ashe and Ferriter. The Earls of Desmond became so powerful that they were able to maintain an independence from the centralizing efforts of the English monarchs right up until the reign of Elizabeth I. They adopted many of the old Irish traditions, language, laws and dress; poetry and music flourished under their patronage. The last Earl took part in a rebellion against Elizabeth and lost his lands and his life, and even in this remote part the Gaelic way of life began to disappear. Another branch of the Fitzgeralds who crop up again and again in Irish history were the Earls of Kildare, eventually the Dukes of Leinster. The son of the first Duke, Lord Edward Fitzgerald, was a United Irishman and very involved in the plans for the Rising of 1798, although he died in prison, after the organization was infiltrated by informers. The county was reorganized in 1606 into the shape we know today, and the new landowners were largely English Protestants. The political destruction of the 17th century is wonderfully recorded in the laments and satires of the poets of Munster. This short verse of David O'Bruadair (*c.* 1625–98) sums up what the poets felt:

> Sad for those without sweet Anglo-Saxon
> Now that Ormonde has come to Erin
> For the rest of my life in the land of Conn
> I'll do better with English than a poem.
> version by John Montague

Kerry produced perhaps the greatest Irish leader there has ever been in the shape of Daniel O'Connell, who in 1829 won Catholic emancipation, not only for the Irish, but for all Catholics under British rule. He came from an old Gaelic family who had managed to hold on to their lands and to get along with their Protestant neighbours.

The famine of 1847 and the emigration that followed reduced the population of Kerry as it did all over Ireland. Nowadays Kerry is a land of small farmers and relies on the tourist industry. Other industries include food processing, the manufacture of animal feed, pharmaceutical and small engine manufacturing, dairying and automotive manufacture. The population of County Kerry is approximately 132,500, although this swells considerably during the tourist season.

The Northern Beara Peninsula, Kenmare and Killarney

The route into County Kerry via County Cork is spectacular. However, instead of going straight to the large town of Killarney, you might like to start by exploring Kerry's portion of the quiet Beara Peninsula. Around **Lauragh** and the **Cloonee Loughs**, the waterfalls and lakes are lovely and relatively free of tourists. An unmarked road off the R571 will take you up to a wonderful view over the Beara Peninsula, the

Cloonee Loughs and Inchiquin Lough. Across the lough is **Uragh** (or Lauragh) **Wood**, a survivor of the primeval oak woods that once covered most of Ireland. Uragh is a mixture of native oak and sessile oaks that are distinguished by their curious hunched branches.

There is a beautifully planted garden at **Derreen Gardens** (*open April–Oct Fri–Sun 10–6, daily in Aug; adm adults €5, children €2; t (064) 83588*), near Lauragh on the R571, where the moist climate gives the plants a tropical vigour. As you walk through the winding paths and tunnels of deep shade cast by the delicate bamboo, blue eucalyptus and tousled rhododendrons, there are glorious glimpses of sea and wild mountain country. Stately North American conifers and New Zealand tree ferns also decorate the garden. The land, and thousands of acres around it, used to belong to Sir William Petty, who was responsible for the mapping of two-thirds of Ireland after the Cromwellian Conquest. He is blamed for denuding many of the oak woods over a large area, especially around Caragh, as fuel for his ironworks, although his descendants (who were further ennobled with the marquisate of Lansdowne) planted the gardens and woods you see today, and also laid out Kenmare.

Leave yourself at least a couple of hours to wander around **Kenmare** (*Neidín*), a pretty, colourful 19th-century market town at the head of the River Kenmare's broad estuary. The town is full of excellent cafés, pubs, restaurants and shops. The colours of woven rugs, jerseys and tweeds on sale here echo the beautiful surrounding countryside perfectly. Fine silver jewellery and good quality ceramics by local artists are to be found in the many craft shops, and there is a wide range of books of local interest to enhance your background knowledge.

It is worth seeking out the Neolithic **stone circle**, reputedly the biggest in Southwest Ireland, along the banks of the River Finnihy. To get there, walk up the road to the right of the Market House (home to the tourist office); the stone circle is signposted and you'll see it on the right overlooking the river.

Back on the town square and above the tourist office is the **Heritage Centre** (*open Easter–Sept Mon–Sat 10–6; July–Aug Sun 11–5*), where an exhibition explores the career of Sir William Petty and the history of the area. Another attraction of note is the **Kenmare Lace Centre** (*open Mon–Sat 10–5.30; adm; t (064) 41491*), also on the square, where you can look at a display of the point lace made locally, and even see demonstrations. The shop sells some wonderful examples of delicate Irish laceware.

This is marvellous walking country, and you can base yourself in Kenmare to savour the views of the rolling Kerry Hills, the Macgillycuddy's Reeks and the Caha Mountains on the Cork border. It's an ideal location because two of Ireland's long distance walking routes, the Kerry Way and the Beara Way, converge in the town. In May, Kenmare is busy with keen walkers taking part in the **Walking Festival** (*see* p.145). This also links to the West Cork Walking Festival (see p.185), which takes place in different locations in West Cork each year (Rosscarbery in 2005).

On the main road to Cork is the village of **Kilgarvan** (*Cill Gharbháin*). Just outside, towards Kenmare, is the **Michael J. Quill Centre**, based in the former St Peter's Church (*t (064) 85511*). This training centre for people with learning difficulties has a gift shop

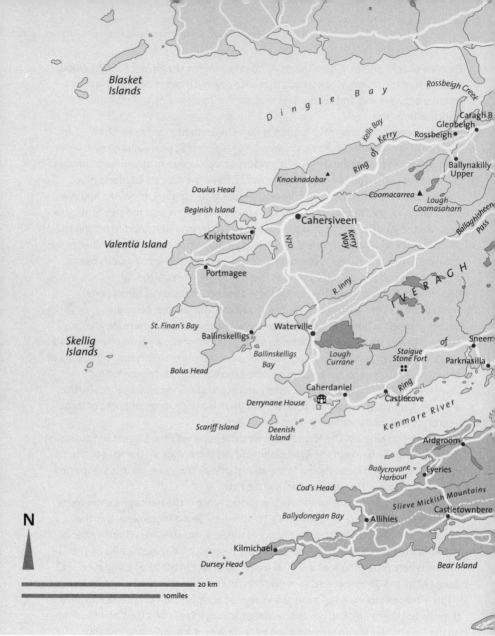

Blasket
Islands

Dingle Bay

Rossbeigh Creek

Kells Bay

Ring of Kerry

Caragh B
Glenbeigh
Rossbeigh

Ballynakilly
Upper

Knocknadobar ▲

Doulus Head

Coomacarrea ▲
Lough
Coomasaharn

Beginish Island

Ballaghisheen Pass

Cahersiveen

Kerry
Way

Knightstown

Valentia Island

N70

Portmagee

IVERAGH

R. Inny

St. Finan's Bay

Waterville

of

Skellig
Islands

Ballinskelligs

Sneem

Ballinskelligs
Bay

Lough
Currane

Staigue
Stone Fort

Parknasilla

Bolus Head

Caherdaniel

Ring

Derrynane House

Castlecove

Kenmare River

Scariff Island

Deenish
Island

Ardgroom

Ballycrovane
Harbour

Eyeries

Cod's Head

Slieve Mickish Mountains

Ballydonegan Bay

Allihies

Castletownbere

Kilmichael

Dursey Head

Bear Island

N

20 km
10 miles

selling handcrafts, some of which are made by the trainees, and also provides guided walks of the area, of between two and four hours. Its name commemorates the founder of the Transport Workers Union of America, who was a native of the village.

The family-run **Kilgarvan Motor Museum** (*open Tues–Sat 9.30–6; adm adults €3.17, children €1.27;* **t** *(064) 85346, www.kenmare.net/jjmitchell*), at Slaheny, contains a passionately built collection of classic and vintage cars including examples from Rolls Royce, MG and Alvis.

The Beara Peninsula and the Ring of Kerry

The N71 from Kenmare to Killarney is very twisty and very steep, but you'll see the landscape is quite spectacular as you find yourself borne high aloft green fields and rock-strewn hills.

On the way, outside Kenmare, is **St Mary's Holy Well**, which is still much visited since the waters are reputed to have strong healing powers. Once you have climbed to the top of the mountain and through Moll's Gap, you get wonderful views of Killarney's lakes and woods.

Tourist Information

Kenmare: Kenmare Heritage Centre, **t** (064) 41233, *www.corkkerry.ie*; *open June–Sept.*

Shopping

Art and Crafts

Black Abbey Crafts, 28 Main Street, Kenmare, **t** (064) 42115. Unusual, tasteful handcrafts.

De Barra, Main Street, Kenmare. Silversmith producing unique Celtic jewellery.

Anam Cré, Rusheens, Ballygriffin, Kenmare, **t** (064) 41849, *www.kenmare-pottery.com*. Beautiful handmade ceramics and crafts.

Michael J Quill Centre, **t** (064) 85511, Kilgarvan. Charity-run centre selling handmade crafts.

Books

Noel and Holland Books, 3 Bridge Street, Kenmare, **t** (064) 42464.

Food

The Pantry, 30 Henry Street, Kenmare, **t** (064) 42233. Organic produce, home-made bread and Capparoe goat's cheese – everything you need for a picnic.

Textiles

Cleo's, 2 Shelbourne Street, Kenmare, **t** (064) 41410. Very tempting shop for top quality, modern tweeds, linen and woven rugs.

Kenmare Lace Centre, The Square, Kenmare, **t** (064) 41491. Locally made lace.

Nostalgia, 27 Henry Street, Kenmare, **t** (064) 41389. New and antique linen and lace.

Quill's, Kenmare **t** (064) 41078. Old-style shop selling Aran sweaters, golfing gear, shoes and gifts.

Avoca, Moll's Gap, *www.avoca.ie*. Woven fabrics and knitwear in beautiful colours.

Sports and Activities

Golf

Kenmare Golf Club, Killowen, Kenmare, **t** (064) 41291, *www.kenmaregolfclub.com*. Parkland course.

Ring of Kerry Golf & Country Club, Templenoe, **t** (064) 42000, *www.ringof kerrygolf.com*.

Pony Trekking

Dromquinna Stables, Kenmare, **t** (064) 41043.

Spas

Sámas, The Park Hotel, Kenmare, **t** (064) 41200, *www.samaskenmare.com*. Stylish, modern day-spa where you can indulge in facials, massage, body wraps and thermal treatments, or bathe in the tranquil outdoor 'infinity' pool, which has views over Kenmare bay.

Sheen Falls Lodge Health Spa, Kenmare, **t** (064) 41600, *www.sheenfallslodge.ie*. Massage, body wraps, beauty treatments and fitness facilities, including a 15m pool.

Water Sports

There is excellent deep-sea fishing in the Kenmare River Estuary. Brown trout fishing takes place on the Kenmare River.

Seafari, 3 The Pier, Kenmare, **t** (064) 42059, *www.seafariireland.com*. Guided cruises introducing the local marine wildlife. Other activities include fishing expeditions, kayaking and water-skiing.

Kenmare Bay Diving Centre, Kenmare, **t** (064) 42238.

Dromquinna Manor, Kenmare, **t** (064) 41657. Fishing, water-skiing, tube riding, windsurfing, canoeing or tennis.

Where to Stay

Kenmare **t** (064) –

The Park Hotel, High Street, **t** 41200, *www.parkkenmare.com* (*luxury*). Château-style, well-reputed hotel with a de luxe spa, *Sámas* (*see above*), and modern comforts in rooms furnished with antiques. The dining room serves an outstanding seafood-oriented menu compiled by chef Joe Ryan.

Sheen Falls Lodge, **t** 41600, *www.sheenfalls lodge.ie* (*luxury*). Set in a beautiful location with sunny, low-key décor. The rooms are elegant, the **restaurant** is lavish and imaginative and there is even a helipad for visiting dignitaries. There's also an on-site health spa (*see above*).

Sallyport House, **t** 42066, *www.sallyporthouse. com* (*expensive*). Spacious 1930s house, built by the Arthur family, now completely modernized and refurbished. Set in peaceful surroundings overlooking Kenmare Harbour.

Brook Lane Hotel, t 42077 (*moderate*). Self-branded 'boutique' hotel with reasonable prices and modern, neutral decor. Pleasant, but other places have more character.

Dromquinna Manor, t 41657 (*moderate*). Very comfortable Victorian manor with lovely views over the water and water-skiing and horse-riding nearby.

Hawthorne House, Shelbourne Street, **t** 41035 (*moderate*). Extremely comfortable, modern house with *en suite* rooms. The food is delicious and lavish.

Lansdowne Arms, William Street, **t** 41368 (*moderate*). Friendly, family-run hotel.

The Lodge, Kilgarvan Road, **t** 41512, *www.thelodgekenmare.com* (*moderate*). Ten rooms in a newly built, smartly styled guesthouse opposite Kenmare Golf Club. Wheelchair-adapted room available.

Muxnaw Lodge, t 41252, *www.muxnawlodge.com* (*moderate–inexpensive*). Hannah Boland's attractive house was built in 1801 and overlooks Kenmare Bay, within walking distance of town. There is an all-weather tennis court and good gardens and walks.

Shelburne Lodge, t 41013 (*moderate–inexpensive*). Georgian farmhouse with lovely rooms, individually furnished, with antiques and polished wooden floors. Run by two of the best restaurateurs in Kerry, Tom and Maura Foley, who provide scrumptious home-made breakfasts.

Atlantic Lodge, t 42666, *www.atlanticlodge-kenmare.com* (*inexpensive*). Newish, family-run hotel set in fields, five minutes' walk from the town. It has large rooms and a relaxed atmosphere.

Driftwood, Killowen, **t** 89147, *www.driftwoodkenmare.com* (*inexpensive*). Lovely B&B with bright, airy rooms, stripped pine furniture and a log fire in the guest lounge.

Lake House, Cloonee, Tuosist, **t** 84205 (*inexpensive*). Friendly pub and restaurant with guest accommodation above, run by Mary O'Shea. Highly recommended, especially for its beautiful lakeside setting. *Open Easter–Oct.*

Rose Cottage, t 41330 (*inexpensive*). Family-run B&B in the town centre, in an old stone terraced cottage.

Eating Out

Kenmare **t** (064) –

The Park Hotel, High Street, Kenmare, **t** 41200 (*luxury*). Delicious French cuisine in grand surroundings. Ideal for a special occasion or a treat.

An Leath Phingin, 35 Main Street, Kenmare, **t** 41559 (*moderate*). Northern Italian chef, Maria, makes her own fresh pasta, *risotti* and scrumptious sauces. The stone-oven pizzas are also popular.

The Boathouse Restaurant, Dromquinna Manor, The Quay, Kenmare, **t** 41788 (*moderate*). Fine seafood and sweeping views down by the harbour.

Darcy's Old Bank House, Main Street, Kenmare, **t** 41589 (*moderate*). Well-established, local favourite with constantly innovative specialities and colourful décor.

The Lime Tree, Shelbourne Street, Kenmare, **t** 41225 (*moderate*). American-style café with plenty of atmosphere.

Packies, 35 Henry Street, Kenmare, **t** 41508 (*moderate*). Excellent fish restaurant: unpretentious, skilful cooking with the best ingredients. *Reservations essential.*

Café Indigo, The Square, Kenmare, **t** 42356 (*inexpensive*). Very trendy daytime haunt for beautiful, young locals and tourists, with an esoteric seafood menu and minimalist decoration. The pub downstairs, **The Square Pint**, is good for traditional entertainment on summer evenings.

The Horseshoe Bar and Restaurant, 3 Main Street, Kenmare, **t** 41553 (*inexpensive*). Friendly, informal bistro with a charcoal grill.

The New Delight, 18 Henry Street, Kenmare, **t** 42350 (*inexpensive*). A big treat for vegetarians and vegans is this wholesome café, serving imaginative food and organic wine.

The Purple Heather, Henry Street, Kenmare, **t** 41016 (*inexpensive*). Good for lunch-time snacks, home-made soups and seafood. There is a very cosy fire in the bar to relax in front of.

The Wander Inn, 2 Henry Street, Kenmare, **t** 42700 (*inexpensive*). Perfect venue for the classic combination of a plate of Irish stew, a pint of Guinness and traditional Irish music.

Killarney

Killarney (*Cill Áirne*, church of the sloes) is a resort town that only began to grow up in the 1750s, when tourism in Kerry first became popular. The town itself is not the attraction but the combination of lakes, woods, mountains and the stunning light and skies in the surrounding countryside, which remain beautiful and unspoiled. If you are prepared to walk in the mountains and the National Park, away from well-worn tracks, you will find that the luxuriant green of the woods, the soft air, the vivid

Tourist Information

Killarney: *Áras Fáilte*, Beech Road, **t** (064) 31633, *www.corkkerry.ie*; *open all year*.

Shopping

Crafts

Brian de Staic, 18 High Street, Killarney, **t** (064) 33822, *www.briandestaic.com*. Craft jewellery.
Bricín Craft Shop & Restaurant, 26 High Street, Killarney, **t** (064) 34902.
Blarney Woollen Mills, Main Street, Killarney, *www.blarney.com*.
Kerry Crafted Glass, Kilcummin, **t** (064) 43295, *www.irishkerryglass.com*.
Kerry Woollen Mills, Beaufort, **t** (064) 44122. The real thing – a woollen mill producing proper scratchy blankets. *Open daily 9–5, closed Sat–Sun during Nov–Feb.*

Sports and Activities

Golf

Killarney Golf and Fishing Club, Mahony's Point, **t** (064) 31034, *www.killarney-golf.com*. Championship courses next to Lough Leane.
Beaufort Golf Club, Churchtown, Beaufort, **t** (064) 44440, *www.beaufortgolfclub.com*.

Spas

Killarney Park Hotel, Kenmare Place, **t** 35555, *www.killarneyparkhotel.ie/thespa*. Eight therapy suites, offering beauty, massage and relaxation treatments, as well as a pool, outdoor hot tub and fitness suite.

Touring Around the Gap of Dunloe

Tours in Killarney National Park and through the Gap of Dunloe can be booked in town or at

the Gap. You can take a horse-drawn 'jaunting car' from Killarney or Kate Kearney's. The cost will depend on the distance (€30–50). During the trip the jarveys (drivers) will regale you with stories; they have gained a reputation for telling visitors exactly what they expect to hear: stories of legends, leprechauns, you name it. If the expense of a **boat trip** down the three lakes doesn't appeal, you can always hire a **bike**, walk or catch a bus. There are half- or full-day **coach trips**, and **ponies** can be hired to explore the Gap of Dunloe, on the outskirts of Killarney (only advised for experienced riders).
Tangney Tours, Kinvara House, Muckross Road, **t** (064) 33358. Jarvey tours from Kenmare Place, opposite the International Hostel.
Castlelough Vintage Tours, 17 High Street, Killarney, **t** (064) 32496. Combined day tour of the area by bus, jaunting car and boat.
Lily of Killarney, 3 High Street, Killarney, **t** (064) 31068. Covered 'water coach' tours of Lough Leane with commentary; daily departures in summer from Ross Castle 10.30–5.45.
Killarney Stables, Ballydowney, **t** (064) 31686, *www.horsevacationireland.com*. Pony treks around Killarney National Park.
O'Sullivan's Cycles, Bishop's Lane, New Street, **t** 31282. Bicycle hire.

Walking

Killarney National Park and the country around the Macgillycuddy's Reeks has some of the best, most arduous ridge-walking country in Ireland. The **Glen of Cummeenduff** leads to the heart of the Reeks, or there's the equally desolate and stunning **Glen of Owenreagh**. The **Kerry Way** is a hiking trail that begins in Killarney and passes Muckross Lake before climbing to some dramatic scenery around Torc Mountain and Windy Gap. The trail goes on to Kenmare and from there clean around the Iveragh Peninsula – the hiker's version of blue of the lakes and the craggy mountains above will have the same charm for you as they have for countless travellers since the 18th century.

Killarney does have one thing to offer sightseers: the Gothic Revival **St Mary's Cathedral**, built in silvery limestone by Augustus Pugin in the 1840s. You will find it in Cathedral Place, a continuation of New Street, possibly on the site of the 'church of the sloes' from which Killarney takes its name. It is a successful building: austere and graceful, with good stained glass. The cathedral was not finished completely until 1908, partly because it served as a hospital during the famine. Pugin's fine interior

the Ring of Kerry. Take waterproof gear because the weather comes straight in off the Atlantic. Visibility is often very poor, with wreaths of mist on the hills.

Where to Stay

Killarney t (064–)

Hotel *Ard na Sidhe*, Lough Caragh, t (066) 976 9105, *www.killarneyhotels.ie* (*luxury–expensive*). Beautiful 1913 manor on Lough Caragh with country-house décor: antiques, chintz and fresh flowers. The dining room serves international and Irish cuisine.

Cahernane House Hotel, Muckross Road, t 31895, *www.cahernane.com* (*luxury*). 19th-century residence built for the Earls of Pembroke, now an elegant hotel. The reputed dining rooms offer good menus.

Killarney Park Hotel, Kenmare Place, t 35555, *www.killarneyparkhotel.ie* (*luxury*). Glamour in the heart of Killarney – marble floors, antiques, a spa (*see* left) and huge suites.

Killarney Royal Hotel, College Street, t 31853, *www.killarneyroyal.ie* (*luxury*). Small boutique hotel with individual rooms, marble bathrooms and attentive staff. The dining room and bar menus are excellent.

Castlerosse Hotel, t 31144, *www.castlerossehotelkillarney.com* (*expensive*). Great lake and mountain views from a hotel that caters well for disabled guests. Includes golf and accommodation packages and an inviting **leisure centre** offering Swedish massage.

Coolclogher House, Mill Road, t 35996, *www.coolclogherhouse.com* (*expensive*). Victorian house in a secluded walled estate, with tranquil rooms and a great conservatory.

Killarney Great Southern Hotel, t 31262, *www.gshotels.com* (*expensive*). Stylish, with landscaped gardens and good facilities.

Gleann Fia **Country House**, Deerpark, t 35035, *www.gleannfia.com* (*moderate*). Victorian-style guesthouse in a 30-acre wooded valley.

Killeen House Hotel, Aghadoe, t 31711, *www.killeenhousehotel.com* (*moderate*). Friendly, cosy little hotel up in the hills. Their restaurant, **Rozzers**, serves very good food.

Carriglea House, Muckross Road, t 31116 (*inexpensive*). Comfortable rooms with *en suite* bathrooms. Close to Muckross House.

Crab Tree Cottage, Mangerton Road, Muckross, t 34193, *www.crabtreebnb.com* (*inexpensive*). Interiors are gaily decorated in this B&B, with an attractive, plant-filled garden.

Hillcrest Farmhouse, Gearahmeen, Black Valley, t 34702, *www.hillcrestfarmhouse.com* (*inexpensive*). Truly a homely feel at this farmhouse out in the wilds.

Eating Out

The Strawberry Tree, 24 Plunkett Street, t 32688 (*expensive*). Easily one of the best restaurants in Killarney.

Blue Door Bistro, High St, t 33755 (*moderate*). Modern menu in a casual setting with wood floors and simple, well-cooked dishes.

Foley's Seafood and Steak Restaurant, 23 High Street, t 31217 (*moderate*). Serves delicious seafood, lamb and good vegetarian dishes.

Gaby's Restaurant, 27 High Street, t 32519 (*moderate*). Mediterranean-style café with delicious seafood. Very popular locally. They don't take bookings, so arrive early.

The Granary Restaurant and Bar, Touhills Lane, Beech Rd, t 20075, *www.granaryrestaurant.com* (*moderate–inexpensive*). Great place for hearty food, and a venue for live music.

Stonechat Restaurant and Café, Flemings Lane, t 34295 (*inexpensive*). Very good home-made soups and organic dishes here.

plasterwork was almost completely destroyed, except in one small chapel. Killarney's fine **Franciscan Friary** (completed 1867), built by Augustus Pugin's eldest son, Edward, lies in College Street. It has a simple style with a vaulted, oak-beamed ceiling and a Flemish-style altar (1871) by a Belgian, J. Janssen. Look out for the vivid south window from the studio of Harry Clarke (1930). Facing the church is the *Sky Woman* monument (1940) to four great Kerry poets: Pierce Ferriter, Geoffrey O'Donoghue, Aodhagán O'Rahilly and Owen Roe O'Sullivan, who lived in the 17th and 18th centuries. (It is worth reading their poetry; the translated versions are excellent.)

It is quite fun to wander down some of the old lanes branching off the main street that survive from Killarney's Victorian era. There are plenty of banks, shops, craft shops, pubs and restaurants to choose from, but avoid staying in the centre as it gets quite crowded. Expect to be approached by the **jarveys**, who gather with their ponies and traps on the street corner as you enter town on the N71; they will guide you around the valley and take you for as long or as short a trip as you want. Be sure to negotiate the price for the ride before you start, and be prepared for a certain amount of chat; most of them have a host of stories about the famous landmarks that have been polished and embroidered since Killarney first became a tourist destination in the 18th century. Some of it is tongue-in-cheek, as is this hoary old phrase about the constant rain: "Twasn't rain at all, but just a little perspiration from the mountains!'

Some geography of the area: the underlying rock varies from old red sandstone to limestone, whilst the scooping action of glaciers in the Ice Age created the precipitous mountain corries. Lower down, the indented lakes are softened by oak, holly and arbutus, interspersed with the alien *rhododendron ponticum*, which splashes mauve amongst the dark leaves in late spring.

Killarney National Park, the Gap of Dunloe and Around

The Killarney Valley runs roughly north to south through a break in the great Macgillycuddy's Reeks. **Killarney National Park** (*visitor centre at Muckross House,* see *opposite, t (064) 31440, http://homepage.tinet.ie/~knp*) covers a large part of the valley. It was once the Muckross Estate: its 11,000 acres, including Muckross House and Abbey, were given to the nation by Mr Bowers Bourne of California and his son-in-law, Senator Arthur Vincent, who had owned the property for 31 years.

The Reeks rise up to the west of three famous lakes. The **Upper Lake** (*An Loch Uachtarach*) is narrow, small and very impressive; it is enclosed by mountains and scattered with wooded islands, on which cedars of Lebanon stand high among the trees. A narrow passage leads into a connecting stretch of water called the **Long Range**, which flows under the Old Weir Bridge and rushes over some rapids, giving a *frisson* of fear and excitement to those on a boat tour (*see* p.152). The river then divides at the 'Meeting of the Waters': the left branch flows into the Lower Lake, **Lough Leane** (*Loch Léin*), and the right branch empties into Middle Lake, **Lough Muckross** (*Loch Mhucrois*). The limestone which underlies Lough Muckross has been worn away into a series of fantastically shaped rocks and cliffs. On Lough Leane's western side is **O'Sullivan's Cascade** which, with all the blessed rain, is always a pretty sight.

Ross Castle (*open April daily 10–5; May and Sept daily 10–6; June–Aug daily 9–6.30; Oct Tues–Sun 10–5; guided tours only, adm adults €5, children €2; t (064) 35851/2, www.heritageireland.ie*) is 1½ miles (2.5km) southwest of Killarney, on a peninsula with pretty, wooded paths to the edge of Lough Leane. The castle is a fine ruin dating from the 15th century, consisting of a tower house surrounded by a *bawn*. The castle was built by the O'Donoghues and taken by the Cromwellians; it was one of the last strongholds to fall. It has been restored and there are guided tours with much historical information. Evidence of copper deposits can be seen in Lough Leane's green waters here; these deposits were worked in the Bronze Age and the 18th century. On its south side is an 18th-century house built by the Brownes, who became Earls of Kenmare.

From Ross Castle you can hire a boat to **Innisfallen Isle** (*book in advance during high season; return costs around €5*), an isle like a country in miniature, with hills, valleys and dark woods. Holly and other evergreens grow very thickly here. Near the landing stages are the extensive ruins of **Innisfallen Abbey**, founded about AD 600, as a refuge for Christians during the Dark Ages in Europe. *The Annals of Innisfallen*, a chronicle of world and Irish history written between 950–1380, are now in the Bodleian Library, Oxford. The monastery lasted until the middle of the 17th century, when the Cromwellian forces held Ross Castle.

At the centre of Killarney National Park you will also find **Muckross House** (*house open daily 9–5.30, until 6 during July–Aug; working farms open Mar, April and Oct, Sat, Sun and bank hols 1–6; May daily 1–6; June–Sept daily 9–7; adm to house adults €5.50, children €2.25, gardens free; additional fee for farms; t (064) 31440, www.muckross-house.ie*), which was built in Tudor style in 1843. On the death of the last MacCarthy (the family who were landlords of this area) in 1770, the Muckross lands passed to an Anglo-Norman family, the Herberts, who had already leased it for 200 years. This, their fourth house, was built for Henry Arthur Herbert, who hosted a visit by Queen Victoria in 1861. The main rooms are furnished in splendid Victorian style; the rest of the house has been transformed into a museum of Kerry folklore with a craft shop in its basement. You can see a potter, a weaver, a bookbinder and a blacksmith at their trades. There is a very informative film on the geology and natural beauties of the park, which is shown every half-hour. It is worth paying the extra to tour the **traditional working farms**, especially if you have children with you; they will love the chickens, pigs and little black Kerry cows, which give such sweet milk. The gardens around the house are delightful; here you can see the native Killarney strawberry tree (*arbutus unedo*), an evergreen with creamy white flowers followed by strawberry-like fruit.

Close by, overlooking Lough Leane, is **Muckross Abbey**, a graceful early English ruin founded in 1448 for the Observatine Franciscans. After being dispossessed by Cromwell in 1652, the Franciscans had to go into hiding, but they returned in more tolerant times and set up a boys' school and a new church in Killarney. In fact, the abbey area is almost like a stage set for everything the tourist wishes to see, and its natural beauty is enhanced by the superb gardens and arboretum. There is a gigantic yew tree in the centre of the cloister. The walks laid out in the park lead you through a mature oak and yew wood and to the very end of the peninsula, to the cliff known as Eagle Point, named after the golden eagles that used to be seen here. The path crosses the wooded Dinis Island. You are now 2.3 miles from Muckross House, and if you do not want to retrace your steps, you can join the N71 Kenmare road (about a mile away).

The **Gap of Dunloe** (*Bearna an Coimin*) is six miles west of Killarney and about eight miles in length, a wild gorge bordered by the dark Macgillycuddy's Reeks, the Purple Mountain and Tomies Mountain. The **Macgillycuddy's Reeks** (*Na Cruacha Dubha*) include **Carrantuohill** (*Corrán Tuathail*), at 3,414ft (1,040m) the highest mountain in Ireland. Cars are not welcome on the dirt track until after 7pm during the tourist season, as the route is taken up with horses, cyclists and walkers. Seeing the sights by pony and trap, also known as a jaunting car, or taking a boat trip along the lakes, is great fun instead (*see* p.152).

The mouth of the Gap starts at **Kate Kearney's Cottage** (*t (064) 44146, www.kate kearneyscottage.com*). Kate was a local beauty renowned for her potent brew of poitín, though some say she was a witch. Today her cottage has grown to become a café, restaurant and shop. The road continues through to **Moll's Gap**, on the Kenmare road (N71). The journey through the Gap is spectacular, with steep gorges and deep glacial lakes. It can be a good idea to approach the Gap from the opposite way to the crowds, especially if you are walking or biking. Take the main Killarney–Kenmare road (N71); there is plenty to stop for en route. Notice the strawberry tree, or *arbutus*, growing among ferns and oaks, and the pink saxifrage on the wayside.

All of the following sights are well signposted.

You can stop and take an easy walk up the woodland path to the **Torc Waterfall**, found by following a rough road on the left just before a sign cautioning motorists about deer. The walk is very short, leading you through splendid fir trees to the 60ft falls. It is also possible to drive there and park.

Back on the main road, for another little detour to some falls, continue on past the Galway Bridge where you can follow the stream up into the hills to the **Derrycunnihy Cascades**. Maybe you will come upon a few sika (Japanese deer) or native red deer. The cascades are set in primeval oak woods, and this is a rich botanical site of ferns and mosses. This area has its own Killarney fern, *trichomanus speciosum*.

Go back to the main road again (N71) and continue for six miles to **Ladies' View**, which gives you a marvellous view of the Upper Lake. Now turn off right before Moll's Gap and right again along the dirt track. You are now close to the Gap of Dunloe. A path leads you along the river to **Lord Brandon's Cottage** (*refreshments available*) where tour groups coming from the Gap join the boats back to Killarney.

To the west is a continuation of the Gap: the **Black Valley**, a wild and remote corner of Kerry. Nearly the entire population died off here during the potato famine and the place counts only a few inhabitants today.

Other Excursions

If you are interested in seeing a fine example of **ogham stones**, take the R562 road towards Killorglin, past the Dunluce Castle Hotel. Turn right down a hill to a

T-junction, and right again, over the bridge and up the hill. A signpost points left to a collection of ogham stones in a wired enclosure high on the bank. This is the best place in Kerry to see the weird ogham writing, the only form that existed in Ireland before the arrival of Christianity. The lateral strokes, incised into the stone and crossing a vertical line, give the name of a man long, long dead.

The **Dunloe Castle Hotel gardens** (*ask at reception; t (064) 44111*) are well worth a visit. It is claimed that your walk will take you around the world in a botanical sense, such is the variety of plants. The nearby village of **Beaufort** is very pretty and has a good golf course.

Another fine view of the Killarney lakes and mountains can be seen from **Aghadoe Hill**, about 2½ miles west of Killarney. It is not at all touristy. In pagan times, the hill was believed to be the birthplace of all beauty, and lovers still meet here. The legend goes that whoever falls in love on Aghadoe Hill will be blessed for a lifetime. From here you can be seen the voluptuous pair of hills known as the **Paps of Anu** (Danu), the mother of the gods. (James Stephens is said to have remarked jokingly, 'I think those mountains ought to be taught a little modesty.') Lower down the hill are the ruins of a round tower, a castle and the remains of a 12th-century church with a Romanesque doorway. To get there from the centre of Killarney, take the Tralee road until you see a sign for Aghadoe Heights Hotel. The view opens up around the hotel. One of the youth hostels is also in this direction.

Halfway between Killarney and Killorglin are the **Kerry Woollen Mills** (*see* p.152), which were first established in the 17th century, and produce the woollen goods sold in the mill shop.

The Ring of Kerry

The narrow road that makes up the Ring of Kerry is 112 miles (180km) long, and takes about three hours to drive without any detours. Starting at Kenmare (*see* p.147), you can take the N70 and follow the coiling road south around the coast, stopping to enjoy the views or going down the tiny R roads to get a better look at St Finan's Bay, Bolus Head and Doulus Head. The Ring ends at Killorglin. You can travel the Ring anticlockwise if you prefer, starting from Killarney on the Killorglin road. The views are equally good but the route gets clogged with tourist traffic in July and August – coaches usually tour the Ring this way.

The Southern Ring, to Waterville

Parknasilla is a sheltered wee place on the Kenmare River, where it widens out into a sea inlet of islands and lovely bathing places fringed by woods and flowers. The coves are favoured sunning places of the Atlantic seal. A lovely climb can be made up Knocknafreaghane (1,350ft/412m) and also the less demanding Knockanamadane Hill. **Sneem** (*An Snaidhm*) is a quiet village out of season, divided by the Sneem River. It has a good pub and was attractively laid out by an 18th-century landlord around a green, through which the river runs. On the green is a recently erected **monument** to De Gaulle, who once spent two weeks here. Locals refer to it affectionately as 'De Gallstone'. Other modern sculptures are positioned around the place, the most memorable being the modern beehive huts beside the church, which have stained glass panels by James Scanlon.

Tourist Information

Waterville: t (066) 947 4646; *open June–mid-Sept.*
Cahersiveen: RIC Barracks, t (066) 947 2589; *open all year.*

Shopping

Crafts

Waterville Craft Market, t (066) 947 4212.
Cill Rialaig **Project**, Dungeagan, Ballinskelligs, t (066) 947 9277, *cillrialaig@esatclear.ie.* Art gallery; also runs drawing, ceramics and painting workshops. *Open April–Sept daily 11–5.*
Fuchsia Cottage Pottery, Dooneen, Cahersiveen, t (066) 947 3456, *http://fuchsia cottagepottery.com.* Family business selling watercolours, pottery, sculpture and gifts.
Boyle's, Langford Street, Killorglin, t (066) 976 1110. Hardware shop that also sells pottery and angling gear.

Sports and Activities

For information on **boat trips** to the **Skelligs**, *see* 'Getting to Islands off Kerry', p.144–5.

Fishing

There is excellent **deep-sea fishing** on Valentia Island and **shore-angling** all round the Ring of Kerry. **Sea trout** fishing is available on the Inny River; **Salmon** fishing is also very popular. There's excellent fishing on Lough Currane, near Waterville, and **brown trout fishing** takes place on Lough Leane and Lough Avaul. Contact one of the following:
Michael O'Sullivan, Waterville, t (066) 74255.
Butler Arms Hotel, Waterville, t (066) 947 4144, *www.butlerarms.com.*
Glencar Hotel, Glencar, t (066) 976 0102. For the River Laune and River Caragh.

Golf

Waterville Golf Links, Waterville, t (066) 947 4102, *www.watervillegolflinks.ie.*
Dooks Golf Links, Glenbeigh, t (066) 976 8205, *www.dooks.com.*
Killorglin Golf Club, Stealroe, Killorglin, t (066) 976 1979, *www.killorglingolf.ie.*

Pony Trekking

Burkes Activity Centre, Faha, Rossbeigh Road, Glenbeigh, t (066) 976 8386, *www.burkesactivitycentre.ie.* Right on Rossbeigh Strand, with treks across the sand.

Walking

Into The Wilderness Tours, The Climbers Inn, Glencar, t (066) 976 0101, *www.climbersinn.com* . Walking, boating and biking tours.
Countryside Tours, Glencar House, Glencar, t (066) 976 0211. Walking and hiking tours.

Water Sports

Activity Ireland, Caherdaniel, t (066) 947 5277, *www.activity-ireland.com.* Scuba diving lessons and equipment. Also, sea-angling and guided hill-walking on the Kerry Way.
Ballinskelligs Watersports, t (066) 947 9182, *www.skelligsboats.com.* Offers world-class diving off the Skellig Islands; packages include accommodation.

Where to Stay

Caragh Lodge, Caragh Lake, t (066) 976 9115, *www.caraghlodge.com (luxury).* Pleasant, well-furnished country house in a wonderful situation overlooking the lake, with a fine garden. Try to get rooms in the main house, not the yard.
Parknasilla Great Southern Hotel, Parknasilla, t (064) 45122, *www.gshotels.com/parknasilla (luxury).* Comfortable hotel in a 19th-century mansion on the banks of Kenmare River,

About 10 miles west of Sneem, continuing on the N70, there is a signpost right to **Staigue Fort** (*the farmer who owns the field requests a donation from those crossing his land*), isolated at the head of a desolate valley, and between 1,500 and 2,000 years old. This circular stone fort rises out of a field, and a large bank and ditch surround it. Its thick dry-stone walls are in good condition and the place has a tremendous

with a well-established garden. Ask for a room in the older part.

Carrig House, Caragh Lake, t (066) 976 9100, *www.carrighouse.com* (*expensive*). Good food and friendly accommodation in Frank and Mary Slattery's delightful, historic country house on the shore of Caragh Lake.

Butler Arms Hotel, Waterville, t (066) 947 4144, *www.butlerarms.com* (*expensive–moderate*). Intimate, family-run, pleasantly old-fashioned, Grade A hotel. A lovely place to stay if you like salmon or trout fishing.

Glanleam House, Valentia Island, t (066) 947 6176 (*expensive–moderate*). Splendid subtropical gardens surround the Knight of Kerry's elegant old manor. Antiques, slate fireplaces and a grand library adorn the interior.

Glencar House Hotel, Glencar, t (066) 976 0102, *www.glencarhouse.com* (*moderate*). Remote, comfortable, clean and efficient country-house hotel with stunning surroundings.

Glendalough House, Caragh Lake, Killorglin, t (066) 976 9156, *www.glendaloughhouse. com* (*moderate*). Josephine Roder-Bradshaw is an excellent hostess and has furnished her house lovingly. Great views over the lake.

Iskeroon, Caherdaniel, t (066) 947 5119, *www. iskeroon.com* (*moderate*). Large bungalow in a very remote setting – you have to drive across a beach to get to it – with spectacular views over Derrynane Harbour. Great seafood, turf fires, interesting books, and a semi-tropical garden leading to a private pier.

Smugglers' Inn, Cliff Road, Waterville, t (066) 947 4330, *www.welcome.to/thesmugglersinn* (*moderate*). Friendy and on the beach.

Tahilla Cove, near Sneem, t (064) 45204, *www.tahillacove.com* (*moderate*). 1960s flat-roofed guesthouse with a Caribbean feel, in an idyllic location on the Ring of Kerry shore.

The Climbers' Inn, Glencar, t (066) 976 0101, *www.climbersinn.com* (*inexpensive*). Wild mountain location, 30mins and a million miles from Killarney. The Inn has cottage-style bedrooms and a hostel behind, and a walking, cycling and climbing centre offering wilderness tours.

The Moorings Guesthouse, Portmagee, t (066) 947 7108, *www.moorings.ie* (*inexpensive*). Comfortable rooms in a cosy guesthouse, with views over the harbour, plus a restaurant and friendly bar (*see* below).

Mount Rivers, Carhan Road, Cahersiveen, t (066) 947 2509 (*inexpensive*). Comfortable rooms with *en suite* bath in Mrs McKenna's Victorian house.

Eating Out

Nick's Restaurant and Pub, Lower Bridge Street, Killorglin, t (066) 976 1219 (*expensive*). Serves large portions of seafood and steaks. Often packed with local people singing round the piano; very friendly and great fun.

The Blue Bull, South Square, Sneem, t (064) 45382 (*moderate*). Quality seafood in an old-style building; delicious seafood platters.

Stone House, Sneem, t (064) 45188, *www. sneem.net/stonehouse* (*moderate*). Offers reasonable Irish food, with fresh oysters and lobsters on the menu. Dinner only.

The Moorings Restaurant and **The Bridge Bar**, Portmagee, t (066) 947 7108, *www.moorings.ie* (*moderate–inexpensive*). Welcoming venue; both serve mouthwatering fresh seafood, with simpler dishes in the bar and hearty fare in the restaurant. They have an 'Irish Night' in the bar on Tuesdays, and set dancing and music every Friday and Sunday.

The Blind Piper, Caherdaniel, t (066) 947 5126 (*inexpensive*). Good, lively atmosphere in this pretty hamlet, with hearty fare.

QC's Seafood Bar Restaurant, 3 Main Street, Cahersiveen, t (066) 947 2244, *www.qcbar. com* (*inexpensive*). Good grills using local meat and fish on a Spanish theme.

atmosphere of ancient strength. It was probably built by late Bronze Age people, but has never been excavated or restored. Elaborate stairways lead to the defensive platform; it is fun to climb to the top, look out over the coast and wonder where it fits in amongst the myths and legends of these parts. Two miles away, at the Staigue Fort Hotel, there is a small exhibition centre about the fort. Beyond Castlecove village on the N70 is **White Strand**, which is superb for bathing.

West again on the N70, a mile from **Catherdaniel** (*Cathair Donall*), is **Derrynane House** (*open May–Sept Mon–Sat 9–6, Sun 11–7; April and Oct Tues–Sun 1–5; Nov–Mar Sat–Sun 1–5; adm adults €2.75, children €1.75; t (066) 9475113, www.heritageireland.ie*),

The Kerry O'Connells

The O'Connells were hereditary constables of Ballycarberry Castle in the Middle Ages. Later they fought against Cromwell and William of Orange. You might think they would have lost everything after being on the losing side twice but, although they had to leave Kerry, they kept up their connections in a pattern which happened more often than is recorded. By good management and cordial relations with their neighbours they managed to acquire land and cattle herds despite the penal laws, because sympathetic Protestants would buy land for them. They also made money by smuggling goods between France and Spain; the forces of law and order must have seemed far off in Dublin, and families such as this were left to their own devices.

Daniel O'Connell's family typified the old Irish ways of hospitality. They got on easily with all their neighbours, whether the hard-drinking gentry or the fisherfolk. Daniel himself was fostered out as a baby to island people, a custom which has its roots in ancient Ireland. However, the family did not escape the corrosive effects of the political and religious norms of the time. Daniel O'Connell's aunt Eileen wrote a wonderful lamentation on the death of her husband, Art O'Leary, who was killed for refusing to sell his fine mare to a Protestant named Morris for the sum of £5. (Catholics, under the penal laws of the time, were not allowed to own a horse of greater value than this.) This extract is from the beginning, when she entreats his dead body to rise up:

*My love and my delight
Stand up now beside me,
And let me lead you home
Until I make a feast,
And I will roast the meat
And send for company
And call the harpers in,
And I will make your bed
Of soft and snowy sheets
And blankets dark and rough
To warm the beloved limbs
An Autumn blast has chilled.*
translated by Frank O'Connor

the home of Daniel O'Connell (*see* box, opposite), 'the Great Liberator', who won Catholic emancipation in 1829. It contains many of his possessions, including his desk, duelling pistols and rosary amongst the plain furniture which he seems to have favoured, and is beautifully kept as a museum. The mellow simplicity of the house is very appealing, with its low ceilings and tiny Gothic-style chapel. Part of the house has been demolished, having got beyond repair. The video of his life is well worth watching and the historical background very interesting. He believed that 'no political change whatsoever is worth the shedding of a single drop of human blood'. The grounds have exceptionally fine coastal scenery and form part of a national park of hundreds of acres. **Derrynane Bay** has one of the most glorious strands in the country, a wonderful place for a long walk. A shorter walk can be taken to **Abbey Island** and its ruined 10th-century abbey, along a cliff path with the rocky outline of the Skelligs framed by the sea and sky. Nearer to land are the isles of **Deenish** (*Dúinis*) and **Scariff** (*An Scairbh*). Access to the abbey is only possible at low tide. Several O'Connell graves can be seen in the graveyard.

Waterville

A few miles further round the coast, **Waterville** (*An Coireán*) is the main resort of the Ring; palm trees and fuchsia imbue it with a Continental air and hotels line the waterfront. Some people speak Gaelic here (the Munster variety) and Ballinskelligs Bay is a favourite place for Gaelic-speaking students. The beach here and at St Finan's Bay is very beautiful, with splendid views.

The *Cill Rialaig* **Arts Centre** (*t (066) 947 9297*) in **Ballinskelligs** (*Baile an Sceilg*) is a small gallery and tearoom in a thatched building. It's associated with an artists' retreat (*see* 'Shopping', p.158) in the restored pre-famine village of *Cill Rialaig* nearby, where the revered folklorist and storyteller Sean O'Connell was born in 1853. Inland is **Lough Currane** (*Lough Luioch*), popular with anglers; the mountain streams that feed it are well known for brown trout.

This area is a rich source of legend. It was near Waterville that Cesair, the grand-daughter of Noah, landed with her father, two other men and 49 women. They were hoping to escape the Great Flood of the Bible story. The year, apparently, was 2958 BC. The women divided the three men amongst them, but two of them died and the third, Fintan, was so reluctant to remain with the women that he fled and later turned himself into a salmon.

The peninsula was also the landing point of another invasion; the coming of the Celts. The 12th-century manuscript *The Book of Invasions*, or *Lebor Gabala*, describes it as follows: the Milesians arrived in Spain, where they built a watchtower from which they saw Ireland, and it looked so green and beautiful that they set sail for it. Their poet, Amergin, sang a poem of mystical incantations when he first touched the Irish shore. The poem itself is rather beautiful, and this is part of what he sings:

I am the womb: of every holt,
I am the blaze: on every hill,
I am the queen: of every hive,

I am the shield: for every head,
I am the grave: of every hope.
version by Robert Graves

The Book of Invasions states that the Celts arrived on 1 May, 1700 BC. As you enter Waterville on the N70, on the skyline to your right is an alignment of four **stones**. This is supposed to be the burial place of Scene, wife of one of the eight leaders of the Milesians. Perhaps Staigue Fort has something to do with them.

The Skellig Islands

A trip to the Skellig Islands will take a whole day and is a high point of any visit to this part of the country. These jagged, rocky islands lie out to sea from St Finan's Bay and rise dramatically from the sea.

Little Skellig (*An Sceilg Bheag*) is home to thousands of gannets and other sea birds, and its dark surface is splashed white – a mixture of birds and droppings. It is a nature reserve and the boats do not land there. **Skellig Michael** (*Sceilg Mhichíl*, or Great Skellig), has on it an almost perfect example of an early monastic settlement, which was in use between the 6th and 12th centuries. The Gaelic word *sceilig* means 'splinter of stone', and you can only wonder at the skill of those who cut and shaped that stone. The remains still impress with their simplicity – seven beehive huts and oratories which convey something of the indefatigable striving of this community.

A sea cruise around the islands can be taken from Cahersiveen or Dingle, or from the Skellig Heritage Centre (*see* opposite and 'Getting to Islands off Kerry', pp.144–5). If you wish to go yourself and stop off at the island for a couple of hours, boats can be hired at several places around the coast: from Waterville, the closest point, from Portmagee and also at Caherdaniel or Derrynane Pier. (The boats only go out there between mid-March and October, and whether you get there will be determined by the weather. Take a waterproof jacket, flat shoes, a picnic and, if you are keen on birdlife, a pair of binoculars.) The trip out there can be very rough even on a fine day, and the boat will soon be riding great valleys of jade, iridescent water. It illuminates something of the hunger for solitude that those holy men felt. Shearwaters glide past, known locally as 'mackerel cocks' for their knowledge of where the shoals are. Kittiwakes abound, and you may get a chance to see a huge gannet bomb into the water after a fish.

You land to the noisy fury of the seabirds, and approach the monastery up a **stairway** of about 600 steps, 540ft long and hacked out of stone over a thousand years ago. It is thought that St Finan founded the monastery on this barren rock, half a mile long and three quarters of a mile wide, in the 7th century. There was little these holy men could do there except pray and meditate, fish and grow vegetables. The way of life must have been hard; sometimes the waves crashing around the rock reach enormous heights.

You can see **clochans**, **stone crosses**, the **holy well**, **cisterns** for storing rainwater, two **oratories** and **cemeteries**, and the ruins of **St Michael's Church** which, although it is of medieval origin, has not lasted as well as the cells. These are laid out close together on a small plateau and enclosed by a strong wall. The oratories and the medieval church are separated from the six cells or beehive huts by the holy well. Fresh water on this desolate island is provided by the rock fissures, which hold rainwater. The Vikings raided the monastery in 812 and 823; but in 995 Olaf Trygveson, the son of the King of Norway, is reputed to have been baptized here. When he became king he introduced Christianity to Scandinavia. The addition of 'Michael' to the name of the island happened sometime in the 10th century. Since St Michael is the leader of the Heavenly Host against the spirit of wickedness in high places, his name is invoked in many places throughout Europe, for instance at Mont St-Michel in Brittany.

The monastery here grew independent of the authorities in Rome, as did the clerics in Ireland as a whole. The Celtic church refused to follow a 7th-century ruling about the time of Easter, and it was not until medieval times that the Skelligs fell into line. The monastic community appears to have withdrawn from the island in the 13th century, maybe because the weather got harsher or because it was attracting too many pilgrims. It remained a place of penitential pilgrimage, especially during the 18th century. The automated **lighthouse** dates from 1865.

The **Skellig Heritage Centre** (*open daily April–May and Sept–Nov 10–6; Jun–Aug 10–7; adm adults €4.40, children €2.20; for exhibition and Skellig cruise adults €21.50, children €10.70; t (066) 947 6306, www.skelligexperience.com*), on Valentia Island, beside the road bridge that links the island to Portmagee, interprets the life of the monks on Skellig Michael through film, graphics and models. It also gives information about the birdlife, waterlife and the lighthouse service, and has books, crafts and snacks for sale. It is well worth visiting for the background knowledge it gives, before you go out to see for yourself. There are environmental concerns about the number of visitors to the islands, so you may prefer simply to circle the island in one of the tour boats run by the centre.

Inside the Ring: The Iveragh Peninsula's Interior

The Ring does not venture deeply into the interior of the Iveragh Peninsula, but you could do just that by travelling to the lake area of Caragh, Glencar and Lough Cloon, which will take at least half a day. This wild, mountainous landscape was the hunting ground of the legendary giant Finn MacCool (also known as Fionn MacCumhail, of the Giant's Causeway in County Antrim) and it is absolutely delightful. Myriad little roads lead up to these parts. Perhaps the simplest is the lonely road through the **Ballaghisheen Pass** (*Bealach Óisín*), which is unnumbered and runs between Killorglin and Waterville. It actually branches off the N70 just north of Waterville, by Inny Bridge. The River Caragh is famous for its early salmon, and the Macgillycuddy's Reeks cast their great height against the skyline all the way. There is an interesting walk to be had at the north end of **Lough Cloon** (*Loch Cluanach*), where up a small road to some farmhouses and then right along a track you will find an **ancient settlement** with ruined clochans and terraced fields.

Farther up in this wild country, turn right at Bealalaw Bridge and carry on until you come to a right fork over the Owenroe River, which takes you into the **Ballaghbeama Gap** and joins a larger road to Sneem. You travel along a tortuous and breathtaking channel between two mountains, Knocklomena and Knockavulloge, named in Irish after the golden gorse that grows on their slopes. Traces of the early Bronze Age Beaker People have been found here in rock carvings.

Alternatively, follow the Caragh River to Caragh Bridge and on to Killorglin. All these single track roads are lonely but so beautiful; huge boulders lie scattered like sheep on the slopes of the hills. Some were old turf tracks, or led to communities long gone since the famine times. The **Kerry Way**, a signed route for walkers, starts at Glenbeigh and follows a beautiful, desolate route through the Reeks. If you have come for the walking and climbing, note that the summits are challenging; don't attempt them without a good map and take sensible precautions (*see* also 'Walking', p.152).

The Northern Ring: Cahersiveen to Killorglin

A rather theatrical **tower** guards the bridge and the inlet at **Cahersiveen** (*Cathair Saidhbhín*), which is sometimes also spelled Caherciveen. It used to be the Royal Irish Constabulary barracks, but is now a **heritage centre** (*t (066) 947 2777*). The design is grandiose Victorian and was used for many other police barracks all over the British Empire; this one was built to take police reinforcements after the 1867 Fenian Uprising and was burnt down in 1922 by anti-Treaty forces during the Civil War. Now restored through a community project, it houses exhibitions that clearly have had a lot of local input. From the barracks there is a three-mile floral walk along the coast to *Cuas Crom.*

Daniel O'Connell was born in Cahersiveen and the Catholic church has a dedication to him. The long main street has more pubs than you could believe possible, but not of the old-fashioned shop-cum-bar type: these are fast disappearing all over Ireland. It is often difficult to get a meal in any, especially off season. This area is marked by turf-cutting and dominated by **Knocknadobar,** the holy mountain, also known as 'the hill of wells'. From the summit at 2,267ft (690m), you get a wonderful view of the Dingle Peninsula and the Blasket Islands. **St Finan's Well**, on its slopes, was reputed to cure sick cattle. People still take water from **St Fursey's**, at its foot. Once upon a time, on the last Sunday in July, a festival of dancing and singing would take place at the summit in preparation for the harvest festival, *Lughnasa*, but the custom has died out now.

Valentia Island (*Dhairbhre*)

Closer to the sea, **Valentia Island** and its quiet little harbour village of **Knightstown** (*an Chois*) is a pretty place to stay. The village was named after the Knight of Kerry, an improving landlord who owned most of the island. He opened a slate quarry in 1816, and the blue-grey slates were used to roof, among other famous buildings, the British Houses of Parliament. The quarry gave work to four hundred men and women, even during the famine. You can still see the old workings and spoil, although an enormous cavern has been converted into a grotto, with Our Lady of Lourdes placed high up and St Bernadette gazing up at her. Another industry the knight set up was weaving; the small but excellent **Heritage Centre** (*open April–Oct daily; adm adults €2, children €1; t (066) 947 6411*) in the old schoolhouse details the natural dyes that were used, many from plants. The knight also planted a garden at **Glanleam House** (*open June–Sept daily 11–7; adm; t (066) 947 6176*). Tree ferns, bamboos and other subtropical species love it here, because the harbour is very well sheltered by Beginish and Church Island. Himalayan poppies and candelabra primulas give intense colour in the summer, and paths take you down to the sea. You can get a map from the tourist office, on the pier, with marked walks. One of the best is a walk along the **Cliffs of Fogher**; massive slaty shelves pounded by huge waves. You might decide to get out to the little islands in the bay. Shell middens and the remains of an ancient iron smelting industry have been found on the golden strand and dunes at the eastern end of Beginish. Deep-sea fishing and diving can be organized on the island. In Victorian times this sleepy place was right at the hub of action, for Valentia was chosen as the site for the first transatlantic cable in 1858 – after which locals could get in direct contact with New York but not with Dublin. The views across to the mainland are magnificent. A very short ferry trip links Knightstown with Reenard Point, three miles west of Cahersiveen.

Onwards to Killorglin

The N70 continues around the peninsula, passing close to Knocknadobar Mountain and along **Kells Bay**, which is a good place to bathe. This wildly romantic landscape is peopled with heroes from Ireland's legendary past; Fionn MacCumhail and the warrior band, the Fianna, hunted these glens. Close by, in the locality of Rossbeigh and **Glenbeigh** (*Gleann Beithe*), the landscape is rich in memories of Oísín, the son of Fionn, who came back here after his long sojourn in the land of youth. He had left with Niamh, a golden-haired beauty he had met on the Rossbeigh strand; he returned to the desolate glens of the Ballaghisheen Pass looking for his companions in the Fianna, and from this great height surveyed the glens and mountains. He did not understand that three hundred years had passed whilst he was enchanted, and that they were long dead. This area is also strongly associated with the story of Diarmuid and Grainne (*see* p.60 and p.62), who stayed in a cave at Glenbeigh.

A fascinating visit can be made to the **Kerry Bog Village Museum** (*open Mar–Nov daily 9–6; adm €3.80, children €1.90; t (066) 976 9184*) just to the east of Glenbeigh, which depicts life in the rural 1800s. The areas of bogland hereabouts support a wealth of plant and insect varieties; the acid-rich soil and rich, coloured mosses, including the sphagnum mosses, soak up the water and help to create the bog itself. Sundews and bog asphodel, dragonflies and butterflies flourish.

A walk may be made to **Lough Coomasaharn** and beyond. Branch off the N70, southwest of Glenbeigh, by turning left and crossing over the Beigh River, then turn right through the townland of Ballynakilly Upper. This leads you into a landscape of purple mountains and to the tarn itself, full of trout and char. A walk around the lough brings you to **Coomacarrea Mountain** (2,541ft/772m). From its summit you can see a host of mountains, peak after peak, starred with lakes and ribboned with silver rivers draining into Dingle Bay.

An easier walk on the strand of **Rossbeigh** (Rossbehy on some maps) might be appealing; the sand here often looks gold against sapphire in the glancing sun. There are other walks around **Lough Caragh** (*Loch Cárthai*), a place popular with visitors since Victorian times. It is strange to think that the bare bogland here was once covered in oak and holly trees; they were mostly destroyed by Sir William Petty, who used them as fuel for a successful ironworks he created in the 17th century. Only a fringe of trees survive around the lough now. South of the lough is **Glencar** (*Gleann Chárthaigh*), a little village, and a wild glen. The Gaelic ruling family in these parts were the MacCarthys. It was from here that the head of the clan decided to take his title when he submitted to Elizabeth I, and became the Earl of Glencar.

Back on the N70, the Ring of Kerry ends with the attractive town of **Killorglin** (*Cill Orglan*), which grew up around an Anglo-Norman castle on the River Laune. The castle is now ruined, but you can explore a similar one nearby at **Ballymalis**. This has been partly restored, and you can climb to the top of the 16th-century tower, which is great fun. Killorglin is famous for its cattle and horse fair, known as the **Puck Fair** and held in August (*see* p.82 and p.145), when vestiges of an ancient rite are enacted. A wild goat from the mountains is captured and enthroned in a cage in the centre of town. He is a symbol of the unrestricted merrymaking to follow. The event may date from the worship of the Celtic God, Lug. The craic is certainly good; book well in advance if you want to stay overnight in the town at this time.

The Dingle Peninsula

This slender peninsula, the northernmost arm that Kerry stretches out into the sea, has become one of the most popular tourist destinations of the west. Dingle could be the Iveragh Peninsula in miniature, one with an equal helping of natural beauty. There is the same sort of spectacular coastal road; girdling impressive, grand, encircling mountains, and an even greater wealth of ancient remains and localities associated with Irish mythology. At the tip, instead of the Skellig Islands, there are the Blaskets. To the west of Dingle is wonderful, austere country, battered by Atlantic wind and sea.

This area is a government-protected **Gaeltacht** and many local people speak Irish amongst themselves, though you will find that they switch to English when you are around for courtesy's sake. Signposts are in Gaelic, so it's an idea to have a map with both the Irish and the anglicized place names upon, although we have included both where possible in this section. The full name for Dingle is *Daingean Uí Chúis*, usually abbreviated to *An Daingean*.

Annascaul to Dingle Town

From the Ring of Kerry, Dingle is reached by continuing on the N70 to Castlemaine and then to Annascaul on the R561, which passes the vast, beautiful sandy beach at Inch (*Inse*). The most spectacular way to get to Dingle, however, is via **Camp** (*An Com*; west of Tralee on the R559) and the **Glennagalt Valley** (*Gleann na nGealt*, glen of the madmen). Lunatics were brought to Glennagalt for recovery, aided perhaps by the magnificent scenery between the Beenoskee Massifs. It was also once believed many lunatics would find their own way here, no matter what part of Ireland they were from. This is the way the old railway used to go, dropping down to Annascaul on its way over to Dingle.

Entering the peninsula from **Castlemaine** (*Caisleán na Mainge*), the coastal road (R561) passes beneath the **Slieve Mish Mountains** (*Sliabh Mis*), where there is not only wild beauty but a fund of archaeological remains. The light glancing off the sea and the traditional field patterns with silvery stone walls and grey ribbed hills make this a scenic drive. Some big new houses have been built looking out to sea; this is happening all around the coastal parts. Not only are the locals better off than they have ever been, with emigration tailing off, but many newcomers are moving in, attracted by the beauty and way of life here in the southwest.

The Phoenix B&B and organic restaurant (*see* p.171) may catch your eye as you drive along; such enterprises are indicative of the way of life that many young Irish people and foreigners come here to enjoy. In the little towns you will often spot organic food shops with adverts for yoga classes in the windows, and the Saturday morning markets selling crafts, local vegetables and cheeses go from strength to strength.

From the great **Strand of Inch** (*Inse*) you have views across the bay and over the mountains. This immense flat sheet of sand holds the water after the tide goes out and to walk on it while it reflects the sky is a remarkable experience. Unfortunately, people drive on to the beach and litter the area around the entrance, where there is a car park and café-cum-craft shop. In the pubs, after 10pm, you can listen to traditional music or singing, which only happens when the locals get together.

At **Annascaul** (*Abhainn an Scail*) you can get a drink at the **South Pole Inn** (*t (066) 915 7388*) , so called because a former proprietor, Tom Crean, was part of that brave team with Scott in the Antarctic. **Dan Foley's Bar** (*t (066) 915 7252*) is another excellent drinking house and Dan himself is a great source of local knowledge and folklore.

To the northeast of Annascaul, on the right summit of Caherconree Mountain, is a rare example of an inland promontory **fort**. It dates from about 500 BC and is associated with Cú Chulainn, the great Ulster hero. Notorious for his attraction to women, he rescued Bláthnait (a damsel who had been kidnapped by Cú Roí) from here and carried her off to the north of Ireland. A drive or a walk of a few miles can be made to tranquil **Annascaul Lake**; the little tarred roads to it are empty of all but a few tractors, and you scarcely pass a house.

Dingle Town (*An Daingean*, fortress – though nothing remains of one now), a big fishing port and the westernmost town in Europe, has developed in a very attractive way. The population is only about 1,500, but this can treble in the summer months. Gaily painted houses and busy streets lead you to the harbour where the fishing boats move gently in the swell of the tide. The catches off this part of the coast are terrific; the boats are small and high-tech methods have not yet arrived. This adds greatly to the charm of the scene. The Roman Catholic church in the centre of the

The Dingle Peninsula and North Kerry

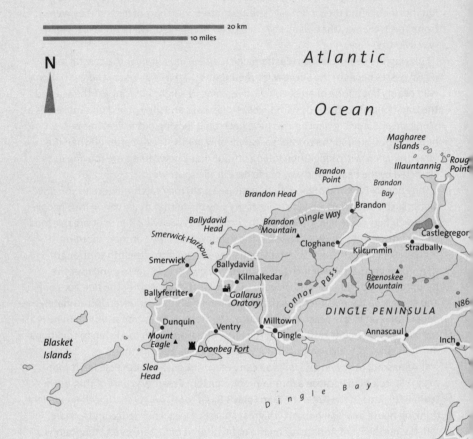

town is a calm place enlivened by narrow stained-glass windows, and is full of welcome. The cafés and bars also invite one to linger and give the town a delightful holiday atmosphere. The choice of restaurants, pub food and traditional music is excellent; there are also several very good craft shops and bookshops to browse in. While here, it is worth buying a good map that shows all the ancient sites in this area.

The local celebrity and major attraction is undoubtedly **Fungi**, a playful bottle-nosed dolphin who wandered into the bay in 1983 and decided to stay. Boats in the harbour take tourists out to visit Fungi daily (*see p.170*); you can swim with him, wet suits are for hire and there is a life-size model of him on display at the **Dingle Aquarium** (*open daily 10–6; adm adults €10, children €6; t (066) 915 2111, www.dingle-oceanworld.ie*). This is not just a tourist attraction but an informative and well laid out exhibition of

the wonders of the deep. The highlight is a walk-through aquarium with all the stars of Kerry marine life in attendance, including small sharks.

Continuing west, **Ventry** (*Ceann Trá*) has a lonely white strand on which, it is said, the King of the Other World, Donn, landed to subjugate Ireland. He had come to help the King of France avenge his honour, as Fionn had run off with his wife and daughter. The great Fionn MacCumhail and his Fenian knights won the day, of course (*see* **Old Gods and Heroes**, pp.61–2). On the road to Slea Head, just off the R559 at Fahan (*Fán*) and about 3 miles (6km) past Ventry, there is a group of early Christian **clochans**, 414 in all. Some were built by hermit monks, others are 19th-century. Until recently, farmers still built clochans as stables for animals, and the continuity of style with the unmortared stone is such that it is difficult to tell the old from the new.

Tourist Information

Dingle: t (066) 915 1188; *open all year*.
Castlegregory: Visitor Centre, Tailor's Row,
Strand Street, **t** (066) 713 9422; *open all year*.

Shopping

Crafts

Annascaul Pottery, Green Street, Dingle,
t (066) 915 7186. Pottery with sea motifs.
Brian de Staic, Green Street, Dingle, *www.
briandestaic.com*. Silversmith.
Dingle Craft Village, *Ceardlann na Coille*, out of
Dingle towards Milltown.
Irish Wild Flowers Ltd, 132 The Wood, Dingle.
Wild flower seeds and gifts.
Lisbeth Mulcahy, Green Street, Dingle, *www.
lisbethmulcahy.com*. Designer weaver: wall
hangings, scarves, table linen and throws.
Louis Mulcahy Pottery Workshop, Clogher,
Dingle, *www.louismulcahy.com*. Large,
distintive pieces with a Grecian influence.
NU (Niamh Utsch) Goldsmith, Green Street,
Dingle, *www.nugoldsmith.com*.
Contemporary designs using precious and
semiprecious stones.
Penny's Pottery, Ventry, **t** (066) 915 9962. Lots
of chunky lavender-blue pottery.

Food

Norreen Curran, Green Street, Dingle.
Delicious smoked bacon and black pudding.
Ted Browne, Kilquane, Ballydavid, **t** (066) 915
5183. Smoked salmon.

Sports and Activities

Fishing

There is excellent **deep-sea fishing** off
Ballydavid Head, and **shore-angling** is possible
all round the Dingle Peninsula.
An Tiaracht, Dingle, **t** (066) 915 5429. Boat
sailing from Smerwick harbour, Ballydavid.

Golf

Dingle Links/*Ceann Sibeal*, Ballyferriter, **t** (066)
915 6255, *www.dinglelinks.com*.
Castlegregory Golf and Fishing Club,
Stradbally, **t** (066) 713 9444. Nine-hole golf
course that also has a freshwater lake filled

with brown trout, available to those with
their own boat and equipment.

Pony Trekking

Most centres offer beach trekking and rides
through woodlands and hills.
Coláiste Íde **Stables**, *Baile an Ghoilin*, Burnham,
Dingle, **t** (066) 915 9100, *www.colaiste-ide-
stables.com*.
Dingle Horse Riding, Ballinaboula, Dingle,
t (066) 915 2199, *www.dinglehorseriding.com*.
Longs Horse Riding, Kilcolman, Ventry, **t** (066)
915 9034, *www.longsriding.com*.

Tours

Hidden Ireland Tours, Dingle, **t** (087) 221 4002,
www.hiddenirelandtours.com. Walking tours.
Sciúird **Archaeology Tours**, Dingle, **t** (066) 915
1606. Guided tours.

Walking Routes

The **Dingle Way** is a circular route around
the Dingle Peninsula (178km). The **Pilgrims
Route** goes from Dingle to Cloghane (64km).
The *Ryan's Daughter* **Route** is at Dunquin.

Water Sports

You can go **diving** in Ventry and Dingle Bays.
In the latter you can swim with a much-loved
friendly **dolphin** called **Fungi**, who has been
living there since 1983 (see *www.fungieforever.
com*). You can walk 1km east of Dingle to the
bay, or boat trips to see him are organized by a
number of operators in Dingle harbour.
Good places for **swimming** include Slea
Head, Smerwick Strand, near Ballyferriter, and
Stradbally. You can also go **surfing** at Inch
Strand and Srudeen Strand, near Dingle, but
bring your own surfboard.
Dingle Boatmen's Association, t (066) 915 1163.
Waterworld, Castlegregory, **t** (066) 713 9292,
www.waterworld.ie. Ireland's largest scuba-
diving centre, with visits to the Blasket and
Magharee Islands.

Where to Stay

Dingle t (066) –
Dingle Skellig Hotel, Dingle, **t** 915 0200,
www.dingleskellig.com (*luxury–expensive*).
Family-friendly hotel with good facilities.

Dingle Benners Hotel, Dingle, t 915 1638, www.dinglebenners.com (*expensive*). Hotel in the centre of town with 52 well-appointed rooms and spectacular views.

The Captain's House, The Mall, Dingle, t 915 1531, *http://homepage.eircom.net/~captigh* (*moderate*). B&B with a seafaring tradition, plenty of awards adorning the walls and wonderful turf fires. Self-catering option of a seaside bungalow available.

Doyle's Townhouse, John Street, Dingle, t 915 1174, *www.doylesofdingle.com* (*moderate*). One of the most enjoyable, comfortable places to stay in the country. Rooms are full of individuality: shelves and tables groan with interesting books you can linger over by a warm fire. The restaurant next door is known for its conviviality and food.

Gorman's Clifftop House, *Glaise Bheag*, Ballydavid, t 915 5162, *www.gormans-clifftop house.com* (*moderate*). Has a breathtaking position. All rooms have waxed wooden furniture, locally-made artworks and weavings, and views over the sea or the mountains. Some even have Jacuzzis. Home-made bread is served for breakfast.

Aisling House, Castlegregory, t (064) 31112, *www.aislinghouse.com* (*inexpensive*). Clean and comfortable, with a delicious breakfast.

Emlagh Lodge, Emlagh West, Dingle, t 915 1922, *www.emlaghlodge.com* (*inexpensive*). Great position overlooking Dingle Bay and harbour; rooms are large and bright with wooden furniture and polished floors.

The Phoenix, Shanahill East, Castlemaine, t 976 6284, *www.thephoenixorganic.com* (*inexpensive*). Dinner, B&B and camping in a dear little stone cottage with organic gardens, bearing vegetables that go on the menu in their vegetarian restaurant.

Self-catering

Cois Cuain, Cooleen, t 915 5151, *www.coiscuain. com*. Lovely 3-bedroom house near the harbour, with wooden floors, gaily decorated rooms and a courtyard garden to the rear.

Criomhthain, Ballinknockane, Ballydavid, t 718 5662. Traditional stone cottage with 3 rooms and views over the sea or Mount Brandon.

The Old Stone House, Chiddaun, Dingle, UK t +44 (0) 1423 860246, *www.irishholiday rentals.com/property.html?id=342*. 19th-century farmhouse cottage, with open fires and well decorated interiors; sleeps 6.

Eating Out

Dingle t (066) –

Beginish Restaurant, Green Street, Dingle, t 915 1588 (*expensive*). Enthusiastic staff and wonderful seafood, with a rear conservatory.

The Chart House, The Mall, Dingle, t 915 1205 (*expensive*). Seriously good food for a memorable experience.

Doyle's Seafood Bar and Restaurant, John Street, Dingle, t 915 1174 (*expensive*). In a room reminiscent of an old Irish kitchen, with stone floor and wooden furniture. Treat yourself to deliciously prepared seafood.

Armada, Strand Street, Dingle, t 915 1505 (*expensive–moderate*). Traditional west coast restaurant with a reputation for quality fare.

Fenton's Restaurant, Green Street, Dingle, t 915 2172 (*expensive–moderate*). Locally-sourced produce (like lamb from their own farm or fresh lobster) is on the menu here.

Gorman's Clifftop Restaurant, *Glaise Bheag*, Ballydavid, t 915 5162, *www.gormans-clifftophouse.com* (*expensive–moderate*). Welcoming restaurant offering delights such as crab claws in butter, wild Atlantic smoked salmon, turbot fillet, beef sirloin or Dingle Bay prawns.

The Forge, Holy Ground, Dingle, t 915 2590 (*moderate*). Steaks and seafood.

The Half-door, John Street, Dingle, t 915 1600 (*moderate*). Excellent, imaginative food.

An Café Liteartha, Dingle, t 915 2204 (*inexpensive*). Combined bookshop and café serving delicious open sandwiches.

Lord Baker's, Main Street, Dingle, t 915 1277 (*inexpensive*). Good quality bar food.

O'Riordan's, Castlegregory t 713 9379 (*inexpensive*). Good lunch spot – unusual dishes, memorable breads and good atmosphere.

Whelans, Main Street, Dingle, t 915 1620 (*inexpensive*). Very good Irish stew and other traditional dishes.

Dick Mack's Pub, Green Street. You can buy a pint or a pair of shoes here. Ireland used to have many such places, but they are rapidly disappearing.

Farther on, at **Slea Head** (*Ceann Sléibhe*), is an old stone and mud cottage, the **Famine Cottage** (*open April–Oct daily 10–6; adm;* **t** *(066) 915 6241, www.faminecottage. com*). Once the home of the Kavanagh family, who emigrated to the US, the cottage has been recreated as it would have been when the family lived there in the 19th to early 20th century. It's a fascinating place and quite chastening to see what harsh lives such people in the west of Kerry would have lived. At the back is a clochan, latterly named *Puicín na Muice* (the pig pen); other buildings nearby were also part of the farm.

Strewn all over the slopes of **Mount Eagle** (*Sliabh an Iolair*) are 19 **souterrains**, 18 **standing stones**, two **sculptured crosses** and seven **ring forts**. The most prominent is the powerful-looking **Doonbeg Fort**, which can be seen from the road, surrounded by the sea on three sides. The fort is dated between 400 and 450 BC. It was well protected by several defensive earthen walls and an inner stone wall. Inside, local people and livestock would have gathered when under threat by rival tribal groups. There is a souterrain leading from the inside of the fort to the entrance.

The road from Fahan winds around the countryside from Mount Eagle to Slea Head, from where you can see the Blasket Islands. The viewing places here allow you to stop and savour the views of traditional sheep fields, walls and dramatic headlands, dark against the ever-changing light of the seas and skies. Aerial photographs reveal how the traditional land-holding patterns of these small farms are changing, and with them the landscape we all cherish. Signs invite you to visit the well known Louis Mulcahy Pottery (*see* p.170), where you can watch a pot taking shape and perhaps make a purchase from the good selection of ceramics on sale.

The Blasket Islands (*Na Bhlascaodaí*)

The Blaskets are made up of several tiny islands plus the Great Blasket, all now uninhabited. Charles Haughey, the former Taoiseach and a fellow still surrounded by seemingly eternal investigations, owns one of them (Inisvickillane) as a holiday retreat. Plans to protect the islands (involving compulsory purchase) were proposed a few years ago – although interestingly, Haughey's island was not included. Great Blasket was established as a national historic park in 1989.

Some beautiful writing has sprung from the **Great Blasket** (*An Blascaod Mór*), produced just before the island way of life collapsed in the 1940s (see *www.blasket islands.com*). The young emigrated because of the harsh living conditions, and the Great Blasket has been uninhabited since 1953. Accounts of island life left to us through the writing record the warmth and the fun, as well as the misery and heartbreak, of their hard way of life. Their acceptance of death and life has great dignity, as does their sense of comradeship with the others on the island. There are three autobiographies written in the 1920s and 1930s: *The Islandman* by Tómas O'Crohan, *Twenty Years a-Growing* by Maurice O'Sullivan, and the autobiography of

Peig Sayers, often taught in schools. All are worth reading for the humour, pathos and command of the Gaelic language, which comes through even in translation.

You can visit the Blaskets from Dingle or Dunquin Harbour (*see* 'Getting to Islands off Kerry', p.144). Regular ferries take about 25 minutes from Dunquin. You might be lucky and persuade a local to take you out there in a curragh, the boat used for centuries by the island men to catch the shining mackerel found in these waters. When you arrive, you will see that the Great Blasket is full of memories. If you have read the literature, you will recognize the White Strand where the islanders played hurling on Christmas morning. Sadly, the stone walls around the intensively farmed fields have now tumbled and the village is a ruin. Tómas O'Crohan wrote at the end of his account, 'Somewhere there should be a memorial of it all... For the like of us will never be again'. It is a pleasant walk up to the ruined hill fort and there are wonderful views; you might also catch a glimpse of Blasket's new inhabitants – red deer, recently transplanted from Killarney.

In **Dunquin** (*Dún Chaoin*), the **Blasket Centre** (*open Easter–Sept daily 10–6; July–Aug 10–7; adm; t (066) 915 6444*) focuses on the story of the Blasket Islands. Unlike Horace's inn, the interior is better than the exterior; even though it looks like an oversized public convenience from the outside (its primary function for the many coach tours that find their way there), the exhibition is excellent. An unusual children's attraction in Dunquin is **The Enchanted Forest** (*t (066) 915 6234*), a fairy-tale museum full of fantasy, fun and friendly bears taking a journey through a mythical forest of the seasons in search of holidays. Dunquin became famous after the film *Ryan's Daughter* was filmed here, and there's a *Ryan's Daughter* walking route around Dunquin (*see* p.170), as well as mementoes from the film *Far and Away* (1991).

Ballyferriter to Tralee

Back on the mainland again, heading north up round the peninsula, you arrive at **Ballyferriter** (*Baile an Fheirtéaraigh*), a small village popular with holiday-makers because of the good beaches close by. It was named after the Anglo-Norman family of Ferriter who built the nearby ruined Castle Sybil. The most famous of that family was Pierce Ferriter, who wrote courtly love poetry; a soldier who was executed in Killarney when Cromwell and his forces rampaged through Ireland. The locals are very keen on preserving their heritage, namely the Irish Gaelic language, antiquities and beautiful scenery. Displays on the archaeology, flora and fauna of the area can be seen at the **Chorca Dhuibhne** **Regional Museum**, Ballyferriter (*open April–Oct daily 10–6; adm; t (066) 915 6333, www.corca-dhuibhne.com*).

At **Ballydavid** (*Baile na nGall*) the ancient industry of curragh-making goes on. The beaches around here are magnificent, in particular **Smerwick Strand**. In any of these you might find 'Kerry diamonds' – sparkly pieces of quartz that make a more attractive souvenir than anything you could buy. Everywhere are signs of past wars and struggles. One such ruin is **Dun an Oir**, or Fort de Oro, built by Spanish forces in

1579 when they and some Irish dug themselves in during the rebellion against Elizabeth I. Lord Grey, her deputy, took the fort, and the garrison was massacred. The road that leads past Castle Sybil towards Ferriter's Cove has many potholes and is not recommended if you are in a car; it is more comfortable to stroll amongst the superb views of the sea cliffs and Smerwick Harbour.

East of Ballyferriter, signs point the way to the oratory of **Gallarus** (*Visitor Centre,* **t** *(066) 915 5333*), the most perfect relic of early Irish architecture, and a sight not to be missed. You approach through a fuchsia-lined path amongst the green fields. This tiny, inverted, tent-shaped church may go back as far as the 8th century; no one knows. There is more art in it than meets the eye; despite their accidental appearance, all the stones in it were carefully shaped, and they fit together so well that not a drop of rain has got in for over a thousand years. The only missing parts of the original building are the crosses that stood at each end of the roof ridge. A visit here, along with a look at the reconstructed plans of the monastery at Ardfert (*see* p.179), provides a vision of the remarkable aesthetic of Irish building in the early medieval golden age – round, walled settlements, round huts and towers, and strange but striking shapes. It's fascinating to speculate how Irish architecture would have evolved had the local traditions not been destroyed by the Vikings and supplanted by foreign forms under the English.

At the crossroads above Gallarus, take a sharp left for **Kilmalkedar Church** (*Cill Maolceadair*), built in Irish Romanesque style in the 12th century. There must have been an earlier pagan settlement here as there are some ancient carved stones around the site, including an ogham stone and an early sundial. Nearby, close to a ruined house for the clergy, is the Saint's Road up **Brandon Mountain** (*Cnoc Bréanainn*, 3,127ft/950m). This ancient track leads up to **St Brendan the Navigator's Shrine**. St Brendan climbed up to its summit to meditate and in a vision saw Hy-Brasil, the Island of the Blessed. Afterwards he voyaged far and wide looking for this ideal land, possibly even as far as America. People still climb up here on the last Saturday in June to pray. An easier climb can be made from the village of **Cloghane** (*An Clochán*). The views from it are magical – it's not surprising St Brendan saw Utopia from here.

The main (unnumbered) road from Dingle to Stradbally and then on to Tralee (R560) takes you over the **Connor Pass** (*An Chonair*, 1,500ft/497m) to reveal great views over Dingle Bay and Tralee Bay. There are dark loughs in the valley and giant boulders strewn everywhere. At the foot of the pass, a branch road leads off towards Cloghane and Brandon, both good bases for exploring and climbing the sea cliffs around Brandon Point and Brandon Head. **Brandon Bay** looks temptingly calm at times, but it is a dangerous anchorage. Mountains encircle it, and the road is high above the sloping fields that edge the long beach. **Tomasin's Bar** in **Stradbally** (*Sráidbhaile*) has framed newspaper cuttings that record the sinking of *The Port of Yorrock*, a barque from Glasgow returning from America which tragically went down with all hands. There is a memorial to the crew on Kilcummin Strand.

This area is well worth spending some time in if you base yourself in or near **Castlegregory** (*Caisleán Ghriaire*). You could explore the sandy spit of the peninsula that ends at Rough Point, whilst the **Magharee Islands** (*Oileán an Mhachaire*), made of

limestone and sometimes called The Seven Hogs, are scattered even farther north. To
the south towers **Beenoskee Mountain** (*Binn os Gaoith*) and beside it the slightly
smaller Stradbally. Beenoskee summit gives you sublime views in every direction.

Surfing and swimming are excellent here, and an interesting trip can be made to
Illauntannig, one of the Magharee islands (*see* 'Water Sports', p.176). On it are the
remains of an old monastic ruin surrounded by a cashel. The limestone gives the
coast distinctive, rough-ridged and fluted shapes. On the spit is Lough Gill, a shallow,
brackish lagoon where the Bewick's swan and other water birds have made their
home. A variety of flowers thrive on the water's edges and in the lough itself are large
yellow waterlilies. On the main road into Tralee you will pass Blennerville (*see* p.177).

Tralee (*Trá Lí*)

Tralee is the chief town and administrative capital of County Kerry, and is invariably
jam-packed with cars and shoppers. It is famous for the sentimental Victorian song
'The Rose of Tralee'.

Tralee was the chief seat of the Desmond family, but nothing remains of their
castle. In 1579 the Earl of Desmond was asked to aid the Commissioners of Munster
against the Spanish, who had landed at Smerwick. But the Desmonds had no love for
the English, and that night Elizabeth's representatives and their entourage were put
to death by the Earl's brother. In the following year a ruthless campaign of retribution
was waged against the Desmonds. Tralee was threatened and the Earl set the town
afire rather than leave anything that might be claimed as a prize by the Queen's men.
In 1583 the Earl of Desmond, then an old man, was hunted from his hiding place in
Glanageenty woods and beheaded. His head was put on a spike on London Bridge, as
was customary in those times. The old Dominican priory that the Desmonds founded
was completely destroyed by Sir Edward Denny, the Elizabethan courtier-soldier, who
was granted the town when the Desmond estates were seized.

The town has suffered continually from wars and burnings, and today is largely
mid-19th-century in character, although there are some elegant Georgian houses in
the centre. The courthouse has a fine Ionic façade, and in Denny Street there is an
impressive 1798 memorial of a single man armed with a pike. In Ashe Street the
Dominican **Church of the Holy Cross** is by Pugin, built after the monks had managed
to re-establish themselves here, long after Sir Edward Denny destroyed their priory.
The priory garden contains some ancient carved stones, amongst them the White
Knight stone and the Roche slab which date from 1685, proof that the foundation was
at least partly in existence in the reign of James II. The interior is very fine, especially
the Chapel of the Blessed Virgin, with exquisite mosaics and altar charts by that great
artist Michael Healy, who worked at the turn of the 20th century. In Abbey Street
there is a modern **church** with a lovely chapel dedicated to the Blessed Virgin Mary,
which contains some fine stained-glass work, also by Healy.

The **Ashe Memorial Hall**, an imposing 19th-century building off Denny Street,
houses the very fine **Kerry County Museum** (*open Jan–Mar Tues–Fri 10–4.30; April–*

Tourist Information

Tralee: Ashe Memorial Hall, **t** (066) 712 1288; *open all year.*

Shopping

Antiques

Antiques & Interiors, 15 Princes St, **t** (066) 712 5635. Georgian house furnished with books, prints and antiques for sale.

Crafts

Carraig Donn Knitwear, 17 Bridge Street, *www.carraigdonn.com.*
John J Murphy Weavers,Currow Road, Farranfore, *www.killarneyweavers.com.*
Úna Ní Shé, *Cathair Bó Sine*, Ventry, *www. unanishe.com.* Unusual felt sculptures.

Food

Sean Cara, 5 Abbey Court. Excellent cheeses, home-made bread and lemon curd.

Sports and Activities

Golf

Tralee Golf Club, West Barrow, Ardfert, **t** (066) 713 6379, *www.traleegolfclub.com.*
Kerries Golf Course, The Kerries, **t** (066) 712 2112

Open Farms

Farmworld, Slieve, Camp, **t** (066) 915 8200. 160-acre hill farm with rare breeds.

Water Sports

The Aqua Dome, Ballyard, **t** (066) 712 8899, *www.discoverkerry.com/aquadome.* Indoor water theme park.
West Kerry Angling and Fenit Sea Cruise Centre, Fenit Pier, **t** (066) 713 6049. Trips to the Magharee Islands.

Where to Stay

Tralee t (066–)

Ballygarry House Hotel, Killarney Road, **t** 712 3322, *www.ballygarryhouse.com* (*luxury*). Elegantly decorated hotel in well-kept

gardens, with renowned dining and attentive service.
Meadowlands Hotel, Oakpark, **t** 718 0444, *www.meadowlands-hotel.com* (*expensive*). Comfortable hotel with charming, elegant interiors. The superb restaurant, *An Pota Stóir*, offers seafood freshly caught by the hotel's proprietor.
Castlemorris House, Ballymullen, **t** 718 0060 (*moderate*). Large, 18th-century house in extensive gardens, with a pleasant drawing room, spacious rooms, welcoming open fires and a friendly atmosphere.
Collis Sandes House, Oakpark, **t** 712 8658, *www.colsands.com* (*moderate*). Victorian country house that also features wonderful, traditional musical entertainment in the evenings. Dorms or private rooms.
The Grand Hotel, Denny Street, **t** 712 2877, *www.grandhoteltralee.com* (*moderate*). Comfortable and plush; though it's more 'smart' than 'grand'.
Tralee Townhouse, High Street, **t** 718 1111, *www.traleetownhouse.com* (*moderate– inexpensive*). Convenient, with plain rooms.
Finnegan's Hostel, 17 Denny Street, **t** 712 7610, *www.finneganshostel.com* (*inexpensive*). 18th-century townhouse B&B.
The Willows, 5 Clonmore Terrace, **t** 712 3779, *www.thewillowsbnb.com* (*inexpensive*). B&B in a pretty terrace with charming interiors.

Eating Out

Brooks Restaurant, Ballygarry House Hotel, Killarney Road, **t** 712 3322 (*expensive*). Great choice of chargrilled meats or fish on a gourmet menu: rack of Kerry lamb, seared peppered yellow fin tuna or Atlantic oysters.
Restaurant David Norris, Ivy House, Ivy Terrace, **t** 712 9292 (*expensive*). International, creative cuisine using organic ingredients where possible. A cut above the rest.
The Tankard, Kilfenora, **t** 713 6164 (*moderate*). Cheerfully decorated inside, with wonderful views over Tralee Bay, this pub and restaurant is very popular with locals for beef and fresh seafood, as well as their extensive wine list.
Duchas House, Edward Street, Tralee, **t** (066) 712 4803. Evening performances of Irish music, song and dance in July–Aug.

May Tues–Sat 9.30–5.30; June–Aug daily 9.30–5.30; Sept–Dec Tues–Sat 9.30–5; adm;
***t** (066) 712 7777).* The display, entitled 'Kerry, The Kingdom', traces the history of Kerry from 5000 BC and the exhibits include archaeological treasures found in Kerry. There is some fascinating film footage taken during the War of Independence and after up to 1965. Thomas Ashe, for whom this building is named, was a native of Tralee and was active in the 1916 Uprising and the IRB. He was arrested and imprisoned in Mountjoy Prison, where he went on hunger strike in protest at being treated like an ordinary convict and not as a political prisoner. After he was force-fed roughly, fluid got into his windpipe and then his lungs, and he died a few hours later. He was a close friend and ally of Michael Collins, who described him as 'A man of no complexes. Doing whatever he did for Ireland and always in a quiet way'. Another attraction in the museum is a life-size reconstruction of a street in medieval Tralee – you travel through it in a 'time car', seeing and smelling what street life was like in the walled Desmond town, so different from the Tralee of today with its supermarket, multi-screen cinema complex and aqua-dome fun centre. The town park surrounding the museum and tourist office is well maintained with pretty trees and, of course, there is a rose garden, which blooms at its best during the Rose of Tralee Festival.

Past the rose garden is the headquarters of **Siamsa Tíre** (**t** *(066) 712 3055, www. siamsatire.com*), the National Folk Theatre, which presents performances of song, dance and mime in an idealized version of rural life. Those with children can carry on around the corner to the **Science Works**, Godfrey Place (**t** *(066) 712 9855*), an interactive science museum.

The **Tralee Steam Train** (*runs May–Oct, on the hour 11–5;* **t** *(066) 712 1064*), a relic of the old Tralee and Dingle narrow-gauge railway, leaves from Ballyard station. The 3km jaunt takes you to **Blennerville Windmill** (*open April–Oct daily 10–6; adm adults €3.49, children €1.90;* **t** *(066) 712 1064*), the largest in the British Isles (1780), complete with restaurant and craft shops. There is access to the **Irish Famine Ship Records** here (*on a trial basis at the time of writing; small charge*) – a database of 19th century emigrants who travelled to the US before and during the Great Famine.

Blennerville used to be the port for Tralee, although it is now silted up. The shipyard includes a **visitor's centre** (*open daily 9–6; adm*), with exhibits on traditional shipbuilding and the emigrant experience. Blennerville was the initial site for the reconstruction of the **Jeanie Johnston**, a replica of an 18th-century sailing ship built from the original plans. The original *Jeanie* was a passenger ship that carried emigrants to America in the years of the famine. The vessel was completed in 2002 and the project team and crew successfully recreated the voyage to the USA and Canada in 2003 (see *www.jeaniejohnston.ie*).

It is interesting to look at the intricate family tree of the Blennerhassetts, a family who ruled over these parts in the 18th century and renamed the place in their honour. One of them tried to abolish Puck Fair in Killorglin, but luckily the locals refused to comply. One of their old homes is at Ballyseedy Castle (now a hotel). North of Tralee near Castleisland is **Crag Cave** (*signposted off the N21 Limerick–Tralee road; open daily mid-March–Nov 10–5.30, July and Aug 10–6; adm;* **t** *(066) 714 1244; www.cragcave.com*), an underground cave system at least 4km long, discovered only in 1983 and now a big tourist attraction.

North Kerry

North Kerry has none of the splendour of Dingle but rather a quiet charm, a taste of which you will get if you drive between Tralee and Tarbert on your way to County Clare. Places to visit in north Kerry include the village of **Spa**, once famous for its

Tourist Information

Listowel: St John's Church, **t** (068) 22590; *open April–Sept.*

Shopping

Art and Crafts
Blue Umbrella Gallery, 21 Church Street, Listowel, **t** 087 611 0499. Local artists' and craftspeople's cooperative.

Sports and Activities

Fishing
John Deady, Fenit, **t** (066) 713 6118. Operates the *Kerry Colleen* from Fenit.
Keltoi Lodge, Ballybunion, **t** (068) 25222, *www. deepseacharters.ie*. Sea angling from Tarbert.

Golf
Listowel Golf Club, Feale View, Listowel, **t** (068) 21592. Nine-hole course.
Old Course and **Cashen Course**, Ballybunion, **t** (068) 27146, *www.ballybuniongolfclub.ie*.

Open Farms
Beal Lodge Dairy Farm, Asdee, Listowel, **t** (068) 41137. Watch farmhouse cheese being made.

Pony Trekking
Curragh Cottage, Spa, Tralee, **t** (066) 713 6320.

Seaweed Baths
Both are on Listowel beach. *See also* p.117.
Collins Family, North Beach, Ballybunion, **t** (068) 27469 *Open June–early Oct.*
Daly's Baths, Ladies' Strand, Ballybunion, **t** (068) 27559 *Open June–end Sept.*

Where to Stay and Eat

Barrow Country House, near Ardfert, **t** (066) 713 6437, *www.barrowhouse.com* (*moderate*). Beautiful 1723 house, once home to the Knights of Kerry and located right on Barrow harbour. Rooms are large and luxuriously appointed; some suites have a Jacuzzi.
Burntwood House, Listowel, **t** (068) 21516, *burntwoodhouse@hotmail.com* (*moderate*). Georgian house attached to a dairy farm on the Ballylongford road, offering B&B.
Listowel Arms Hotel, The Square, Listowel, **t** (068) 21500, *www.listowelarms.com* (*moderate*). Old-fashioned country hotel with elegant interiors. The dining room (*expensive*) serves very good fresh, local produce amidst classical, restrained decor.
Mount Rivers, Listowel, **t** (068) 21494, *www. mountriverslistowel.com* (*moderate*). In a comfortable 19th-century family home just outside Listowel (off the R555), with a family suite and two double rooms.
White Sands Hotel, Ballyheigue, **t** (066) 713 3102, *www.cmvhotels.com* (*moderate*). Surrounded by wonderful beaches. **Jimmy Browne's Pub**, in the hotel, hosts regular traditional music sessions.
Listowel, in particular, has a few award-winning restaurants and is a good place to find gourmet food.
The Oyster Tavern, The Spa, Fenit, **t** (066) 713 6102 (*expensive*). Award-winning seafood, game and steaks (as well as veggie meals) in a beautiful setting.
Allo's Bistro, 41 Church Street, Listowel, **t** (068) 22880 (*moderate*). Great food – far better than just pub grub.
The Literary Café, *Seachai* Centre, The Square, Listowel, **t** (068) 22212. Good café food.

sulphur waters, and **Fenit**, a small fishing port, from where the coastal views on a bright day are stunning. An attraction for those with children is **Fenit Seaworld** (*adm adults €5.08, children €1.90;* **t** *(066) 713 6544*): the aquarium takes as its theme underwater wildlife on and around a shipwreck. On a fine day, the fishing trips and barbecues on the Magheree Islands in Tralee Bay (*see* p.175 and p.176) are bracing.

A very well-known ecclesiastical site built on St Brendan's original foundation is **Ardfert Cathedral** on the R551, a noble Norman building dating from the 13th century and partially restored (*open May–Sept daily 9.30–6.30; guided tours; adm; www. heritageireland.ie*). Exhibits inside detail Ardfert's history as a monastic centre from the earliest times. The great nave remains without a roof, and the authorities have had to put up a sign to forbid locals from making any new burials inside. Besides the cathedral, the grounds contain a picturesque graveyard with those vault-like graves that are common here, and the remains of the early Romanesque church that the cathedral replaced, which has a beautiful carved south window. Beside it is *Temple na Griffin*, a late Gothic ruin. Ardfert was an important settlement in the early Middle Ages, and probably long before then. The surrounding countryside is full of ring forts and other ancient relics, along with an austerely handsome 15th-century **Franciscan friary and church** just down the road from the cathedral.

Banna, about two miles northwest of Ardfert, is a place of dunes, caravans and a beach at least six miles long. **Ballyheige** is a small village on a continuation of Banna Strand; the white sand and views of Kerry Head make it popular with holiday-makers.

Going inland, signposted after the village of Ballyduff, is **Rattoo Round Tower** and ruined priory, rising from among the flat fields. The tower is one of the most perfect examples of its kind and is in good condition. The graveyard has the usual mixture of old and new gravestones and is overgrown with delicate ivy and hart's-tongue fern. **Rattoo Heritage Complex** (*adm;* **t** *(066) 713 1000*) has a display on the local archaeology, history and folklore of north Kerry.

On the main road between Tralee and Listowel at Kilflynn is **A Day in The Bog** (*open daily 9–7;* **t** *(066) 713 2555*). With its thatched roof, a pets' corner, café and an audio-visual show, it re-creates a farmer's life in the boglands. There's also an exhibit on the work of the North Kerry Writers; some evenings they have traditional music sessions.

Listowel has ambitions as a cultural centre and puts on a Writers' Week every spring, with a book fair, art and photography exhibitions and writing workshops (*see* p.145). This attractive town is situated on the River Feale, on the flat Kerry plain, with a ruined 15th-century castle in the square. It belonged to the Fitzmaurice family, Anglo-Normans who later showed consistent disloyalty to the Crown. Also in the square is a handsome Catholic church, and on the outskirts of the town is a racecourse. Many writers came from this area. Of particular note are Bryan MacMahon, whose novel *Children of the Rainbow* is entrancing with its descriptions of the Kerry countryside, and prolific novelist and playwright John B. Keane, whose pub is on William Street. His novel *The Field* became an Oscar-winning film. Listowel has some remarkable plaster shop fronts by Pat McAuliffe (1846–1921), **The Maid of Erin** on Church Street being the most rococo. **St John's Theatre and Arts Centre** (*open daily 9.30–6;* **t** *(068) 22566*), on the Square in the late Georgian Church of Ireland church, has a weekly programme of theatre, music, dance and exhibitions and occasional evening shows.

On the coast, some 10 miles (16km) northwest of Listowel on the R553, is the delightful and popular resort of **Ballybunion**. The golden sand is divided by a black rocky promontory, upon which perch dramatically the remains of a 14th-century castle. Besides good sea bathing, you can have a relaxing hot **seaweed bath** (*see* p.178 and p.117), which leaves your skin feeling like silk and seems to take away any aches and pains. It is very popular with jockeys after the Listowel races. The seaweed is hand-picked from the Blackrocks every day.

The views of Kerry Head and Loop Head in County Clare are magnificent from Ballybunion, and there are long, bracing walks along the cliffs to **Beal Point**, which overlooks the Shannon Estuary. See if you can persuade a boatman to take you out to the intricate and connecting caves within the cliffs; the largest is known as the Pigeon Cave. Most people come here for the beach and the golf, and B&Bs line the road towards the golf course. Slap bang next to the smart-looking clubhouse is the parish burial ground, among the dunes and cropped grass. It's an odd sight, especially when funeral mourners meet golfers. **Ballybunion Heritage Museum** (*adm €1.30; t (088) 654127*), on Church Road, has some interesting relics of the Marconi Station and the Lartigue monorail system, which between 1888 and 1924 ran to Listowel.

Carrigafoyle Castle, north of Ballylongford, is a 16th-century O'Connor castle that stands by the shoreline; it was built of carboniferous sandstone and has weathered well. It's always accessible and you can walk to the battlements by a winding raised stone path (may be submerged during spring tides) to get a stunning view. Rather than take the main road to Ballylongford, you could go on the winding (unnumbered) coastal road, bordered by quiet farms and the lapping sea, where waders pick their way across the shore. This will take you eventually to Carrigafoyle.

If you are taking the car ferry across to County Clare from **Tarbert** (*see* p.232), you can stop to see the **Bridewell Courthouse and Jail** (*open April–Oct daily 10–6; adm adults €5.08, under 12s €2.54; t (068) 36500*). The buildings have been restored with tableaux, exhibits and documents to show what justice and prison were like for local people in Victorian times when the British still ruled. Especially interesting are the accounts of life on transportation ships going to Australia, and the verse of the neglected poet Thomas MacGreevy (1894–1967) who came from around here.

A short, signposted walk leads from the courthouse through mature mixed woods, part of the demesne of **Tarbert House** (*open May–Aug Mon–Sat 10am–12 noon and 2–4pm, Sun 10am–12 noon; adm €5; t (068) 36198*), a fine, grey Georgian Queen Anne house which has been the residence of the Leslie family since it was completed in 1730. Many of the paintings and pieces of furniture inside date from the 18th century. Visitors to the house included Benjamin Franklin, Jonathan Swift, Dan O'Connell, Lord Kitchener and Winston Churchill.

County Cork

12

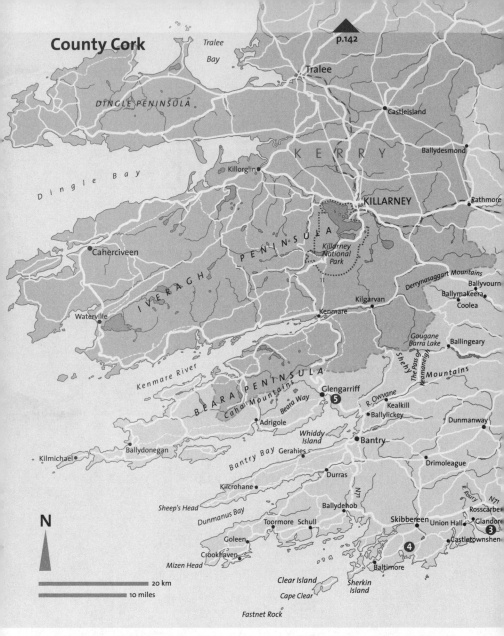

County Cork

p.142

Tralee Bay

Tralee

Castleisland

K E R R Y

Ballydesmond

DINGLE PENINSULA

Dingle Bay

Killorglin

Rathmore

KILLARNEY

Cahirciveen

Killarney National Park

IVERAGH PENINSULA

Derrynasaggart Mountains

Ballyvourn

Ballymakeera

Coolea

Kilgarvan

Kenmare

Waterville

Gougane Barra Lake

Ballingeary

Kenmare River

Shehy Mountains

The Pass of Keamaneigh

BEARA PENINSULA

Caha Mountains

Beara Way

Glengarriff
5

R. Owvane

Kealkill

Ballylickey

Dunmanway

Adrigole

Whiddy Island

Bantry

Ballydonegan

Gerahies

Kilmichael

Bantry Bay

Durras

Drimoleague

Kilcrohane

Ballydehob

N71

R. Roury

N71

Rosscarbery

Sheep's Head

Dunmanus Bay

Toormore   Schull

Skibbereen   Union Hall   Glandore
3

Castletownshend

4

Goleen

Crookhaven

Baltimore

Mizen Head

Clear Island

Sherkin Island

Cape Clear

Fastnet Rock

N

20 km

10 miles

Imagine quiet flowing rivers in green wooded valleys, a coastline which combines savage rock scenery with the softest bays, hill slopes that are purple with heather in the late summer, an ivy-clad castle standing amongst hayricks in a field, and you have captured something of County Cork. This is Ireland's largest county and it includes some of the richest agricultural land (in the northeast), the third largest city in Ireland and the important ocean port of Cobh, as well as the most beautiful coastal and mountain scenery in the country and a famously mild climate because of the warm Gulf Stream. It is also the most suitable spot to indulge in the relaxing

LIMERICK

Mullaghareirk
Mountains

Broadford

Kilmallock

Ardpatrick

TIPPERARY

Galty Mountains

Liscarroll

Buttevant

Kildorrey

N73

Mitchelstown

Knockmealdown Mountains

Doneraile

R. Awbeg

Kanturk

N72

Castletownroche

Glanworth

N8

Kilworth

Mallow

N20

Killavullen

N72

Fermoy

Ballyduff

WATERFORD

River Blackwater

Nagles
Mountains

Lismore

Millstreet

Castlelyons

Conna

River Bride

Boggeragh   Mountains

Glenville

River Blackwater

C O R K

N8

Macroom

Blarney

N20

Knockraha

Dungourney

Youghal

Carrigadrohid

Dripsey

Riverstown

Dunkathel
House

Barryscourt
Castle

N25

Coachford

2

CORK

Midleton

Castlemartyr

Inishcarra
Reservoir

Farnanes

N22

Ballincollig

1

Blackrock

N25

Youghal Bay

Crookstown

Douglas

Passage West

Cobh

Cloyne

Garryvoe

Ballinhassig

Ringaskiddy

Shanagarry

Ballycotton

N71

Crosshaven

Bandon

Inishannon

Myrtleville

Robert's
Cove

Swansea & the
continent

Bandon River

Ballynacarriga

N71

Kinsale

Rossmore
R. Argideen

Kilbrittain

Ballinspittle

Oysterhaven

Clonakilty

Timoleague

Garrettstown

Courtmacsherry

Butlerstown

Old Head of Kinsale

Galley
Head

Highlights

1 Cork City, for the Old English Market,
  Crawford Art Gallery and lively nightlife

2 Blarney Castle and its famous stone

3 Symbolic Drombeg Stone Circle

4 Beautiful Lough Ine nature reserve

5 Subtropical Ilnacullin (Garinish Island)

pastimes of eating and drinking: you'll find some of Ireland's best hotels and restaurants located in attractive settings all over the county. There is wonderful sailing, deep-sea angling, and salmon- and trout fishing amongst its 680 miles of indented coastline, with beautiful stately homes and gardens to visit, and, of course, the Blarney Stone to kiss. The growth of tourism has not yet spoilt the coast, but it has encouraged better quality restaurants, hotels, pubs and shops. Many of the most discerning visitors are the Corkonians themselves, who work hard in the city and enjoy their free time in the pretty coastal resorts such as Kinsale and Crosshaven.

The city is something else: country people may be more laid-back, but city folk have produced a cosmopolitan centre humming with energy and confidence, full of grand buildings and shops, industry and culture, aided by a wit and business sense that is hard to beat. Dubliners alternate between jealousy and heavy sarcasm in trying to describe the place – the best I've heard is, 'God's own place with the devil's

Getting There

A wide selection of airlines flies to Cork from various UK cities; see Travel p.92. You can also get to Cork by ferry: Fishguard–Rosslare, or Swansea–Cork; see Travel p.94 and p.95.

From the Airport

Cork Airport is south of the city on the N27; there is a regular shuttle service from the airport to the bus station on Parnell Place, which takes 20mins and costs €4. A taxi to Cork City centre will cost approximately €15. Cork Airport, t (021) 431 3131, www.cork-airport.com.

Getting Around

Trains include a suburban service to Fota and Cobh. For enquiries call t (021) 450 6766, www.irishrail.ie. Kent Station is 5mins' walk northeast of the city centre on Lower Glanmire Road. The bus station is central, in Parnell Place, with city and rural services. City centre fares are a flat rate; a day pass costs about €6. Call t (021) 450 8188 or use the travel planner on www.buseireann.ie. A central taxi rank can be found in the middle of St Patrick's Street; Cork Taxi Coop t (021) 427 2222.

Car Hire

Alamo/National, t (021) 432 0755, www.carhire.ie.
Thrifty, t (021) 434 8488, www.thrifty.ie.
Murrays, t (021) 491 7300.

Bike Hire

Irish Cycle Hire, Cork rail station, t (021) 455 1430.
Rothar Cycle Tours, 55 Barrack Street, t (021) 431 3133.

Getting to Islands off County Cork

Sherkin Island: from Baltimore, 8 daily sailings in summer (about 10mins, €5); t (028) 20125, www.baltimore-ireland.com.
Cape Clear Island: there are 2 ferries, one from Schull and one from Baltimore (both 45mins). The Baltimore Naomh Ciarán II runs at least once daily, t 086 346 5110, www.capeclearferry.info; the Schull Karycraft sails daily June–Sept (May upon sufficient demand), t (028) 28138, www.westcork coastalcruises.com.
Ilnacullin: the Glengarriff passenger ferry Harbour Queen, Mar–Oct daily every 20mins; t (027) 63116, www.garnishislandferry.com.
Bere Island: 2 ferries operate services to Bere; Bere Island Ferries sail the Misneach or Morvern from Castletownbere, t (027) 75009, www.bereislandferries.com; Murphy's Ferries sail daily from a pontoon 3km east of Castletownbere, t (027) 75014, www.murphysferry.com.
Whiddy Island: Off Bantry in Bantry Bay. Contact Danny O'Leary, t (027) 50310.
Heir Island: from Cunamore Pier, off Bantry Road, Skibbereen, or from Baltimore. Contact Danny Murphy, t 086 888 7799, or Richard Pyburn, t 086 809 2447.
Shearwater Cruises: contact John Petch, t (023) 49610. Cruises from KYC Marina in Kinsale.

own people'. Corkonians think nothing of nipping across to Paris for the weekend, and there is an air of sophistication here that seriously challenges Dublin as the cultural capital. The Triskel Arts Centre in the city centre is excellent and puts on a great variety of events all year, while the Crawford Art Gallery has a memorable collection of Irish and English works.

Corkonians are a mixed bunch, consisting of the down-to-earth working class and the moneyed middle class – which includes a rather genteel Protestant element whose forebears manned the British Empire – as well as quite a few 'blow-ins': Britons, Europeans and North Americans who have settled down to enjoy the way of life. You will notice them particularly in west Cork, where some have restored traditional cottages and farms, and produce their own vegetables, art and crafts.

The Cork accent is very strong, slow and sing-songy – you may have to concentrate to understand it.

Festivals

Cork City was very proud to be designated European Capital of Culture in 2005, so its events calendar has been expanded.

March
St Patrick's Day Festival: in most Cork towns.
Celtfest: Celtic art, music, dance, language and culture, held by Cork University.

April
Cork International Choral Festival: festival of choirs in the City Hall; www.corkchoral.ie.

May
West Cork Walking Festival: www.westcork.ie.
Bantry Mussel Fair: 3 days of mussel-feasting (not in 2005); www.bantrymusselfair.ie.
Denis Murphy's Weekend: in Knocknagree.
Rosscarbery Arts & Literature Festival: www.rosscarbery.ie/arts_and_literature.
Baltimore Wooden Boat and Seafood Festival: www.baltimorewoodenboatfestival.com

June
Cork Midsummer Festival: 12 days of events and performing arts; www.corkfestival.com.
Eurochild: www.tighfili.com.
Bandon Music Festival: www.bandonmusicfestival.com.
Murphy's Uncorked: Irish and UK stand-up comedians; www.murphysuncorked.com.
Innishannon Steam and Vintage Rally: on the bank holiday weekend; www.isvrally.com.
West Cork Literary Festival: at Bantry; www.westcorkmusic.ie.

West Cork Garden Trail: 16 private gardens open; www.westcorkgardentrail.com.

July
Youghal Maritime Festival.
Wild Boar Festival, Kanturk.
Bandon Summer Carnival.
Cahirmee Horse Fair: ancient fair at Buttevant.

August
Courtmacsherry Harbour Festival: sandcastle competitions, talent contests and races.
Ballabuidhe Races and Horse Fair: ancient races in Dunmanway; www.ballabuidhe.com.
Ballingeary Agricultural & Horticultural Show: in a Gaeltacht village, with animals on show.

September
Cork Folk Festival: www.corkfestival.com.
Frank O'Connor Festival of the Short Story: in Cork City; www.munsterlit.ie.
Youghal Through the Ages Heritage Week: Irish heritage; www.youghalchamber.ie.
International Storytelling Festival, Cape Clear Island; http://indigo.ie/~stories.
Midleton Food & Drink Festival: www.ireland-cork.com/midleton.

October
Cork Film Festival: www.corkfilmfest.org.
Jazz Festival: Cork, www.corkjazzfestival.com.
Kinsale Festival of Autumn Flavours: festival of fine food; www.kinsalerestaurants.com.
Cape Clear Storytelling Workshop: Cape Clear Island; http://indigo.ie/~ckstory.

History

The well-watered and fertile lands of Cork attracted human settlement as far back as 6000 BC, when people lived by hunting, fishing and gathering roots and berries. Kitchen middens found around the shores of Cork Harbour date from this time. From the megalithic period there are stone circles, standing stones and wedge tombs to explore; luckily these have survived because farmers did not touch them, believing them to be fairy places.

Waves of invaders brought different peoples, with the Celts arriving between 800 and 500 BC. Written history dates from the coming of Christianity and later clerics recorded the sagas, annals and laws of this Celtic culture, which had been left intact on the edge of the Roman Empire. St Ciaran of Cape Clear is titled 'first-born of the Saints of Ireland'; it is claimed he arrived before St Patrick in the 5th century AD.

Early church sites abound, and the metalwork and carved stone that survives from the 11th and 12th centuries testifies to the mastery and skill of the Celtic artist. With the invasion of the Anglo-Normans in 1169, the Continental religious orders were set up in rich and beautiful abbeys. Some of their ruins remain. The Norsemen or Vikings mounted many raids on the early Christian settlements from the late 8th century onwards. They soon founded their own ports, settling down to trade with the native Irish, accepted Christianity, and so gradually became amalgamated into Gaelic society, especially in the southeast.

The Anglo-Norman invasion brought advanced building techniques to Ireland: the Norman warlords built sophisticated castles, usually on defensive sites that had been used before. Their followers lived in moated farmhouses. The Gaelic ruling families – MacCarthys, O'Sullivans, O'Mahonys, O'Driscolls and O'Donovans – generally lost out to the Norman Barrys and their followers. In the 15th century, the ruling families built tower houses, and many of these grand ruins remain, to add drama and interest to the countryside and coastline (Blarney Castle is one of the best examples).

Comfortable domestic architecture did not develop until the 17th and 18th centuries, because until then the county was very unsettled, as the Celts and Anglo-Normans fought, made alliances with and against each other, and largely ignored the laws issued from London. It was only the area around Dublin, known as 'the Pale', that was really under the thumb of the English.

After the Elizabethan wars of the late 16th century, the land was colonized with families loyal to the Crown, who supported the administrators sent to implement English rule. Huge tracts of land were granted to adventurers; men like Richard Boyle, who became Earl of Cork, and Sir Edmund Spenser, who wrote *The Faerie Queene* at Kilcoman Castle. Beautiful Georgian houses survive from the 18th century, especially in the richer farmlands of Cork, when the new landowners began to feel secure in their properties and to build, plant and garden. It is possible to stay in many of these fine houses, which are not huge, but perfect in proportion and decoration. Nowadays, many have been bought up by the increasingly prosperous Irish and by foreign buyers. There is a new regard for the craftsmanship of the mainly Irish workers who created them, and a reassessment of the landed gentry, who were not necessarily all as bad as they have been portrayed.

By contrast, the oppressive laws introduced to control the Catholic population in the 1690s, the Rising of 1798 and the ghastly famine of the 1840s all combined to create a peasantry that was poverty-stricken. Large families relied almost totally on the potato, and the failure of the crop in successive years brought starvation, disease and death to thousands in County Cork. The fight for fair rents and fixity of tenure was pursued vigorously in the 1880s. The Irish War of Independence was fought with ferocity in County Cork, with burnings and cruelties on both sides. The Civil War split family loyalties in two, and it was especially bitter in County Cork where anti-Treaty forces were in control. Michael Collins (1890–1922), the dynamic revolutionary leader and one of the men responsible for negotiating the Anglo-Irish Treaty of December 1921, was the son of a small farmer from Clonakilty. During the Civil War he was shot in the head by the anti-Treaty forces, in an ambush between Macroom and Bandon.

Today, the memories of the Civil War are still alive, but the people are forward-looking. Industries such as whiskey-making, brewing, clothing, food-processing, computers and pharmaceuticals have boomed around Cork Harbour. The drug Viagra, among others, is made in Ringaskiddy for Pfizer, as well as artificial hips and knees produced for Johnson & Johnson (as you can imagine, a good many jokes circulate in the local bars). A large proportion of the population, which presently stands at about 473,000, is involved in the tourist industry.

Cork City (*Corcaigh*)

The name Cork comes from the Gaelic *Corcaigh*, meaning 'marshy place'. Ireland's second city, with a population of 140,000, is built on marshy land on the banks of the River Lee and has crept up the hills. Over the years, nearly all the islands in this marsh have been reclaimed, their watercourses built over and the city walls removed. The river flows in two main channels, crossed by bridges, so that central Cork is actually on an island. (It can be confusing if you are driving there for the first time, with its one-way roads and the crossing and recrossing of the river.)

Until the Anglo-Norman invasion in 1169, Cork City was largely a Danish stronghold. It was famous from the 7th century for its excellent school under St Finbarr. The Cork citizens were an independent lot and, although after 1180 English laws were nominally in force, it was really the wealthy merchants who were in charge. In 1492 they took up the cause of the Yorkists and Perkin Warbeck, and went with him to Kent where he was proclaimed Pretender to the English crown (by claiming he was Richard IV, King of England and Lord of Ireland). They lost their charter for that piece of impudence, but Cork continued to be a rebel city – although, rather curiously, it offered no resistance to Oliver Cromwell. William III laid siege to it in 1690 because it stood by James II, and it had to surrender without honour. In the 17th and 18th centuries it grew rapidly with the expansion of the butter trade, and many of the splendid Georgian buildings you can still see were built during this time. By the 19th century it had become a centre for the Fenian movement, which worked for an independent republic. During the War of Independence (1919–21), the city was badly

burned by the Auxiliaries, known as 'the Black and Tans' after the colours of their uniform, and one of Cork's mayors died on hunger strike in an English prison. But Cork is also famous for a more moderate character, Father Theobald Matthew (1790–1856), who persuaded thousands of people to go off the drink, though the effect of his temperance drive was ruined by the potato famine and the general misery it brought.

Cork still has a reputation for clannish behaviour amongst its businessmen and for independence in the arts and politics, but it would be hard to find a friendlier city to wander around, and you can easily explore it on foot.

City Centre

Cork's business and shopping centre is crowded onto an island between the twin channels of the River Lee, with elegant bridges linking the north and south sides of the city. The city's elegant skyline is still, like Derry's, 19th-century. Cork has spires and gracious wide streets, and many of its fine buildings, bridges and quays are of a silvery limestone. **St Patrick's Street** curves close to the river; one side of the street is lined with old buildings, the other by uninspiring modern offices, shop fronts and an opera house built since the burning in 1920. Here you will find a statue of Father Matthew. The covered **English Market**, hidden behind the facades of St Patrick's Street, is rather like Smithfield Market in London and displays great pig carcasses and drisheen (a type of black pudding), as well as fresh fish, piles of vegetables, tasty bread and olives of every description. It also has some superb eating places.

Paul Street, north of St Patrick's Street, once the Huguenot quarter, is the trendy corner of Cork, with cafés, bookshops and buskers in an attractive pedestrian area. It joins **Cornmarket Street** with its open-air flea market, usually called **Coal Quay**, where you can bargain for trifles and observe the sharp-tongued stallholders. Also off Paul Street is **St Peter and St Paul Church**, a neogothic building by the younger Pugin.

The **South Mall**, to the south of the island, and the adjoining **Grand Parade** have some pretty buildings. In Washington Street, east of the Grand Parade, is the magnificent Corinthian façade of the 19th-century **Court House**. Just off South Mall is **Holy Trinity Church**, on **Father Matthew Quay**, with a wonderful stained-glass window dedicated to Daniel O'Connell, 'the Great Liberator'. Between South Main Street and Grand Parade is the fine 18th-century **Christ Church**, used today to house the archives of the county. At the south end of the Grand Parade is a monument to Ireland's patriot dead, and the tourist office.

Crawford Art Gallery (*open Mon–Sat 10–5; t (021) 427 3377; www.crawfordartgallery. com*) in Emmet Place has a stunning collection of works by Irish artists such as Sean Keating, Orpen and Walter Osbourne. There are also some very good 18th- and 19th-century paintings – in particular, look out for two magnificent paintings by James Barry, a native of the city, one of which is a self-portrait. The gallery's **café**, well known throughout Ireland for its excellence, is just the place for a civilized lunch after the exhausting pastime of art appreciation (*see also p.193*). Nearby are a couple of excellent craft shops to browse in. Opposite North Mall, on Cork Island still, the **Old Maltings** buildings have been adapted for the use of the University. This complex includes a small theatre called **The Granary** (*see p.193*).

Tourist Information

Cork City t (021–)
Cork City: *Áras Fáilte*, Grand Parade, t 425 5100; *open all year*.
Blarney: t 438 1624; *open all year*.

Shopping

Antiques
McCurtain Street. Antiques and bric-a-brac.
Flea market, Cornmarket Street.

Books
Mercier Bookshop, 18 Academy Street. Wealth of books of Irish interest, and novels by Irish authors.

Crafts
Shandon Craft Centre, The Butter Exchange, Shandon. Wide selection of quality crafts.
Blarney Castle Craft Shop, Blarney.
Cork Crystal, Kinsale Road, t 431 3336, *www.corkcrystal.ie*.
Blarney Woollen Mills, Blarney, *www.blarney.com*.

Food and Flowers
The English Market, located between St Patrick's Street, Grand Parade and Oliver Plunkett Street.
Natural Foods, 26 Paul Street. Sells delicious bread.

Musical Instruments
Crowleys Music Centre, 29 McCurtain Street, t 503426. Bodhráns and other musical instruments.
The Living Tradition, 40 MacCurtain St, t 450 2564, *www.thelivingtradition.com*.

Sports and Activities

Cruises
Cork Harbour Cruises, t 481 1485. Daily in summer, departing from Penrose Quay in Cork and the main Kennedy Pier in Cobh (adults €4, children €2.50).

Fishing
Angling Charters, Kayville, Carrigaloe, Cobh, t 481 2435, *www.anglingcharters.ie*. Day or evening trips.

Golf
Douglas Golf Club, Douglas, t 489 5297, *www.douglasgolfclub.ie*.
Ted McCarthy Municipal Golf Course, Mahon, t 429 4280, *www.corkcorp.ie/ourservices/rac*.
Muskerry Golf Club, Carrigrohane, t 438 5297.
Cork Golf Club, Little Island, t 435 3451, *www.corkgolfclub.ie*.
Harbour Point Golf Complex, Little Island, t 435 3094, *www.harbourpointgolfclub.com*.
Fota Island Golf Club, Carrigtohill, t 488 3710, *www.fotaisland.ie*.
Cobh Golf Club, Ballywilliam, Cobh, t 481 2399.
Monkstown Golf Club, Monkstown, t 484 1376
Fernhill Golf and Country Club, Carrigaline, t 437 2226, *www.fernhillcountryclub.com*.

Tours
OLGA (Official Local Guiding Association) organizes guided tours all over the county. They also run two **walking tours** in Cork City: the **Cork City Trail** (*June–Sept, Sat 11am; 90mins; €7*) takes in most of the city's highlights, and the **Literary and Historical Tour** (*June–Aug, Tues and Thurs, 7pm; 90mins; €7*) explores the city's literary heritage and rounds off with refreshments in *An Spailpin Fanach*.

Swans, the symbol of Cork City, are fed near here, so there are often large flocks of them. Close to the Maltings is the large Mercy Hospital, in Prospect Row, off Grenville Place, which incorporates the 1767 **Mayoralty House**, built as the official residence of the Mayor of Cork, with fine rococo interior plasterwork. It was designed by Davis Ducart, a Sardinian whose work can also be seen in the Limerick Customs House.

Follow the river westwards along Dyke Parade and leafy Mardyke Walk, and then cut south across Western Road, and you will come to the Oxbridge-style **University College Cork**, its buildings grouped around a 19th-century Gothic square. There is an

OLGA Cork, t 488 5405. Walking tours depart from outside the Tourist Office.

Water Sports

International Sailing Centre, 5 East Beach, Cobh, t 481 1237, www.sailcork.com

Where to Stay

Cork City t (021–)

Hayfield Manor, Perrott Avenue, College Road, t 484 5900, www.hayfieldmanor.ie (luxury). Modern building designed in a traditional style, graciously appointed, with a lovely pool, air conditioning and various other self-pampering facilities.

The Metropole Ryan Hotel, McCurtain Street, t 450 8122, www.ryan-hotels.com (luxury). Old-fashioned charm and excellent facilities, including 3 pools, 2 dining areas with great views over the River Lee, and the Met Tavern.

Jury's Hotel, Western Road, t 494 3000, www.jurysdoyle.com (expensive). Modern, slightly dull but practical hotel offering sports facilities and a riverside garden.

Maryborough House, Douglas t 436 5555, www.maryborough.com (expensive). Beautiful 18th-century house with large, comfortable rooms and very good service.

Hotel Isaac's, 48 McCurtain Street, t 450 0011, www.isaacs.ie (expensive–moderate). Cheerful hostel with a self-service restaurant in a converted warehouse.

Commodore Hotel, Cobh, t 481 1277, www.commodorehotel.ie (moderate). Old-fashioned seaside hotel.

Lotamore House, Tivoli, t 482 2344 (moderate). Comfortable rooms with bathrooms.

Garrycloyne Lodge, Garrycloyne, Blarney, t 488 6214 (inexpensive). Welcoming B&B

just north of Blarney, on a 145-acre dairy and sheep farm.

Maranatha Country House, Blarney, t 438 5102, www.maranathacountry house.com (inexpensive). Bizarrely – some might say delightfully – frilly and floral rooms in a lovely 19th-century house B&B.

Sheila's Hostel, 4 Belgrave Place, Wellington Road, t 450 5562, www.sheilashostel.ie (inexpensive). Conveniently central (north of the river) hostel.

Eating Out

Cork City t (021) –

The Ivory Tower, Exchange Buildings, Princes Street, t 427 4665 (expensive). Upstairs restaurant in the heart of the city, perfectly run by its talented chef-patron.

Bawnleigh House Restaurant, Ballinhassig, south of the city on the N71, t 477 1333 (moderate). Has rather grim décor, but don't be put off; the food is delicious and creative.

Greene's, in Hotel Isaac's, 48 McCurtain Street, t 455 2279, www.isaacs.ie/greenes (moderate). Located in a fashionable 18th-century converted warehouse.

Jacques Restaurant, 9 Phoenix Street, t 427 7387 (moderate). Imaginative cooking, with particularly good vegetarian dishes.

Oyster Bar, Market Lane, off St Patrick's Street, t 427 2716 (moderate). Atmosphere of a gentlemen's dining room, with white-aproned waitresses. An excellent seafood menu.

Café Paradiso, 16 Lancaster Quay, Western Road, t 427 7939, www.cafeparadiso.ie (moderate–inexpensive). Great vegetarian food made solely from organic ingredients.

important collection of **ogham stones** here, which you can see in the Stone Corridor. The only modern building in the complex is the **Boole Library**, opened in 1985. It is named in honour of George Boole (1815–1864), who was the first professor of mathematics here and is credited with working out the principles of modern computer logic.

The Roman Catholic **Honan Chapel** is a period piece of Celtic revivalism, copied from Cormac's Chapel on the Rock of Cashel and adorned with exquisite Irish revival stained glass.

Clancy's Bar and Bistro, 15-16 Princes St, t 427 6097 (*inexpensive*). Relaxed, friendly atmosphere. Useful to remember if you are shopping or visiting the city centre.

Crawford's Art Gallery Café, Emmet Place, t 427 4415, *www.crawfordartgallery.com* (*inexpensive*). Run by one of the Allen family of Ballymaloe Restaurant fame, Crawford's serves light, original food for lunch or early supper. They have particularly good fresh orange juice and gooey cakes.

Eastern Palace, t 427 6967 (*inexpensive*). Chinese restaurant in the English Market; take advantage of their excellent lunch menu. Zesty and imaginative food.

The Gingerbread House, Paul St Plaza, t 427 6411 (*inexpensive*). Takeaway or eat-in sandwiches, croissants, and cakes.

Gino's, Winthrop St, t 427 4485 (*inexpensive*). Fabulous pizzas, famous amongst Corkonians. For big appetites.

Oz Cork, Grand Parade, t 427 2711 (*inexpensive*). A taste of Australia in the heart of the city. Very popular, so make a reservation.

Quay Co-op, 24 Sullivan's Quay, t 431 7026, *www.quaycoop.com* (*inexpensive*). Good wholefood, vegetarian restaurant, open for lunch and dinner. Also a wholefood shop and bookshop.

Triskel Arts Café, Triskel Arts Centre, 15 Tobin Street, t 427 2022, *www.triskelart.com* (*inexpensive*). Arts café offering a wide variety of filling lunch-time dishes and very good soups.

The Vineyard, Market Lane, off St Patrick's Street, t 427 4793, *www.vineyard.ie* (*inexpensive*). Traditional, old-fashioned bar ideal for a quiet drink.

Entertainment and Nightlife

Pubs and Clubs

Bodhrán Bar, 42 Oliver Plunkett Street. Specializes in traditional Irish music.

City Limits, Coburg Street. Offers different styles of music, occasionally comedy and disco nights.

Clancy's Bar and Bistro, Princes Street. Victorian style bar and restaurant, lined with gold-leaf advertising mirrors

The Lobby Bar, Union Quay. The place to sample a decent pint of Murphy's Stout.

An Spailpin Fanach, South Main Street. Also a great venue for traditional music.

Theatre, Music and Film

Check the *Cork Examiner* or *Evening Echo* for current listings. In the evenings there is plenty to choose from:

Cork Opera House, Emmet Place, t 427 0022, *www.corkoperahouse.ie*. Open for about eight weeks every summer.

Everyman Palace Theatre, McCurtain Street, t 450 1673, *www.everymanpalace.com*. This theatre does not restrict itself in any way – tragedy, farce and comedy, by any author as long as he or she is good. Go prepared for anything and you won't be disappointed.

Granary Theatre, Mardyke, t 490 4275, *www.granary.ie*. New and experimental work.

Kino Cinema, Washington Street, t 427 1571, *www.kinocinema.net*. Shows first-run and classic films, catering for all tastes.

Triskel Arts Centre, Tobin Street, t 427 7300, *www.triskelart.com*. Hosts a wide range of events – music, exhibitions, drama, film seasons and poetry readings.

Close to the university is the **Cork City Museum** (*open Mon–Sat 9–6; adm free; t (021) 427 0679*), a pleasant Georgian house with an ultramodern new wing in the gardens of **Fitzgerald Park**, north of the Lee. It is worth visiting for local information and history, particularly on the War of Independence. There are displays of silver, glass and lace and, on the first floor, the Garryduff bird, a tiny wren of exquisite gold filigree from the early Christian period. Bus number 8 from the centre will drop you nearby.

Cork is the home of two Irish stouts that rival Guinness – Murphy's and Beamish. The **Beamish Brewery** (*open May–Sept, Tues and Thurs, 10.30am and 12 noon; Oct–April*

Thurs only, 11am; adm €7; t (021) 491 1100; www.beamish.ie), on South Main Street, offers brewery tours throughout the year.

North of the River

St Patrick's Street leads to St Patrick's Bridge. Once over it, you enter a hilly part of the city. Some of the 19th-century streets here are literally stairways on the steep slopes, and so are accessible only to those on foot.

Off Shandon Street, **St Anne's Shandon** church bell tower, with its two faces in white limestone and two in red sandstone, topped by a cupola and distinctive salmon weather vane, looks down into the valley. It is nicknamed the 'four-faced liar', because the clock often tells a different time on each side. The church, which is open daily, was built between 1722 and 1726 to replace a church destroyed during the Williamite siege. The peal of eight bells, which were made in Gloucestershire in 1750, are dear to every Corkonian heart. You may ring the bells of Shandon for a small fee, and conjure up Father Prout's lyrical poem about the spells they wove for him 100 years ago:

> *'Tis the bells of Shandon*
> *That sounds so grand on*
> *The pleasant waters of the River Lee.*

Skiddy's Almshouse, founded in 1584, stands in the churchyard. In about 1620, the Vintners Company of London settled a perpetual annuity of IR£24 (€30) on 12 Cork widows. Part of the 18th-century Butter Exchange is now the **Shandon Craft Centre**, but once it was the largest butter market in the world. The **Cork Butter Museum** (*open Mar–Oct daily 10–5; t (021) 430 0600*), on O'Connell Square, explains the history of butter-making in Cork and Kerry up to the present day through displays of traditional tools, including a 1,000-year-old keg of 'bog butter'. By the Exchange is the **Firkin Crane Centre** (now used by the Institute for Choreography and Dance), built in 1855 as the market expanded. The cattle slaughterhouse was also once in this area; the salted meat provided for the British Navy and many European ships making the voyage to America. By the river is **North Mall**, with some fine 18th-century doorways.

The Dominican **St Mary's Church**, by the River Lee, was completed in 1839 and has a magnificent classical façade. It is in a very prominent position, which allows us to date it as post-Catholic Emancipation (Catholic churches built before that time were built away from the main centre of towns and cities). Farther north is **St Mary's Pro-Cathedral**, begun in 1808, which has a fine tower. To the west of the city is the neogothic **Cork City Gaol** (*open daily Mar–Oct 9.30–6, Nov–Feb, 10–5; adm; t (021) 430 5022, www.corkcitygaol.com*), off Sunday's Well Road. It has been restored as a museum and depicts the life of a 19th-century prisoner, and the social history of the period. Upstairs is the **Radio Museum** with a collection of old-time radios and an exhibition on the impact of radio on our lives.

South of the River

South of the river, between Bishop and Dean Streets, is **St Finbarr's Cathedral**, which was built in the 19th century by wealthy Church of Ireland merchants on the site of the ancient church founded by St Finbarr. (If you don't have time to do much visiting in Cork, this building and the Art Gallery are essential sights.) The cathedral's great spires dominate the city, and it has a beautiful west front, with three recessed doors, elaborate carving and a beautiful rose window. The building itself is in the Gothic style of 13th-century France and was built between 1867 and 1879 by a committed medievalist, the English architect William Burges. His eye for detail was meticulous as well as humorous, and the whole effect is vigorous – a defiant gesture to Catholic Ireland. Also on the south side, off Douglas Street, is the grey limestone tower of **Red Abbey**, a remnant of a 14th-century Augustinian friary. Close by, on Dunbar Street, is **South Chapel**, built in 1766 on an inconspicuous site. At this time, the penal laws may have relaxed, but a show of Catholicism was discouraged and disliked by the ruling classes. It contains most of its original fittings and furniture, and a sculpture of 'The Dead Christ' by John Hogan.

Back on Sullivan's Quay, the **Munster Literature Centre** (*Tigh Litriochta*) (*t (021) 431 2955; www.munsterlit.ie*), at 84 Douglas Street, has gathered together an interesting multimedia exhibition of well-known writers from Cork City and County. Authors such as Elizabeth Bowen, Frank O'Connor, William Trevor and Patricia Lynch (who wrote enchanting children's stories) are all represented. The centre also promotes young poets and writers and is a focus of literary activity in the south.

The Suburbs

The **Church of Christ the King** on Evergreen Road, to the south at Turner's Cross, was designed by an American architect, Barry Byrne, in the 1930s. The carved figure of Christ crucified with his arms spread above the twin entrance doors is very striking.

Riverstown House (*open May–mid Sept Wed–Sat 2–6, or by appointment; adm €5; t (021) 482 1205*), near Glanmire, 3 miles (6km) from the city centre off the old Cork–Dublin road, was built in 1602, and has exquisite plasterwork by the Francini brothers. The brothers were Swiss-Italian stuccoers who came to Ireland in 1734 and adorned the ceiling of the dining room with allegorical figures, representing Time rescuing Truth from the assaults of Discord and Envy. Dr Browne, the Archbishop of Cork, was responsible for remodelling the original house in the 1730s and it remained in his family until the early part of the 20th century. It has been beautifully restored by its present owners, Mr and Mrs Dooley, with the help of the Irish Georgian Society.

This area is well endowed with large houses overlooking the Lee Estuary. One you can visit is **Dunkathel House** (*open May–mid-Oct, Wed–Sun 2–6; adm €3; t (021) 482 1014*), also in Glanmire. It is a fine Georgian Palladian house, worth visiting; afternoon tea here is very pleasant too. The house was built by a wealthy Cork merchant in 1790 and has a wonderful bifurcated staircase of Bath stone. A permanent display of watercolours by Elizabeth Gubbins, a daughter of the house, is hung on the walls. She was a deaf-mute who travelled widely, recording her experiences and the scenery as she went. There is a rare 1880s barrel organ which is still played for visitors.

Across the Glanmire Valley from Dunkathel is Brian Cross's attractive new garden at **Lakemount Gardens** (*open any time by appointment; adm €4.50; t (021) 482 1052, www.lakemountgarden.com*), on Barnavara Hill, Glanmire.

Twenty minutes' walk from the city centre, via Barrack Street and Bandon Road, is the **Lough**, a freshwater lake with wild geese. **Douglas Estuary**, via Tivoli (15 minutes from the centre by car) is home to hundreds of black-tailed godwits, shelducks and golden plovers. The **Cork Heritage Park** (*open May–Sept 10.30–5; adm €4.50; t (021) 435 8854*) in Blackrock illustrates the maritime history of the city and its burning during the War of Independence, as well as the history of a Quaker merchant family, the Pikes, who lived there. Other interesting buildings on the estuary are **Blackrock Castle**, designed by the Pain brothers, and Father Matthew's **Memorial Tower**, on the other side of the water, a neogothic folly.

Around Cork City

Approximately 5 miles (8km) southwest of Cork City on the N22 is **Ballincollig**, where you can visit the 19th-century **Royal Gunpowder Mills** on the banks of the River Lee (*open Easter–Sept daily 10–6; adm; t (021) 874430*). This factory produced huge quantities of gunpowder for the British army. The restored visitor centre details the history of the mills and has an exhibition gallery, craft shop and café.

Blarney is 5 miles (8km) northwest of the city on the R617. This small village has a fame out of all proportion to its size because it is the home of the **Blarney Stone**. According to legend, whoever kisses it will get the 'gift of the gab'. This magic stone is high up in the ruined keep that is all that is left of **Blarney Castle** (*open Mon–Sat Oct–April 9–6 or sunset, May and Sept until 6.30, June–August until 7, Sun 9.30–5.30 in summer or sunset in winter; adm adults €7, under 14s €2.50; t (021) 438 5252, www.blarneycastle.ie*). It is a magnet which attracts almost every visitor to Ireland, so expect to find the place (and the entire town of Blarney) crowded and full of knick-knacks. In the days of Queen Elizabeth I, the castle was held by Dermot MacCarthy, the lord of Blarney, who had the gift of *plamas*, the Irish word for soft, flattering or insincere speech. Elizabeth had asked him to surrender his castle, but he continued to play her along with fair words and no action. In the end the frustrated Queen is supposed to have said, 'This is all Blarney – he says he will do it but never means it at all'. The MacCarthys forfeited their castle in the Williamite wars of 1690, and it was later acquired by the St John Jefferyes family. To kiss the Blarney Stone, climb the stone steps up five flights to the parapet, where an attendant will hold your feet while you drop your head down to the stone. The stone is probably a 19th-century invention, and today you can even buy yourself a certificate which guarantees you have kissed it. The castle is well worth seeing for its own sake, as it is one of the largest and finest tower houses in Ireland, built in 1446 by the MacCarthy clan. The landscaped gardens surrounding it are also superb.

You can also visit **Blarney House and Gardens** (*open for tours June–mid-Sept Mon–Sat 12–6; adm; t (021) 438 5252*), a Scottish baronial mansion built by Charles Lanyon with a charming garden, ancient yew trees, scattered rocks and a lake.

Fota House and Estate (*open April–Sept daily 10–5.30, Sun 11–5.30, Oct–Mar daily 11–4; adm adults €5, children €2; t (021) 481 5543; www.fotahouse.com*) is on magical little

Fota Island in the River Lee Estuary. The arboretum surrounding the house is luxurious and mature, with one of the finest collections of semitropical and rare shrubs in the British Isles. The house, which is mainly Regency in style, was built as a hunting lodge, and has a splendid neoclassical hallway. The house was subject to an award-winning restoration project, completed in 2001. There is also a bee garden and a **wildlife park** (*open Mon–Sat 10–6, Sun 11–6, last adm 1hr before close; adm adults €10.50, children €6.50; t (021) 481 2678, www.fotawildlife.ie*). The park is an ideal expedition for children as the animals (giraffes, zebras, ostrich, antelope, kangaroos, macaws and lemurs) roam freely – only the cheetahs are in a large pen. The splendid scimitar-horned oryx, extinct in its native North Africa, is being bred here.

Cobh

Cobh (*An Cóbh*, pronounced *Cove*) is 15 miles (24km) southeast of Cork City on the R624 off the N25 and served by regular trains – though the shortest and most interesting way to reach it, if you can find your way through Cork's southern suburbs, is by the little car ferry at **Passage West**, an inexpensive five-minute crossing to Carrigaloe, just beside **Cobh**. Cobh is the great harbour of Cork and handles huge ships. In the 18th century, it was a great naval base for the British; later, nearly all the transatlantic ships and liners stopped here – it was the last port of call for the *Titanic*, and the destination of the *Lusitania* when it was torpedoed nearby off Old Head. For many thousands of people, it was the embarkation port for the new worlds of North America and Australia.

Despite the industry that surrounds it, Cobh is a rather nice place to stay, near to the city but without its bustle. The colourful town centre is almost entirely 19th-century and is dominated by the Gothic **St Colman's Cathedral**, the work of Pugin and Ashlin. It dates from 1868, but it was not completed until 1919, and has a soaring spire and a glorious carillon of some forty bells – the largest in the British Isles – which can be heard at 9am, 12 noon, 4pm and 6pm. Between 1848 and 1950 two and a half million people emigrated to America from here with many a sad scene enacted by the quay. The history of the port and the story of the emigrants is recorded at the **Cobh Heritage Centre** (*open daily 10–6; t (021) 481 3591, www.cobhheritage.com*), a converted Victorian railway station. A genealogical information centre has been set up here for those with Irish antecedents. There is a long, proud yachting tradition here: the Royal Yacht Club was founded in 1720, and is the oldest in Ireland and Great Britain, although it has moved from its original home near the railway station to Crosshaven. It has a very good regatta in the summer. The old Yacht Club in Cobh is now the **Sirius Arts Centre** (*open Wed–Fri 11–5, Sat–Sun 2–5; t (021) 481 3790, www.iol.ie/~cobharts*) and is used for contemporary art exhibitions and a permanent exhibition on local maritime history. The view from the hill above Cobh facing south on to the harbour, peppered with islands (one of which is a prison) and edged with woods, is superb. If you want a stroll, make for the old **churchyard of Clonmel**, a peaceful place where many of the dead from the *Lusitania* are buried. Also buried here is the Rev. Charles

Wolfe, 1791–1823, who is remembered for one poem, 'The Burial of Sir John Moore', a stirring poem extravagantly praised by Byron. Sir John Moore died a hero in the Peninsula Wars, but he was closely connected to Ireland through his role in quelling the 1798 Rebellion. Unlike many of his superiors, he was successful in disarming parts of the south with restraint, and he is remembered for his clemency and humanity; he found the behaviour of his own Irish troops disgraceful.

> Not a drum was heard, not a funeral note
> As his corpse to the ramparts we hurried
> Not a soldier discharged his farewell shot
> O'er the grave where our hero we buried.

One of the finest public monuments in the country is the **Lusitania Memorial** in Casement Square. It depicts two mourning sailors and, above them on a stone pedestal, the Angel of Peace. It was sculpted by Jerome Connor (1876–1943), born in County Kerry but raised in Massachusetts. Also in Cobh, the former Presbyterian church, known as the **Scots Church**, is a museum with many interesting artefacts from former industries, including the Belvelly Brickworks. Models of Cork harbour coasters, marine paintings and maritime photographs are also in the collection.

Crosshaven, 13 miles (21km) southeast of Cork city on the Cork Harbour Estuary, a crescent-shaped bay filled with yachts and boats of every description, is the playground of the busy Cork businessmen and their families. There are small delightful beaches at Myrtleville and Robert's Cove, farther along the coast.

Around County Cork

West of Cork: The Lee Valley and Gougane Barra to Bantry Bay

Heading west from Cork for Killarney, the N22 and the more scenic R618 meet at **Macroom** (*Maigh Chromtha*: sloping plain), a busy market town on the Sullane River. Macroom once belonged to Admiral Sir William Penn, whose son founded Pennsylvania, and it has a small folk **museum** (*t (026) 41840*).

This is a gorgeous part of Ireland, lush with green pasture and bright-flowered with fuchsia and heather. The Lee and Inishcarra reservoirs swell the river. The R618 follows the lovely River Lee from Cork City through Dripsey and Coachford. (The Dripsey woollen mills once produced excellent wool.) Just beyond Macroom, to the south off the R584, is a marshy area of water known as **The Gearagh**, which is a haven for water birds, and woodlands of oak, ash and birch. It forms part of the Lee hydroelectric works and is an expansion of the river into a maze of rivulets. The overall effect is of dreary flooded land, but it is a bird-watcher's dream.

If you are heading for Killarney, try to include the **Pass of Keamaneigh**, 5 miles (8km) west of Ballingeary on the R584, which takes you on a loop into the wild countryside.

Follow the N22 up the Sullane Valley through Ballymakeera (*Baile Mhic Íre*) and Ballyvourney (*Baile Bhuirne*), passing the ruins of **Carrigaphuca Castle**, a MacCarthy tower house, on the way. Turn off the N22 where it is signposted Kilgarven and Kenmare on the left. In **Ballyvourney**, stop at the **shrine and holy well of St Gobnait**, who has many devotees. She established a monastery here in the 6th century, after being led to this spot by a vision of nine white deer. St Gobnait is said to have kept the plague away from the village by consecrating the ground so that the disease could not pass. She is also known as the patroness of bees. In the church is a wooden 13th-century statue of Gobnait, which is displayed to pilgrims on her feast day, 11 February. *Tomhas Ghobnata* (Gobnait's measure) is still observed: a length of wool is measured against her statue, and then used for curing ailments.

Nearby, in **Killeen**, is **St Gobnait's Stone**, an early cross pillar; carved on one face is a figure bearing a crozier. Having turned left off the N22, the road climbs up to Coolea

Tourist Information

Macroom: Castle Gates, The Square, t (026) 43280. *Open May–Sept.*

Shopping

Prince August Toy Soldier Factory, Kilnamartyra, Macroom, t (026) 40222, *www.princeaugust.ie*. Ireland's only lead soldier factory in a wild and remote setting, well off the beaten track.
Milmorane Basketry, Milmorane, Ballingeary, Macroom. Quality handmade baskets.
Macroom Country Market. Time your visit for a Tuesday morning when the market is in full swing and you can stock up with delicious farm-produced cheese.

Sports and Activities

Golf
Lee Valley Golf and Country Club, Clashenure, Ovens, t (021) 433 1721, *www.leevalleygcc.ie*.
Macroom Golf Club, Lackaduve, Macroom, t (026) 41072.

Open Farms
Muskerry Farm Museum, Ryecourt Meadows, Farnanes, t (021) 733 6462. On the Cork–Killarney Road, with displays of horse-drawn machinery.

Water Sports
Carrig Water Ski Club, Carrigadrohid, Macroom, t (021) 487 3027, *open May–Oct*, has wheelchair facilities.

Where to Stay

Farran House, Farran, Macroom, t (021) 733 1215, *www.farranhouse.com (expensive)*. Patricia Wiese's elegant country house is set in 12 acres of mature beech woods, and the rooms have huge bathrooms.
Bridelands Country House, Crookstown, Macroom, t (021) 733 6566, *bridelunds@eircom.net (moderate)*. Comfortable accommodation in this attractive old house.
The Castle Hotel, Macroom, t (026) 41074, *www.castlehotel.ie (moderate)*. Impressive service, choice and quality in this welcoming hotel, with its own leisure centre facilities and award-winning restaurant.
Gougane Barra Hotel, Ballingeary, t (026) 47069, *www.gouganebarra.com (moderate)*. Quiet hotel in a perfect setting on the shores of the beautiful Gougane Barra Lake.

Eating Out

The Auld Triangle, Killarney Road, Macroom, t (026) 41940. Popular amongst locals for its extensive à la carte dinner menu.
Café Muesli, South Square, Macroom, t (026) 42455. An interesting variety of vegetarian and Italian cuisine.

(*Cúil Aodha*), a tiny place which was the home of Sean O'Riada (1931–1971), a composer and musician who did much to awaken a strong interest in Irish musical heritage by reviving traditional dances and tunes.

Continuing through the moorland, you come to a fork in the road: make a sharp left and you will ascend steeply to **Ballingeary** (*Béal Atha an Ghaorthaidh*) via Inchee Bridge. From here it is a short distance to **Gougane Barra**, 'the rock cleft of Finbarr'. This is a dramatic glacial valley with a shining lake in its hollow into which run silvery streams, and the source of the River Lee. In the lake is a small island, approached by a causeway, where St Finbarr set up his oratory in the 6th century. At the entrance to the causeway are **St Finbarr's Well** and an ancient cemetery. The island has a few 18th-century remains, some Stations of the Cross, and a tiny modern Irish Romanesque chapel which is often used for weddings. A popular pattern (pilgrimage) is made here every year on the Sunday nearest to the feast day of St Finbarr (25 September). After the **Pass of Keamaneigh,** strewn with massive boulders, you come into the colourful valley of the Owvane River, with a view of Bantry Bay. At **Kealkill,** 5 miles (8km) before you reach Bantry, there is an ancient

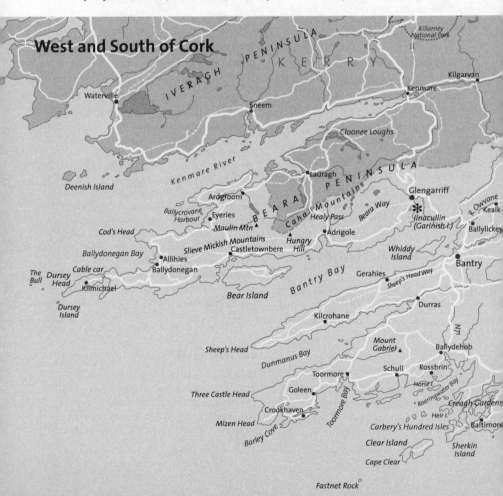

stone circle, reached by an exciting hilly road just off the R584. Ask someone locally for directions, as it isn't easy to find.

South of Cork: Kinsale to Mizen Head

Kinsale and Around

Kinsale (*Cionn tSáile*, tide head) is 18 miles (29km) southwest of Cork City on the R600. A sheltered port on the Bandon Estuary, its fame was established years ago as a quaint seaside town with excellent restaurants and carefully preserved 18th-century buildings, clad often as not with grey slates to keep out the damp, or painted cheerful colours. A few far-sighted people restored the dilapidated buildings in the 1960s, so that Kinsale avoided the usual fate of a town with a lot of ancient history and decaying houses – piecemeal demolition. In recent years it has become unquestionably the smartest, poshest and most expensive corner of rural Ireland, with music and cinema stars bidding up local property values, and wealthy Cork folk

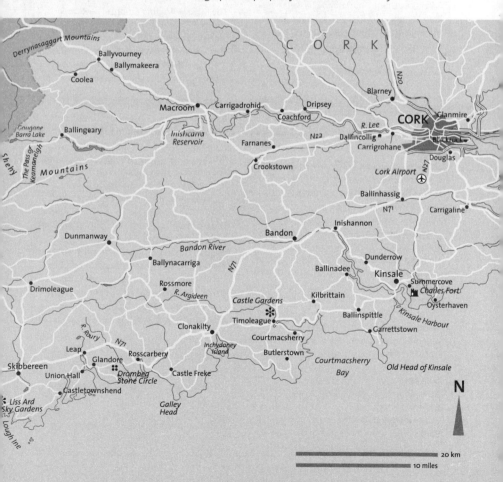

Tourist Information

Kinsale: Pier Head, **t** (021) 477 2234; *open all year.*
Skibbereen: North Street, **t** (028) 21766; *open all year.*
Bantry: t (027) 50229; *open June–Sept.*

Shopping

Books
Fuchsia Books, Schull.

Crafts and Pottery
Kinsale Crystal Glass, Market Street, Kinsale.
Keane on Ceramics, Pier Road, Kinsale.
Jagoes Mill Pottery, Farrangalway, Kinsale.
Bandon Pottery, St Finbarr's Place, Lauragh.
Norbert Platz, Ballymurphy, Inishannon, near Bandon. Unique handmade baskets.
Rory Connor, Ballylickey. Handmade knives.
Ardigole Arts, Droumlave, Ardigole.
Courtmacsherry Ceramics, Courtmacsherry.
Rossmore Country Pottery, Clonakilty.
Ian Wright, Corsits Pottery, Kilnaclasha, Skibbereen.
Leda May Studios, Main Street, Ballydehob.
Great Barrington Pottery, Eyeries.
Bantry House Craftshop, Bantry.

Food
Gubbeen Cheeses, Gubbeen House, Schull. Wonderful soft cheese made on the farm.
Durras Farmhouse Cheese, Croomkeen, Durras. Semi-soft raw milk cheese.
Milleens Cheese, Eyeries, **t** (027) 74079. Good cheese, garlic or plain semi-soft. Call first.
Quay Food Co., Market Quay, Kinsale.
Ummera Smoked Products, Ummera House, Timoleague, Bandon, **t** (023) 46187. Delicious smoked salmon sausage; call before visiting.
Twomey's Butchers, 16 Pearse Street, Clonakilty. Famous Clonakilty black pudding.
Adele's, Schull, for cakes and breads.
Manning's Emporium, Ballylickey, Bantry. Local cheeses and whiskey cake.

Markets
Carrigaline: GAA Hall, Fridays 10–11.
Bandon: Fridays 2–4.
Skibbereen: Fridays 12 noon–2.
Bantry: Friday mornings; fair in the market square on the first Friday of the month.

Sports and Activities

Art Galleries
Kent Gallery, Quayside, Kinsale, **t** (021) 477 4956, *www.kentgal.com.*
West Cork Arts Centre, North Street, Skibbereen, **t** (028) 22090.
Harling Gallery, Cotter's Yard, Main Street, Schull, **t** (028) 28165.

Courses and Tours
Ballydehob Historical, Archaeological and Landscape Tours, *Teach Dearg,* Ballydehob, **t** (028) 37282.
The Ewe Art Centre, Glengarriff, near Mizen Head, **t** (027) 63840, *www.theewe.com.* Art retreat with pottery courses and a shop.

Fishing
The Kinsale Angling Co-op, 1 The Ramparts, Kinsale, **t** (021) 477 4946, *www.kinsale angling.com.* In the Blackwater River.
Bandon Angling Association, Bandon **t** (023) 41674, *bandonangling@eircom.net.* For fishing in the Bandon River.
Fallon's Sport Shop, North Street, Skibbereen, **t** (028) 22246. For state licence and permit.
Baoite Mara Teo, Cape Clear, Skibbereen, **t** (028) 39146. Chartered trips.

Golf
Fernhill Golf and Country Club, Carrigaline, **t** (021) 437 2226, *www.fernhillcountryclub.com.*
Kinsale Golf Club, Kinsale, **t** (021) 477 4722, *www.kinsalegolf.com.*
Old Head Golf Links, Kinsale, **t** (021) 477 8444, *www.oldheadgolflinks.com.* Open April–Oct.
Bandon Golf Club, Castle Bernard, **t** (023) 41111.
Skibbereen and West Carbery Golf Club, Skibbereen, **t** (028) 21227, *www.skibbgolf.com.*
Bantry Golf Club, Bonenark, Bantry, **t** (027) 50579, *www.bantrygolf.com*
Glengarriff Golf Club, Glengarriff, **t** (027) 63150

Pony Trekking
Ballinadee Pony Trekking, t (021) 477 8152.
Bantry Horse Riding, Coomanore South, Bantry, **t** (027) 51412, *www.eventingireland.com.*

Spas
Inchydoney Island Spa, Clonakilty, **t** (023) 33143, *www.inchydoneyisland.com.* Luxury

thalassotherapy centre offering beauty and massage treatments.

Walking
The Sheep's Head Way, 90km circular route from Bantry.
The Beara Way, 196km circular route around the Beara Peninsula from Glengarriff.

Water Sports and Cruises
Oysterhaven Holiday and Activity Centre, Kinsale, t (021) 477 0738, *www.oysterhaven.com*.
Kinsale Harbour Cruises, t (021) 477 8946, *www.kinsaleharbourcruises.com*.
Sail Ireland Charters, Kinsale t (021) 477 2927, *www.sailireland.com*. Bare or skippered.
Kinsale Dive Centre, Castlepark Marina, Kinsale, t (021) 477 4959.
Kinsale Outdoor Education Centre, Kinsale, t (021) 477 2896, *www.kinsaleoutdoors.com*. Instruction in all water sports.
Baltimore Sailing School, The Pier, t (028) 20141, *www.baltimoresailingschool.com*. Courses on ketches and day boats.
Glenans Irish Sailing Club, Baltimore, t (028) 20154, *www.glenans-ireland.com*. Residential sailing courses.
Aquaventures, Lifeboat Rd, Baltimore, t (028) 20511, *www.aquaventures.ie*. Impressive new dive centre with abundant marine life and wrecks, including a German U Boat and the infamous Kowloon Bridge.
Baltimore Diving Centre, Baltimore, t (028) 20300, *www.baltimorediving.com*.
Schull Watersports, Schull, t (028) 28554. Dinghies and windsurfing.

Where to Stay
Inchydoney Island Lodge, Clonakilty, t (023) 33143, *www.inchydoneyisland.com* (*luxury*). Luxurious hotel that comes complete with a thalassotherapy spa (*see* above).
Marine Hotel, Glandore, west of Rosscarbery, t (029) 58900, *www.cmvhotels.com* (*luxury*). Simple hotel with lovely views of the cove. The restaurant has a good reputation.
Seaview House Hotel, Ballylickey, near Bantry, t (029) 58900, *www.cmvhotels.com* (*luxury*). Luxuriously appointed Victorian house with spacious bedrooms, antique furniture, and a high quality dining-room menu.

Sovereign House, Newmans Mall, Kinsale, t (021) 477 2850, *www.sovereignhouse.com* (*luxury*). Striking converted Queen Anne house, on cobbled streets leading down to the harbour.
Blairs Cove House, Durrus, near Bantry, t (027) 61127 (*expensive*). Georgian house in a spectacular setting on Dunmanus Bay. 3 courtyard suites and a self-catering cottage (*available Mar–Nov*) in the grounds.
The Blue Haven, Kinsale, t (021) 477 2209, *www.bluehavenkinsale.com* (*expensive*). The best hotel in Kinsale: small, cosy and comfortable with excellent food.
Casey's Hotel, Baltimore, t (028) 20197, *www.caseysofbaltimore.com* (*expensive*). The best type of small hotel: welcoming, comfortable and with excellent food.
Perryville House, Kinsale, t (021) 477 2731, *www.perryvillehouse.com* (*expensive*). Sophisticated accommodation, with stunning views and super breakfasts.
Westlodge Hotel, Bantry, t (027) 50360, *www.westlodgehotel.ie* (*expensive*). Scenic location just outside town. Includes fully-refurbished leisure centre and gym.
Bantry House B&B, Bantry, t (027) 50047, *www.bantryhouse.ie* (*moderate*). Converted wing of an interesting country pile (*see* p.215), where the library, billiard room and extensive gardens are at guests' disposal.
Butlerstown House, Butlerstown, south of Courtmacsherry, t (023) 40137 (*moderate*). Georgian country house with fine rooms and excellent breakfasts.
The Castle, Castletownshend, t (028) 36100, *www.castle-townshend.com* (*moderate*). B&B in a gentrified 18th-century castle; or, a selection of apartments in its towers, or 3 terraced cottages in the village (sleep 2–6).
Castle Salem, near Rosscarbery, t (023) 48381, *www.castlesalem.com* (*moderate*). Atmospheric B&B, where William Penn once slept. Donations gratefully received to preserve this impressive 15th-century castle.
Fortview House, Gurtyowen, Goleen, t (028) 35324, *www.fortviewhousegoleen.com* (*moderate*) Friendly farmhouse in a remote setting, with airy rooms and fresh, tasty breakfast options: home-made bread and preserves, pancakes, and freshly laid eggs.

Glebe Country House, Ballinadee, Kinsale
t (021) 477 8294, *http://indigo.ie/~glebehse*
(*moderate*). Family-run Georgian rectory,
informal and relaxed.

Grove House, Ahakista, Durras, t (027) 67060
(*inexpensive*). Pretty old farmhouse on the
Sheep's Head Peninsula. Sample delicious
honey from the garden and free-range eggs.

Grove House, Skibbereen, t (028) 22957,
www.grovehouse.net (*moderate*). Pleasant
Georgian house with four-poster beds, and
a 200-year-old bath in room 3.

Kilbrogan House, Bandon, t (023) 44935,
www.kilbrogan.com (*moderate*). This lovingly
restored Georgian B&B home has 5 airy en
suite rooms with wooden floors, sash
windows and inviting beds.

O'Donovans Hotel, 44 Pearse Street, Clonakilty,
t (023) 33250, *www.odonovanshotel.com*
(*moderate*). Wonderful, old-fashioned hotel
in the town centre, with a fine public bar.

Dromcloc House, Relane Point, 2km southwest
of Bantry, t (027) 50030, *www.dromcloc
house.com* (*inexpensive*). Dairy farm B&B. A
warm and friendly welcome in a wonderful
location; fishing and boat trips arranged.

Duvane Farm, Ballyduvane, Clonakilty, t (023)
33129, *www.duvanefarm.com* (*moderate–
inexpensive*). Lovely country house décor at
this working farmhouse B&B; fresh eggs are
served for breakfast. *Open Mar–Nov.*

Heron's Cove, The Harbour, Goleen near Mizen
Head, t (028) 35225, *www.heronscove.com*
(*inexpensive*). Well-run B&B right on the
water, with a super seafood restaurant
(*see* below).

Hillcrest Farm, Ahakista, Bantry, t (027) 67045,
www.ahakista.com (*inexpensive*). Traditional
farmhouse with lovely views.

Kilfinnan Farm, Glandore, t (028) 33233
(*inexpensive*). Rooms in a traditional
farmhouse.

Leighmoneymore House, Dunderrow, Kinsale,
t (021) 477 5312, *www.leighmoneymore.ie*
(*inexpensive*) Friendly farmhouse looking
out over the River Bandon.

Maria's Schoolhouse, Glandore, t (028) 33002,
www.mariasschoolhouse.com (*inexpensive*).
Great hostel hospitality and striking interior
decoration.

Schull Central B&B, Schull, t (028) 28227
(*inexpensive*). Efficiently run, comfortable,
central B&B. All rooms en suite.

Seacourt, Butlerstown, t (023) 40151
(*inexpensive*). Beautiful historic house (1760),
with views of the Seven Heads Peninsula.

Seamount Farm, Goat's Path Road, Glenlough
West, Bantry, t (027) 61226, *www.sea
mountfarm.com* (*inexpensive*). Well-kept
farmhouse B&B overlooking Bantry Bay.

Shiplake Mountain Hostel, Dunmanway,
t (023) 45750, *www.shiplakemountainhostel.
com* (*inexpensive*). Traditional farmhouse
hostel in the mountains, with a self-catering
kitchen where you can cook up organic
vegetables sold by the owners. They also sell
wholemeal bread and delicious pizzas.

Travara Lodge, Courtmacsherry, t (023) 46493
(*inexpensive*). Comfortable rooms with views
of the bay and good home cooking.

Self-catering

Courtmacsherry Coastal Cottages, t (023)
46198. Eight luxury coastal cottages
overlooking Courtmacsherry Bay.

Grove House Courtyard Cottages, Skibbereen,
t (028) 22957, *www.grovehouse.net*. Three
lovely stone cottages sleeping 2–7.

Hollybrook Cottages, Hollybrook House,
Skibbereen, t (028) 21245. Several 19th-
century properties on a wooded estate.

Lumina Farm Cottages, Cahermore,
Rosscarbery, t (023) 48227, *www.lumina
farm.com*. Five self-catering cottages
sleeping 4–8.

Eating Out

Liss Ard Lake Lodge, Liss Ard, Skibbereen,
t (028) 22635 (*luxury*). Refined cuisine,
ranging from Mediterranean to oriental, in a
lovely location.

Blairs Cove House, Durras, t (027) 61127
(*expensive*). Situated in the stable building of
a Georgian mansion and run by a French-
Belgian couple. Steaks and fish are cooked
before your eyes on an open wood-fired grill.
Open mid Mar–Oct Tues–Sat, dinner only.

The Blue Haven, 3 Pearse Street, Kinsale, t (021)
477 2209, *www.bluehavenkinsale.com*
(*expensive*). Very good restaurant in this cosy
hotel. Seafood is a speciality, and the steaks
are good too.

Good Things Café, Durras, Ahakista Road,
t (027) 64126, *www.thegoodthingscafe.com*

(*expensive–moderate*). Michelin award-winning café-style restaurant with a fantastic, modern Irish-Continental menu, with chef Carmel Somers using the freshest of local produce. Not to be missed.

Mews Bistro, Baltimore, t (028) 20390 (*expensive–moderate*). Impressive, upscale contemporary cooking. Dinner only.

The Rectory, Marine Hotel, Glandore, t (029) 58900, *www.cmvhotels.com* (*expensive–moderate*). Regency house with views over the harbour; excellent food in elegant surroundings.

The Altar Restaurant, Toormore, Schull, t (028) 35254 (*moderate*). Tasty pâté and seafood.

Annie's Restaurant, Main Street, Ballydehob, t (028) 37292 (*moderate*). Good value set meals and special portions for children.

Casey's, Baltimore, t (028) 20197, *www.caseysofbaltimore.com* (*moderate*). Bar and seafood restaurant with a wide choice of freshly caught fish, and music on Saturdays.

Casino House, Coolmain Bay, Kilbrittain, near Kinsale, t (023) 49944 (*moderate*). In a lovely old house; specializes in Continental dishes using seasonal ingredients where possible.

Customs House Restaurant, Baltimore, t (028) 20200 (*moderate*). Elegant restaurant that conjures up imaginative, excellent seafood dishes in a seaside setting.

Heron's Cove Restaurant, Goleen, near Mizen Head, t (028) 35225, *www.heronscove.com* (*moderate*). Cosy restaurant in a harbour setting, serving very good fish and shellfish dishes: langoustines, mussels and salmon, plus meat and veggie dishes.

Island Cottage Restaurant, Heir Island, Skibbereen, t (028) 38012 (*moderate, plus the boat fee*). Great cooking in an unlikely, remote setting at the only restaurant in Cork you need a boat to reach. Evenings only.

Larchwood House, Pearson's Bridge, Bantry, t (027) 66181 (*moderate*). Good home cooking in a friendly and informal atmosphere.

Lawrence Cove House, Bere Island, Castletownbere, t (027) 75063 (*moderate*). Fabulous fish restaurant on the island, with its own ferry service.

Max's Wine Bar, 48 Main Street, Kinsale, t (021) 477 2443 (*moderate*). Set in an attractive old house, offering a varied menu.

The Old Bakery, West End, Castletownbere, t (027) 70869 (*moderate*). Last espresso machine before New York.

Kicki's Cabin, 53 Pearse Street, Clonakilty t (023) 33384 (*moderate–inexpensive*). Maritime-themed restaurant with unusual menus.

The Baybery, Union Hall, Glandore Bay, t (028) 33605, *www.churchillandco.com/baybery* (*inexpensive*). Wholesome food; handcrafted pine furniture and pottery also on sale.

La Brasserie, O'Donovan's Hotel, 44 Pearse Street, Clonakilty, t (023) 33250, *www.odonovanshotel.com* (*inexpensive*). Simply-cooked hearty grub. The bar has a huge Guinness mural and a collection of old bottles and glasses.

The Courtyard Restaurant & Deli, Main Street, Schull, t (028) 28390 (*inexpensive*). Combined restaurant, bar, craftshop and deli, serving simple yet delicious lunches.

Dillon's Pub, Mill Street, Timoleague, t (023) 46390 (*inexpensive*). Continental-style bar/café with good snacks.

Holly Bar, Ardgroom, Beara Peninsula, t (027) 74433 (*inexpensive*). Decent soup and sandwiches. A holly tree grows in the middle of the bar.

Levi's Bar, Main Street, Ballydehob, t (028) 37118 (*inexpensive*). The old-fashioned type of bar that used to be common: a dim friendly room with two long counters; on one side the bottles and glasses, on the other, groceries.

Mary Anne's Bar, Castletownshend, t (028) 36146 (*inexpensive*). Serves excellent bar food in a friendly atmosphere. Beware of the rather boisterous Hooray Henrys at the height of the summer season.

The Snug, The Quay, Bantry, t (027) 50057 (*inexpensive*). Eccentric bar opposite the harbour with simple home-cooked dishes.

Entertainment and Nightlife

Traditional Music

The Lord Kinsale, 4 Main Street, Kinsale. Also hosts music evenings.

The Shanakee Bar, Market Street, Kinsale. Popular venue for music sessions.

dining out in its restaurants. It can become quite crowded in the summer, and some new holiday homes jar a little, but for all that it's still a very agreeable place. There is a lot to see in the area, as well as good quality craft shops, delis, restaurants, antique shops and art galleries.

Kinsale was once an important naval port. In 1601 the Irish joined forces with Spain against the English after the Ulster chieftain Hugh O'Neill called for a national rising and support of the Catholic cause. He met with success at first, and appealed to Spain for help. In September 1601, a Spanish fleet anchored here with 3,500 infantry aboard. They planned to meet with the Gaelic lords O'Neill and Tyrconnell, who were marching south to meet them. In November, the forces of O'Neill met with the forces of Mountjoy, Elizabeth's deputy, who was beseiging the Spaniards. Within hours, the Gaelic army had been defeated at the disastrous Battle of Kinsale, which led to the Flight of the Earls and put an end to the rebellion against Queen Elizabeth I, which in turn led to her reconquest of Ireland. It was the beginning of the end for Gaelic Ireland; anglicization was now inevitable, and though the peasantry still spoke Irish, the language of power was English.

Afterwards, Kinsale developed as a shipbuilding port. It declared for Cromwell in 1641, but James II landed and departed from here after his brief and unsuccessful interlude fighting for his throne between 1689 and 1690.

St Multose Church is the oldest building in town, with parts of it dating from the 12th century. Inside, take a look at the Galway slab, in the south aisle, and the old town stocks. The churchyard has several interesting 16th-century gravestones which in spring are covered in whitebells and bluebells, and in summer red valerian grows out of crevices in every wall. **Desmond Castle** (*open mid-April–mid-June Tues–Sun 10–6, mid June–Oct daily 10–6; adm adults €2.75, children €1.25; t (021) 477 4855, www. heritageireland.ie*), a tower house from the 1500s, was once used as a customs house and later as a prison for captured American sailors in the War of Independence as well as for the French. The castle now accommodates an **International Museum of Wine** which details the Irish links of some major vineyards in Europe. There is also the **Kinsale Regional Museum** (*open Sat 10–5, Sun 2–5; adm; t (021) 477 7930, http:// homepage.tinet.ie/~kinsalemuseum; town tours for groups of 8+ available*) in the Dutch-style old courthouse and market building, with an interesting collection of material associated with the life of the town and port through the centuries, especially the Siege and Battle of Kinsale.

By the harbour are the ruined remains of **King James Fort**, built some time after 1600. A much better example of a military fort can be seen on the opposite shore near the attractive village of Summercove, 3km away from Kinsale: the spectacular **Charles Fort** (*open mid-Mar–Oct daily 10–6, Nov–mid-Mar Sat–Sun 10–5; adm adults €3.50, children €1.25; t (021) 477 2263, www.heritageireland.ie*) was built in the 1670s (during the reign of Charles II) as a military strongpoint. It is shaped like a star and you can wander round its rather damp nooks and crannies. It was breached by Williamite forces under Marlborough after a 13-day siege. The severe 18th- and 19th-century houses inside were used as barracks for recruit training, and the fort was burned by the IRA in 1921. It is possible to walk to Charles Fort: follow the Scilly Walk from the middle of Kinsale. It takes about 45 minutes. Farther to the east is the little port of **Oysterhaven**.

To the southwest, on the R604, near **Ballinspittle**, is a **ring fort** built in around AD 600. This tiny village is now famous for its **shrine** to Our Lady: the statue of her is said to have moved in 1985; since then thousands of people have come to pray here and already, miracles have been associated with the statue. Unfortunately, also in 1985, the statue was attacked and badly damaged by a Christian sect from California. It has been repaired but apparently has not moved since.

There are some superb sandy beaches at the resort of **Garrettstown** on the wide expanse of Courtmacsherry Bay, a little farther south on the R604, and splendid cliff scenery at the **Old Head of Kinsale**, at the end of the road (to see the cliffs and an old lighthouse on the point, you'll need to pay an admission fee to the golf course, which occupies most of Old Head). The *Lusitania* was sunk off here, with 1,198 lives lost. Round the Old Head the remains of a 15th-century De Courcy castle, known as **Ringnone Castle**, overlooks the blue and white-flecked sea.

A good drive or cycle ride can be made along the River Bandon from Kinsale to **Inishannon**, once an 18th-century Huguenot weaving village. You will pass several ruined castles on the way. Take the unnumbered route via Ballinadee by crossing the Western Bridge. From Inishannon you can get to Bandon on the N71.

Bandon to Clonakilty

The market town of **Bandon**, 20 miles (32km) southwest of Cork City on the N71, was founded in 1608 by Richard Boyle, the Earl of Cork. Over the gate of the then-walled town it is said that there were once the words, 'Turk, Jew or atheist may enter here, but not a papist'. A Catholic wit responded, 'He who wrote this wrote it well, the same is written on the gates of hell'. The ownership of the town passed to the Dukes of Devonshire through marriage and they constructed most of its public buildings. The Maid of Erin Monument commemorates the Rebellions of 1798, 1848 and 1867. West of Bandon, the river skirts the demesne of **Castle Bernard**, originally called Castle Mahon. It was a large mansion with a Gothic façade, but it was burnt down in the summer of 1921, one of fifteen houses burnt around Bandon in the same week. The owner, Lord Bandon, was kidnapped by the IRA, but released a few days later after talks between De Valera, Arthur Griffith and the leaders of the Southern Unionists where safeguards for the Protestant and Unionist minority were agreed. The River Bandon and its tributaries make for good fishing and walking and, if you want to explore, Kilbrittain, Timoleague and Courtmacsherry Bay are unspoilt.

Courtmacsherry, a peaceful place with a lovely setting on the bay, is a sea-angling centre. Motorists can get a good view of the wooded valleys and rolling fields, which do not have the high hedges you find in Tipperary. **Timoleague** is dominated by the ruins of a **Franciscan Abbey** founded in 1312 overlooking the mud flats of the estuary. It has a fairly complete cloister and an outer yard, and is always accessible to the public. The mud flats are the temporary home of birds from the far north, Russia and beyond. On the banks of the Argideen River are the varied and lush **Timoleague Castle Gardens** (*open June–Aug Mon–Sat 11–5.30, Sun 2–5.30; adm €3.80, t (023) 46116*) with many rare and tender plants. The 13th-century Barry Castle is in ruins, but the more modern house sits comfortably amid the landscaped gardens. Both the Catholic and Protestant **churches** are worth seeing in the village, the latter for its Harry Clarke window, and the former for its richly decorated walls covered in mosaic decorated by an Indian Maharajah. **Dillon's Pub** in Timoleague (*see* p.204) is a good stopping place for a coffee or lunch.

Clonakilty (*Cloich na Coillte*), birthplace of Michael Collins (*see* below), received its first charter in 1292. It was a thriving linen town in the 18th century, but was given the label 'Clonakilty, God help us' during the Great Famine, such was the horror and suffering of the people there. Nowadays it is an attractive place, with traditional hand-painted signs swinging from the pubs and shops. You could linger in the **West Cork Regional Museum** (*open May–Oct; adm €1.27; t (023) 33115*) on Main Street, or in the craft centre, or look at the statue of the pikeman, a monument to 1789. A **model railway village** (*open Mon–Fri 11–5, Sat–Sun 1–5pm; adm; t (023) 33224; www.clon.ie/ mvillage.html*) has been built on the Inchydoney Road and recreates the world of the long-closed West Cork Railway. Clonakilty is also famous for its black puddings, which you can buy at **Twomey's** (*t (023) 33733; www.clonakiltyblackpudding.ie*), the butcher's shop in Pearse Street.

Lisnagun Ring Fort (*Lis na gCon*, fort of the hound); (*open Mon–Fri 9–5, from 10 at weekends; adm*), a reconstructed 10th-century defensive farm, is signposted on the N71, just outside town on the Cork Road. Just off the N71 near Ballinascarty are **Lisselan Gardens** (*open Jan–Feb and Nov–Dec 8–5, Mar–April and Oct 8–6, May–June and Sept 8–7, July–Aug 8–8; adm; t (023) 33249, www.lisselan.com*). Mature rhododendrons and unusual, exotic trees and plants are cultivated here in an informal 25-acre landscape, around a simple French château-style house built in 1851.

Other attractions include a small **stone circle** at **Templebrian**, north of the village off the N71, and a fine, broad beach at **Inchydoney** (it is becoming a bit overdeveloped, but if you are looking for solitude there are plenty of other coves and inlets around Clonakilty). Inland from here, if you fancy a drive or bike ride away from the coast, you can follow small, uncrowded roads going northwest amongst scenic farmland, past wooded demesnes, to **Ballynacarriga Castle** southeast of Dunmanway (*Dún Mánmhaí*), a well-preserved ruin on the edge of a small lough, with a Sheila-na-Gig on the outside wall and fine stone carvings within.

The reputation of Michael Collins, the energetic and much loved strategist of the War of Independence, is growing with the years, rather as Dev (De Valera) himself had prophesied (*see* pp.82–3). He was born a few miles outside Clonakilty, and bus tours now run from Clonakilty to **Woodfield**, the family homestead near Pike's Cross, where there is a small memorial to him. Only the older building remains, as the new farmhouse was burnt down in a revenge attack by a regular army officer, Major A.E. Percival, and his troops in 1921 after an IRA attack on Rosscarbery. Michael Collins went to see the ruins on the last day of his life, and had a drink in his cousin's bar where he met up with friends and relatives. He was confident that he would not be attacked in his own county despite the warnings of friends who told him that something was planned; later he was ambushed by anti-Treaty forces and shot in the head on the road between Bandon and Clonakilty. A little further west is Sam's Cross, where there is a bronze roundel of him by Seamus Murphy.

Rosscarbery to Glandore

The N71 now leads to **Rosscarbery**, which is a charming old-fashioned village with a pretty square, famous for its good eating houses, lively pubs, and a strange saying – 'Rosscarbery, where they buried the elephant' – which nobody seems to understand. It had a famous school of learning founded by St Fachtna in the 6th century, and a medieval Benedictine monastery. The very attractive 17th-century **Protestant church** is on the site of the old cathedral; it was mostly rebuilt in the 19th century, although the tower dates from 1612. It was raised to a bishopric in the 12th century. Inside the church is a marble statue of the sixth Baron Carbery in Elizabethan dress, and a fine carving on the west doorway. The nationalist Jeremiah O'Donovan Rossa (1831–1915) was born in the grounds of the Celtic Ross Hotel (which has delicious bar food). He was active in the Fenian movement, arrested in 1865, and sentenced to penal servitude, but was freed in 1871 on the condition that he left Ireland. He went to America where he published, among other things, recollections of his prison life. When O'Donovan Rossa died, he had an enormous funeral in Dublin, at which Patrick Pearse proclaimed, in his famous oration, 'The fools, the fools, they have left us our dead, and while Ireland holds these graves, Ireland unfree shall never be at peace'.

Castle Freke, the home of the Barons of Carbery, is a sad Gothic ruin to be found on the road out to **Galley Head**. It was in fine shape for the 10th baron's coming-of-age ball in 1913, for it had just been restored, after a fire, with reinforced steel window frames and reinforced concrete between the walls. The 10th Lord Carbery was rather a spoiled young man who is remembered for his daring looping of the loop in his monoplane, his beautiful wife Jose, and his devilment in shooting out the eyes of his neighbours in a group painting of the Carbery Hunt which used to hang in the hall of Castle Freke. After the end of the First World War he, like many Anglo-Irish, left, sold the estate and settled elsewhere, in his case in Kenya, where he married twice more. The castle just grew more dilapidated with the passing years.

Inland to the west, in the valley of the little River Roury, stands the ruin of **Coppinger's Court**, an Elizabethan or Jacobean mansion burned out in 1641, which gives shelter to cows in winter. It stands to the left, off an unclassified road between **Leap** (pronounced 'lep') and Rosscarbery. It was built by Sir William Coppinger, who sprang to prominence after the defeat of the Irish chieftains and Spaniards at the Battle of Kinsale. At that stage he was valet to one of the O'Driscolls, but used the time and position to amass an empire from the confiscated lands of the defeated chieftains, only to lose it to Cromwell in his old age.

Northwest of Rosscarbery, signposted off the N71 Skibbereen road, is **Castle Salem** (*open for tours by appointment; adm; t (023) 48381, www.castlesalem.com*), a 15th-century tower house built for the MacCarthys and known as Benduff. It was confiscated from Florence MacCarthy in 1641 and given to a Cromwellian soldier, a Major Apollo Morris, who became a Quaker and renamed it Castle Shalom, meaning 'peace', which over the years has become Salem. During the 17th century, a farmhouse was built into the thick castle walls, and now the entrance into the first floor of the castle is through a small door at the top of the farmhouse stairs. It is slowly crumbling away, but perhaps your entrance money will help to keep its roof on. It also offers B&B accommodation (*see* p.203). The graves of a community of Quakers are in the grounds.

From Roury Bridge, a country road (R507) winds to **Drombeg Stone Circle**, from where you can see across pastures and cornfields to the sea. Erected between the 2nd century BC and 2nd century AD, it may have been used for some kind of fertility rite and worship of the sun. A cremated body was discovered in the centre of the circle when it was excavated. Close beside the circle are the remains of an open-air roasting oven and cooking pit, so it must have been a place of feasting. The cooking pit would have been filled with water and hot stones added to bring the water to boiling point.

The beaches of Owenahincha and, to the east, the Longstrand have wonderful sand. **Union Hall** and **Glandore** are two pretty and colourful resort villages on a narrow inlet 5 miles (8km) west of Rosscarbery, whose harbours are filled with highly painted boats. Their grey-steepled Protestant churches add to their prettiness, although the congregations have dwindled to a handful. Union Hall was named after the 1800 Act of Union, which the British Government and most of the Ascendancy sought after the eruption of 1798. Glandore is fashionable with the rich; its south-facing seaside houses form a street known as 'millionaire's row'. Jonathan Swift was a visitor to Glandore while writing *Rupes Carberiae*. Hardy fuchsia adorns the hedges here as it does in so much of west Cork; the bright red-and-purple-flowered plant was brought from Chile.

Castletownshend to Cape Clear Island

Round the next headland, **Castletownshend** is a neat Georgian village on a steep hill, in the middle of which grows a huge sycamore tree. The bar and restaurant **Mary Anne's** is a popular tourist spot, with a beer garden at the back (*see* p.205). The village's claim to fame is that it used to be the home of Edith Somerville (1858–1949), author of *The Real Charlotte* and the humorous *Reminiscences of an Irish RM* and other novels. She is buried in the pretty Church of Ireland graveyard here, with her cousin and co-author Violet Martin (1862–1915), who wrote under the pen name Martin Ross. In their day, Castletownshend was made up of 'the gentry', who were all vaguely related to each other: the Coghills, the Chavasses and the Alymers all lived in good stone houses at various points throughout the village. At one end lived the Somervilles in Drishane House and, in the castle on the shore, lived the Townshend family. They still do to this day – you can even stay in **The Castle** (*see* p.204).

Park your car in the village and walk up to **St. Barrahane's Church** to visit the graves of Edith Somerville and Violet Martin, and look down on the wooded Castlehaven shore. It is one of the prettiest graveyards in the country, planted with autumn-flowering cyclamen, gnarled cherry trees and the stately yew. The church itself has a very fine Harry Clarke window and a four-spired turret. The history of these Protestant families reveals itself in the gravestones and memorials in the church. They hoped for service to the British Empire and retirement to Ireland for their sons and, if they were lucky, intermarriage with local families for the daughters. Edith Somerville did not put her energies into marriage and children, and we are all the better off for it. She and Violet Martin managed to collaborate to produce brilliantly funny yet serious novels. Their talent for remembering and polishing the well-turned word or phrase, as well as the idiosyncrasies of their neighbours, is irresistible. Edith was the organist in the church and at one time master of the Carbery Hunt (still going strong). Her brother, Admiral Boyle Somerville, was shot dead on his doorstep in 1935, in a sad afternote to the War of Independence. The Somervilles got on well with all the locals but, after the establishment of the Irish Free State, the IRA were operating spasmodically against the status quo. The admiral had been asked what life was like in the British navy by young local men and had also provided them with references. The IRA accused him, in a note thrown in the door by his murderer, of being a British recruiting agent. In response to this outrage, De Valera reinstated the ban on the IRA which he had lifted in 1932.

On the outskirts of the village is a pleasant Catholic church on the road to Skibbereen, and farther on is **Knockdrum Fort**, a stone-built cashel. Opposite the fort is an alignment of standing stones known as 'the fingers' – a prehistoric calendar. A road follows the coast westwards to Castlehaven where, in the little glen leading up to the 18th-century rectory (of the first Somerville to come to Cork), there's a holy well dedicated to St Barrahane. It is still venerated: locals hang threads from the branches of the tree that overhangs it, and as the thread rots, their ailment disappears.

Skibbereen, linked to Castletownshend by the R596, is a market town famous for its weekly newspaper, the *Southern Star*, previously called the *Skibbereen Eagle*. It's a good read and sheds light on local preoccupations. The old phrase, 'Skibbereen, where they ate the donkey', came about during the Famine. From 1846 to 1848 over a million people died in Ireland, yet foodstuffs worth £17 million were being exported to England every year. The soup kitchens run by the gentry could not possibly feed the thousands of starving people who poured into Skibbereen from the countryside.

Between Skibbereen and Drimoleague, off the R593, is an exciting and thoughtful enterprise, **Liss Ard Gardens** (*open summer Sun–Fri 10–8, winter Wed–Sun 1–6; adm; t (028) 22368, www.lissard.com*): a combination of artistic spaces, water and wildlife gardens extending for forty acres. The 'Sky Garden' was designed by the American James Turrell.

Three and a half miles (5.6km) south of Skibbereen on the Baltimore Road are the **Creagh Gardens** (*open daily 10–6; adm adults €3.80, children €2.50; t (028) 22121*), a romantic and informal garden planted amongst woods which lead to the river estuary, best seen between April and June, although the grounds are lovely all year. The walled garden is cultivated organically and contains a variety of hens and other fowl. All around Skibbereen, and particularly to the west, is some lovely countryside where knuckles and fingers of land reach out into the sea, breaking off into islands like Sherkin and Clear.

Baltimore is an attractive fishing village perched at the end of one of these fingers. It looks out on to the humpy shape of Sherkin Island and beyond to the wonderful expanse of Roaringwater Bay and Carbery's Hundred Isles. In the summer, the trawlers are outnumbered by sailing boats and the place is buzzing with visitors who come for the sea sports, hotels, bars, eating places and to visit the islands. Holiday cottages have been built here, as they have in many of these coastal villages, which jar slightly among the local architecture, but there are not enough of them yet to spoil the area. It is also the place to get a boat for the islands – negotiate with the local fishermen or take the regular ferryboat.

The O'Driscolls ruled all this area, but by 1200 their power had dwindled and their chief kept up his revenues by plundering ships and exacting harbour dues. You will notice that many people you come across here have the surname O'Driscoll, and in August, in the week before the annual regatta, there is always an O'Driscoll get-together. The O'Driscolls built nine castles around Baltimore in order to secure themselves; these are now all dramatic ruins, especially those on Cape Clear and on Sherkin Island. This area has many tales of blood and treachery – one such story describes a retaliatory attack on Baltimore in 1537 by some soldiers from Waterford, after the O'Driscoll chief of the time had plundered a ship loaded with Spanish wine bound for Waterford City. Another recounts the disappearance of a hundred and fifty people who were carried off as slaves by Algerian pirates in 1631. A number of them were English settlers who arrived in 1607 during the time of Sir Fineen O'Driscoll (who was on good terms with the English). The pirates had been guided into Baltimore by a man from **Dungarven**, just up the coast. The abducted settlers and the native Irish who were also taken were never seen again. Thomas Davis speculated on their fate in his poem *The Sack of Baltimore*:

> *Oh! Some must tug the galley's oar and some must tend the steed,*
> *This boy will bear the sheik's chibouk; and that a bey's jereed.*

Not surprisingly, people moved farther inland and Skibbereen was founded. Baltimore later became a rotten borough in the gift of Lord Carbery, sending two MPs to the English Parliament. After the Famine, during which time people here suffered terribly, a boat-building industry was set up, and there are still two or three boat-builders locally. You can learn to sail at the sailing schools based here, or even better, if you have your own boat, arrive that way and explore the islands with their sandy beaches and tranquil green fields. Diving, windsurfing and deep-sea fishing are all easy to organize. There are also regular ferries to the islands.

East of Baltimore on the mainland is the beautiful **Lough Ine**, just the place for a walk or picnic; or you could walk from the village up to the navigational beacon at the tip of the peninsula – a beautiful spot, with dramatic cliffs of shiny slate, which breaks off in big sheets and piles up on the shore below. Lough Ine is a remarkable stretch of salt water connected to the sea by a very narrow channel, and the channel is partially blocked by a sill of rock, which prevents the lough from ever dropping below the halfway mark. Very little fresh water flows into it and it is extremely deep, especially on its western side. This unusual geography has produced a marine life more typical of the Mediterranean Sea: the red-mouthed goby fish, a variety of sponges, coral and the purple sea urchin thrive in its warm waters. Sea water rushes in and out of the channel with the pull of the tide and the water is very clear. In the shallows you can see the spiky sea urchins and the pearly saddle oyster in profusion. The lough is a nature reserve and divers have to obtain a government permit. The water is scattered with humpbacked islands and the road that leads down to the car park is edged in September with arches of brilliant red fuchsia. The hilly woods behind are often hung with dramatic wisps of cloud, great conifers mixed with beech give way to oaks and holly, and the walks are edged with ferns and bell heather.

Sherkin Island (*see* 'Getting to Islands off Cork', p.184) encloses Baltimore harbour. It is very small with three sandy beaches. Murphy's Bar on the island rents bicycles, and you can head off to visit one of the excellent sandy beaches on the far side of the island or the ruins of a 15th-century Franciscan Abbey which was destroyed by the expeditionary raid from Waterford in 1537. There are several B&Bs on the island and bars serving food.

St Ciaran was born on **Cape Clear Island** (*see* 'Getting to Islands off Cork', p.184) where the remains of a cross and holy well mark the site of his church. There are several other ancient stones at the eastern end of the island, in the townland of St Comillane; one is known as the trysting stone because of the hole bored through it. About one hundred and forty people live on the island, which is Irish-speaking. There is a B&B, a camp site, a couple of hostels, three bars, a small heritage centre and a pottery. Of special note here is Ed Harper's goat's cheese and, even better, his ice cream (*t (028) 39126*). The cars that the islanders use are very ancient, and a lot of dead cars litter up the place. A visit to the island makes a wonderful day trip (it takes about 45 minutes on the ferry) but you might like to stay for a day or so to go walking or bird-watching.

There is an important **bird observatory** here by the harbour and it is worth asking about organized bird-watching trips, as the island is on a major bird migration route and many birds are blown in by the autumn gales. You may well see Manx shearwaters which live on the rocky islands off the Kerry coast; in the mornings and evenings during July and August huge numbers fly past, skimming the water on their way back and forth from their feeding grounds.

The familiar **Fastnet Rock**, mentioned in the shipping forecasts, is just off Cape Clear, and you can get a fine view of it from the hill of Clear and its south-facing sea cliffs. This is especially dramatic in the winter, when the wind often reaches force 10 and the seas are huge with waves and spume. The list of ships lost in these waters makes chilly reading, but it is a diver's paradise. The diving centre in Baltimore organizes diving around the reefs of Fastnet.

Ballydehob to Mizen Head

Ballydehob is on the next finger of land, stretching into Roaringwater Bay and the Atlantic. It is a colourful little village 10 miles (16km) away from Skibbereen on the N71, distinguished by a fine 12-arch railway bridge, now defunct, which lies at the head of Roaringwater Bay. Quite a few 'blow-ins' have come to live around here: Germans, Dutch and English who have bought up neglected cottages in spectacular situations. About 2 miles (3.2km) south at **Rossbrin Cove**, the ruin of an O'Mahony castle stands by the sea, home of the 14th-century scholar Finin. **Gurtnagrough Folk**

Museum, 3 miles (5km) north of Ballydehob (*open daily in summer; adm; t (028) 37274*) contains a delightful haphazard collection of bygone agricultural and domestic tools.

Schull (pronounced 'skull'), west of Ballydehob on the coast, is a small boating and tourist centre with a deep harbour; ferries (*see* p.184) run out to Clear Island and along the coast to Baltimore. Schull has a good selection of craft shops, food shops, restaurants and cafés. It also has a wonderful second-hand bookshop, Fuchsia Books, in which you could while away hours on the many books of Irish and local interest. It also has the small **Schull Planetarium** (*call for opening times; adm adults €5, children €3.50; t (028) 28552/28315, www.westcorkweb.ie/planetarium*), in Schull Community College, since the night skies here are so free of light pollution. Diving and sailing are also offered in the village.

A spectacular road runs from Schull up to **Mount Gabriel** (1,339ft/407m). If you decide to climb it, be careful of the prehistoric copper mines dug into the slopes. The view is out of this world. The R591 curls round the head of lovely **Toormore Bay**, and past **Goleen** with its sandy beach (the Gulf Stream means that swimming is quite possible here) and the Ewe Art Centre nearby (*see* 'Courses and Tours', p.202). The road winds on in its spectacular way to **Crookhaven** with its boat-filled harbour. O'Sullivans Bar is a good place for a jar, its walls decorated with sketches of well-known locals. This was once a busy anchorage for fishing and sailing fleets. Marconi built the first transatlantic telegraph station here in 1902, before moving it to Valentia Island in Kerry.

Farther on, **Barley Cove**, one of the best beaches in the southwest, stretches down to the splendid, sheer heights of **Mizen Head**, the southwesternmost point of Ireland. The soft red sandstone cliffs banded with white fall down to the sea while flurries of birds glide on the air currents beneath you. The cliffs are high and nearly vertical, so be careful. A lighthouse on the islet below is linked to the mainland by a suspension bridge. Many ships have been wrecked here in the past. The old fog signal station, now controlled automatically, has been opened to visitors (by the former keeper) as the **Mizen Head Signal Station Visitor Centre** (*open mid-Mar–May and Oct daily 10.30–5, June–Sept daily 10–6, Nov–mid-Mar 11–4; adm adults €4.50, children 5–12 €2.50; t (028) 35115, www.mizenhead.ie*).

Farther around is **Three Castle Head**, where on the edge of the sheer cliffs is a dramatic ruin, an O'Mahony castle. On its other side is a supposedly haunted lough. You can walk out to it, but do not bring any dogs, and ask permission at the farm house. (From the Barley Cove Hotel car park turn right, then left at the T-junction, right at the next junction, ignoring the sign for the B&B on the left. Pass through the farm gate and on up the track.)

From Mizen Head, the R591 goes to **Durras** at the head of Dunmanus Bay, which has another ruined medieval castle. The drive to Kilcrohane and Sheep's Head, over Seefin Pass then on to **Gerahies** is magnificent and very untouristy. The views extend across Bantry Bay and the Beara Peninsula. The **Sheep's Head** peninsula is relatively unvisited and, as you stand on the hilliest parts of the rocky promontory, little farmhouses lie below, built into the side of the slopes. The small village of **Kilcrohane** is famous for its early potatoes. You can have a good walk or bike ride along the Goat's Path and the north side of the peninsula. From Durras, an amazing route (part-road part-track but quite drivable) leads past the Durras Cheese Farm and over the top of the peninsula down into Bantry.

Bantry (*Beanntraí*) has one of the finest views in the world, out over the bay. There is a deep-water harbour between the Beara and Dunmanus Peninsulas, which in 1796 attracted a French fleet of 47 ships and 14,000 troops under General Hoche with Wolfe Tone on board. They were all set to support the planned United Irishmen's uprising but what became known as the 'Protestant wind' foiled their attempt at landing and they had to return to France. Don't miss **Bantry House** (*open March–Oct, daily 10–6; adm €10; tearoom and craftshop; see also 'Where to Stay', p.204;* **t** *(027) 50047, www.bantryhouse.com*) which has a glorious view, and is directly above the town so you do not see the ugly petrol stations below it. You can go around the house on your own (accompanied only by the faint strains of classical music), with a detailed guide written by the owner. Rare French tapestries, family portraits and china still have a feeling of being used and loved. The house and garden have definitely seen better days, but nevertheless, this is one of the most interesting houses in Ireland open to the public, and certainly one of the least officious. The house was built in 1740, and added to in 1765. The owner, Mr Egerton Shelswell-White, is always at work on various restoration projects in and around the house. He is an enthusiastic patron of music, and many fine concerts are held in the library. The dining room is a stunning shade of bottle-blue, against which the gold-framed portraits and the china and silver look magnificent. Two of the portraits are of King George II and Queen Charlotte. They were painted at the sovereign's order and given to the first Earl of Bantry, from whom Mr Shelswell-White is descended, as a token of thanks for his efforts in helping repel the French invasion force of 1798. In the side courtyard of the house is an **Armada Exhibition** devoted to the 1796–78 Bantry Bay Armada. There is a 1:6 scale model of a frigate in cross section and extracts from Wolfe Tone's journal.

Offshore is **Whiddy Island**, used for oil storage by Gulf Oil, which brought prosperity in the 1970s (some of the bungalows along the shore of Bantry Bay were built then). Unfortunately, tragedy struck in 1979: fifty people were killed when a tanker exploded, and Gulf Oil suspended their operations. The tanks are now used for long-term storage. West of the town is the 9th-century **Kilnaruane Pillar Stone** (take the N71 Cork road and turn left by the West Lodge Hotel), carved with figurative and interlaced panels, including one of a boat with oarsmen which some think is a depiction of St Brendan.

Glengarriff's (*An Gleann Garbh*) humpy hills and wooded banks look over still water and isles. The average annual temperature here is 11°C (52°F). **Ilnacullin Gardens**, alias Garinish Island (*see p.184 for details of ferry; open March and Oct Mon–Sat 10–4.30, Sun 1–5; April Mon–Sat 10–6.30, Sun 1–6.30; May–June and Sept Mon–Sat 10–6.30, Sun 11–6.30; July–Aug Mon–Sat 9.30–6.30, Sun 11–6.30; adm adults €3.50, children €1.25;* **t** *(027) 63040, www.heritageireland.ie*), used to be covered only in rocks, birch, heather and gorse until it was made into 37 acres of garden by a Scotsman, John Allen Bryce, in 1910, and designed by Harold Peto. Now it is a dream island full of subtropical plants, with a formal Italian garden, rock gardens and a marble pool full of goldfish. It is an exceptional place, perfectly structured and full of outstanding plants; well worth the return boat fare from Glengarriff. Bernard Shaw often stayed here. You will find that there are many boatmen willing to take you out to the island.

The village itself consists of a main street lined with craft shops selling woollens of every description, and soft sheepskins. Wonderful walks can be taken in the **Glengarriff Forest**, full of every shade of green – mossy trees and stones, ferns growing in every crevice and on the trees, mostly oak, beech and holly. Also growing in wild profusion is *Rhododendron ponticum*; here, as in Killarney, it has become a threat to native plants. There is a steep drive to **Barley Lake** (*Lough na Heornan*), which is up in mountainous bogland crossed by rushing streams. The tourist office stocks a local walking map.

You might walk in **Glengarriff Valley**, 'the bitter glen', and up to the hills hidden in the Caha Range, or continue westwards into the **Beara Peninsula** – one of the less touristy parts of the western coasts. The Beara presents rougher, rockier landscapes than its neighbours to the north and south, under the sombre peaks of the **Caha Mountains**, some of the highest in Ireland. From **Adrigole**, the first town west of Glengarriff, you can drive up the **Healy Pass Road**, with its lovely mountain scenery gazing down on the indented sea line and the green woods. It is quite a testing zigzag drive following the R574 road to Lauragh in County Kerry (*see* p.146).

Castletownbere, the only town of any size, is a fishing village built around a deep-water harbour where you can get a boat across to Bear Island (Bere on some maps). It is busy in the summertime with sailors, walkers and cyclists and festivals, especially during the regatta on the first weekend of August. Hungry Hill (2,251ft/686m) and Sugarloaf Mountain (1,887ft/575m) are very popular with climbers and hill walkers, offering beautiful views in every direction. To the west are the looming **Slieve Mickish Mountains** with equally lovely views. Bear Island is used by the Irish army for training; it has a pub, shop, splendid restaurant and B&B, and the opportunity for long, peaceful walks.

Just outside Castletownbere is the ruined castle of **Dunboy** (*on private land; possible adm*), on a small wooded peninsula. In fact there are two buildings here: the ancient ruin was the castle of the O'Sullivan Bere, the powerful chief of the O'Sullivans, who played a leading role in organizing the revolt against English rule. He fought in the disastrous Battle of Kinsale, and his castle was besieged by Sir George Carew. It held out bravely under the leadership of MacGeohegan, a subsidiary chief, but was eventually stormed and its inhabitants hanged. Donall waited in hiding for more help from the Spanish but, when he learnt that Philip III of Spain had abandoned all thoughts of another expedition, he decided Ulster was his safest refuge. He set off from Glengarriff in late December 1602 with 400 fighting men, 600 women and children and servants. They were continually attacked by the English and other hostile chiefs; only 35 survived to reach the protection of the O'Rourke chief in Leitrim Castle. Donall hoped for a pardon from James I in 1603, but got none, so he sailed to Spain with his family. Philip gave him honours and a pension, but he was murdered in Madrid by John Bathe, an Anglo-Irishman. J.A. Froude based his Irish historical romance *The Two Chiefs of Dunboy* (1889) on this story. The other ruin on the peninsula is a 19th-century **Puxley Mansion** in the Scottish Baronial style, built by the Puxleys, a family who became very wealthy through copper-mining. They were burned out in 1921, although they had lived latterly mainly in England. Daphne du Maurier used them as an inspiration for her novel *Hungry Hill*. Exotic garden escapees grow wild in the hedgerows and roadsides here – gunnera, buddleia, orange monbretia – and every garden sports spiky New Zealand flax, and the pretty myrtle with its cinnamon-coloured bark.

A scenic drive can be made to the end of the Beara Peninsula, where another sparsely inhabited island, **Dursey Island**, at the tip of the peninsula, is connected to the mainland by a **cable car** (*open Mon to Sat 9–11, 2.30–5 and 7–8; Sun 9–10.30, 1–2.30 and 7–8; also June–Aug Sun 4–5pm; arrive 30mins before departure*) at Ballaghboy. The cable car was set up in the 1970s and is designed to take six passengers, or one person and a cow, and is said to be the only working example of its kind in Ireland. The islanders graze cattle and try to earn a living through fishing. About twenty people live on the island full time, but Irish is no longer spoken here although it was recorded in 1925 as being a Gaeltacht area. A road leads through the village of **Kilmichael** and across the middle of the island to a Martello tower. Tracks lead around the cliffs to **Dursey Head**, which has wonderful views: from here you can see the three rocks in the ocean known as the Bull, the Cow and the Calf.

As the road winds around the coast, there is barely a tree to be seen; only thorn and fuchsia hedges, and astonishingly beautiful coastal views all the way through Allihies, Eyeries and Ardgroom. Between Castletownbere and Allihies, at the junction where the road goes left for Dursey, is a wedge **grave** in a field, and from here you can see the beach at Ballydonegan.

The village of **Allihies** is a tiny place along one street, with a fine hostel and friendly pubs. Fresh fish is fried up in the simple Atlantic restaurant, bikes can be hired from O'Sullivan's and the beach at Garinish is of white crystalline sand. There is a café and camp site by the beach and as yet the place is unspoiled. Allihies has always been a fishing village, but during the 19th century it was also a busy copper-mining centre which formed part of the Puxley empire. The mines closed in 1930 but used to employ 1,200 people, some of whom were skilled workers brought in from Cornwall to oversee the locals. This caused great resentment and the community boycotted the Cornish workers – their food supplies had to come from Wales on the boats that took the copper ore to Swansea. Their ruined stone cottages and the remains of a Nonconformist chapel are still there. There is easy walking around the copper mines, which are above the village. Part of the **Beara Way** runs above Allihies; a track continues from the copper mine, and it is a glorious walk to Eyeries. (Look at *West Cork Walks* by Kevin Corcoran.)

Back on the tarmac road to Eyeries, you will pass a sign for globe artichokes (pick your own), delicious for those doing their own catering. The café on the beach sells handmade crafts, and you might want to stop in at **Great Barrington Pottery** (*the shop is open in the afternoon, but they are flexible*). The drive to Eyeries is as different as the weather; you might be impressed by churning seas, black rocks, rough bracken and wind-torn skies or, if the weather is fine, by the idyllic cerulean water, the brilliant green fields, the wild flowers and silvery rocks. Massive rocks are scattered around this area and recent archaeological research has shown that many date from the earliest days of Christianity in Ireland. Some also date from penal times, when Catholics had to hold their services in secret places. The scenery is barren and hard, with exciting juxtapositions of colour, and the Slieve Mickish Mountains are a constant brooding presence.

The village of **Eyeries** is painted in strong Mediterranean colours, and behind it rises Maulin Mountain (2,044ft/620m). Above **Ballycrovane Harbour**, on a little hill, looms the tallest **ogham stone** in the country: it stands over 17ft (5m) high. Milleens, a distinctive and delicious farmhouse cheese, is made around here. As you approach **Ardgroom** the seas are calmer, and in the bay you will notice the lines of seaweed-covered ropes and rafts that indicate mussel farming. The road continues to Lauragh and Derreen Gardens (*see* **County Kerry**, p.146).

East of Cork: Midleton and Youghal

Approximately 11 miles from Cork City going east on the N25 is the attractive town of **Midleton** (*Mainistir na Corann*), which has benefited from the restoration of an

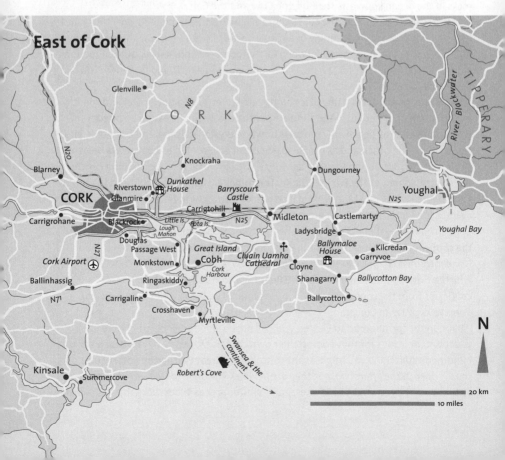

Tourist Information

Midleton: Jameson Heritage Centre, **t** (021) 461 3702; *open June–Sept.*
Youghal: Market House, on the harbour, **t** (024) 92447, *info@youghalchamber.ie; open June–mid-Sept.*

Shopping

Ballymaloe Craft & Kitchen shop, Shanagarry (*see* below). For handmade kitchen knives.
Stephen Pearce Pottery, Shanagarry, *www. stephenpearce.com.*
Ardsallagh goat's cheese and milk, Ardsallagh, Youghal. Cheese is also bottled with olive oil.

Sports and Activities

Activity Centres

Trabolgan, Midleton, **t** (021) 466 1551, *www. trabolgan.com.* Children's indoor and outdoor fun.

Courses and Tours

Ballymaloe Cookery School, Kinoith House, Shanagarry, Midleton, **t** (021) 464 6785, *www.cookingisfun.ic.* Cookery, gardening and wine courses at the famous hotel.

Golf

East Cork Golf Club, Gurtacrue, Midleton, **t** (021) 463 1687, *homepage.eircom.net/~east corkgolfclub.*
Water Rock Golf Course, Midleton, **t** (021) 461 3499, *www.waterrockgolfcourse.com.*
Youghal Golf Club, Knockaverry, Youghal, **t** (024) 92787, *homepage.eircom.net/~youghalgc.*

Open Farms

Cnoc A Ceo **Leahy's Open Farm and Farm Museum**, Condonstown, Dungourney, **t** (021) 466 8461. *Open Easter–Sept daily 11–6.* Plenty of opportunities to feed the animals, play games or visit the agricultural museum.

Spas

Midleton Park Wellness Centre and Spa, Midleton, **t** (021) 463 5153, *www.midleton park.com/wellness.* A range of treatments and alternative therapies (facials, hydrotherapy, wraps, reflexology, hot stone massages and reiki), plus state-of-the-art facilities: an 18m pool, gym, steam room, outdoor hot tub, sauna and aerobics room.

Where to Stay and Eat

East of Cork t (021) –
Aherne's Hotel and Seafood Restaurant, North Main Street, Youghal, **t** (024) 92424, *www.ahernes.net* (*luxury–expensive*). Well-appointed rooms, with a good atmosphere; wonderful fresh fish, local meat and produce are used in the restaurant.
Ballymaloe House, Shanagarry, **t** 465 2531, *www.ballymaloe.ie* (*expensive*). Beautiful Georgian house near the fishing village of Ballycotton; elegant rooms, friendly service, fabulous food and generous helpings. The whole Allen family are involved – you may be inspired to take a course (*see* above).
Midleton Park Hotel, Midleton **t** 463 5100, *www.midletonpark.com* (*expensive*). Quite luxurious for the price. The décor is beautiful, the atmosphere relaxed and the restaurant food superb.
Glenview House, Ballinaclasha, Midleton, **t** 463 1680, *www.glenviewmidleton.com* (*moderate*). 18th-century house with homely décor, good food and lovely grounds. 2 self-catering mews apartments available.
The Old Parochial House, Castlemartyr, **t** 466 7454 (*moderate*). Elegantly restored Victorian house on the edge of the village.
Spanish Point Seafood Restaurant and Guesthouse, Ballycotton, **t** 464 6177, *www. spanishpointballycotton.com* (*moderate*). Comfortable rooms in this Georgian house with wonderful views. John Tattan catches the fish and Mary cooks it for their delicious restaurant menu.
The Clean Slate, Midleton, **t** 633655 (*moderate*). Adventurous food in a striking building.
The Farm Gate, Broderick Street, Midleton, **t** 463 2771 (*moderate–inexpensive*). Emphasis on local ingredients and traditional dishes.
Finin's Restaurant and Bar, Main Street, Midleton, **t** 463 2382 (*moderate*). Attractive pub with an excellent restaurant.

18th-century whiskey distillery as the **Old Midleton Distillery**, off Distillery Road (*open for tours Mar–Oct daily 10–6; Nov–Feb Mon–Fri 11.30, 2.30 and 4; adm; t (021) 461 3594, www.whiskeytours.ie*). It's a fine building, self-contained within 11 acres, and you can take a tour around all the major parts – mills, maltings, corn stores, still houses and kilns. The water wheel is still in perfect order, and you can see the largest pot still in the world with a capacity of more than 30,000 gallons and sample some of the delicious stuff. It stopped as a working distillery in 1975, and there is a mass of information charting the history of Irish whiskey. Southwest of Midleton is the impressive 15th-century **Barryscourt Castle** (*open June–Sept daily 10–6, Oct–May Fri–Wed 11–5; adm adults €2, children €1; t (021) 488 2218/3864, www.heritageireland.ie*) at Carrigtohill, which contains an exhibition on the history of the Barrys and the castle. It is a quadrangular keep with square towers surrounded by a lawn, overlooking the inner reaches of Cork harbour. The 18th-century farmhouse in its *bawn* sells crafts, antiquarian books and teas.

The fast main road (N25) to Midleton and Youghal means that many people do not explore the peninsula opposite Crosshaven. Turn off at Midleton and follow the R629 to *Cluain Uamha* (the meadow of the cave) where an ancient bishopric was founded by St Colman in the 6th century. There are some large limestone caves close to the village, but it is chiefly interesting for its vast and ancient cathedral. This dates from the 13th century, and the round tower beside it is one of the only two surviving round towers in the county. You are allowed to climb to the top where the view is superb; its castellated top is more modern. Among the monuments in the cathedral is an alabaster tomb to George Berkeley, the philosopher who was bishop here from 1734 to 1753, and a 17th-century Fitzgerald tomb. The carved decoration on the north door represents the pagan symbols of life.

The R629 from Cloyne leads down to **Ballycotton**, a little fishing village set in a peaceful, unspoiled bay. There is a pretty view out to the Ballycotton Islands, which protect the village from the worst of the sea winds, and a bird sanctuary on the extensive marsh by the estuary. Close by is the welcoming **Ballymaloe House** (signposted in Castlemartyr on the Cork–Waterford road), which is famous for its hotel, restaurant, cooking school and kitchen/craft shop (*see* p.219). The **gardens** (*open daily 9–6; adm; t (021) 465 2531*) are new, though laid out within the old grounds, and designed to resemble a series of 'rooms', including a potager in geometric patterns, a formal fruit garden, a herb garden, a rose garden and herbaceous borders. At Ladysbridge, near Garryvoe, are the ruins of a grand fortified house built of the local limestone, **Ightermurragh Castle**. Over one of the fireplaces is a Latin inscription which tells that it was built by Edmund Supple and his wife, 'whom love binds in one', in 1641.

Two miles (3.2km) southeast in **Kilcredan**'s 17th-century Church of Ireland church are some fascinating limestone headstones with a variety of imaginative motifs. Sadly, the church has suffered the fate of many of that faith and is without a roof, and the carved tomb of Sir Robert Tynte has been ravaged by the weather. Just to the south is **Shanagarry**, famous for Stephen Pearce's pottery (*see* p.219), and the old home of the father of William Penn, the founder of Pennsylvania. You can buy simple earthenware and glazed pottery from his studio and tearooms or at the Ballymaloe House craft shop, which is one of the best kitchen shops in the country.

Youghal (pronounced 'Yawl'; *eochaill*, yew wood) is approximately 30 miles (48km) east of Cork City on the N25. It is an important medieval town which used to be a centre for the carpet industry, but has become one of the most attractive seaside towns in Ireland. It is set on the estuary of the River Blackwater, and has many fine bathing places and a long sandy beach. The river scenery between here and Cappoquin is memorable for its pretty woods, the silver twisting Blackwater and the attractive houses along its banks.

Youghal was founded by the Anglo-Normans in the 13th century and was destroyed in the Desmond Rebellion of 1579. The Fitzgeralds, Earls of Desmond, were a powerful Anglo-Norman family who joined forces with the Gaelic lords from Ulster to try and repulse the armies of Elizabeth I. Ruthless coercion and martial law put down the rebellion – 'man, woman and child were put to the Sword' wrote Raleigh's half-brother. The ruined town was handed over to Sir Walter Raleigh, as he had played an important part in the suppression, along with 42,000 acres of the Earl's forfeited estate in the Elizabethan plantation period. Raleigh became an 'undertaker', agreeing to repopulate his lands with English settlers and drive out the native Irish. He became mayor of the town and lived in the gabled **Myrtle Grove House** (*private*) at the end of William Street. He later sold Youghal to Richard Boyle who became the Earl of Cork. Thereafter, it was a prosperous place, supporting Oliver Cromwell and so avoiding another sacking. Raleigh reputedly planted the first potato in the garden, an act which was to have far-reaching consequences for Ireland's population.

In nearby Church Street is the 15th-century Church of Ireland collegiate **Church of St Mary**. The inside of this large cruciform church is crowded with interesting monuments, including one to the Earl of Cork, Richard Boyle, looking very smug, surrounded by his mother, his two wives, and nine of his 16 children. A memorial stands to an extraordinary lady, the Countess of Desmond, who apparently died in 1604 at the age of 147 after falling out of a tree when gathering cherries. The church was built around 1250, rebuilt in 1461 by Thomas, the 8th Earl of Desmond, and restored in 1884, after lying partially derelict since the Desmond Rebellion. The most notable features are its early English west doorway, the massive pulpit with its canopy of carved bog oak, and the large stained glass east window (*c.* 1468) with the arms of the Desmonds, Sir Walter Raleigh, the Earl of Cork and the Duke of Devonshire. Nearby on Main Street is the ruined 15th century tower house, **Tynte's Castle**. Large sections of the old town walls still stand, up on the crest of the hill, but even in 1579 they were in a bad state, and were easily breached by the rebellious Earl of Desmond.

The old part of town lies at the foot of a steep hill, whilst the new part has grown along the margin of the bay. The main street is spanned by Youghal's landmark, a tower known as the **Clock Gate** and erected in 1771. Other buildings of note are the **Red House**, an early 18th-century Dutch-style brick building, and, on the corner of Church Street, a group of medieval **almshouses** which have been restored. Youghal's harbour is close by. When you see it, try to imagine it fixed up with picket fences and clapboard siding to look like New Bedford, Massachusetts – that's what John Houston did to it when he filmed *Moby Dick* here in 1954, with Youghal's old salts, housewives and children pressed into service as extras. Paddy Linehan's Moby Dick bar facing the harbour is full of photos and mementos. The tourist office, in the old market house, includes a heritage centre with exhibits on Youghal's rich history, and in summer they offer walking tours of the town. Across the road in Foxes Lane is a small folk museum.

Leaving Youghal for the east, you might wish to take a detour up the lovely **Blackwater Valley**, which has some of the best driving and walking country in Ireland – if you like wooded banks, green fields, old buildings and twisting, unfrequented roads. You may be tempted to follow the Blackwater River to **Lismore** in County

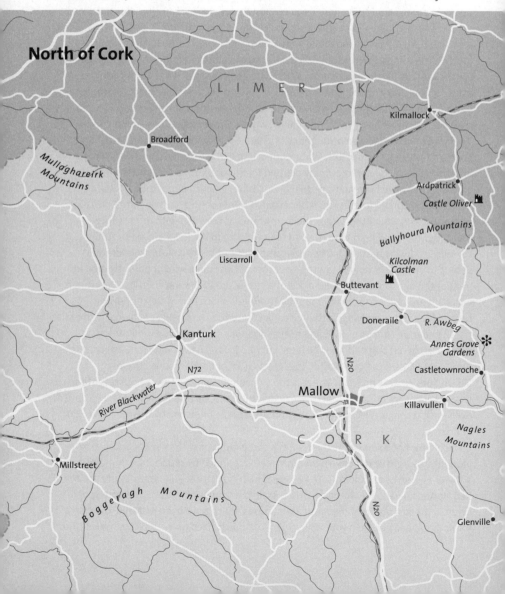

North of Cork

Waterford, which is well worth a tour: the cathedral is very impressive with fine monuments, Georgian glass, Gothic vaulting, and a window by Burne-Jones, made by William Morris. The town itself shows the planned approach of the local landlord family, the Dukes of Devonshire, who inherited the castle and estates through the Boyles. The 14th child of Richard Boyle, Earl of Cork, is famous for establishing Boyle's law, which is a basic tenet of physics. To the east is the Great Rath (*Lios Mor*) after which the town is named. The demesne of **Lismore Castle** dominates the town; when it was being rebuilt between 1812 and 1821, the 13th-century Lismore Crosier and the 15th-century *Book of Lismore* were found built into the walls of the castle. Both are now in the National Museum, Dublin. The castle can be rented, and the general public can visit the gardens, with a stately eight-hundred-year-old yew walk, which edge the

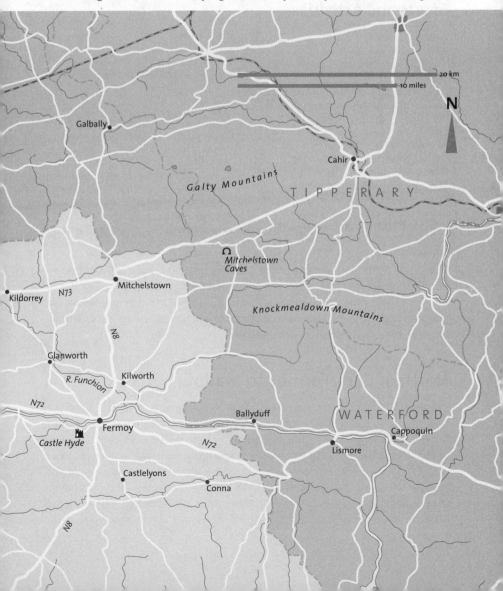

Tourist Information

Fermoy: Brian Toomey Sports, McCurtain St,
t (025) 438 1624; *open Mon–Sat 9–1 and 2–5.*
Mallow, Bridge Street, t (022) 42222; *open all
year Mon–Fri 9.30–1 and 2–5.30.*

Shopping

Ardrahan Cheese, Ardrahan House, Kanturk.
Mitchelstown Market, Thurs, 10.30–4.

Sports and Activities

Fishing

Ballyvolane House, Castlelyons, near Fermoy,
t (025) 36349, *www.ballyvolanehouse.ie.*
Speycast Ireland, Ghillie Cottage, Kilbarry
Stud, Fermoy, t (025) 32720, *www.speycast-
ireland.com*. Salmon fly-fishing tuition.

Golf

Fermoy Golf Club, Corrin, Fermoy, t (025)
32694, *fermoygolfclub@eircom.net*
Mitchelstown Golf Club, Limerick Road, t (025)
24072, *www.mitchelstown-golf.com.*
Doneraile Golf Club, Doneraile, t (022) 24137.
Mallow Golf Club, Ballyellis, Mallow, t (022)
21145, *golfmall@gofree.indigo.ie.*
Kanturk Golf Club, Kanturk, t (029) 50534.

Open Farms

Rambling House Farm Museum and Folk Park,
Mallow, t (029) 76155. *Open May–Sept.*
Kanturk Rural Farm Museum, Mealehara,
Kanturk, t (029) 51319.
Millstreet Country Park, Millstreet, t (029)
70810, *www.millstreetcountrypark.com.*
500-acre park with nature trails and
archaeological reconstructions.

Pony Trekking

Green Glens Equestrian Centre, Millstreet,
t (029) 70707, offers 1–6 day trail rides.

Walking

The Ballyhoura Way: Limerick Junction to
John's Bridge near Kanturk (90km).
The Blackwater Way: the Knockmealdown
Mountains to Muckross Park (168km).

Where to Stay

Castlehyde Hotel, Fermoy, t (025) 31865,
www.castlehydehotel.com (*luxury*).
Beautiful, renovated 18th-century
woodland hotel. The dining room offers
bistro-style lunches and a richer dinner
menu. In summer, eat alfresco on a terrace
in the woodland garden.
Longueville House, Mallow, t (022) 47156,
www.longuevillehouse.ie (*luxury*). Stylish

Blackwater. To the west, along the R666, back towards Fermoy, you will pass the
turreted Gothic tower gatehouses and bridge of **Ballysaggartmore** (1834), all that is
left of the Kiely estate. This folly was built to the design of their gardener; locals say
that after building it, the Kielys ran out of money and had to live in a less significant
house on the estate (demolished in the 1930s.)

North of Cork: Fermoy to Mallow

Fermoy (*Mainistir Fhearmuighe*, abbey of the plantations), 30 miles (48km) north of
Cork City on the N8, used to be a garrison town for the British army. People here are
familiar with every fascinating detail of salmon-catching. The town, built along both
sides of the dark River Blackwater, has seen more prosperous days and retains an air
of shabby gentility. Lord Fermoy, an ancestor of the late Princess of Wales, is said to
have gambled away his Fermoy estates in an evening. The Protestant church, built in
1802, contains some grotesque masks; however, the Catholic church is rather elegant:
it was designed by E.W. Pugin in 1867, with an interior by the Pain brothers.

manor with views to the river and Callaghan Castle ruin. Luxuriously appointed rooms are decorated in warm hues; the food is superlative, and the service attentive. Off the dining room is a marvellous curved iron conservatory, built by Richard Turner in 1866.

Assolas Country House, Kanturk, t (029) 50015, *www.assolas.com* (*expensive*). Set among mature trees reaching down to the river. Offers tennis, fishing and croquet in the grounds, and delicious food.

Ballyvolane House, Castlelyons, near Fermoy, t (025) 36349, *www.ballyvolanehouse.ie* (*expensive*). Lovely old Georgian house set in beautiful grounds, with lots of local seasonal produce, cheese and meats served in the dining room. They also have a self-catering cottage which sleeps 6.

Glanworth Mill, Glanworth, Fermoy, t (025) 38555, *www.glanworthmill.ie* (*expensive*). Riverside inn with excellent food, and rooms named after writers associated with the area – including one cut into the cliff face.

Glenlohane, Kanturk, t (029) 50014, *www.glenlohane.com* (*expensive*). Comfortable, informal Georgian house in parkland.

Hibernian Hotel, Mallow, t (022) 21588, *www.hibhotel.com* (*moderate*). Comfortable décor in an old, family-run hotel in Mallow.

Springfort Hall, Mallow, t (022) 21278, *www.springfort-hall.com* (*moderate*).

Comfortable 18th-century manor house set in woodlands, with simple décor.

Self-catering

Cashman Thatched Cottage, Garrison, t (029) 50197, *www.irelandselfcatering guide.com*. Charming thatched cottage with gardens to front and rear. Sleeps 6 comfortably.

Eating Out

Glanworth Mill, Glanworth, Fermoy, t (025) 38555 (*moderate–inexpensive*). Café serving delightful soups, salads, and wicked desserts; and a formal restaurant for dinner.

Castlehyde Hotel, Fermoy, t (025) 31865, *www.castlehydehotel.com* (*expensive–moderate*). Imaginative bar food at lunch time and modern Irish cuisine in the evening.

La Bigoudenne, 28 McCurtain Street, Fermoy, t (025) 32832 (*moderate*). Quintessentially French bistro, with filled crêpes a speciality.

Paki Fitz's, Cork St, Mitchelstown, t (025) 84926 (*moderate*). A café, a 3-storey bar serving food, and a sophisticated restaurant with an extensive dinner menu.

Longueville House, Mallow, t (022) 47156, (*luxury–expensive*). Exciting cuisine in generous portions (*see left*).

Just outside Fermoy, overlooking the river to the west, is one of the most beautiful houses in Ireland, the late-Georgian mansion, **Castle Hyde** (*now owned by Michael Flately of 'Riverdance' fame; private*). This was the ancestral home of Douglas Hyde, the first President of the Irish Republic and the founder of the Gaelic League, although he was actually born at French Park in County Roscommon. **Castlelyons**, a few miles outside the town (turn left off the N8 going towards Cork), is a quiet and pretty hamlet where intimations of past history compel you to stop. Here is the great ruined house of the Barrys, a Norman family, burned down in 1771, and the remains of a 14th-century Franciscan Friary. In the graveyard of Kill St Anne is a roofless 15th-century church, and within it is the ruin of an 18th-century parish church. The classical **Barrymore Mausoleum** is quite impressive, especially the white marble bust of the Earl of Barrymore.

To the north, **Mitchelstown** is famous in Ireland for butter and cheese, an industry which employs a lot of people, although the cheese is rather boring – Cheddar and a sort of soft bland spread. It is also famous for its limestone **Mitchelstown Cave** (*open daily throughout the year, 10–6; adm adult €5, children €2; t (052) 67246*), which have good examples of stalactites and stalagmites, and are very extensive. They are a further 10 miles (16km) to the north on the Cahir road (N8). The Lord of Kingston planned Michelstown in the grand manner with important buildings at the end of vistas. If you have some time to spare, walk through **Kingston Square** where there are 18th-century almshouses for decayed Protestant gentlefolk, and a central chapel designed by John Morrison of Cork. His son and grandson were also architects and responsible for some of the finest buildings in the county. A tree-lined street leads to the Church of Ireland church, which was designed by G. R. Pain.

The castle, which was the focus of all this grandeur, has unfortunately been demolished and replaced with a huge dairy factory. The old castle was founded by the White Knights of Desmond, and passed to the Kingstons through marriage around 1660. The old castle was replaced with a Gothic mansion by G. R. Pain in 1823, but the estates were heavily mortgaged owing to the extravagance of the Regency earl. Mary Wollstonecraft (1759–1797), who wrote *Vindication of the Rights of Women* and was the mother of Mary Shelley, spent time as a governess here; her libertarian and feminist ideas were deeply disapproved of by the family.

By the reign of Anna, Countess of Kingston, the land wars were brewing; her tenants wanted their rents reduced and refused to pay her. Her finances were already straitened; it was well known that you would get barely a raisin in her barmbrack (*see* recipe, p.89) if you were invited to tea. In 1880, some 1,600 of her tenants demanded a rent reduction, and there was a huge demonstration in Michelstown in 1881. The dispute ended with evictions; most of the tenants paid up and were reinstated by the summer of 1882. But the whole thing started up again in 1887, and a meeting in Mitchelstown of Land Leaguers, tenants, nationalist MPs and Radicals from England turned into a riot which ended when two people were killed and twenty others were seriously wounded by shots from the police. There is a statue of John Manderville, a leader of the agitation for fair rents, and stone crosses to commemorate the dead in the Market Square. Elizabeth Bowen describes the last garden party at Mitchelstown in her recollections, *Bowen's Court* (*see* below).

The countryside around becomes richer as you travel west and enter the Golden Vein, a fertile plain that extends north of the **Galty Mountains**. At Kildorrey, turn right off the N73 on to the R512 to go to **Doneraile**. Near here was the home of novelist Elizabeth Bowen (1899–1973) whose works so beautifully describe the shades and subtleties of the Anglo-Irish. Her house, Bowen's Court, a beautiful 18th-century mansion, was demolished in the 1960s – a victim of the government's lack of interest in historic buildings at that time. The farmer who bought it was only interested in the land and the timber.

Doneraile and Buttevant are in Edmund Spenser country, 40 miles (64km) north of Cork City, between the Blackwater and the **Ballyhoura Mountains**. Here the poet served the Crown in various positions, and wrote most of *The Faerie Queene*, trying desperately (and unsuccessfully) to flatter Elizabeth I enough to get the grant of a bigger manor, one closer to London. While spinning his learned Renaissance fantasies he also found time to write *A View of the Present State of Ireland* in which he advocated a policy for the island that was uncomfortably close to genocide. Spenser had just been appointed Sheriff of Cork when a revolt broke out in 1598, and the Irish repaid him by sacking and burning his home and chasing him back to England, where he died the following year.

His home, **Kilcolman Castle**, is now a sombre ruin, hard to find, in a field beside a reedy pool northeast of Doneraile. There is a sad essay by Yeats on Spenser and the irony of the poet as oppressor. 'Could he have gone there as a poet merely,' he wrote, 'he would have found among wandering storytellers...certainly all the kingdom of Faery, still unfaded, of which his own poetry was often but a troubled image.'

From 1895 to 1913 Doneraile was the parish of Canon Sheehan, who wrote wise and funny books about Irish rural life. His statue stands outside the Catholic church. **Doneraile Court and Wildlife Park** (*open mid-April–Oct, Mon–Fri 8am–8.30pm, Sat 10–8.30, Sun 11–7; Nov–mid-April Mon–Fri 8–4.30, Sat–Sun 10–4.30; adm adults €1.50, children 75 cents; t (022) 24244, www.heritageireland.ie*) has a wonderful Georgian house that has been saved from ruin by the Irish Georgian Society (*under restoration at time of writing; completion date unknown*). Here, Elizabeth Barry, wife of the first Viscount Doneraile, hid in a clock case to observe a masonic lodge meeting held in the house. Perhaps she laughed, but whatever happened she gave herself away, and all the masons could do to keep her quiet was to elect her as a mason – the only woman mason in history. A sadder story concerns a 19th-century viscount who kept a pet fox, which bit him and his coachman one day. The fox was found to have rabies, and both men travelled to Paris to be treated by Pasteur, but although the coachman continued with his treatment, Lord Doneraile gave it up. He soon developed the disease and died a terrible death in 1887. The beautiful surrounding parkland has been developed for tourists, and there are nature walks, cascades, and herds of deer in the park. Enter through the grand stone gates just outside the town.

Nearby is the unique alkaline **Kilcolman Bog** (*see* p.68), home to many birds, and you can visit it if you are involved in bird study. Contact the tourist office for details. At **Buttevant** during July is the **Cahirmee Horse Fair**, which has been held here for hundreds of years and is always good craic, with lots of other events happening at the same time.

Mallow, 10 miles (16km) south, used to be a famous spa where the gentry of Ireland came to take the waters and have a good time. In the 18th century the spa inspired the anonymous verse which begins:

Beauing, belling, dancing, drinking,
Breaking windows, damning, singing,
Ever raking, never thinking,
Live the rakes of Mallow...

The old spa house in Spa Walk is now privately owned and the once-famous water gushes to waste. The town has some pretty 18th-century houses and a timbered, decorated Clock House. **Mallow Castle** is a still-impressive, although roofless, ruin of a fortified 16th-century tower house. The Catholic **St Mary's Church** has a pretty interior and Romanesque revival façade. Davis Street is named after the poet and nationalist Thomas Davis (1814–1845) who was born in No. 72. The **Mallow Races**, which happen intermittently throughout the spring, summer and autumn, are the only times the place really comes alive, though it is frequented by anglers and the **Folk Festival** in July is very cheerful. Just outside the town is **Longueville House**, which produces delicious wine, and where you can eat and stay in great style.

At **Castletownroche** on the N72, 10 miles (16km) east of Mallow, notice the pretty Church of Ireland church on a rise above the river. It is also worth stopping to wander around the ruins of Bridgetown Abbey founded by FitzHugh Roche in the 13th century. To the north of the pretty church is **Anne's Grove** (*open Easter–Sept, Mon–Sat 10–5, Sun 1–6; adm adults €6, children €2; t (022) 26145*), with its tranquil woodlands and walled garden (*see* pp.76–7). The sloping grounds surrounding the beautiful 18th-century house are planted in the style made popular by William Robertson in the late 19th century. Nothing is contrived and the massed plants lead along winding paths to the river and gardens. Rhododendrons, magnolias, eucryphias, abutilons and primulas obviously love it here, so vigorously have they grown. Just south of the Blackwater River at Castletownroche is **Killavullen** where **Ballymacmoy House**, the original home of the Hennessys of cognac fame (and now in their ownership again), is being restored. The extensive caves beneath the estate are already open during the summer. Northeast of Castletownroche is **Glanworth**, a sleepy village dominated by the imposing remains of Roche's castle above the River Funchion, on which stands an 18th-century water mill that has recently opened as an attractive inn.

From Mallow, the country lanes which take you through the **Boggeragh Mountains** are a maze, and rather fun if you have time to get lost for a while. They have a wild mystery, heightened by the green glow from the overgrown hedges which form an arbour overhead. The road from Mallow to Killarney meanders past the haunted shell of the O'Callaghan's castle at Dromaneen. **Kanturk**, to the north of the main road, is an attractive 18th-century planned town. **Kanturk Castle** is a huge building, begun around 1609, but never finished. It is said that the Privy Council ordered the work to stop and the owner, McCarthy, flew into a rage and ordered that the blue glass tiles with which the castle was to be roofed be thrown into the river.

A little diversion to the northwest will take you to **Liscarroll**. This small and remote village has the third-largest **Norman Castle** in Ireland, probably built by the Barrys. It also has the largest concentration of donkeys in the country for outside the village is the home of a **donkey sanctuary** (*open Mon–Fri 9–4.30, Sat–Sun 10–5; t (022) 48398, www.thedonkeysanctuary.ie*). Back on the main road (N72) to Killarney (which bypasses **Millstreet**, famous for its equestrian centre) the second road to the left after Rathmore, about a mile from the town, goes to the base of the **Paps Mountains**, dedicated to the ancient fertility goddess Danu. At the end of that road, by the school, turn left and then first right where a small signpost points to 'The City'. This extraordinary site, enclosed by a dry-stone cashel 10ft (3m) high, is the setting for what is perhaps the oldest uninterrupted religious ceremony in Europe. Certainly since the early Iron Age, people have gathered here in May. Time stands still; uninterpreted and without a gift shop in sight, this is the sort of place that makes a tour of Ireland memorable.

County Clare

13

County Clare

Galway Bay

Inishmore

Inishmaan

Aran Islands

Inisheer

10 km
5 miles

N

Black Head

Ballyvaughan Bay

Fanore

Ballyvaughan

Burren Way

Corkscrew Hill

Aillwee Caves

The Burren

N67

Poulnabrone Megalithic Tomb

Lisdoonvarna

Doolin

Ballykinvarga Stone Fort

Kilfenora

R. Dealagh

Leamaneh Castle

O'Brien's Tower

Cliffs of Moher

Hags Head

St Brigid's Holy Well

Liscannor

Lahinch

Ennistymon

R. Cullenagh

Liscannor Bay

Atlantic

N67

Miltown Malbay

Ocean

Spanish Point

Slievecallan

N85

The Hand Cross Roads

Quilty

Lake Boolynagreana

Doonbeg

R. Doonbeg

N68

Corbally

Cooraclare

Kilkee

N67

Kilrush

Killadysert

Carrigaholt

Killimer

Scattery Island
p.142

River Shannon pp.126–7

Loop Head

Tarbert

Until the 4th century Clare was part of Connacht, after which it became known as the Kingdom of Thomond. It is a wild and beautiful county, still marked with signs of a tempestuous past; there are 2,300 stone forts or *cahers* dating back to pre-Celtic times. Clare is bounded by water on three sides – the silvery Shannon Estuary and River widen into Lough Derg on its south and east side, its western side is edged by the pounding Atlantic Ocean, and on its northern border it meets County Galway.

GALWAY

Athenry

GALWAY

Loughrea

Aughinish

Burren

Corcomroe
Abbey

Bealaclugga

Kinvarra

Turlough

N66

Slieve Aughty Mountains

Gort

Lough Derg

Carran

Cahercommaun
Stone Fort

Lough Cutra

R. Owendalulleegh

Killinaboy

Inchiquin
Lough

Lough
Graney

Corofin

L. Atedaun

Mountshannon

3 Dysert O'Dea

Ballinruan

R.

R. Bow

Holy Island

Dromineer

Crusheen

C L A R E

Inchicronan Lough

Graney

Feakle

Scarriff

Tulla

Ennis

2

Craggaunowen
Megalithic Centre

Ogonnelloe

Doon
Lough

Slieve Bernagh

St Molua's
Oratory

Arra
Mountains

Quin

R. Rine

Clarecastle

N18

Broadford

Killaloe

Ballina

Dromoland Castle

Knappogue Castle

Mooghaun Fort

N18

Newmarket on Fergus

Sixmilebridge

TIPPERARY

River
Fergus

Deer
Island

Deenish
Island

1 Bunratty Castle
Folk Park

Clonlara

Shannon Airport

N19

Shannon

Cratloe

Castleconnell

Bunratty

Cratloe Woods House

Canon Island

N18

pp.126–7

LIMERICK

Ann

Askeaton

L I M E R I C K

It is unspoilt by tourism, even though it has some unattractive ribbon development and the urban sprawl of huge Shannon Airport in the flatlands of the River Shannon and its estuary to the south. The locals earn money from farming, tourism and fishing; the airport and the industries that have grown up around it also give a lot of employment to the surrounding area. It benefits further from the Shannon Scheme, the largest hydroelectric scheme in the country. The population is approximately 103,000, with most people living in the flat central plain from which the county takes its name, *An Clar*. It is separated by the Shannon Estuary from County Kerry, its neighbour in the south, though there is a car ferry from Tarbert to Killimer.

Most people go inland, almost to the centre of Ireland, to find the Limerick bridge, and then only shoot through Clare on their way to the delights of Connemara. But Clare has its plunging cliffs and strange limestone karst landscapes to attract the

Getting There and Around

By Air

Shannon Airport (t (061) 471 444, *www.shannonairport.com*) is 15 miles south of Ennis town. *Bus Eireann* runs a regular **airport bus service** to Ennis (30mins, around €5).

By Bus and Rail

Buses leave Ennis from the station (t (065) 682 4177) in the centre, with connections to Shannon Airport, Limerick, Galway and Dublin. Ennis **train station** (t (065) 684 0444) is in Station Road; services mirror the bus lines. You can get to most smaller towns by bus. **Burren Coaches**, t (065) 707 8009. Guided tours of the Burren.

By Ferry

The **Shannon Car Ferry** sails between **Tarbert** in Kerry and **Killimer** in Clare. There are daily, hourly (May–Sept half-hourly) crossings. Cars €14 single/€22 return; pedestrians €4 single; t (065) 905 3124, *www.shannonferries.com*.

By Bike

Michael Tierney, 17 Abbey Street, Ennis, t (065) 682 9433, *www.ennisrentabike.com*.
Irish Cycle Hire, in the train station, Ennis, t (065) 682 1992, *www.irishcyclehire.com*.

Getting to Islands off Clare

Aran Islands: Aran Islands Fast Ferries, t (065) 707 4550, *www.aranislandsfastferries.com*, offer 20min sailings Doolin–Inisheer in high season, €20 return; **Doolin Ferries**, t (065) 7074455, *www.doolinferries.com*, go from Doolin or Galway to Inishmore, Inisheer and Inishmaan by request, all year. **Willie O'Callaghan** also runs cruises in summer from Liscannor Pier, t (065) 682 1374.
Scattery Island: Shannon Dolphins, t (065) 905 1327, *www.discoverdolphins.ie*, operate the daily ferry *St Senan II* from Kilrush marina.

Festivals

May
Fleadh Nua Ennis: *www.fleadhnua.com*.
Iniscealtra Festival of Arts: Mountshannon.
Clare Festival of Traditional Singing: Miltown.

June
Clare County *Fleadh*: in Ennis.
Spancil Hill Fair: traditional horse fair.

July
Féile Brian Ború: 5-day event on a Viking theme in Killaloe; *www.killaloe.ie*.
Scariff Harbour Festival: *www.scariff.com*.

August
Lisdoonvarna Matchmaking Festival: now 'Europe's biggest singles event' (runs to Oct); *www.matchmakerireland.com*.
Feakle International Traditional Music Festival: *www.feaklefestival.ie*.
Eigse **Mrs Crotty, Festival of Concertina Music**: in Kilrush; *www.eigsemrscrotty.com*.

September
Dan Furey Weekend: set and step dancing in Labasheeda; *www.labasheeda.net*.

more adventurous. The west Clare coast ends in the dramatic Cliffs of Moher, and besides gazing at the splendid seascapes you can go sea-fishing, diving, walking, rock-climbing, golfing and dolphin-watching along this part of the coast. To the north, overlooking Galway Bay, the Barony of the Burren looks like some misplaced section of the moon, white, crevassed and barren; but springy turf and calcium-loving plants grow in the earth-filled fissures, and cattle manage to graze quite happily around the cracks that could catch them in a leg-breaking fall. The archaeological and botanical interest and the mysterious and evasive charm of this rocky place make many converts. There are numerous places to bathe and fish on the coast, whilst the scenery and walking around the lakes and hills of Slieve Bernagh, which rise on the west side of the long stretch of Lough Derg, and the Slieve Aughty Mountain Range, are some of the best in the county.

Walking and caving attract the more active visitors, but many regard County Clare as the best place in Ireland to hear traditional music. Doolin, a little fishing village and port for boats to Inisheer, one of the Aran islands, became the place to hear it in the late 1970s, and still continues to attract many European and American backpackers. However, spontaneous creativity and musical excellence is not tied to any one place. It has long moved on from Doolin to other places in Clare; a shifting energy, not easily contained, and nothing like the debased form of traditional music that is served up to bus tours.

Recently, a few of the wonderful carved stone heads to be found in the ancient holy sites have been stolen, apparently hacked off and driven away. The Office of Public Works may have to substitute replicas for the originals if this continues.

History

The 12th-century *Book of Invasions*, or *Lebor Gabala*, connects Clare with the Fir Bolgs, but we know little about these shadowy people. Many centuries later, it was a Clare man, Brian Boru of the clan O'Brien, who conducted a vigorous and successful campaign against the Vikings and defeated them at Clontarf in 1014. He became High King of Ireland in 1002, and built the Palace of Kincora as his royal residence in 1012. Sadly, he was killed in his tent after the battle of Clontarf, and the fragile national unity he had managed to create disappeared very fast. There is nothing left of Kincora today, that palace of feasting and music; in fact nobody is really sure exactly where it was located (it was probably close to Killaloe).

In the tales of ancient Ireland the countryside was fraught with the battles of the landowning Celtic clans: the O'Briens, the O'Deas, the MacNamaras and the MacMahons, who, when they were not waging fierce war on foreigners, passed the time by fighting amongst themselves. In 1172 the incumbent chief of the O'Briens, Donal Mor, enlisted the help of a new group of invaders, a party of Norman mercenaries, in his war against the O'Conors of Connacht. Despite this initial foothold in the country, the Norman-English forces did not make much of a mark in County Clare until the accession of Henry VIII in 1534 and his acknowledgement as King of Ireland. The O'Briens were made Earls of Thomond, and remained more or less loyal to the English crown until the Cromwellian conquest (*see* **History**, p.14). After that time,

Clare and its neighbouring county, Connacht, became a seat of rebellion against English rule. Clare is part of the wild west of Ireland; when Cromwell heard that a substantial part of Clare had no trees to hang a man, nor enough water to drown him, nor enough earth to bury him, he thought it would be just the place to banish the rebellious Irish whom he had thrown off the land in other parts of the country.

Later, in the 19th century, Daniel O'Connell was able to exploit this burning sense of injustice and channel it into his campaign for Catholic emancipation in which he was enthusiastically supported by the peasantry, who gave his organization the 'penny a month' that they could afford. He became the MP for Ennis and used his position in the English Parliament to campaign for the repeal of the Union with England. The Great Famine and emigration hit the population of Clare very hard: its population fell from 286,000 in 1841 to less than half this number thirty years later.

East Clare and Ennis

Around Lough Derg

Broadford, **Tulla** and **Feakle** are all pleasant villages where you can stay in farms or town and country houses and explore the Clare Lakelands. **Lough Graney** is especially beautiful, with its wooded shores. Most of the loughs are well stocked with bream, brown trout and pike. Near Feakle the witty and outrageous 18th-century poet Brian Merriman earned his livelihood as a schoolmaster (*see* **Introduction**, pp.2–3). Here also is the cottage of Biddy Early, the wise woman about whom at the turn of the century Lady Augusta Gregory collected stories for her book, *Visions and Beliefs of the West of Ireland*.

From the neat and pretty village of **Mountshannon** on Lough Derg it is possible to get a boat to **Holy Island**, also known as *Iniscealtra*, about half a mile from the shore. Regular ferries run in summer or you could hire a boat at the harbour, which is a main stopping place on the lake for hire-cruisers and sailing boats. The view of Tountinna Mountain from the lough is magnificent. The giant cross on its summit was erected to the Irishmen who fell in 'the Troubles' of 1916–22. This mountain is in County Tipperary; the Gaelic meaning of the name *Tul tuinne* is 'the hill above the wave'. The Christian settlement on the island is attibuted to St Cairmin, who lived here *c.* AD 640. Today there are five ancient churches, a round tower, a saint's graveyard, a hermit's cell and a holy well. St Cairmin's Church, beside the incomplete round tower, has a wonderful Hiberno-Romanesque chancel arch, impressive in its simplicity. St Mary's Church, much altered in the 16th century, contains a monument to Sir Turlough O'Brien and his wife. This O'Brien was infamous for butchering the Spanish Armada survivors who were washed up on the coast of Clare. The festival at the holy well was famous for the bacchanalian revelry that accompanied it. It was stopped by the priests some time in the 19th century, because the local squireens would seduce the girls attending. The memorial stones are still in place in the saint's graveyard for the period covering the 8th to the 12th centuries. Unfortunately the whole effect is rather spoiled by modern tombstones and garish plastic wreaths.

Tourist Information

Ennis: Arthur's Row, t (065) 682 8366, *tourist officeennis@shannondev.ie; open all year.*
Killaloe: The Bridge, t (061) 376866; *open Mar–Sept.*
Shannon Airport: t (061) 471664, *touristoffice shannon@shannondev.ie; open all year.*

Shopping

Crafts
Ballymorris Pottery, Cratloe, *www.ballymorris pottery.com.*
Bunratty Folk Park, Bunratty Castle. Woven clothing, candles and prints.
Bunratty Village Mills, Bunratty. Shopping complex including a Tipperary Crystal shop, Meadowes & Byrne clothing store, and a restaurant.
Clare Business Centre, Ennis. Peadar O'Loughlin's fiddles and violins.
Clare Craft and Design, Parnell Street, Ennis. Displays and sells the art, pottery and crafts of a number of Clare craftspeople.
Cratloe Woods House, northwest of Limerick, t (061) 327028.

Delicacies
Bunratty Winery, Bunratty, *http://homepage. eircom.net/~bunrattywinery/.* Sells a particularly good mead.
Open Sesame, 35 Parnell Street, Ennis. Organic vegetables and local cheeses.

Sports and Activities

Cruising
Mountshannon Harbour, on Lough Derg, is a great place to begin boat trips up the lovely River Graney (also known as the Scariff).

Shannon Castle Line, Williamstown Harbour, Whitegate, t (061) 927042, *www.shannon cruisers.com.* Cruiser hire for 3 nights minimum. Instruction available.

Fishing
O'Callaghan Angling & Cruising, Ennis, t (065) 682 1374, *www.ocallaghanangling.com.*

Golf
Dromoland Castle Golf Club, Newmarket on Fergus, t (061) 368144, *www.dromoland.ie.*
East Clare Golf Club, Scarriff, t (061) 921322, *www.scariff.com/east.htm.*
Ennis Golf Club, Drumbiggle, Ennis, t (065) 682 4072, *http://homepage.tinet.ie/~egc.*
Shannon Golf Club, Shannon Airport, t (061) 471551, *www.shannongolf.com.*
Woodstock Golf and Country Club, Woodstock House, Ennis, t (065) 682 9463, *www.woodstockgolfclub.com.*

Pony Trekking
Cahergal House, Newmarket on Fergus, t (061) 368358, *www.cahergal.com.*
Carrowbaun Farm Trekking Centre, Killaloe, t (061) 376754.
Clare Equestrian Centre, Ennis, t (065) 684 0136, *www.clareequestrian.com.*
Clonlara Equestrian Centre, Clonlara, t (061) 354172, *www.clonlaraequestrian.com.*

Walking
The Mid-Clare Way. A circular route from Quin, 100km.

Water Sports
The swimming is good in Lough Graney.
Shannon Sailing Centre, Dromineer, Co. Tipperary, t (067) 24499. Windsurfing, canoeing, water-skiing, day cruises and sailing on Lough Derg.

Around Killaloe and Bunratty
Killaloe is right on the great Shannon River and surrounded by the **hills of Slieve Bernagh** and the **Arra Mountains**. It is connected to Ballina in Tipperary by an elegant bridge of 13 arches. Not far from the bridge, on the west bank of the river, is the gem of Killaloe, **St Flannan's Cathedral**, a fine 12th-century building built by Donal O'Brien on the site of an earlier church founded in the 6th century by St Lua. There is a magnificent Hiberno-Romanesque door which is better than anything else of its kind

University of Limerick Adventure Centre, Killaloe, t (061) 376622, *www.ulac.ie*. Water sports facilities and instruction available. Call well in advance to book sessions.

Where to Stay

Dromoland Castle, Newmarket on Fergus, t (061) 368144, *www.dromoland.ie* (*luxury*). Owned by the consortium that also operates Ashford Castle, the hotel has beautiful grounds, a golf course and delicious food; however, the atmosphere can be a bit impersonal.

Old Ground Hotel, O'Connell Street, Ennis, t (065) 682 8127, *www.flynnhotels.com* (*luxury*). Well-appointed rooms in an 18th-century building in Ennis. Good food is served in the café and **O'Brien Room** restaurant; the **Poets' Bar** hosts traditional music sessions.

Thomond House, Dromoland, Newmarket on Fergus, t (061) 368304, *www.thomondhouse.com* (*luxury*). Conor O'Brien, the 18th Baron Inchiquin, is the O'Brien of Thomond. His Georgian-style house overlooks Dromoland Castle and its lake, the original home of the O'Briens which is also now a hotel (*see above*). There is salmon-fishing, deerstalking, riding and golf, all of which need to be arranged in advance.

Bunratty Castle Hotel, Bunratty, t (061) 478700, *www.bunrattycastlehotel.com* (*expensive*). Instinct suggests that this is a tourist trap, but in fact it offers excellent accommodation and traditional music every night. The main irritation is that the bar can be so full of people that one cannot be served.

Tinarana House, Killaloe, t (061) 376966, *www.tinaranahouse.com* (*expensive–moderate*). Beautifully decorated B&B in a

Victorian mansion amidst park; they can set you up with horses and boats and all manner of cures, as it is also a health farm.

Ardsollus Farm, Quin, t (065) 682 5601 (*moderate*). Rooms in a 300-year-old farmhouse overlooking Dromoland estate, with antique furnishings.

Carrygerry House Hotel, Shannon, t (061) 360500, *www.carrygerryhouse.com* (*moderate*). 18th-century house with lots of space and elegant, homely décor, yet only 5mins from Shannon Airport. The restaurant serves delicious meals (*see below*).

Smyths Country Lodge Hotel, Feakle, t (061) 924000, *www.iol.ie/~smythvil* (*moderate–inexpensive*). Cosy fishing hotel.

Mooghaun Farmhouse, Newmarket on Fergus, t (065) 682 5786, *mooghaunfarmhouse@eircom.net* (*inexpensive*). Family farmhouse B&B in a great location.

Rathmore House B&B, Ballina, Killaloe, t (061) 379296, *www.rathmorehouse.com* (*inexpensive*). Warm, comfortable B&B with five *en suite* rooms.

Self-catering

Ballyhannon Castle, near Quin, t 086 814 5837, *www.ballyhannon-castle.com*. Stunningly restored and decorated 15th-century castle, with massive stone walls and crafted stout oak beams. Sleeps 8.

Leapfield House, Laccaroe, Feakle, t (061) 924111, *www.cottageguide.co.uk/leapfield*. 18th-century farmhouse with a pretty garden; sleeps up to 7, plus a baby. Contact Christine Guilfoyle.

Mountshannon Village Cottages, close to Mountshannon Harbour and Sailing Club, t 087 907 9564, *www.mountshannon villagecottages.com*. Attractive, traditional-style cottages with 3/4 bedrooms, overlooking Lough Derg.

in Ireland and is said to be the entrance to the tomb of Murtagh O'Brien, King of Munster, who died in the same century the cathedral was built. The bold and varied carvings of animals and foliage on the shafts and capitals, and the pattern of the chevrons on the arches, are not merely decoration; they are modelled to make the entire conception an organic whole. Nearby is **Thorgrim's Stone**, the shaft of a cross bearing a runic and ogham inscription of about the year AD 1000. The view from the top of the square cathedral tower is superb. You can see all the mountains

Strasburgh Manor Cottages, Inch, Ennis,
t (065) 683 9125, *homepage.eircom.net/~
strasburgh*. Restored 18th-century stone-cut
cottage building in 5 acres of woodland.
Sleeps 4; newly equipped and furnished.

Eating Out

Game Keeper's Restaurant, Smyth's Country
Lodge Hotel, Feakle, **t** (061) 924000
(*moderate*). Impressive fare in an intimate
setting.
Flappers, Tulla, **t** (065) 683 5711 (*moderate–
inexpensive*). Interesting menus and
flavoursome food, including vegetarian
dishes, in a simple setting.
Lantern House, Ogonnelloe, south of Scarriff,
t (061) 923034 (*moderate*). Excellent home
cooking in a lantern-lit room overlooking
Lough Derg. *Dinner only.*
Goosers Bar and Eating House, Ballina, near
Killaloe, **t** (061) 376791 (*moderate*). Popular,
award-winning restaurant serving local
produce, meat and fish, with plenty of
intimate character and inviting open fires.
Galloping Hogan's, Ballina, near Killaloe,
t (061) 376162 (*moderate*). Ideal for relaxed
alfresco dining on the shores of tranquil
Lough Derg.
Muses Restaurant, Bunratty House Mews,
Bunratty, **t** (061) 364082 (*expensive*). In the
cellars of an attractive house built in 1846 by
a hopeful son waiting to inherit the castle
from his father. The décor and atmosphere
reflect that feeling of a vanished, leisurely
way of life. The menu offers a choice of local
fresh produce, and a good wine list. *Open
Tues–Sat 6pm–9pm.*
Gallagher's Seafood Restaurant, Bunratty,
t (061) 363363 (*moderate*). Charming,
thatched cottage, specializing in local
seafood. *Open Tues–Sat.*

Durty Nelly's, Bunratty, **t** (061) 364861,
www.durtynellys.ie (*inexpensive*). Pub
and eating house popular with locals as
well as visitors. Choose from the **Loft
Restaurant** (*expensive–moderate*), a quieter
venue offering à la carte, mostly meat
dishes; or the **Oyster Restaurant** (*moderate*),
which specializes, of course, in seafood.
Mac's Pub, Main Street, Bunratty, **t** (061)
360788 (*moderate*). Right in the middle of
Bunratty Folk Park, serving good seafood
with music in the evening.
Castle Banquets, **t** (061) 360788 (*moderate*).
Medieval banquets at Bunratty and
Knappogue Castles (*see* pp.238 and 240).
The Conservatory, Carrygerry Country House,
Newmarket on Fergus, **t** (061) 360500,
www.carrygerryhouse.com (*expensive*).
Country-house charm and marvellous, rich
local meat, fish and vegetarian dishes that
are worth seeking out. *Open Tues–Sat
6.30–9.30.*
Cloister Restaurant and Bar, Abbey Street,
Ennis, **t** (065) 682 9521 (*inexpensive*). Old-
world bar. Good soups, local cheeses and
nutty brown bread during the daytime; at
night it becomes more formal (and
expensive) as a restaurant.

Entertainment and Nightlife

Traditional music
Clare is particularly famous for its music
sessions. **Ennis** boasts some good venues. Try:
Brogan's, O'Connell Street.
May Kearney's Bar, 1 Newbridge Road.
Tailor Quigley's Pub, Auburn Lodge, Galway
Road, Ennis, **t** (065) 682 1247. Named after a
famous local tailor of the song 'Spancil Hill'.
Nightly music and song in summer.

that crowd round the gorge of Killaloe, and the beautiful Lough Derg. In the grounds
of the cathedral is **St Flannan's Oratory** with a lovely high stone roof; its Gothic
doorway is a splendid contrast to the cruciform cathedral. The oratory, which dates
from the 12th century, has a Romanesque west door, but the inside is quite dark
and gloomy.

The Roman Catholic **church** standing high above the town is believed by some to be
on the site of Kincora, the great palace of Brian Boru where riotous banquets were

the order of the day. (Others believe Kincora to have been at Beal Boru, an ancient earthen mound to the north of the town.) Inside the church are some fine stained-glass windows by Harry Clarke, who worked on many church windows in the early decades of the 20th century. His style is fantastical and fairy-like, in the manner of the English illustrator Aubrey Beardsley, and the colours are exceptionally vivid. In the grounds is **St Molua's Oratory**, a very ancient ruin reconstructed here after being removed from an island in the Shannon before it was flooded by the Shannon Hydroelectric Scheme in 1929. Killaloe is a centre for fishing and boating; there are facilities for water-skiing and sailing, and a large marina (see 'Sports and Activities', p.235). **Ballina**, over the bridge, has better bars and restaurants.

A mile or so out of Killaloe on the R463 is **Crag Liath** (*always accessible, free entry*), known locally as the Grianan, overlooking the road northwards to Scarriff. It was written in 1014 in the annals of *Loch Ce* that this fort was the dwelling place of Aoibheal (also known as Aibell), the celebrated banshee of the Dalcassian Kings of Munster, the O'Briens. (In Irish, *Dal gCais* means sept or tribe of Cas.) A banshee (*bean-sidhe*), or fairy woman, is a ghost peculiar to people of old Irish stock; her duty is to warn the family she attends of the approaching death of one of its members. Thus it was that Aoibheal appeared to Brian Boru on the eve of Clontarf and told him that he would be killed the next day, though not in the fury of the battle. This is exactly what happened, for he was murdered in his tent when the battle was over and the victory his. It is a lovely, short climb to the fort. All around is beauty: woods, water and mountain.

If you cross the Shannon at Limerick, you will find yourself heading for **Bunratty Castle and Folk Park** (*open daily, Sept–May 9.30–5.30, June–Aug 9–6; adm adults €11, children €6.25; t (061) 360788, www.shannonheritage.com*) on the Newmarket road (N18). Allow yourself the best part of a day to tour the castle and the folk park here, for it is a very interesting and well-conceived set up. Bunratty is a splendid tower house standing beside a small stone bridge over River Ratty; a perfect, restored example of a Norman-Irish castle keep. The present castle dates from 1460, though it is at least the fourth to have been built on the same spot. It was built by the McNamaras, who were a sept of the O'Briens, and it remained an O'Brien stronghold off and on until 1712 and played an important part in the struggle between the Anglo-Norman de Clares and the Thomonds. It was then occupied by the Parliamentarian Admiral Penn, the father of William Penn who founded Pennsylvania. After years of neglect it was bought by Lord Gort in 1954, who restored it with the help of *Bord Fáilte* and the Office of Public Works.

They have managed to recreate a 15th-century atmosphere and there is a wonderful collection of 14–17th-century furniture, tapestries and early portraits. The stairs to the upper apartments are very narrow and steep, which can be annoying when the place is crowded, but you get a real feeling of what it was like to be one of the privileged in those times, and the mellow simplicity of the furnishings is very attractive. In the evenings, the castle provides a memorable setting for medieval-style banquets; some people dismiss these as 'paddywackery' but they are great fun, though certainly not cheap.

The folk park has gradually grown up in the castle grounds, with examples of houses from every part of the Shannon region; many of them were re-erected here after being saved from demolition during the Shannon Airport extension. The various types of cottage range from the wealthier small farmer's house, with a small parlour, down to the cabin of a landless labourer. They are all furnished with authentic cottage pieces; one constant is the dresser-cum-henhouse, keeping the fowl snug in the house at night. Patchwork quilts, utensils, ornaments and pictures tell a million stories about life in the olden days, while outside the cottages you can wander around the vegetable patches and hay stooks, and watch the pigs, donkeys, doves and chickens. Inside some of the cottages there are people who can tell you about the old life that has all but disappeared now; you may even get a taste of the scones baking on the open turf fire. The teashop here sells these fresh scones and delicious home-made apple pie. You can see butter-making, basket-weaving and all the traditional skills that made people nearly self-sufficient in days gone by. Village life too is depicted; the school, the musty-smelling doctor's house with its oilcloth on the floor, the post office selling stamps and sweets and various shops selling crafts and old linens, as well as a bar where you can have a good glass of creamy Guinness. Further into the park there is also an excellent collection of agricultural machinery. There are good craft centres close to the folk park and at the Ballycasey Workshops about 3 miles (5km) west on the N18.

It is also worth making an expedition to **Cratloe Woods House** (*open June–mid-Sept, Mon–Sat 2–6; adm €3.50; t (061) 327028*), on the main Limerick/Shannon–Ennis road (N18), about 5 miles (8km) from Limerick. Cratloe Woods is an ancient O'Brien house, and the only surviving example of an Irish long house that is still lived in as a home. It is packed with interesting history, and there is a good tea and craft shop. The woods themselves are a remnant of the only primeval oak forest left in Ireland, and if you climb Woodcock Hill you will get a fine view. Timber from these woods was used for the roof of Westminster Abbey in London in 1399, and further back in the mists of time we know that the men of Ulster came down and cut the oaks and carried them back to make a roof for the Grianan of Aileach, near Derry.

Towards Ennis

Beyond Bunratty is the entirely modern sprawl of buildings that makes up Shannon town and airport. The roads around here are large and busy, but they soon get smaller and more attractive as you get further into the county. On the road to Newmarket on Fergus, you will pass by **Kilnasoolagh Church**; if you can get in, it is worth it to see the exuberant baroque monument (*c. 1717*) by William Kidwell. It is a sculptured figure of an obese O'Brien – this time Sir Donat, the son of Maire Ruadh, who is rather a legend in Clare; a tough, hatchet-faced woman who kept her castle at Leamaneh in the Burren against all the odds. Their descendant was Lord Inchquin who built **Dromoland Castle**. This line of O'Briens became loyal servants of the Crown and they were rewarded well. But in the 19th century William Smith O'Brien (1803–1864) of Dromoland bucked the trend, became a leading member of the Young Irelanders and planned a revolt. He and others decided on an armed rising, despite the fact that many of them had been arrested and the preparations for the rising were not complete. In July 1848, O'Brien and a small party clashed with 46 policemen in the widow McCormack's cabbage patch at Ballingarry, in County Tipperary. That was the end of the uprising; O'Brien was sentenced to death, but this was commuted to penal servitude, and later he was given an unconditional pardon.

Newmarket on Fergus takes its name from a 19th-century O'Brien, Lord Inchiquin, who was very enthusiastic about horses. In the grounds of his neogothic mansion, now a luxury hotel, is **Mooghaun Fort** (also spelled Maughaun), one of the largest Iron Age hill forts in Europe, enclosing 27 acres with three concentric walls. Maybe it was people from this fort who buried the enormous hoard of gold ornaments discovered nearby in 1854 by workmen digging the way for a railway line. Unfortunately, much of it was melted down, probably by dealers, but a few pieces of 'the great Clare gold find' have found their way to the National Museum in Dublin. You can reach the fort through Dromoland Forest. Access is by foot via a forestry car park signposted to the left off the N18 road between Newmarket on Fergus and Dromoland.

At **Craggaunowen** off the Quin–Sixmilebridge Road (R469) there is a reconstructed Bronze Age crannog or lake dwelling, including a ring fort and farmers' houses, built on a pond next to a four-storey tower house. This house contains an important collection of medieval art donated by John and Gertrude Hunt, who were involved in setting up **Craggaunowen, the Living Past** (*open April and Sept–Oct daily 10–6, May–Aug 9–6; adm adults €7.50, children €4.50; t (061) 367178, www.shannonheritage. com*). This is a fascinating centre that gives a good idea of how our ancestors lived. On display is the *Brendan*, a replica of the original boat used by St Brendan on his voyages. Tim Severin, a modern-day adventurer, sailed it to North America via Iceland and Greenland, with the purpose of demonstrating that St Brendan could have been the first to discover America, in the 6th century. Rare and ancient breeds of poultry and livestock, including Kerry cattle, graze in the reconstructed pens and fields. The valley surrounding it is beautiful, and if you are there at teatime, the scones at the reception cottage are delicious. Nearby, at **Quin** (about 8 miles/13km northwest of Bunratty), is **Knappogue Castle** (*open April–Oct daily 9.30–7.30; adm; t (061) 368103, www.shannonheritage.com*), run on the same lines as Bunratty Castle with medieval banquets in the evening (*nightly at 6.30*). The ribbon development between Sixmilebridge and Quin may disappoint you; this is a feature around all expanding towns in Ireland.

At the next crossroads, to the east of the town, a right turn leads to **Quin Abbey** (*always accessible; free entry*) which is well preserved and subject to countless coach tours. It was founded for the Franciscans in 1402 and incorporated into a great castle built by one of the de Clares. The monastic buildings are grouped around an attractive cloister and there is a graceful tower. Buried here is a famous duellist with the wonderful name of Fireballs MacNamara. Northeast of Quin, on the unmarked road between the R469 and the R352, you can walk up to the **Mound of Magh Adhair**. This was the crowning place of the kings of Thomond, and a battle was fought here in 877 between Lorcan, the Thomond king, and Flan, High King of Ireland.

Ennis

Ennis (*Inis*, river meadow), the busy and attractive county capital, is sited on a great bend of the River Fergus. The streets are narrow and winding, and in the centre is a hideous monument to the great Daniel O'Connell, who successfully contested the Clare seat in 1828 even though the repressive laws of the time disqualified Catholics from standing. Right in the middle of the town is the substantial ruin of **Ennis Friary** (*open April–May and mid-Sept–Oct Tues–Sun 10–5, June–mid-Sept daily 10–6; adm adult €1.50, children 75 cents; t (065) 682 9100, www.heritageireland.ie*). The friary was founded for the Franciscans by Donchadh O'Brien, King of Thomond, just before his death in 1242. It is rich in sculptures and decorated tombs, although the building itself has been rather mucked about, with additions and renovations. On one of the tombs is the sculptured device of a cock crowing. The story goes that, standing on the rim of a pot, he cries in Irish, 'the son of the Virgin is safe', a reference to the story of the cock that rose from the pot in which it was cooking to proclaim that, 'Himself above on the Cross will rise again', to the astonishment of the two Roman soldiers who had questioned the prophecy. There is a small **Clare Museum** (*open Mon–Fri; adm adults €4, children €2; t (065) 684 2119*) in a former convent in Arthur's Row, which specializes in objects associated with famous Clare people. De Valera has strong connections here, as he represented Clare from 1917–59. Fans of Percy French (1854–1920), the painter and entertainer, can look at the old steam engine immortalized in his song, 'Are you right there, Michael, are you right?' This song about the West Clare Railway, and the engine's habit of stopping at places other than stations, led to a libel action with the directors.

Northeast of Ennis are the **Slieve Aughty Mountains**, and it is really worthwhile to drive up into the foothills for the view, perhaps to **Ballinruan**, a small village with a stunning panorama. The huge plain of Clare, interspersed with loughs, bright green fields of irregular shapes, bogs, woodland and tracts of limestone, is spread before you, with the odd church spire or tumbled castle adding romance. Beyond this rises the barren limestone mass of the Burren, stretching as far as Galway Bay, while to the south are the wide Shannon River and the hills of Limerick.

The Burren and the Clare Coast

North of Ennis

On the way from Ennis to Corofin (off the N85 to Ennistymon, and 2 miles off the R476) is the famous religious settlement of **Dysert O'Dea**. It was started in the 7th century by St Tola, but he probably lived in a cell of wattle and daub. The present ruin is a much-altered, 12th-century, Hiberno-Romanesque church with a badly reconstructed west doorway that now stands in the south wall. The door is sumptuously carved, and the arch has a row of stone heads with Mongolian features and proud but rather sad expressions. The idea for the heads came from northern France. (Monks and scholars moving between Ireland and the Continent had much

Tourist Information

Cliffs of Moher: Liscannor, t (065) 708 1565; *open March–Oct.*
Kilkee: The Square, t (065) 905 6112, *open June–Aug.*
Kilrush: Moore Street, t (065) 905 1577, *open May–Sept.*
An informative website, *www.burrenbeo.com*, offers background information about the Burren, its geology, heritage, agriculture and ecology.

Shopping

Crafts
The Burren Perfumery, Carron t (065) 708 9102, *www.burrenperfumery.com*. A still room, herb garden, shop and organic tearoom in the middle of the Burren. They can also organize field trips to the Burren in the company of experts living in the area.
Doolin Crafts Gallery, Doolin, t (065) 707 4309, *www.doolincrafts.com*. Batik, books, fine art, glass, clothing and an excellent café.
Eugene Lambe, Fanore. Uilleann pipes.
Kenny Woollen Mills, Main Street, Lahinch. Designer woollens, tweeds, Arans, Waterford crystal and Belleek china.
Manus Walsh Craft Shop, Ballyvaughan. Paintings, silver, jewellery and enamels.
The Rock Shop, Liscannor, t (065) 708 1930, *www.therockshop.ie*. The history of Liscannor stone and common, semiprecious and precious stones.
Whitethorn Crafts, Ballyvaughan. Old, refurbished fish factory with a wide range of ceramics, glass, jewellery and clothes.

Delicacies
The Burren Smokehouse, Lisdoonvarna. Sells home-smoked salmon plus other local produce, and offers guided tours through its visitor centre.
The Farmshop, Aillwee Caves, Ballyvaughan. Food for picnics or to take home – all the delicacies are made by the Johnston family. They also bottle the natural spring water from the caves, produce honey and Ben makes his own cheese, Burren Gold; other Irish cheeses, pickles and preserves are also for sale.

Unglert's Bakery, Ennistymon. German rye breads and strudels.

Sports and Activities

Courses
Berry Lodge, Miltown Malbay, t (065) 708 7022, *www.berrylodge.com*. Weekend cookery courses with Rita Meade. Themes include 'fish and shellfish', 'a taste of Irish cooking', 'Mediterranean kitchen' and 'game cooking'. Rita's favourite proverb is 'Serve fresh young food and mature drink'.
Willie Clancy Summer School, Miltown Malbay, t (065) 708 4281, *www.setdancing news.net/wcss*. Held as a tribute to Clare's greatest piper, Willie Clancy (1921–73), who was a musician, folklorist and master carpenter. He was noted for his beautiful rendering of slow Irish airs on the uilleann pipes. The summer school, starting on the first Sat of July for 10 days, comprises lectures, concerts, workshops in Irish dance and traditional music.

Fishing
Atlantic Adventures, Cappa, Kilrush, t (065) 905 2133. For deep-sea fishing.
Burke's Shop, Main Street, Corofin, t (065) 683 7677. Tom Burke will take you brown-trout fishing on the lakes.
O'Callaghan Angling & Cruising, Liscannor, t (065) 682 1374, *www.ocallaghanangling. com*. Family-run business offering deep-sea fishing and trips to the Aran Islands.

Spas and Seaweed Baths
Spa Wells Centre, Lisdoonvarna, t (065) 707 4023. Little-changed Victorian spa well. Sulphur water is also available by the glass in the Edwardian pump room.
Thalassotherapy Centre, Gratton Street, Kilkee, t (065) 905 6742, *www.kilkeethalasso.com*. Enjoy a relaxing seaweed bath or a full range of other treatments.

Golf
Kilkee Golf Club, Kilkee, t (065) 905 6048, *www.kilkeegolfclub.ie*.
Kilrush Golf Club, Ballykett, Kilrush, t (065) 905 1138, *www.kilrushgolfclub.com*.

Lahinch Golf Club, Lahinch, t (065) 708 1003, *www.lahinchgolf.com*

Pony Trekking

Burren Riding Centre, Fanore, t (065) 707 6140.
Willie Daly Riding Centre, Ennistymon, t (065) 707 1385, *http://homepage.eircom.net/~ williedaly*. Riding holidays at a horse whisperer's centre.

Walking

If you are planning to walk in the Burren, the best **map** of the area is a large-scale one by local cartographer Tim Robinson. It should be easy to buy locally. The **Burren Way** runs for 42km between Liscannor and Ballyvaughan.
Burren Outdoor Education Centre, Bell Harbour, Turlough, t (065) 78033, *www.oec.ie*.
Burren Hill Walks, Ballyvaughan, t (065) 707 7168, *http://homepage.eircom.net/~ burrenhillwalks*.

Water Sports

The swimming is good at Fanore, **Lahinch** (in the sea or at the leisure centre on the promenade); **Spanish Point** and **Doonbeg**. *See also* p.232 for information on **cruises** to the Aran Islands.
Dolphinwatch, Carrigaholt, t (065) 905 8156, *www.dolphinwatch.ie* Two-hour cruises in the Shannon Estuary to observe the large colony of dolphins that live there and listen to their conversations with underwater microphones.
Kilkee Dive Centre, The Pier, Kilkee, t (065) 905 6707, *www.diveireland.com*. Highly rated scuba-diving, snorkelling and boat-handling courses available.
Lahinch Surf School, Lahinch Promenade, t 087 960 9667, *www.lahinchsurfschool.com*. Learn to surf with an Irish surfing champion.

Where to Stay

Gregan's Castle, near Ballyvaughan, t (065) 707 7005, *www.gregans.ie* (*luxury*). Not actually a castle, but an old manor house, with wonderful food and beautiful, individual rooms. Set at the top of Corkscrew Hills amidst verdant gardens, in fantastic contrast to the Burren moonscape, with wonderful views over Galway Bay.

Ballinalacken Castle Hotel, Coast Road, Lisdoonvarna, t (065) 707 4025 (*moderate*). Beautifully situated in front of the castle, overlooking the beach, with open fires and an award-winning restaurant (*booking essential*).
Clifden House, Corofin, t (065) 683 7692, *www.clifdenhouse-countyclare.com* (*moderate*). Highly eccentric house full of character, associated with Richard Burton, translator of the *Arabian Nights*. Was once described as 'being slowly coaxed into compromise with the 20th century'.
The Falls Hotel, Ennistymon, t (065) 707 1004, *www.fallshotel.net* (*moderate*). Large hotel with a spectacular view right over the river. Full of atmosphere and faded charm; a previous owner's daughter, Caitlin, became Dylan Thomas's wife. A Leisure and Wellness Centre is planned for 2005.
Fernhill Farmhouse, Doolin Road, Lisdoonvarna, t (065) 707 4040, *www.fernhill farm.net* (*moderate*). Welcoming owners at this comfortable B&B on a working cattle farm close to the Burren, with nine rooms and characterful décor.
Halpin's Hotel, 2 Erin Street, Kilkee, t (065) 905 6032, *www.halpinsprivatehotels.com* (*moderate*). Good service and comfort, with plain but not unpleasant décor.
Sheedy's Country House Hotel, Lisdoonvarna, t (065) 707 4026 (*moderate*). Friendly, family run hotel with a popular restaurant.
Berry Lodge, Miltown Malbay, t (065) 708 7022, *www.berrylodge.com* (*moderate– inexpensive*). This is the place to stay. Rita Meade's Victorian house has very prettily decorated rooms, several with iron bedsteads, shutters, rugs and wood features, and excellent food in the **restaurant** (*expensive–moderate*; she also runs a cookery school, *see* opposite). *Dinner served each evening July–Aug, rest of year on request.*
Crotty's Bar, Kilrush, t (065) 905 2470, *www. crottyskilrush.com* (*moderate–inexpensive*). Traditional Irish music in a friendly, cosy traditional bar with accommodation above. Rooms are a little intimate, and it can be noisy, but a great place for atmosphere.
The Old Parochial House, Cooraclare, t (065) 905 9059, *www.westclare.net/parochial*

house (*moderate–inexpensive*). Wonderful old house with spacious, individual rooms, polished wooden floors and old wooden furniture; the walls are painted in a marvellous shade of blue. The parish priest certainly never had the four-poster beds! They also have 3 quaint self-catering cottages in the old stables, sleeping 2–4.

Fergus View, Kilnaboy, Corofin, t (065) 683 7606 (*inexpensive*). Farmhouse with good home cooking. Mary Kelleher makes all her own yogurt and muesli.

Inchiquin View, Kilnaboy, Corofin, t (065) 683 7731, *bkellinchfmho@eircom.net* (*inexpensive*). Farmhouse overlooking the Fergus River and Lake Inchiquin.

Lismactigue, Ballyvaughan, t (065) 707 7040, *mike-g.keane@analog.com* (*inexpensive*). Thatched farmhouse in a ring fort on a green road in the Burren.

Self-catering

Clifden House, Corofin, t (065) 683 7692, *www.clifdenhouse-countyclare.com*. Two charming apartments in the stable wing of a Georgian manor, also a hotel (*see opposite*). One sleeps 6; the other, 8.

Oughtdarra Thatch Cottages, Doolin/Lisdoonvarna, t (065) 707 4154, *www.harbourviewthatchedcottages.com*. Three individual thatched cottages in the heart of the Burren, with lovely bright décor, wooden flooring and furniture, and exposed beams. Contact Kathleen Cullinan.

Eating Out

Barrtrá **Seafood Restaurant**, Lahinch, t (065) 708 1280 (*expensive, but much less so for lunch*). Simple but good seafood restaurant just outside Lahinch with views of the bay.

The Gairdin, Market Street, Corofin, t (065) 683 7425 (*expensive*). Small restaurant with delightful, modern, award-winning cooking.

Orchard Restaurant, in Sheedy's Country House Hotel, Lisdoonvarna, t (065) 707 4026 (*expensive*). Surprisingly sophisticated food in this family-run hotel; pub lunches too.

The Cape Restaurant, Armada Hotel, Spanish Point, t (065) 708 4110 (*expensive–moderate*). Hearty, traditional Sunday roast or bar food

in a variety of settings, with uninterrupted views over the Atlantic.

The Cottage Restaurant, St Brigid's Well, Liscannor, t (065) 708 1760 (*expensive–moderate*, lunches *inexpensive*). Lunches and serious evening dining in a rustic setting.

Gregan's Castle Hotel, Ballyvaughan, t (065) 707 7005, *www.gregans.ie* (*expensive–moderate*). Delicious food all day in the **Corkscrew Bar**, where the cosy fire and low-beamed ceiling are especially welcoming.

The Black Oak Restaurant, Rineen, near Miltown Malbay, t (065) 708 4403 (*moderate*). Perched on the coast road, with beautiful views down on to Liscannor Bay and an extensive, international menu.

The Long Dock, Carrigaholt, t (065) 905 8106 (*moderate*). In a beautiful fishing village, a traditional pub with flagstone floors and a good reputation for its local fresh seafood.

Mr Eamon's Restaurant, Lahinch, t (065) 708 1050 (*moderate*). Unpretentious, popular steak and seafood house.

O'Looney's, on the Promenade, Lahinch, t (065) 708 1414 (*moderate*). Good seafood, also bar food, sandwiches and music nightly.

Trí na Cheile, Ballyvaughan, t (065) 707 7029 (*moderate*). Small and unpretentious with lots of seafood and a vegetarian dish as standard; great atmosphere. Very popular.

Linnane's Lobster Bar, New Quay, Burren, t (065) 707 8120 (*moderate–inexpensive*). Authentic Irish pub, overlooking Galway Bay, that specializes in seafood: chowder, lobster and oysters.

Roadside Tavern, Kincora Road, Lisdoonvarna, t (065) 707 4494 (*moderate–inexpensive*). Wood-panelled pub-cum-smokehouse. Delicious smoked salmon and chowder.

Aillwee Cave Restaurant, Ballyvaughan, t (065) 707 7036/77067 (*inexpensive*). Eating in a cave; delicious soups, pies, cakes. *Open April–Sept 10–6.30, Oct–Mar 10–5.*

Cassidy's, Carron, Burren, t (065) 708 9109 (*inexpensive*). Very remote pub in the wildest part of the Burren, with tasty lunches using local produce such as excellent farmhouse cheeses.

Monk's Bar, Ballyvaughan, t (065) 707 7059 (*inexpensive*). Delicious mussels and brown bread. Traditional music at night.

more influence on building and style than was once thought.) Beside the church is the stump of a round tower, and about a hundred yards east is a high cross from the 12th century. Christ is shown in a pleated robe, and below him is a bishop with a crozier. A decisive battle fought here in 1318 drove the Anglo-Normans out of the surrounding area for several centuries, when the O'Brien chief of the time defeated Richard de Clare of Bunratty and expelled him. Dysert O'Dea Castle (*adm*; *t (065) 683 7401*) has a heritage centre and is the start of a short signposted walk around the archaeological remains of the vicinity.

Corofin village lies between two pretty lakes, the Inchiquin and Atedaun. There is good game and coarse fishing here, and plenty of caves, for this is marginal shale and limestone countryside in which the River Fergus plays some tricks. The **Clare Heritage and Genealogical Centre** (*open all year Mon–Fri 9–5.30; t (065) 683 7955, http://clare. irish-roots.net*) in the old Church of Ireland hall offers a 'trace your ancestors' service (*fee*), and displays give a very interesting guide to rural Ireland 150 years ago.

About 2 miles further up on the R476 is **Killinaboy** (Kilnaboy on some maps), a small village close to the northern tip of Lough Inchiquin. The remains of a round tower rest in the graveyard of a ruined church which dates from the 11th century. Over the south door is a Sheila-na-Gig, a grotesque and erotic figure of a woman. These Sheila-na-Gigs are often carved and fixed to ecclesiastical buildings, probably as a sort of crude warning to the monks and laity of the power of female sexuality. There are many gallery graves around here. A mile northwest of Killinaboy at Roughan, just over a stile and in a field, is the Tau Cross, shaped like a T with a carved head in each of the arms. Several like this have been found in a Celtic sanctuary at Roquepertuse in France, and it is likely that this is pre-Christian. The minor roads around **Lough Inchiquin** are a delight either to walk or cycle along. Songbirds fill the woods and there are little farms where nature and agriculture seem to coexist harmoniously. You will notice a few deserted farmhouses, each usually with a new bungalow sheltering in its lee. The intensity of colour in the skies at sunrise and sunset burns into the mind's eye, along with the dark rounded hills and woods.

If you wish to continue to avoid the main roads, several little roads from Killinaboy meander right into the heart of the Burren. Take the first road to the right after leaving Killinaboy, which will take you between Glasgeivnagh Hill and Mullaghmore, where a huge visitor centre was planned. Luckily, opposition to the centre was successful and this secret place has not been turned into a large car park. The **Cappaghkennedy** megalithic tomb is near the summit on Glasgeivnagh. At the next junction take a left and continue back in a wide circle to Carran and pass by the great stone fort of **Cahercommaun**. To get to it, turn left in Carran village and left again at the next junction. Look out for an avenue to the left which leads to a car park. From here you go a short way on foot. The fort is situated on a cliff edge across some ankle-breaking country, but while you pick your way across, notice the flower life between the stones. A Harvard excavation team reached the conclusion that the fort was occupied during the 8–9th centuries by a community that raised cattle, hunted red deer and cultivated some land for growing grain. This route brings you back to the main road (R480).

On the main road leading to Kilfenora (R476) is the ruined **Leamaneagh Castle** which belonged to the O'Briens. It's a lovely old ruin with a tower dating from 1480 and an early 17th-century fortified house. Sir Conor O'Brien, who built the four-storey house, had a very strong-minded wife called *Maire Ruadh* (Red Mary), many of whose exploits have passed into folklore. After Sir Conor died, she married an influential Cromwellian to ensure the inheritance of her son, Donat, and to prevent the expropriation of her lands. The story goes that when one day he made an uncalled-for remark about her first husband she promptly pushed him out of the window.

The Burren

This district is generally called 'the Burren' after the ancient Barony of that name. Burren, in Gaelic *An Bhoieann*, means 'the stony district'. It extends some 25 miles (40km) from east to west and 15 miles (24km) from north to south, between Galway Bay and the Atlantic Ocean, with the villages of Doolin, Kilfenora, Gort and Kinvarra forming its southeastern border. One of the amazing things about the Burren is that its 50 square miles are dotted with signs of ancient habitation – stone forts, walls and megalithic tombs, which blend perfectly with a landscape strewn with strangely shaped rocks, left behind as the glaciers retreated.

You really have to get out of your car and walk here, for the Burren's appeal is gradual rather than dramatic. The Burren is a plateau riven by valleys, some of which lead to the sea; others go nowhere, only into themselves. The **Aran Islands** (*see* 'Getting to Islands off Clare', p.232) rise from Galway Bay, sometimes appearing dark and close to shore, at other times in a shimmering misty haze, far away. They were part of the Burren many ages ago and share the same geology and flora. In late May the place becomes starred with sky-blue gentians, bloody cranesbill, geraniums and orchids. Arctic-alpine mountain avens sprawl lavishly over the rocks and Irish saxifrage tufts cover sea-sprayed boulders. Sheltered in the damp clefts of limestone are shade-loving plants such as the maidenhair fern. The plentiful rainfall disappears into the limestone pavements and down into a potholer's dream: a subterranean maze of passages and caverns. No rivers meander through these valleys. Impermanent lakes, known as turloughs (from the Irish *tur*, dry), appear when the ground water floods through the fissures after a lot of rain. No one has yet been able to explain fully how such a profusion of northern and southern plants came to grow together, some of them unknown in continental Europe; seeds must have survived from a warmer age, despite the actions of the glaciers and fracturing movement of the earth that shaped this rock. The present temperate winters and warm limestone beneath the turf suit the plants, and their colonies have grown up unhindered because the arid land has never been cultivated, only grazed by cattle.

The Burren is very rich in antiquities – portal and megalithic tombs, *cahers* and cooking places left by Stone Age farmers who cleared the hills of forest (it is probable that the place was not such a desert then). By medieval times, the hills were treeless, and the wide expanses of fissured rock exposed. The Burren certainly stimulates many questions. Botanists and geologists as well as tourists come here, but happily the plan to site an interpretative centre right in the middle of one of its most beautiful and untouched places was shelved after local people and environmentalists objected to it. How to maintain the traditional ways of farming which have preserved the unique character of the Burren is, as yet, an unresolved issue. The bulldozer is busy clearing the mythical landscape of ancient stone patterns, and mechanized spraying creates a sward of modern flowerless grasses. The farmers are encouraged in this by EU grants: after all, they have to make a living, and there is no support system in place to stop the destruction; only the opportunities for profit that farmers themselves can make in opening up their land and houses to tourists.

It would be easy to drive through the Burren, never stopping to see and feel its magic. You have to walk in its moss-softened hazel woods and see close up the profusion of colour and scented plants in early summer that somehow thrive on the thin soil of the limestone pavements. The black wiry fronds of the maidenhair ferns and the bright green hart's tongue hide in the shelter of the grikes, while wild goats and rabbits nibble at the succulent grass. Many of the stone ring forts where the ancients kept their cattle for safety are covered in a mass of brambles or hazel, and you could easily pass them by. The farmers still practice 'booleying' (*see* p.251), although here it is the opposite of the usual transhumance: because of the mild climate and the summer warmth stored in the limestone, the grass grows well, so cattle are brought to the uplands in the winter; whereas in the summer months the Burren is a desert with no surface pools or streams and the cattle are brought back down to be close to the farmhouses and water.

Kilfenora is a place of ancient importance on the fringe of the Burren. It is worth staying a while, not only to look at the **Burren Centre** (*open daily, mid-Mar–May and Sept–Oct 10–5, June–Aug 9.30–6; adm; t (065) 708 8030, www.theburrencentre.ie*), which explains the flora, fauna, butterflies and rock formations of the area, but also because in the graveyard of the ruined church are four 12th-century, carved high crosses, all of the same excellent standard, which suggests they might have been produced by the same workshop or even by a single carver. The small, 12th-century church of St Fachnan is called 'the Cathedral', and its bishopric is still held by the Pope. A fifth cross with elaborate carvings, including that of the crucifixion, stands in a field to the west. Close to it is a holy well.

On the R480 to Ballyvaughan, 6 miles (9.7km) past Leamaneagh Castle, is the great dolmen of **Poulinabrone** (pool of sorrows) with a massive capstone; it is one of the most photographed sites of the Burren. Excavations in 1986 produced the remains of fourteen adults and six children and dated the tomb as middle Neolithic. Not surprisingly, the farmer who owns the land on which it lies has decided to get something out of the huge crowds of people who trail up to it, occasionally leaving their litter behind them. A couple of men in a battered car, complete with lurking sheepdog, will probably wave a plastic bucket at you in which they want you to put a donation to help keep the stone walls up and the gate up to the dolmen open. Also on the road to Ballyvaughan, a mile out of Kilfenora, is one of the finest stone forts in Ireland, known as **Ballykinvarga**. This has a very effective trap for those trying to launch an attack: a cheval-de-frise, sharp spars of stone set close together in the ground. The great fort of Dun Aengus on the Aran Islands has a similar arrangement.

At **Ballyvaughan**, an attractive fishing village on the north edge of the Burren, you can rent yourself an Irish cottage and explore **Black Head**, which looks over the shimmering Galway Bay with clear views of the Aran Islands and the Cliffs of Moher. The islands are made of the same grey limestone as the Burren and have the same bright flowers in the springtime. Ballyvaughan village is set in a green wooded vale, an oasis after the bleached plateaux of limestone, mighty terraces and escarpments to the south. The village has good craft shops, and the harbour is the starting point for boat trips to the islands. There are a couple of tower houses built in the 16th century to explore: Gleninagh, signposted between Ballyvaughan and Lisdoonvarna, was occupied by the O'Loughlins (whose family name is often spelled O'Loghlen) until 1840; close by is a deserted and ruined village which in the 1930s still had a thriving community and 85 men fishing from their curraghs out in the bay. **Newtown Castle** *(open Easter–early Oct daily 10–6; adm;* **t** *(065) 707 7200)*, also an O'Loughlin stronghold, has been restored and is unusual in that it is round with a square base. You will find it down a lane, off the N67 and 2 miles south of Ballyvaughan; the buildings around it house the Burren College of Art. The castle tours take about 40 minutes; a trail around the surrounding area includes bardic poetry recitals and extracts from ancient annals, as well as archaeology and geology.

While in Ballyvaughan, take some time to explore the Burren uplands and the inlets of **Ballyvaughan** and **Aughinish Bays**, quiet beaches where the oystercatcher whistles. A long tramp can be made into the stony fastness of Turlough Hill or the higher Slievegarron where all the Burren features make their appearance. The pass between Turlough and Corcomroe Abbey is called Mám Chatha, the Pass of Battle. This is the path Donagh O'Brien took on his way to battle against his rival and kinsman Dermot O'Brien in 1317. He was forewarned of defeat by the Hag of the Burren as he passed Lough Rask, close to Bealaclugga; she was washing a grisly pile of heads and limbs in the waters, and she told Donagh that his head was in the pile. After raining foul curses upon his head, she disappeared in the air. Donagh tried to dismiss the prophecy but, sure enough, later that day he and his followers were dead. Dermot O'Brien went on to defeat Richard de Clare, which kept the Normans out of the Burren for nearly two hundred years. **Corcomroe Abbey** was founded by the Cistercians in 1195; in the north wall of the choir is an effigy of King Connor O'Brien. To the south on a hill are the remains of the three ancient churches of Oughtmama.

The **Aillwee Cave** *(open daily 9.30–5.30; guided tours only; adm adults €10, children €5;* **t** *(065) 707 7067/36, www.aillweecave.ie)* is 2 miles southeast of Ballyvaughan on the N67. All over the Burren there are hundreds of caves formed by the underground rivers, which give great sport for the speleologist. Aillwee dates back two million years BC. When the river dried up, or changed its course, they became the dens of wild bears and other animals. Today the entrance has been tamed to make it easier for the less intrepid, and the caverns are festooned with stalagmites and stalactites. The food shop and craft shop here are excellent, and the centre itself is built sympathetically to blend with its surroundings, though there is a charge to enter even the car park.

The Clare Coast

By taking the corkscrew road to **Lisdoonvarna** (*Lios Duin Bhearna*, 'the enclosure of the gapped fort'), you get a series of lovely views of Galway Bay. Since the decline of Mallow, Lisdoonvarna is the most important spa in Ireland. The waters are said to owe much to their natural radioactivity; there are sulphur, magnesium and iron springs, a pump room and baths for those who come to take the waters. Hotels, guesthouses and B&Bs have sprung up everywhere and the town could not be described as attractive, but it has a certain energy when the place is very crowded in the summer. Traditionally it was the place to which moderately prosperous farmers came to arrange marriages for their children; and there is still much courting, inspired no doubt by the invigorating properties of the water. There are also plenty of dances and concerts during the spa season. Excitement peaks in August with the Matchmaking Festival, which is hyped up for all it's worth (*see* p.232). There is a sandy cove at **Doolin**, 3 miles away, good for fishing but dangerous for bathing. This long straggling little fishing village (really two hamlets divided by a field) became famous for its traditional music in the late 1970s, and is still a mecca for music-lovers. Several hostels have sprung up to cater for all these visitors, and the pubs do a fine trade, with traditional music every night in the summer. On the outskirts of the village is the very fine Doolin Craft Gallery (*see* 'Shopping', p.242). You can get a boat from here to Inisheer, the smallest of the Aran Islands, a crossing that takes about 40 minutes and goes 3 times a day in the summer months (*see* 'Getting to Islands off Clare', p.232).

In this area you find curious mineral nodules formed by limestone and shale that look just like tortoise shells. There are three of these built into the wall beside the Imperial Hotel in Lisdoonvarna. From here, the coast road (R478) leads to the **Cliffs of Moher**, which drop down vertically to the foaming sea. Seabirds somehow manage to nest on the steep slopes: there are guillemots, razorbills, puffins, kittiwakes, various gulls and choughs; and sometimes even peregrines can be seen. The cliffs stretch for nearly 5 miles (8km) and are made of the darkest yellow sandstone and millstone grit, which can be seen in bands near the top. On a clear day there is a magnificent view of the Twelve Bens, the mountains of Connemara and the three Aran Islands. **O'Brien's Tower**, on the cliff edge, was built in 1835 by Cornelius O'Brien, a local landlord around whose reputation a lot of stories have been woven. In reality, he was a bit of a do-gooder as well as being a builder of follies and bridges, not a ruthless tyrant and womanizer as he has been portrayed. He wanted the tower as an observation post from which to watch the turbulent seas, and he also got his peasants to build a three-mile-long wall of limestone flags to prevent visitors being sucked over the edge of the cliffs by the downdraughts. Behind it is an **Information Centre** (*open – weather permitting – Mar–May and Sept–Oct 9.30–6, June–Aug 9.30–8*).

On the R478 southeast of the cliffs is **Liscannor**, a little fishing village where a few of the fishermen still use curraghs. It is on the north shore of Liscannor Bay, where the River Dealagh flows into the sea. The famous limestone flags of Clare were exported from here, and it is easy to spot these lovely striated stones propping up a gateway, or used as lintels, roofing slates or paving. Under the waters of the bay, it is said, there lies a submerged city. Down on the shore of Liscannor Bay (just off the R478) is the tumbledown ruin of St Macreehy's Church (he was a destroyer of plagues, eels, and dragons), and there is also a holy well. John P. Holland (1841–1914), who invented the submarine, was born here, the son of a coastguard. Holland was a nationalist who went to America, where Irish friends and *Clan na Gael* helped him with funds to build and operate a small submarine. He hoped that his invention would be used in the War of Independence against England. However, Liscannor is more famous locally for the **Holy Well of St Brigid**, about 2 miles northwest of Liscannor on the R478, near the Cliffs of Moher. The well is an important place of pilgrimage: on the last Saturday in July a vigil is held there and the 'patron' (celebration) continues on into Lahinch on the Sunday with racing and sports on the strand. It was the end of the 'hungry month' and the beginning of the festival of *Lughnasa*, when all the crops were harvested, so the 'patron' was celebrated with a feast of new potatoes.

Around the well an aura of faith and devotion lingers in the damp air and amongst the trivial offerings of holy pictures of bleeding hearts and saints, plastic statues of the Pope, rosaries and other bits and pieces left by the sick. You approach by a narrow stone passage, probably still feeling slightly amazed by the life-size painted plaster model of St Brigid next to the entrance of the well, which is sufficiently naturalistic to be macabre when first glimpsed. Sir Cornelius O'Brien is buried under the Victorian memorial and he also built the monument on the hill with the urn on top. The remains of his house and demesne are within sight of the well; apparently a curse was put on the place because he gave up going to Mass.

Lahinch, a mile south of Liscannor, is a small seaside resort with a pretty arc of golden sand and waves big enough for surfing. The part of town devoted to entertainment is a bit tacky, but it has a fine promenade. The golf course at Lahinch is championship-standard, but as a guest you are most welcome. There is an amusing story of one enthusiast who putted a winner and got the trophy. He remarked with the skill and colour only the Irish can summon, 'I declare to God I was that tense I could hear the bees belchin'.' The clubhouse barometer is very basic: players scan the links for goats – if there is none, it is not worth going out to play, you will get too wet! During the War of Independence in 1920, Lahinch was partially burnt and two men shot by the Black and Tans and Auxiliaries, in reprisal for the ambushing and killing of four RIC by the republican army. The townspeople took refuge in the sand dunes.

On the promenade is the **Lahinch Seaworld Centre** (*open daily 10–6; adm adults €7, children 4–16 €5, children 2–4 yrs €3; t (065) 708 1900, www.iol.ie/~seaworld*), where you can see and experience the underwater life of the Atlantic Coast and the unusual Clare coastline. There is also a 25m indoor pool, children's pool and soft play area.

Ennistymon, with its colourful shop fronts, is 2 miles inland on the N85, in a wooded valley beside the cascading River Cullenagh. The Falls Hotel, which was previously known as Ennistymon House, was the home of Francis MacNamara, a bohemian character and a friend of Augustus John, whose daughter Caitlin married Dylan Thomas. MacNamara was a supporter of Sinn Féin and an advocate of free love. He generally shocked local sensibilities – the parish priest let fly at him from the pulpit for letting his children play naked on the beach at Doolin. In 1919 his father, who was

an ardent unionist, was shot in the neck when one of his shooting parties was
ambushed; later Francis' own house at Doolin was burnt by the Black and Tans.

Southwards, following the N67 down the coast from Lahinch, you come to **Spanish
Point** (just off the R482), a good spot for surfing, where a great number of ships from
the Spanish Armada were wrecked. Those sailors who struggled ashore were
slaughtered by the locals on the orders of the Governor of Connacht, Sir Richard
Bingham, and a local man, Sir Turlough O'Brien. **Miltown Malbay**, opposite Spanish
Point on the N67, is noted for its Willie Clancy Summer School in July (*see* 'Courses',
p.242). It is a splendid time to visit for all the fun; the standard of traditional music in
the bars is good all year round (*see* 'Festivals', p.232).

From Miltown Malbay, which was a rather smart Victorian resort, you can have a
swim at the silver strand of **Freach**, just to the north of the town, or climb
Slievecallan, the highest point in west Clare, which has a megalithic tomb on its
southeast slopes. On the way you could rest at the little lake at **Boolynagreana**, which
means 'the summer milking place of the sun'. To get there, follow the R474
southwards for 6 miles (9.6km) to the Hand Cross Roads, and then walk over rough
land for about a mile. All round these foothills the ancient agricultural practice of
transhumance was pursued. This is known in Ireland as 'booleying' and involves
moving livestock to mountain pasture during the summer months. Booleying has
fallen into disuse with modern feeding methods.

Back on the coast road (N67) you will find **Quilty**, a strange name for an Irish village:
it comes from the Irish *coillte*, woods, but there are no trees on this flat part of the
coast. The great lines of stone walls are bestrewn with seaweed being dried for kelp-
making. The seaweed is either burned, and the ash used for the production of iodine,
or exported for the production of alginates which produce the rich, creamy head on
Guinness. The church here is reminiscent of the early Christian churches, but in fact it
was built in 1907, with money given by some French sailors who were rescued by the
villagers when their ship was wrecked one stormy night.

Southwest Clare

Kilkee (*Cill Chaoidhe*, church of St Caoidhe), about 12 miles (19km) south on the N67,
is a favourite resort for Irish holiday-makers, though a recent orgy of tasteless
building has rather changed its Victorian ambience. It is built along a sandy crescent-
shaped beach; the Duggerna Rocks, acting as a reef, make it safe for bathing at any
stage of the tide. Within the rocks are natural swimming pools and further to the
south is a large sea cave. A cliff walk starts from the seafront, from where you can get
a good view of these sights. Diving off the Duggerna Rocks is well organized by a
watersports centre at the harbour. The coast southwest for about 15 miles (24km),
from here to **Loop Head**, is an almost endless succession of caverns, chasms, sea
stacks and weirdly and wonderfully shaped rocks. The cliff scenery is on a par with the
Cliffs of Moher. Walkers can explore the coast between Kilkee and Loop Head, a path
of some 15 miles (24kms). There is a colourful legend about Ulster's hero Cú Chulainn,
who was generally well loved by women, but this time was being pursued relentlessly
by a termagant of a woman called Mal. Eventually he came to the edge of the cliffs

on Loop Head and leapt on to a great rock about 30ft out to sea. Mal was not to be outdone and made the same leap with equal agility and success. Cú Chulainn straightaway performed the difficult feat of leaping back to the mainland and this time Mal faltered, fell short, and disappeared into the raging ocean below. Out of this legend came the name Loop Head, Leap Head in Irish. As for poor Mal, she must have been a witch, for her blood turned the sea red and she was swept northwards to a point near the Cliffs of Moher called **Hag's Head**. The R487 takes you close to Loop Head, but you will really have to branch off down the minor roads to get a view of all its splendour. If dolphin-watching appeals, head for **Carrigaholt** where boat trips go out to a resident population of sixty bottlenose dolpins who hang around the Shannon Estuary. You can also go from Kilrush.

Kilrush (*Cill Rois*, the church of the promontory) is a busy market town overlooking the Shannon Estuary. It has a large marina and a heritage centre that explores the role of the landlords, the Vandeleurs, in shaping the town. There is also the recently restored **Vandeleur Walled Garden** (*open daily summer 10–6, winter 10–5; adm adults €5, children €2; t (065) 905 1760*), where you can walk through 420 tranquil acres of woodland.

The Catholic **church** has some Henry Clarke stained glass windows. He was part of the movement to revive the art of stained glass in Ireland, which was nurtured by a workshop in Dublin founded by Sarah Purser. About a mile away is the harbour, centred around Cappagh Pier.

Two miles out into the estuary, **Scattery Island** (Cathach's Island), founded by St Senan in the 6th century, has some interesting monastic remains. An island in the broad Shannon was easy meat for the Vikings, who raided it several times. The round tower is very well preserved and has its door at ground level, so the unsuspecting monks must have been surprised by the aggressive Norsemen. The five ruined churches date from medieval times. Boat trips from Kilrush to Scattery Island are available in the summer (*see* 'Getting to Islands off Clare', p.232), and the **Scattery Island Centre** in Kilrush, on the Marina on Merchant's Quay (*open mid-June–mid-Sept daily 10–1 and 2–6; t (065) 905 2139, www.heritageireland.ie*), offers an introduction to the island before you go.

The **Fergus Estuary**, where the mouth of the River Shannon gapes its widest, is a paradise of forgotten isles, untouched and deserted, with names like **Deer Isle**, **Canon Isle** and **Deenish**. You can base yourself near **Killadysert**, on the R473 going north to Ennis, and have great fun exploring them. If you make enquiries you may find someone to take you out there in a boat.

Glossary

Anglo-Norman: the name commonly given to the 12th-century invaders of Ireland, who came in the main from southwest Britain, and also their descendants, because they were of Norman origin.

Bailey: the space enclosed by the walls of a castle, or the outer defences of a motte (*see* Motte-and-bailey).

Barrel-vaulting: simple vaulting of semicircular form, such as in the nave of Cormac's Chapel, Cashel, County Tipperary, where the vault is strengthened with transverse arches.

Bastion: a projecting feature of the outer parts of a fortification, designed to command the approaches to the main wall.

Battlement: a parapet pierced with gaps to enable the defenders to discharge missiles at the enemy.

Bawn: a walled enclosure forming the outer defences of a castle or towerhouse. As well as being an outer defence, it also provided a safe enclosure for cattle. There is a good example at Dungory Castle, Kinvara, County Galway.

Beehive hut: a prehistoric circular building, of wood or stone, with a dome-shaped roof, called a clochan.

Bronze Age: the earliest metal-using period from the end of the Stone Age until the coming of the Iron Age in Ireland, 2500 BC.

Caher: a stone fort.

Cairn: a mound of stones over a prehistoric grave; they frequently cover chambered tombs.

Cashel: a stone fort, surrounded by a rampart of dry-stone walling, usually of late Iron Age date (*see* ring fort).

Chancel or choir: the east end of a church, reserved for the clergy and choir, and containing the high altar.

Chapterhouse: the chamber in which the chapter or governing body of a cathedral or monastery met. One of the finest Irish examples is the 14th-century chapterhouse at Mellifont, County Louth.

Cheval-de-frise: a stone or stake defence work set upright and spaced. It occurs at Dun Aengus, Inishmore, Aran Islands, County Galway.

Cist: A box-like grave of stone slabs to contain an inhumed or cremated burial, often accompanied by pottery. Usually Bronze Age or Iron Age in date.

Clochans (1): little groups of cottages, too small to be villages, grouped in straggly clusters according to land tenure and the ties of kinship between families. The land around the clochan forms the district known as a townland. A familiar sight is deserted or ruined clochans in mountain and moorland areas where huge numbers of people left with the land clearances and the potato famine during the 19th century.

Clochan (*clochaun*) (2): a small stone building, circular in plan, with its roof corbelled inwards in the form of a beehive. There are many examples in the west, especially in County Kerry. The word clochan comes from the Irish *cloch*, for stone. The structures were early monks' cells and nowadays they are used for storage.

Cloisters: a square or rectangular open space, surrounded by a covered passage, which gives access to the various parts of a monastery. Many medieval cloisters survive in Ireland, e.g. at Quin, County Clare.

Columbarium: a dovecote, as seen at Kilcooly Abbey, County Tipperary.

Corbel: a projecting stone in a building, usually intended to carry a beam or other structural member.

Corbelled vault: a 'false dome', constructed by laying horizontal rings of stones that overlap on each course until finally a single stone can close the gap at the centre. It is a feature of prehistoric tombs.

Corinthian: the third order of Greek and Roman architecture, a development of the Ionic. The capital has acanthus-leaf ornamentation.

Court cairn: a variety of megalithic tomb consisting of a covered gallery for burials and one or more open courts or forecourts for ritual purposes. Very common in the North of Ireland.

Crannog: an artificial island constructed in a lake or marsh to provide a dwelling place in an easily defended position for isolated farming families. Large numbers of crannogs (from *crann*, tree) have been discovered as a result of drainage operations at Lough Gara, near Boyle, County Roscommon. These dwelling places would have been in use until the 17th century.

Curragh or **currach**: a light canoe consisting of skins or, in more recent times, tarred canvas, stretched over a wickerwork frame.

Curtain wall: the high wall constructed around a castle and its bailey, usually provided at intervals with towers.

Demesne: land/estate surrounding a house which the owner has chosen to retain for his own use.

Dolmen: the simplest form of megalithic tomb, consisting of a large capstone and three or more supporting uprights. Some appear to have had forecourts.

Doric: the first order of Greek and Roman architecture, simple and robust in style. The column had no base and the capital was quite plain.

Dun: a fort, usually of stone and often with formidable defences, e.g. Dun Aengus, Inishmore on the Aran Islands.

Early English: the earliest Gothic architecture of England and Ireland, where it flourished in the 13th century. It is characterized by narrow lancet windows, high pointed arches and the use of rib vaulting.

Esker: a bank or ridge of gravel and sand, formed by subglacial streams. The most notable esker in Ireland stretches from the neighbourhood of Dublin to Galway Bay: Clonmacnoise and Athlone stand on offshoots of it.

Fleadh: feast, banquet, entertainment.

Folly: structure set up by a landlord to provide work for poor tenants in the 19th century.

Fosse: a defensive ditch or moat around a castle or fort.

Gaeltacht: government-protected Irish Gaelic-speaking area.

Gallaun: *see* standing stone.

Gallowglass: Scottish mercenary soldier hired by Irish clan leaders to fight their enemies.

Hill fort: a large fort whose defences follow a contour round a hill to enclose the hill top. Hill forts are usually early Iron Age.

Hospital: in medieval times, an almshouse or house of hospitality with provision for spiritual as well as bodily welfare, usually established to cater for a specific class of people. The foundation of the Royal Hospital, Kilmainham, at Dublin for aged soldiers, was in the medieval tradition.

Ionic: the second order of Greek and Roman architecture. The fluted column was tall and graceful in proportion and the capital had volutes (spiral scrolls in stone) at the top.

Irish-Romanesque or **Hiberno-Romanesque**: the Irish variety of the Romanesque style in architecture (*see* Romanesque). Cormac's Chapel, Cashel, County Tipperary and Clonfert, County Galway, provide examples.

Iron Age: the early Iron Age is the term applied to the earliest iron-using period; in Ireland, from the end of the Bronze Age, *c.* 500 BC, to the coming of Christianity in the 5th century.

Jamb: side of a doorway, window or fireplace. Early Irish churches have characteristic jambs inclined inwards towards the top. The incline is called the 'batter'.

Keep: the main tower of a castle, serving as the innermost stronghold. There is a fine rectangular one at Carrickfergus, County Antrim, and at Trim, County Meath. Round keeps are rare in Ireland, but occur at Nenagh, County Tipperary. Castles with keeps date from the late 12th century until about 1260.

Kern: an Irish foot soldier of Tudor times.

Kitchen midden: a prehistoric refuse-heap, in which many articles of bronze, iron, flint and stone have been discovered; also shellfish debris, which indicates what our ancestors ate.

Lancet: a tall, narrow window ending in a pointed arch, characteristic of Early English style. Often occur in groups of three, five or seven.

La Tène: a pre-Christian Irish classic ornamental style, which is linked to ornamental designs found in France.

Lunula: a crescent-shaped, thin, beaten gold ornament, of early Bronze Age date; it is an Irish speciality.

Megalithic tomb: a tomb built of large stones for collective burial, Neolithic or early Bronze Age in date.

Misericord or **miserere**: a carved projection on the underside of a hinged folding seat which, when the seat was raised, gave support to the infirm during the parts of a church service when they had to stand. Good examples can be found in St Mary's Cathedral, Limerick.

Motte-and-bailey: the first Norman for tresses, which were made of earth. The motte was a flat-topped mound, shaped like a truncated cone, surrounded by a fosse and surmounted by a wooden keep. An enclosure, the bailey, bounded by ditch, bank and palisade, adjoined it. The bailey served as a refuge for cattle and in it were the sheds and huts of the retainers. This type of stronghold continued to be built until the early 13th century.

Nave: the main body of the church, sometimes separated from the choir by a screen.

Neolithic: applied to objects from the New Stone Age, which was characterized by the practice of agriculture; in Ireland, between 3000 and 2000 BC.

Ogham stones: early Irish writing, usually cut on stone. The characters consist of strokes above, below or across a stem line. The key to the alphabet may be seen in the *Book of Ballymote*, now in the library of the Royal Irish Academy, Dublin. Ogham inscriptions occur mainly on standing stones. The inscription is usually commemorative in character. They probably date from c. AD 300.

Pale: the district around Dublin, of varying extent at different periods, where English rule was effective for some four centuries after the Norman invasion of 1169.

Passage grave: a type of megalithic tomb consisting of a burial chamber approached by a long passage and covered by a round mound or cairn.

Patron or **pattern**: festival celebration of a saint, held on the anniversary of his death.

Plantation castles: a name given to defensive buildings erected by English and Scottish settlers under the plantation scheme between 1610 and 1620, which were very common in Ulster.

Poitín or **poteen**: illegal spirit, often made with barley or potatoes, distilled in small pots (translates as 'small pot'; *uisce poitín*: 'water from the little pot').

Portcullis: a heavy grating in a gateway, sliding up and down in slots in the jambs, which could be used to close the entrance quickly. There is a good example at Cahir Castle, County Tipperary.

Rath: the rampart of an earthen ring fort. The name is often used for the whole structure.

Rib vaulting: roofing or ceiling in which the weight of the superstructure is carried on comparatively slender intersecting 'ribs' or arches of stone, the spaces between the ribs being a light stone filling without structural function.

Ring fort, rath or **lis**: one or more banks and ditches enclosing an area, usually circular, within which were dwellings. It was the typical homestead of early Christian Ireland, but examples are known from c. 1000 BC– AD 1000. The bank sometimes had a timber palisade. Some elaborate examples were defensive in purpose.

Romanesque: the style of architecture, based on late classical forms, with round arches and vaulting, which prevailed in Europe until the emergence of Gothic in the 12th century. *See* Irish- (Hiberno-) Romanesque.

Round towers: slender stone belfries, also used as refuges and built between the 9th and 12th centuries.

Rundale: a system of holding land in strips or detached portions. The system has survived in parts of County Donegal.

Sedilia: seats recessed in the south wall of the chancel, near the altar, for the use of the clergy. A richly carved example may be seen in Holycross Abbey, County Tipperary.

Sept: in the old Irish system, those ruling families who traced their descent from a common ancestor.

Sheila-na-Gig: a cult symbol or female fertility figure, carved in stone on churches or castles. No one is sure of its origin.

Souterrain: artificial underground chambers of wood, stone or earth, or cut into rock. They served as refuges or stores and in some cases as dwellings. They occur commonly in ring forts and, like these, date from the Bronze Age to at least early Christian times.

Standing stone: an upright stone set in the ground. These stones may be of various dates and served various purposes, marking burial places or boundaries, or serving as cult objects.

Stone fort: a ring fort built of dry-stone walling.

Sweat houses: an ancient form of sauna. Sometimes the mentally ill were incarcerated within them, in an attempt to cure them.

Teampull: a church.

Torc or **torque**: an ornament from the middle to late Bronze Age, made of a ribbon or bar of gold twisted like a rope and bent around to form a complete loop. Two very large examples were found at Tara, County Meath.

Tracery: the openwork pattern formed by the stone in the upper part of middle or late Gothic windows.

Transepts: the 'arms' of a church, extending at right angles to the north and south from the junction of nave and choir.

Tumulus: a mound of earth over a grave; usually the mound over an earth-covered passage grave, e.g. Tara, County Meath.

Undertaker: one of the English or Scottish planters given confiscated land in Ireland in the 16th century. They 'undertook' certain obligations designed to prevent the dispossessed owners from reacquiring their land.

Vaulting: a roof or ceiling formed by arching over a space. Among the many methods, three main types were used: barrel vaulting, groin vaulting and rib vaulting. Rib vaulting lent itself to great elaboration of ornament.

Zoomorphic: describing decoration based on the forms of animals.

Language

The Irish language is the purest of all the Celtic languages, and Ireland is one of the last homes of the oral tradition of prehistoric and medieval Europe. It was preserved by the isolated farming communities, along with many expressions from the dialects of early English settlers. Irish was spoken by the Norman aristocracy, who patronized the Gaelic poets and bards. But with the establishment of an English system of land tenure and an English-speaking nobility, Gaelic became scarce, except in the poorer farming areas. The potato famine in the 1840s hit the people who lived in such areas; thousands died and emigrated, and Gaelic speaking was severely reduced. The Gaelic League, founded in 1870, initiated a new interest and pride in the language and became identified with the rise of nationalism. In 1921 its survival became part of the new State's policy. It was decided that the only way to preserve Gaelic was to protect and encourage it where it was still used.

The areas where it is spoken today are mostly in the west, and around the mountainous coast and islands. They form the Gaeltacht. Here everything is done to promote Irish-speaking in industry and at home. Centres have been set up for students to learn among these native speakers. There are special grants for people living in Irish-speaking areas but the boundaries are rather arbitrary. In Galway there's a boundary line through a built-up area so there's a certain amount of animosity towards those living on one side of the line, Irish speakers or no. There is also the problem of standardizing Irish, for the different dialects are quite distinct. The modern media tend to iron out these with the adoption of one region's form of words in preference to others. County Donegal seems to get the worst deal, being so much further from the centre of administration, although it has the largest number of native speakers.

One can appreciate all the reasons for promoting Irish, but it is only in the last few generations that the language has become popular. Before, it was left to Douglas Hyde and Lady Gregory to demonstrate the richness of Irish language and myth, and they had the advantage of being far away from the grim realities of hunger and poverty that the Irish speakers knew. Gaelic, like certain foods (usually vegetables), had associations with hunger and poverty, and belonged to a hard past. The cultural coercion of the 1930s had a negative effect on most Irish people. It was only in Ulster that Gaelic speaking and culture kept its appeal in the face of Protestant and official antipathy. Even now, people prefer to use English rather than stay in the Gaeltacht, existing on grants and other government hand-outs. Gaelic is a compulsory subject in schools in the Republic, and there is a certain amount in the newspapers, on television, radio, signposts and street names (with English translations). The use of Gaelic amongst the more intellectual of the middle classes is now on the increase, and this is being reinforced by the establishment of Gaelic-speaking primary schools throughout the country. Irish Gaelic is one of the official languages of the European Union.

The carrying over of Irish idiom into English is very attractive and expressive. J.M. Synge captured this in his play *Riders to the Sea*. In fact, English as spoken by the Irish is in a class of its own. Joyce talked of 'the sacred eloquence of Ireland', and it is true that you could hardly find a more articulate people. Their poetry and prose is superb, and the emotions that their ballads can release is legendary. Great hardship and poverty have not killed the instinctive desire within to explain life with words. The monk who scribbled in the margin of his psalter wrote with oriental simplicity the following poem entitled 'Winter':

My tiding for you: The stag bells
Winter snows, summer is gone.
Wind is high and cold, low the sun,
Short his course, sea running high.
Deep red the bracken, its shape all gone,
The wild goose has raised his wonted cry.
Cold has caught the wings of birds;
season of ice – these are my tidings.

9th century, translation by Kuno Meyer

That hardship brings forth great poetry is a theory strengthened by the school of contemporary northern Irish poets who have become known all over the world: Seamus Heaney, James Simmons, Derek Mahon, Medbh McGuckian. The cutting criticisms of Brian O'Nolan (known as Flann O'Brien), the gentle irony of Frank O'Connor and the furious passion of Sean O'Casey, Patrick Kavanagh, Liam O'Flaherty and John McGahern, to name only a few, have become part of our perception of the Irish spirit since Independence. The list of recent writers could go on and on. One can only urge you to read them. There is a particularly good anthology of short stories edited by Benedict Kiely (Penguin) and an anthology of Irish verse, edited by John Montague (Faber and Faber).

Even though the disciplined cadences of the Gaelic bardic order was broken by the imposition of an English nobility in the 17th and 18th centuries, the Irish skill with words has survived, and is as strong as ever. As a visitor to Ireland, you will notice this way with words when you have a conversation in a pub, ask the way at a crossroads, or simply chat to the owners of the farmhouse where you spend the night.

The Meaning of Irish Place Names

The original Gaelic place names have been complicated by attempts to give them an English spelling. In the following examples, the Gaelic versions of the prefixes come first, followed by the English meaning.

abhainn, avon, owen a river
achadh, agh, augh a field
aglish, eaglais a church
ah, áth, atha a ford
ail, aill, all a cliff

anna, canna, éanarch a marsh
ard, ar a height
as, eas, ess a waterfall
atha, aw, ow a river; also a ford
bal, béal, bel the mouth (of a river or valley)
bal, balli, bally, baile a town
balla, ballagh, bealach a way or path
bán, bane, bawn white
barn, bearna a gap
beag, beg small
boola, booley, booleying, buaile movement of cattle from lowland to high pastures
boy, buidhe yellow
bun the foot (of a valley) or mouth (of a river)
caher, cahir, carraig, cathair a rock
caiseal, caislean, cashel a castle
can, ceann, ken, kin a headland
cill, kil, kill a church
cloch, clogh, cloich a stone
clon, cluain, clun a meadow
cnoc, knock a hill
dearg, derg red
disert, dysert a hermitage
doo, du, dubh, duf, duv black
dun, dún a fort
glas, gleann, glen a valley
illaun, oileán an island
lios, lis, liss a fort
loch, lough a lake or sea inlet
ma, magh, may, moy a plain
mainistir, monaster a monastery
mona, móna, mone turf or bog
mor, mór, more big or great
rath a ring fort
reen, rinn a point
roe, ruadh red
ros, ross a peninsula, or a wood
sean, shan, shane old
see, suidhe a seat, e.g. Ossian's seat
sliabh, slieve a mountain
tir, tír, tyr country
tobar, tobrid, tubber, tubbrid a well
tra, trá, tráigh, traw a strand or beach

Some Expressions

an oul sceach crosspatch
assay attention, as in Hi!
auld flutter guts fussy person
balls of malt whiskey
ballyhooley a telling off (in Cork)
blow-in stranger to the area

boreen country lane

brave commendable, worthy, e.g. a brave wee sort of a girl

bravely could be worse, e.g. business is doing bravely

caution (as in 'He's a caution'), a devil-may-care-type

chawing the rag bickering

chick child

cleg horsefly

clever neat, tight-fitting, usually refers to a garment

coul wintry, cold

craic fun, lively chat

cranky bad-tempered

craw thumper a 'holy Mary' or hypocrite

cut insulted, hurt

dead on exactly right

deed passed away, dead

destroyed exhausted

dingle dent, mark with an impression

dip bread fried in a pan

dither slow

doley little fella he's lovely

dulse edible seaweed

eejit fool

fairly well, e.g. 'that wee lad can fairly sing'

feed meal

fern foreign

in fiddler's green (you're) in a big mess

fierce unacceptable, extreme, e.g. it's fierce dear (expensive)

figuresome good at sums

fog feed lavish meal

foostering around fiddling about

guff impertinence, cheek

half sir landlord's son

harp six tumble

he hasn't a titter of wit he has no sense at all

jar a couple of drinks

lashins plenty

mended improved in health

mizzlin raining gently

mullarkey man

neb nose

nettle drive (someone) barmy

ni now, this moment

not the full shilling half-witted

oul or auld not young, but can be used about something useful, e.g. my oul car

owlip verbal abuse

palsie walsie great friends

paralytic intoxicated

plamas sweet words

playboy conceited fellow

poless (*po*-lis) police

put the caibosh on it mess things up

quare memorable, unusual

qurrier or *cowboy* bad type, rogue

rare to bring up, educate

rightly prospering, e.g. 'he's doing rightly now'

scalded bothered, vexed; badly burned

she's like a corncrake chatterbox

skedaddled ran quickly

skiff slight shower or rain

slainte drinking toast

soft rainy, e.g. it's a grand soft day

spalpeen agricultural labourer

spittin' starting to rain

terrible same use as 'fierce'

themins those persons

thick as a ditch stupid

thundergub loud-voiced person

wean pronounced wain, child

wee little

you could trot a mouse on it strong (tea)

Proverbs and Sayings

Wise, and beautifully expressed with a delightful wry humour, these sayings and proverbs have passed into the English language. They highlight the usual Irish preoccupations with land, God, love, words and drinking, as well as every other subject under the sun.

These are just a few examples; for a comprehensive collection read *Gems of Irish Wisdom*, by Padraic O'Farrell.

On God

It's a blessing to be in the Lord's hand as long as he doesn't close his fist.

Fear of God is the beginning of wisdom.

God never closes the door without opening another.

Man proposes, God disposes.

On the Irish Character

The wrath of God has nothing on the wrath of an Irishman outbid for land, horse or woman.

The best way to get an Irishman to refuse to do something is by ordering it.

The Irish forgive their great men when they are safely buried.

It is not that the Ulsterman lives in the past... it is rather that the past lives in him.

Advice

No property – no friends, no rearing – no manners, no health – no hope!

Never give cherries to pigs, nor advice to a fool.

Bigots and begrudgers will never bid the past farewell.

When everybody else is running, that's the time for you to walk.

You won't be stepped on if you're a live wire.

If you get the name of an early riser you can sleep till dinner time.

There are finer fish in the sea than have ever been caught.

You'll never plough a field by turning it over in your mind.

Don't make a bid till you walk the land.

A man with humour will keep ten men working.

Do not visit too often or too long.

If you don't own a mount, don't hunt with the gentry.

You can take a man out of the bog but you cannot take the bog out of the man.

What is got badly, goes badly.

A watched pot never boils.

Enough is as good as plenty.

Beware of the horse's hoof, the bull's horn and the Saxon's smile.

Time is the best storyteller.

On Marriage and Love

Play with a woman that has looks, talk marriage with a woman that has property.

After the settlement comes love.

A lad's best friend is his mother until he's the best friend of a lassie.

A pot was never boiled by beauty.

There is no love sincerer than the love of food. (G.B. Shaw)

It's a great thing to turn up laughing having been turned down crying.

Though the marriage bed be rusty, the death bed is still colder.

On Argument and Fighting

Argument is the worst sort of conversation. (Jonathan Swift)

There is no war as bitter as a war amongst friends.

Whisper into the glass when ill is spoken.

If we fought temptation the way we fight each other we'd be a nation of saints again.

We fought every nation's battles, and the only ones we did not win were our own.

On Women

It takes a woman to outwit the Devil.

A cranky woman, an infant, or a grievance, should never be nursed.

A woman in the house is a treasure, a woman with humour in the house is a blessing.

She who kisses in public often kicks in private.

If she is mean at the table, she will be mean in bed.

On Drinking

If Holy Water was porter he'd be at Mass every morning.

It's the first drop that destroys you; there's no harm at all in the last.

Thirst is a shameless disease, so here's to a shameless cure.

On the Family

Greed in a family is worse than need.

Poets write about their mothers, undertakers about their fathers.

A son's stool in his father's home is as steady as a gable; a father's in his son's, bad luck, is shaky and unstable.

On Old Age

The older the fiddle, the sweeter the tune.

There is no fool like an old fool.

On Loneliness

The loneliest man is the man who is lonely in a crowd.

On Bravery

A man who is not afraid of the sea will soon be drowned. (J.M. Synge)

On Flattery

Soft words butter no turnips, but they won't harden the heart of a cabbage either.

Further Reading

Biography

Bence-Jones, Mark, *Twilight of the Ascendancy* (Constable and Robinson).

Davis-Goff, Annabel, *Walled Gardens: Scenes from an Anglo-Irish Childhood* (Eland Books).

Kelly, A. A. (Ed.), *The Letters of Liam O'Flaherty* (Merlin).

Kenny, Mary, *Goodbye to Catholic Ireland* (New Island Books).

Krause, David, *A Self Portrait of the Artist as a Man: Sean O'Casey's letters* (Dolmen).

Lyons, J. S., *Oliver St John Gogarty, A Biography* (Bucknell University Press).

McCourt, Frank, *Angela's Ashes* and *'Tis* (Flamingo).

Moore, George, *Hail and Farewell* (Colin Smythe).

Murphy, Maura, *Don't Wake Me at Doyles* (Hodder Headline).

Murphy, William M., *Yeats Family and the Pollexfens of Sligo* (Dolmen).

Ni Shuilleabhain, Eibhlis, *Letters from the Great Blasket* (Mercier).

O'Crohan, Thomas, *Island Cross-talk, The Islandman, A Day in Our Life* (OUP).

Osborne, Chrissy, *Michael Collins: Himself* (Mercier).

O'Sullivan, Maurice, *Twenty Years a-Growing* (OUP).

Sayers, Peig, *An Old Woman's Reflections* (OUP).

Somerville-Large, Peter, *Irish Eccentrics* (Lilliput Press).

Taylor, Alice, *To School through the Fields: an Irish Country Childhood* (Brandon).

Thomson, David, *Woodbrook* (Vintage).

Walsh, Marrie, *Irish Country Childhood* (Blake).

Yeats, W. B., *Synge and the Ireland of his Time* (Irish UP).

Cookery

Allen, Darina, *Darina Allen's Ballymaloe Cookery Course* (Pelican); *A Year at Ballymaloe Cookery School* (Kyle Cathie); *Ballymaloe Seasons* (Roberts Rinehart).

Allen, Myrtle, *The Ballymaloe Cook Book* (Gill & Macmillan); *Cooking at Ballymaloe House* (Steward, Tabori & Chang).

Arnold, Hugo, *Avoca Café Cookbook* 1&2 (Avoca Handweavers).

Cotter, Denis, *The Café Paradiso Cookbook* (Atrium).

Flynn, Paul, *An Irish Adventure with Food: the Tannery Cookbook* (Collins).

McKenna, J. and S., *The Bridgestone Irish Food Guide* (Estragon Press).

Rankin, P. and J., *New Irish Cookery* (BBC Books).

Fiction

Banville, John, *The Untouchable* (Picador).

Berry, James, *Tales of the West of Ireland* (Colin Smythe).

Bowen, Elizabeth, *Elizabeth Bowen's Irish Stories* (Poolbeg) and *Bowen's Court* (Vintage).

Carleton, William, *Black Prophet* (Irish UP).

Carpenter and Fallon (Eds), *The Writers: A Sense of Ireland* (O'Brien Press).

Crone, Anne, *Bridie Steen* (Blackstaff).

Du Maurier, Daphne, *Hungry Hill* (Penguin).

Edgeworth, Maria, *The Absentee* (Penguin, Oxford Paperbacks).

Farrell, J. G., *Troubles* (New York Review of Books).

Kennelly, B. (Ed.), *The Penguin Book of Irish Verse* (Penguin).

Kiely, B. (Ed.), *The Penguin Book of Irish Short Stories* (Penguin).

Lavin, Mary, *In a Café: Selected Stories* (Penguin).

McGahern, John, *The Barracks* (Faber, Penguin) or any other novels by him.

Montague, John (Ed.), *The Faber Book of Irish Verse* (Faber).

O'Faolain, Sean, *The Heat of the Sun* (Penguin).

O'Flaherty, Liam L., *Famine* (Merlin).

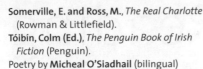

Somerville, E. and Ross, M., *The Real Charlotte* (Rowman & Littlefield).

Tóibín, Colm (Ed.), *The Penguin Book of Irish Fiction* (Penguin).

Poetry by **Micheal O'Siadhail** (bilingual)

Plays by **John M. Synge**, stories and plays by **Brian Friel**.

Novels by **Sam Hanna Bell**, George Birmingham, **Roddy Doyle**, Kate O'Brien, Colm Tóibín or William Trevor.

Folklore, Music and Tradition

Donegan, Maureen, *Fables & Legends of Ireland* (Mercier).

Estyn Evans, E., *Irish Folk Ways* (Dover).

Flower, Robin, *The Irish Tradition* (Lilliput).

Gaffney, S. and Cashman, S., *Proverbs and Sayings of Ireland* (Merlin).

Gregory, Lady Isabella Augusta, *Gods and Fighting Men* (Colin Smythe).

Healy, James N., *The Songs of Percy French* (Ossian).

Henry, Sean, *Tales from the West of Ireland* (Mercier).

McLaughlin, John, *One Green Hill: Journeys Through Irish Songs* (Beyond the Pale).

O'Farrell, Padraic, *Folktales of the Irish Coast* (Mercier).

O'Flaherty, Gerry, *A Book of Slang, Idiom and Wit* (O'Brien).

O'Keeffe, D. and Healy, J. N. (Eds), *Book of Irish Ballads* (Mercier).

O'Sullivan, Patrick, *A Country Diary: Year in Kerry* (Anvil).

O'Sullivan, Sean, *The Folklore of Ireland* (Batsford).

Wilde, William, *Irish Popular Superstitions* (Irish UP).

History

Boylan, Henry (Ed.), *A Dictionary of Irish Biography* (Gill & Macmillan).

Connolly, S. J. (Ed.), *The Oxford Companion to Irish History* (OUP).

Corkery, Daniel, *Hidden Ireland* (Gill & Macmillan).

Dudley Edwards, Ruth, *An Atlas of Irish History* (Routledge).

Ferriter, Diarmuid, *Transformation of Ireland, 1900–2000* (Profile).

Fitzgerald, Mairéad, *The World of Colmcille, Also Known as Columba* (O'Brien Press).

Foster, R. F. (Ed.), *The Oxford History of Ireland* and *Modern Ireland 1600–1972* (OUP).

Gray, Peter, *The Irish Famine* (Thames & Hudson).

Kee, Robert, *The Green Flag: a History of Irish Nationalism* (Penguin).

Lyons, F. S. L., *Ireland Since the Famine* (Fontana).

MacLysaght, Edward, *Irish Families: Their Names and Origins* (Irish Academic Press).

O'Farrell, Padraic, *How the Irish Speak English* (Mercier) and *Irish Surnames* (Gill & Macmillan).

Pakenham, Thomas, *The Year of Liberty: History of the Great Irish Rebellion of 1798* (Abacus).

Stephens, James, *The Insurrection in Dublin* (Colin Smythe).

Thomas, Cahill, *How the Irish Saved Civilization* (Hodder & Stoughton).

Woodham Smith, Cecil, *The Great Hunger: Ireland 1845–1849* (Penguin).

Travel Literature

Böll, Heinrich, *Irish Journal* (Vintage).

Hawks, Tony, *Round Ireland With A Fridge* (Ebury).

Irwin, Colin, *In Search of the Craic: One Man's Pub Crawl Through Irish Music* (André Deutsch).

McCarthy, John, *A Ghost Upon Your Path* (Black Swan).

McCarthy, Pete, *McCarthy's Bar: A Journey of Discovery in Ireland* (Hodder & Stoughton).

Walking Guides

Bardwell, S., *The Kerry Way* (Rucksack Readers).

Bardwell, S., and Megarry, J., *The Dingle Way* (Rucksack Readers).

Corcoran, Kevin, *West Cork Walks, Kerry Walks* and *West of Ireland Walks* (O'Brien Press).

Cronin, Joe, *Rambles in Cork City and County* (Collins).

Dillon, Paddy, *Irish Coastal Walks* and *The Mountains of Ireland* (Cicerone).

Jones, Carleton, *The Burren and the Aran Islands: Exploring the Archaeology* (Collins).

Lynam, Joss, *Best Irish Walks* (Gill & Macmillan).

Lynch, Denis, *Munster's Mountains: 30 Walking, Scrambling and Climbing Routes* (Collins).

Teegan, Sean, *Scenic Walks in Cork* (Mercier).

Index

Main page references are in **bold**. Page references to maps are in *italics*.

Southwest Ireland
touring atlas

N

40km
20 miles

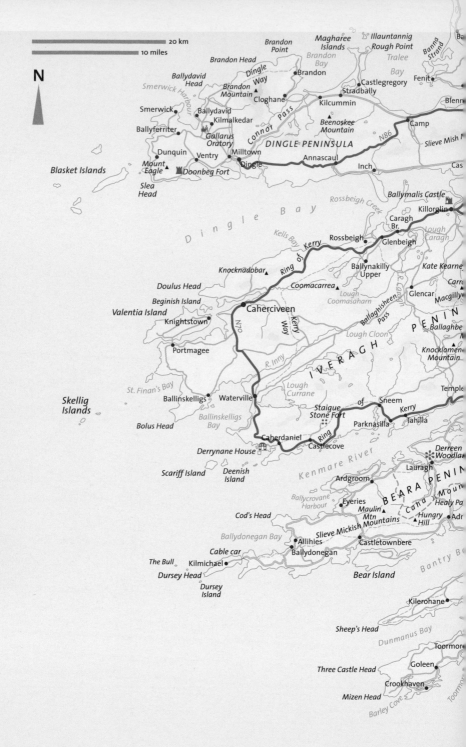

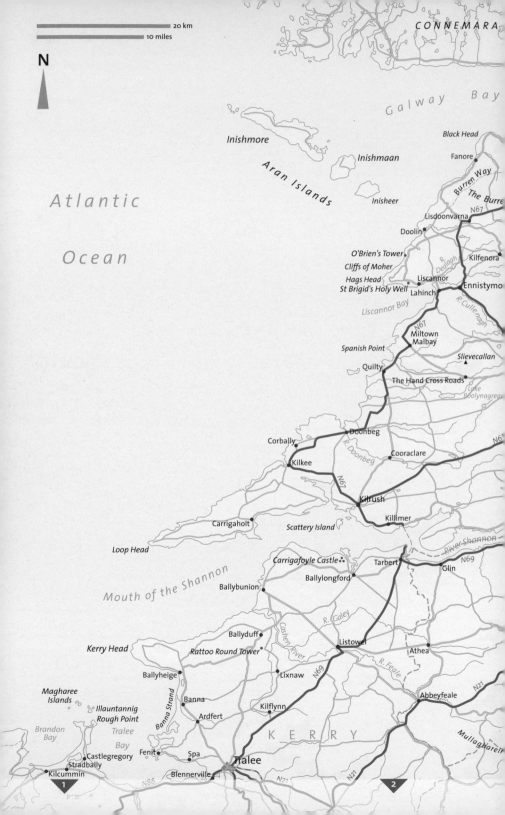

N

20 km
10 miles

CONNEMARA

Galway Bay

Inishmore

Inishmaan

Aran Islands

Inisheer

Black Head

Fanore

Burren Way

The Burre

Atlantic

N67

Lisdoonvarna

Doolin

Ocean

O'Brien's Tower

Kilfenora

Cliffs of Moher

R. Dealagh

Hags Head

Liscannor

Ennistymo

St Brigid's Holy Well

Lahinch

R. Cullenagh

Liscannor Bay

N67

Miltown
Malbay

Slievecallan ▲

Spanish Point

Quilty

The Hand Cross Roads

*Lake
Boolynagreg*

Doonbeg

Corbally

R. Doonbeg

Cooraclare

N6

Kilkee

N67

Kilrush

Killimer

Carrigaholt

Scattery Island

River Shannon

Loop Head

Carrigafoyle Castle

Tarbert

N69

Glin

Mouth of the Shannon

Ballybunion

Ballylongford

R. Galey

Ballyduff

Cashen River

Listowel

Athea

Kerry Head

Rattoo Round Tower

R. Feale

*Maghuree
Islands*

Lixnaw

N69

*Illauntannig
Rough Point*

Ballyheige

Abbeyfeale

N21

Tralee
Bay

Banna

Banna Strand

Kilflynn

*Brandon
Bay*

Ardfert

K E R R Y

Mullaghareil

Castlegregory

Fenit

Spa

Stradbally

Kilcummin

Blennerville

Tralee

N86

N21

N21

1

2

GALWAY

Athenry

N84

N7

N6

R. Clarinbridge

N6

R. Suck

Grand Canal

N6

R. Dunkellin

GALWAY

Loughrea

N65

N6

ughinish

Burren

Corcomroe Abbey

Kinvarra

Slieve Aughty Mountains

han

Bealaclugga

N67

N66

Lough Cutra

R. Owendalulleegh

Turlough

Gort

llwee Cave

Poulnabrone

Megalithic Tomb

Cahercommaun

Stone Fort

Lough Graney

N52

arran

nvarga

Fort

maneh Castle

Killinaboy

Lough Derg

Ballinruan

R. Graney

Feakle

R. Bow

Mountshannon

Drumineer

rofin

Atedaun

Crusheen

N18

Inchicronan Lough

Scarriff

Holy Island

Dea

Tulla

Ogonnelloe

CLARE

Ennis

Quin

Craggaunowen

Megalithic Centre

Doon Lough

R. Rine

Slieve Bernagh

St Molua's

Oratory

Arra

Mountains

N7

Clarecastle

N18

Knappogue Castle

Broadford

Killaloe

Ballina

N7

Dromoland Castle

Mooghaun Fort

Newmarket on Fergus

River Fergus

Sixmilebridge

Deenish Island

Bunratty Castle

Folk Park

Clonlara

TIPPERARY

Shannon Airport

Shannon

Cratloe

Castleconnell

Canon Island

Bunratty

Cratloe Woods House

rt

Annacotty

Clonkeen

LIMERICK

Murroe

Clare Glens

Pallaskenry

Dromore

Castle

N69

Clarina

Slievefelim Mountains

Kilcornan

Askeaton

R. Mulkear

Franciscan

friary

N21

Ballyneety

e Matrix

Rathkeale

Adare

R. Maigue

R. Dead

N24

LIMERICK

Croom

R. Camoge

Lough Gur

astle West

Ballingary

N20

Limerick Junction

Tipperary

N74

Knockfierna

Hill

Bruree

Duntryleague

Hill

N24

Broadford

Kilmallock

Galbally

Galtymore Mountain

ins

Kilfinane

CORK

Ardpatrick

Castle Oliver

Galty Mountains

N8

2

DUBLIN
Mary-Anne Gallagher

VENICE
Dana Facaros & Michael Pauls

CADOGANguides

BARCELONA
Dana Facaros & Michael Pauls

CADOGANguides